COMMANDER OF THE ARMADA

Commander of the Armada

✳ ✳ ✳

The Seventh Duke of Medina Sidonia

✳ ✳ ✳

Peter Pierson

Yale University Press   New Haven & London

PUBLICATION OF THIS BOOK HAS BEEN AIDED BY GRANTS FROM THE PROGRAM
FOR CULTURAL COOPERATION BETWEEN SPAIN'S MINISTRY OF CULTURE AND
UNITED STATES' UNIVERSITIES.

DESIGNED BY JAMES J. JOHNSON
AND SET IN GALLIARD ROMAN TYPES BY
MARATHON TYPOGRAPHY SERVICE, INC.,
DURHAM, NORTH CAROLINA.
PRINTED IN THE UNITED STATES OF AMERICA BY
BOOKCRAFTERS, INC., CHELSEA, MICHIGAN.

LIBRARY OF CONGRESS CATALOGING-IN-PUBLICATION DATA

PIERSON, PETER.
COMMANDER OF THE ARMADA : THE SEVENTH DUKE OF MEDINA SIDONIA /
PETER PIERSON.
P. CM.
BIBLIOGRAPHY: P.
INCLUDES INDEX
ISBN 0-300-04408-9 (ALK. PAPER)
I. MEDINA SIDONIA, ALONSO PÉREZ DE GUZMÁN, DUQUE DE, 1550-1619.
2. SPAIN—HISTORY—PHILIP II, 1556-1598. 3. SPAIN—HISTORY,
NAVAL—16TH CENTURY. 4. ARMADA, 1588. 5. GREAT BRITAIN—HISTORY,
NAVAL—TUDORS, 1485-1603. 6. CADIZ (SPAIN)—HISTORY. 7. SPAIN—
NOBILITY—BIOGRAPHY. 8. SPAIN. ARMADA—BIOGRAPHY. I. TITLE.
DP181.M43P54 1989
946'.04'0924—DC19   89-5258
                                                     CIP

THE PAPER IN THIS BOOK MEETS THE GUIDELINES FOR
PERMANENCE AND DURABILITY OF THE COMMITTEE ON
PRODUCTION GUIDELINES FOR BOOK LONGEVITY OF THE
COUNCIL ON LIBRARY RESOURCES.

I 3 5 7 9 10 8 6 4 2

To Harry de Wildt

Contents

Illustrations

Preface

On the stage of world history the seventh Duke of Medina Sidonia makes but two brief appearances: as Spain's Captain General of the Ocean-Sea in 1588, when he commanded the Armada that sailed against England and met defeat; and as Captain General of the Coast of Andalusia in 1596, when an Anglo-Dutch expedition captured and sacked Cádiz.

He was blamed for both failures, and as a result his reputation has suffered. His long career of service to the Spanish Crown, attested by extensive correspondence in state and private archives, was forgotten, and his appointment by Philip II to command the armada seemed in retrospect to make no sense. Historians decided that the Prudent King acted imprudently and must have based his choice on the Duke's wealth or some other reason that was less than satisfactory.

It was the grandfather of the present Duchess of Medina Sidonia, Don Gabriel Maura y Gamazo, Duke of Maura, who began to set accounts right. Maura was a historian and academician who had written a masterly study of the reign of Carlos II. Working with papers from the Medina Sidonia ducal archive, he reconstructed the career of the seventh Duke to the time of his appointment to command the armada and thereby made Philip II's choice appear more reasonable.[1] In his splendid *Armada*,[2] Garrett Mattingly used Maura's work to paint a sympathetic portrait of Medina Sidonia, and since his book appeared, more work on the armada and Medina Sidonia has further clarified the problems that faced both Philip II and the Duke.[3] But Maura's work is thin and stops in 1588, and Mattingly's marvelously proportioned study focuses almost exclusively on 1587 and 1588. Medina

Sidonia continued to render significant service to the Crown into 1615, the year of his death.

Medina Sidonia's public career began in 1569, before he was twenty, and he was a major participant in important events apart from those of 1588 and 1596. His career also knew much routine. Because of its broad scope, it offers valuable insights into the political, military, and public life of the Spain of Philip II and Philip III as well as the world of a grandee of the epoch. For some forty years Medina Sidonia acted as Captain General of western Andalusia and was the Crown's single most important agent in the region. I offer here a study of his career that, like Stirling Maxwell's *Don John of Austria* (1883), might be aptly subtitled "Passages from the History of the Sixteenth Century."

The longest passage by far will treat the Invincible Armada of 1588, from the time of Medina Sidonia's first work with its preparation through his conduct of the campaign. While Medina Sidonia's own account of the campaign remains central to my narrative, I have tried to reconstruct what happened from many sources. I believe the account he wrote for the King describes a relatively faithful adherence to the King's instructions, certainly to the time when the armada approached Calais. While he informed the King in a letter from the Channel that he intended to seek shelter in the lee of the Isle of Wight, he makes no mention of attempting to do so in his account. Why? I suspect he did not because he had to explain defeat, and his effort to shelter off Wight was contrary to the King's instructions, which ordered him to proceed directly to his rendezvous with the Duke of Parma's invasion force off Flanders. Yet the battles that raged between Plymouth and Wight suggest that he aimed at gaining an anchorage off Wight and that the English knew it and did all they could do to keep him from it. The account I offer is thus ultimately my own, and in this I join a long line of others before me who have written the history of the great Enterprise. I have learned all I could about Spanish battle tactics and have used lists of ships, battle plans, and mentions of individual ships in the accounts of the campaign to plot, with a marker for each ship involved, the battles. The discovery in the Karpeles Manuscript Library, Santa Barbara, California, of a list of ships assigned to the armada's main battle formation from Medina Sidonia's own papers has proved extraordinarily useful in determining the armada's order of battle.

Because the bureaucratic habit at the time was more entrenched with the Spaniards, my reconstruction was somewhat easier for their side than for the English. Because I am writing about Medina Sidonia,

I have dealt with the English side only as necessary. The Spaniards were never sure whom or which ship they fought. They identified several vessels at different times as the English flagship (*capitana*) and did not know where the best-known Englishmen, Sir Francis Drake (Draque) and John Hawkins (Aquines, Juan Acles), fought.

This work could not have been written without access to the Medina Sidonia archive in Sanlúcar de Barrameda, for which I thank the twenty-first Duchess of Medina Sidonia, Doña Isabel Alvarez de Toledo y Gamazo. I also thank the Fulbright Program, which permitted me first to study in Spain; its assistant director in Madrid, Doña Matilde Medina, for her special encouragement; and its director, Don Ramón Bela. And because many of the seventh Duke's papers are now held by the Karpeles Manuscript Library, I wish to thank David and Marsha Karpeles for giving me access to them and for their kind help. Also helpful for my study of Medina Sidonia and Spain's armadas were grants from the Del Amo Foundation, the National Endowment for the Humanities, the American Philosophical Society, and a Presidential Research Grant and other support from Santa Clara University. I want to give particular thanks to Geoffrey Parker, above all for letting me read the typescript of his and Colin Martin's *The Spanish Armada*,[4] and for the long, provocative, and helpful discussions we have had on the subject. We agree on much but do differ here and there. Others who contributed to this effort include my mentor at the University of California, Los Angeles, Andrew Lossky, who got me thinking about Europe of the Old Regime; Don José Valverde, who introduced me to Sanlúcar; Geoffrey Symcox, who read my earliest efforts to write about Medina Sidonia and offered good advice; the staff of the Museo Naval, Madrid; and friends and colleagues in early modern history and Spanish history: John H. Elliott, Manuel Fernández Alvarez, J. F. Guilmartin, Richard Herr, Richard Kagan, Henry Kamen, Ursula Lamb, Albert Lovett, William S. Maltby, Helen Nader, Stanley Payne, Carla Rahn Phillips, William Phillips, David Reher, David Ringrose, Lewis W. Spitz and I. A. A. Thompson, all of whom shared lively discussions with me and posed intelligent questions over the years. For their help with the figures and maps I thank Kirk Frederick and Scott Rankin. I also thank Susanna Barrows, Kevin Starr, former UCLA Dean of Students Byron Atkinson, Harry and Margot de Wildt, and my parents.

COMMANDER OF THE ARMADA

CHAPTER ONE

An Andalusian Grandee

WHEN Philip II appointed the Duke of Medina Sidonia to command the armada assembled in Lisbon harbor in February 1588, the Venetian Ambassador Hieronimo Lippomano noted in his dispatch to the Doge and Senate, "This nobleman is the first Grandee of Spain; he has excellent qualities and is generally beloved. He is not only prudent and brave, but of a nature of extreme goodness and benignity. He will be followed by many nobles and by all Andalusia. Only one might desire in him a wider experience at sea, but all other possible appointments presented greater difficulties."[1] In making his astute summary Lippomano reported what his well-informed contemporaries knew and thought about the Duke. He had on occasion spoken with Medina Sidonia and was familiar with his record of service to the King and his recent activities in Andalusia.

In February 1588, Don Alonso Pérez de Guzmán el Bueno, seventh Duke of Medina Sidonia, was in his thirty-ninth year. He had been born on the first day of September 1549 in the ducal palace at Sanlúcar de Barrameda, which stands at the confluence of the river Guadalquivir and the waters of the Gulf of Cadiz. His parents were Don Juan Claros de Guzmán, Count of Niebla, and Doña Leonor Manrique de Zúñiga y Sotomayor, daughter of the fourth Duchess of Béjar and her consort, the Count of Belalcázar. His paternal grandfather was Don Juan Alonso de Guzmán, sixth Duke of Medina Sidonia, his grandmother Doña Ana de Aragón, a natural granddaughter of King Ferdinand of Aragon. Don Alonso and Philip II were third cousins, once removed.[2]

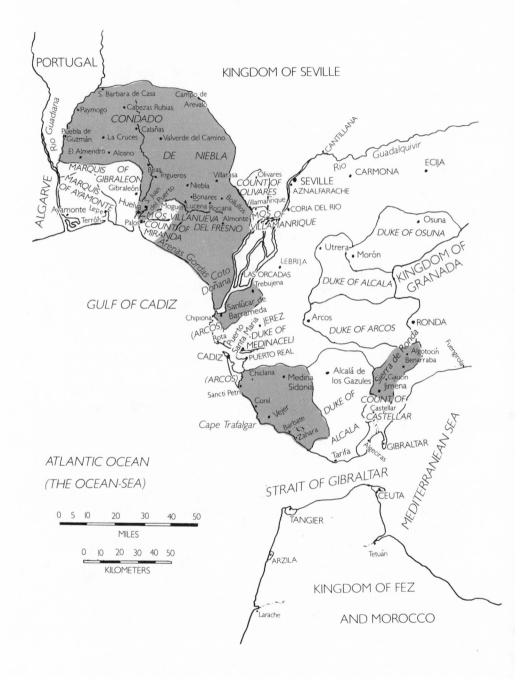

ANDALUSIA IN THE LATE XVI CENTURY

PORTUGAL

KINGDOM OF SEVILLE

S. Barbara de Casa
Campo de
Arevalo
Paymogo
Cabezas Rubias
CONDADO
Puebla de
Guzmán
Calañas
La Cruces
El Almendro
Alosno
Valverde del Camino

Rio Guadiana

CANTILLANA

Guadalquivir

Rio
CARMONA
ECIJA

DE   NIEBLA

Beas
MARQUIS   OF
MARQUIS
OF AYAMONTE
GIBRALEON
Trigueros
Villarasa
Olivares
COUNT OF
OLIVARES
SEVILLE
AZNALFARACHE

ALGARVE
Gibraleón
Niebla
Ayamonte
Lepe
Huelva
S. Juan
del Puerto
Bonares
Moguer
Bollullos
Villamanrique
CORIA DEL RIO
Terrón
Lucena
Rociana
Palos
MOS VILLANUEVA
DEL FRESNO
Almonte
MOS OF
VILLAMANRIQUE
COUNT OF
MIRANDA
Arenas Gordas   Coto
LEBRIJA

DUKE OF OSUNA
Osuna

Utrera
Morón
KINGDOM OF
GRANADA

DUKE OF ALCALA

Doñana
LAS ORCADAS
Trebujena

GULF OF CADIZ

Chipiona
Sanlúcar de
Barrameda
JEREZ
Arcos
DUKE OF ARCOS
RONDA

(ARCOS)
Rota
Puerto
Santa María
DUKE OF
MEDINACELI

CADIZ
PUERTO REAL

Sierra de Ronda
Algotocín
Benarraba

(ARCOS)
Chiclana
Medina
Sidonia
Alcalá de
los Gazules
Gaucín
Jimena

Sancti Petri
Conil
Vejer
DUKE OF
COUNT OF
CASTELLAR
Castellar

Cape Trafalgar
Barbate
Zahara
ALCALA
Tarifa
Algeciras
GIBRALTAR

MEDITERRANEAN SEA

ATLANTIC OCEAN

(THE OCEAN-SEA)

STRAIT OF GIBRALTAR
CEUTA

0 5 10   20   30   40   50
MILES

TANGIER

0   10   20   30 40   50
KILOMETERS

ARZILA
Tetuán

KINGDOM OF FEZ

AND MOROCCO

Larache

The Count of Niebla was stricken ill suddenly in the midst of his family and died in January 1556. His title, the courtesy title carried by Medina Sidonia heirs, passed to Don Alonso. The Duchess Doña Ana died late the same year, and on 26 November 1558 the disconsolate sixth Duke died. Don Alonso inherited his titles and estates to become seventh Duke of Medina Sidonia, fifth Marquis of Cazaza in Africa, and twelfth Señor (Lord) of Sanlúcar de Barrameda, as well as tenth Count of Niebla.

Over four hundred folio pages were needed to catalogue the estates he inherited and his properties, rights, and jurisdictions within each.[3] Legally his estates were known as *señoríos* because over them he held seigneurial jurisdiction.[4] His señoríos embraced both his own properties and the properties of others and stretched from the Portuguese frontier to the mountains behind Gibraltar. They covered about half of today's provinces of Huelva and Cádiz, then part of what was called the Kingdom of Seville, and a corner of the province of Málaga, then in the Kingdom of Granada. His largest señorío was the Condado (County) de Niebla, a region of olives, figs, and grains, of pigs, sheep, and evergreen oak; it embraced some twenty *términos* (townships).[5] Other señoríos included Sanlúcar de Barrameda, Medina Sidonia, Conil, Chiclana, Vejer, and Jimena de la Frontera.[6] Between fifty and fifty-five thousand people[7] lived under the Duke's jurisdiction and were referred to customarily as his *vasallos* (vassals).

In his señoríos the Duke was responsible for the provision of local government, the administration of justice, and the maintenance of the militia, which included the collection of taxes needed to support these functions. In those towns which stood on the frontier of Portugal or faced the sea, the Duke maintained citadels and provided them with artillery. On several occasions he loaned cannon to the Crown.[8]

What properties the Duke possessed in each señorío varied. In the condado he possessed a good amount of land which, combined with dues and other incomes, reportedly brought him 60,000 ducats in 1572.[9] If the arms brought to muster by the militiamen of the condado are any indication, its inhabitants were the poorest of the Duke's vassals.[10]

South of the condado Medina Sidonia possessed the coastal duneland called the Arenas Gordas, and the great hunting preserve

Map 1. Andalusia in the late sixteenth century. Shaded areas indicate the estates of the seventh Duke of Medina Sidonia.

known as the Coto Doñana. Across the Rio Guadalquivir close to Sanlúcar he held a *salina* (salt flat), and in nearby Trebujena he raised cattle on fertile pastureland.

Sanlúcar de Barrameda was the historic seat of the House of Medina Sidonia, and in the sixteenth century became the customary residence of the dukes, who before had often lived in Seville. From the ducal palace perched on a bluff overlooking the town Medina Sidonia could watch the comings and goings of Indies *flotas* (merchant and treasure fleets) and ships of every nation that congregated in the Guadalquivir's broad estuary from Sanlúcar upriver to Bonanza, sheltered from ocean swells by Sanlúcar's bar.

The value of Sanlúcar, a lively center of foreign commerce, to the Duke was estimated in 1582 at 80,000 ducats per year.[11] At least 10,000[12] of this was due directly to his control of the royal customs house, which he lost in 1583 when the Crown renegotiated the administration of the Almojarifazgo Mayor (Greater Royal Customs) of Seville, of which the Sanlúcar customs were legally a part. The merchants of Seville and Cádiz had long complained about special favors granted to foreign merchants who traded in Sanlúcar and about its semiannual fairs during which duties were lowered.[13] "The two fairs," ran a report, "last for three months, and those who ought to go to Seville go there. His Majesty loses each year in customs and *alcabalas* [tax on sales and business transactions] more than 20,000,000 [*maravedís*, about 53,000 ducats], apart from the violation of the law of the realm. To Sanlúcar they bring more than 400,000,000 [*maravedís*, about 1,200,000 ducats], including to foreigners."[14] The report hinted that the Duke's secretary was taking bribes.

About foreigners a local joke ran "in Sanlúcar, the Bretons find their Indies," in pointed reference to the merchants of Brittany and England doing business there. Until the 1580s, when matters between Philip II and Queen Elizabeth took a decided turn for the worse, English merchants enjoyed special favor.[15] In 1578 ninety-three English ships called at Sanlúcar. And even after the outbreak of war, a report of 1592 listed four Englishmen as resident in Sanlúcar, two Catholic and two suspected of being heretics.[16] Today the street that winds downtown from the ducal palace is still known as the Calle de los Bretones.

Both Charles V and Philip II had ordered the Andalusian *señores* not to fix duties at lower rates than those of Seville and Cádiz, but Seville and Cádiz were not satisfied until all Andalusian customs houses came directly under the Almojarifazgo Mayor of Seville. Even when his case was lost, the Duke did not accept it gracefully and in 1587 accused the agent posted to Sanlúcar by the Crown of "robbing Spain."[17] He tried in 1593 and afterward to regain control of the customs, and in 1600 had some small success when he acquired through Philip III's favorite, the Duke of Lerma, the office of chief customs clerk of Sanlúcar.[18] Pedro de Valverde, for many years the royal judge in charge, became a virtual member of the Duke's household and a trusted collaborator.

From Sanlúcar it is some thirty-five miles to the hill town which lent its name to his ducal title, Medina Sidonia. There the Duke owned an inn, a fulling mill, and a grain mill, in addition to lands in the neighborhood. At Chiclana, which lies at the end of Cadiz Bay, he had another salina, while in the rolling hills near Vejer he owned pastures. He derived further income from pastures in the foothills of the Sierra de Ronda that surrounded Jimena and from Jimena's privilege of provisioning the royal fortress of Gibraltar.

Apart from his señoríos Medina Sidonia possessed in Seville a splendid palace and several blocks of urban property, which he proudly showed the King during the royal progress of 1570, receiving in return the King's compliments.[19] He also had blocks of property in Granada and Madrid and according to tradition owned in Madrid a tavern called the Siete Diabolos.[20]

A special property was his *almadraba* (tunny fishery). By royal privilege he enjoyed the right to fish the coast from Conil to Zahara and barrel, preserve, and sell the catch. The value of the almadraba in the 1560s was estimated at some 40,000 ducats per year,[21] and when he lost control of the Sanlúcar customs, his tunny haul was exempted from duties.[22] The almadraba took place annually in the late spring, when Atlantic tunny seeking entrance to the Mediterranean come close inshore south of Cádiz. A 1765 color sketch in the ducal archive depicts two stages of the almadraba, as it had been conducted from time immemorial and would continue to be into the early twentieth century. In the first, fishermen in boats drive the tunny toward the beach and shallow lagoons of Conil, where trumpeters in a tower summon people who make great pens of nets to trap the fish; in the second scene the trapped tunny are speared, hauled ashore with hooked staves, and loaded on ox-drawn carts. Often four or five men were needed to beach a flailing tunny. The fish were butchered, some sold fresh, but most salted, dried, and barreled. Miguel de Cervantes in his novella *La Ilustre Fregona* (The Illustrious Kitchenmaid) described the fishing camp at Zahara, where vagabonds found seasonal employment, as the ultimate stage in the picaresque life.

The income from the Duke's almadraba, domains, and properties made him the richest grandee in Spain. His annual income in the year he acceded to his estates was reported at 75,000 ducats, which seems low given what was claimed for the Condado, the almadraba, and Sanlúcar at various times.[23] But 1558 was a year of war, corsairs menaced the coasts, and royal agents were laying heavy hands on the wealth of Seville. Twenty some years later the Duke's income was reckoned at over 150,000 ducats[24] and in 1600, at 170,000,[25] despite the loss of the Sanlúcar customs house to the Crown.

The debts of the house were also large. Medina Sidonia claimed in 1588 that he owed 900,000 ducats.[26] In 1581 he lost a lawsuit brought against him by *vecinos* (heads of households) of the town of Medina Sidonia and was fined 400,000 ducats, though he did obtain from the King a six-months' suspension on its payment while he appealed the case, which dragged on for some years.[27] Aristocratic debt has lately been much studied, and its roots are many.[28] While extravagance played its part, debts were often contracted in unremunerated service to the Crown, for contributions to local defense, and sometimes for investment purposes in hope of future profit.

The management of the Duke's estates was supervised by his mother, Doña Leonor, until her death in April 1582. She also saw to his education, for which she employed the humanist scholar Pedro de Medina, author of renowned books on cosmography, navigation, and history.[29] Medina, who had tutored the Duke's father, found the young Duke bright and full of promise. The curriculum the Duke followed was that prescribed by humanist educators, particularly Luis Vives, based on the study of Latin and the liberal arts. Medina had been born in the ducal palace in 1493 and before 1538 entered Holy Orders. That year he accompanied the sixth Duke of Medina Sidonia and his son to the assembly of the Cortes of Castile at Toledo. Familiar with the world of letters, he helped to increase the number of volumes in the excellent ducal library, where he himself had first discovered erudition.

Medina seems to have been successful with his pupil. In reading the Duke's later correspondence, one can detect a man of considerable education, though his style seems more convoluted than normal in an age when baroque subtleties and indirect discourse were typical. He could converse in Latin, and Philip II's personal secretary, the priest Mateo Vázquez, studded his letters to the Duke with Latin phrases. Medina Sidonia knew history and followed the affairs of the world. He had a good idea of what was happening most everywhere, and in his letters one encounters news from such varied places as Barbary, England and Scotland, Constantinople, the Low Countries, Sweden, the New World, and the Far East. His geographic knowledge was vast, as might be expected of a pupil of Medina.

In matters of religion the Duke appears to have been devout in the Erasmian tradition of Luis Vives. A list of books his confessor Fray Diego Calahorrano brought with him during the armada campaign of 1588 includes works by Fray Luis de Granada, a mystic whose writings were considered suspect by the Inquisition. The Duke's correspondence often reveals concern for the plight of the poor, especially during the famine years of the 1590s, and a sense of anger at those who neglected or exploited them. Most interesting is a comment the Duke made on black slavery, not long after King Sebastian of Portugal and his army had been annihilated in Morocco: "Speaking in conscience, I consider the trade and captivity of these blacks an evil and iniquitous thing, and understanding that God has punished the Kingdom of Portugal for it, I pray to God that He not likewise punish our Spain."[30] Medina Sidonia did fulfill his ordinary religious obligations, and in some of his correspondence mentions the rituals of Holy Week.

Properly devout, the Duke also developed a keen sense of pride in his station and place in the world. While he got along well with most people, he was sometimes tetchy with his fellow titled nobles: with hidalgos and commoners he usually proved affable. Royal officials, most often of the petty nobility, frequently praised his willingness to pay attention to detail and work long hours. Medina Sidonia believed in what we call noblesse oblige, and the topics of nobility, honor, and correct deportment interested him. Pedro de Medina treated them in his *Libro de la Verdad* (Book of Truth), and Captain Jerónimo Carranza, who in 1589 became governor of Honduras, published in Sanlúcar several editions of his *Filosofía de las armas*, about honor and the redress of injury, dedicated to Medina Sidonia.[31] Carranza saw no conflict between arms and erudition and quoted Medina Sidonia's physician, Doctor Pedro Peramato, that "letters do not sully arms, but rather enhance them."[32]

Medina Sidonia's pride and self-esteem were further nurtured by the history of the dukes of Medina Sidonia, written by Pedro de Medina and dedicated to him and his mother, the Dowager-Countess of Niebla.[33] From it can be gleaned what he understood about the growth in wealth and influence of his house and its place in the history of Andalusia.

Figure 1. Genealogy of the seventh Duke of Medina Sidonia.

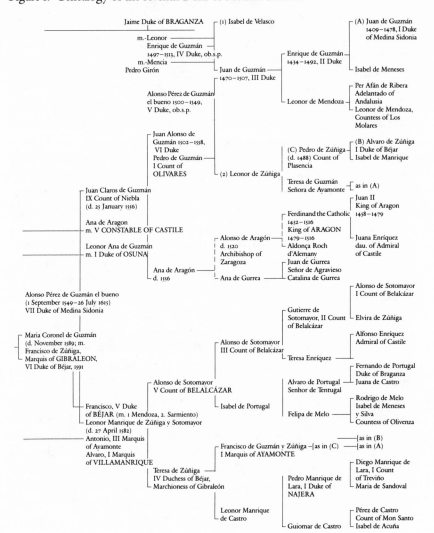

The founder of the house was Guzmán el Bueno, whose historic deeds in the late thirteenth century merge with legend. The family coat of arms displaying two cauldrons, each containing seven serpents, derived from his dragon-slaying derring-do in Morocco. What won Guzmán the epithet el Bueno and the señorío of Sanlúcar was his steadfast loyalty to King Sancho el Bravo in the civil wars of the 1290s. Spanish schoolboys still hear the tale about how Guzmán, besieged in Tarifa by Sancho's enemies, was given the choice of surrendering the town or seeing his captive son killed before his eyes. From the battlements he hurled his dagger and exclaimed, "If you will kill him, here is the knife!"

Guzmán's niece Leonor became the celebrated mistress of King Alfonso XI and mother of his royal bastard Henry of Trastámara. When Henry rebelled against his legitimate brother King Pedro, his Guzmán kin joined him. They reaped their rewards in 1369 when Henry won the throne, and the third Señor of Sanlúcar became first Count of Niebla.

The counts of Niebla enlarged their domains by purchase and border combats, which included a failed attempt on Gibraltar in 1436 that cost the second Count of Niebla his life. In 1445, King Juan II awarded the third Count what now is the oldest ducal title in Spain, that of Medina Sidonia.

The newly created Duke took Gibraltar from the Moors in 1462 and supported Queen Isabella's succession to the throne a dozen years later. He died in 1478, leaving his titles and estates to a legitimized son, whose mother he married in his old age. The counts of Alba de Liste, descendants of a daughter of an earlier marriage, litigated to get the title, a litigation that continued as late as the 1580s. The seventh Duke admitted in 1572 that the whole business so irritated him that he burnt the relevant papers.[34]

The second Duke of Medina Sidonia participated in the War of Granada but died in 1492, leaving as third Duke his twenty-four-year-old son. In 1497 the third Duke organized an expedition that captured Melilla in North Africa, but soon after faced the determined effort of the Crown to strip him of Gibraltar. He died in 1507. His heir was aged nine.

Gibraltar went to the Crown and the remainder of the inheritance entered a period of trouble and litigation. The nine-year-old Duke was soon caught in the schemes of the ambitious Count of Ureña, who was extending his influence from Old Castile to Andalusia. Ureña arranged for his daughter to marry the Duke and his son Pedro Girón to marry the Duke's sister. King Ferdinand of Aragon, Regent of Castile, moved to prevent the Ureña marriages and wanted Medina Sidonia to marry instead Doña Ana de Aragón, the King's natural granddaughter. Pedro Girón fled with the Duke to Portugal, where the Duke died at age sixteen.

Ferdinand of Aragon now took charge. There remained three brothers from the third Duke's second marriage, on whom he settled the Medina Sidonia inheritance. Because the eldest was feebleminded, Ferdinand allowed him the title and set him aside; he arranged for the second, Don Juan Alonso de Guzmán, to exercise all pertinent authority and rights and marry Doña Ana. From 1538 Don Juan Alonso shared the ducal title, and on his older brother's death in 1549, he became sole Duke, ranked sixth in the succession. The youngest brother, Don Pedro de Guzmán, became in 1539 Count of Olivares.

Beholden to the Crown as guarantor of their inheritance, the brothers stood in 1520 by Ferdinand's grandson, King Carlos I (Holy Roman Emperor Charles V), against the rebellious Comuneros; Pedro Girón, still hoping to corner the inheritance, became a Comunero leader. The Guzmán brothers swiftly cowed Comunero sympathizers in their neighborhood and kept Seville and Andalusia safely in the royal camp. Don Pedro then joined the royalist forces at the taking of Toledo.

For his loyalty, his wealth, and his influence in Andalusia, Don Juan Alonso de Guzmán basked in the royal favor. The Medina Sidonia title appeared in the 1520 list of twenty-five that Charles V recognized as *grandes de España* (grandees of Spain). In 1526 Don Juan Alonso headed the cavalcade that escorted Isabel of Portugal to her marriage with Charles in Seville; and in 1543 he helped organize the celebrations that attended the marriage of Prince Philip to Princess Maria Manuela of Portugal.

He also assumed the role of his forebears in overseeing the defense of western Andalusia. During the last years of the wars of Habsburg against Valois, French privateers infested the Gulf of Cadiz, threatened the treasure route to the Indies, and plundered coastal shipping. In 1540 the Ottoman Turkish fleet attacked Gibraltar, and annually corsairs from Morocco and Algiers menaced Andalusia's shores. Alarms were constant. Local militias had to be mustered and drilled, watchtowers had to be manned, provisions had to be collected for royal garrisons, patrol galleys, and armadas bound for the Indies. Orders from court rained on the sixth Duke, urging him to get these things done.

The death of the Duke's son, the Count of Niebla, in 1556 made the

Duke's grandson heir not only to the ducal titles and estates, but also to the responsibilities. The sixth Duke rid himself of the most onerous and least profitable, the provisioning of Melilla. By the time he died two years later, aged fifty-six, peace was in sight. Medina's history ends with the accession to his titles of Don Alonso Pérez de Guzmán el Bueno, at age nine the premier nobleman of Andalusia.

The province the boy Duke surveyed from his palace in Sanlúcar, the Kingdom of Seville, had a population reckoned to number some half million souls.[35] It was watered by the Rio Guadalquivir, called by the poet Luis de Góngora "el gran rey de Andalucía" (the great king of Andalusia) and its capital, Seville, was a teeming city of an estimated 120,519 persons. At the top were wealthy nobles and merchants and an influential clergy; at the bottom thrived the world of vagabonds and *pícaros*, cutpurses and brigands, celebrated in the novellas of Mateo Alemán, Miguel de Cervantes, Luis de Góngora, and others unknown. In 1597 Medina Sidonia referred to this world when he complained that the post carrying his dispatches and those of others was robbed a league from Seville, "a new case and worthy of punishment."[36]

Seville's corregidor carried the resounding title *Asistente Real* (Royal Assistant) and was most often a titled nobleman. In times past dukes of Medina Sidonia had dominated the city's public life from their palace on the Calle de las Sierpes, and the seventh Duke continued to play an active part. He owned the office of *Escribano Mayor* (Chief Clerk) of Seville's municipal council, which he sold in 1581 to a person the council did not appreciate.[37] But two years later, in order "to serve better His Majesty," the Duke purchased the office of *Alférez Mayor* (Chief Ensign-bearer) of Seville's militia from his prominent kinsman Don Francisco Tello de Guzmán, Judge of the Indies, for the sum of 16,000 ducats.[38]

Of Seville's institutions what most interested the Duke, apart from the Almojarifazgo Mayor, was the Casa de Contratación (House of Trade) which regulated commerce with the Indies, and the closely related Prior and Consuls, who certified pilots and ships. He often complained to the King that the presidency of the casa routinely went to jurists with no experience of the Indies or annual flotas, and that the Prior and Consuls looked only after their own interests.

After Seville the largest city in the province was Jerez de la Frontera, which had historically supported the dukes of Arcos, the chief rivals in Andalusia of the dukes of Medina Sidonia.[39] Jerez counted over six thousand vecinos (from which can be reckoned a population of more than twenty-five thousand) and had long produced the sack favored by

Falstaff. Cádiz, which had become important for its position on the deep-water side of Cadiz Bay, had at best six hundred vecinos, and in 1592 the Council of War complained that it had a bare four hundred, not sufficient for its defense.[40] By the late sixteenth century many of the ships that formed the flotas to the Indies had become too large to sail the Guadalquivir to Seville or even comfortably cross the bar at Sanlúcar, and anchored and were loaded in Cadiz Bay. Medina Sidonia complained often about the growing size of ships in the Indies flotas and argued that vessels of three hundred to five hundred tons' burden were more suitable than larger vessels. To lend weight to his arguments and avoid accusation of self-interest, he filled his memorials with horror stories of nine-hundred-ton vessels lost on their first voyage and similar relevant examples.[41]

Apart from western Andalusia's many cities and towns, both royal and seigneurial, Medina Sidonia had to deal with the church and the provincial nobility. When Don Rodrigo de Castro, a son of his distant relation the Count of Lemos, became Archbishop of Seville in 1583, Medina Sidonia hurried "to kiss his hands."[42]

The most closely related to Medina Sidonia of the Andalusian nobility was the Marquis of Gibraleón, a first cousin who became his brother-in-law by marriage to his only surviving sister, Doña María Coronel de Guzmán, with whom he was very close.[43] Gibraleón inherited in 1591 the titles and estates of his father, the fifth Duke of Béjar. His domain on the coast, centered on Gibraleón, was small; his ducal inheritance in west-central Spain was vast, and as Duke of Béjar he joined Medina Sidonia among the grandees of Spain.

The marquises of Ayamonte and the counts of Olivares were also close blood relations of Medina Sidonia. Ayamonte's estates lay on the coast by the Portuguese border; those of Olivares lay a short distance west of Seville. In 1575, a younger brother of Medina Sidonia's mother became Marquis of Villamanrique, a small señorío he possessed between the Olivares estates and the County of Niebla.

Apart from Medina Sidonia and Béjar, other grandees with Andalusian estates were the dukes of Osuna, Arcos, Alcalá de los Gazules, and Medinaceli. The title Duke of Osuna was awarded by Philip II in 1562 to Don Pedro Girón,[44] already Count of Ureña and a grandee. Osuna married one of Medina Sidonia's aunts on his father's side. Osuna's extensive Andalusian estates centered on the town of Osuna, east of Seville. The dukes of Arcos, of the Ponce de León family, were historic enemies of the dukes of Medina Sidonia, but by

Medina Sidonia's lifetime past enmity had become gentle rivalry, and the dukes of both lines were closely related as the result of frequent intermarriage between the two houses made in search of peace. The dukes of Alcalá were of the Ribera family and had held previously the title Marquis of Tarifa. The second Marquis in 1558 was created duke and made a grandee by Philip II. The dukes of Medinaceli, whose chief estates lay on the border of Aragon, possessed in Andalusia only the señorío of Puerto Santa Maria. That, however, had put them at odds with the dukes of Medina Sidonia, and the two houses fought in the streets and the lawcourts over its possession until Ferdinand and Isabella put an end to the contest and left Medinaceli with the town.

Medina Sidonia's other aunt on his father's side married into the powerful Velasco family, and her husband became in 1559 Constable of Castile and Duke of Frias. The Velasco estates stretched from Burgos, their seat, to the Cantabrian coast, where the royal customs had long been in their hands. Because the royal customs of Sanlúcar were at the time controlled by the Duke of Medina Sidonia, the two houses were in a position to reciprocate.

In 1559, when peace came and King Philip II returned from the Low Countries to Spain, among his first acts were maneuvers to recover for the Crown the collection of customs duties that had been alienated by the Trastámara kings before Ferdinand and Isabella. The Crown targeted both the Constable's and Medina Sidonia's customs houses.

The death in November 1559 of the fourth Constable of Castile gave the King his opportunity to seize control of the Cantabrian customs in the course of confirming the inheritance of the fifth Constable, Medina Sidonia's uncle by marriage. After an unequal battle, the Constable lost. Medina Sidonia was probably lucky that in November 1558, when his grandfather died, the King had not yet returned to Spain.

Though Medina Sidonia had already been confirmed in his inheritance, the Crown nonetheless began to search for ways to obtain legally his customs house of Sanlúcar de Barrameda and also his salinas. The Royal Council of Castile went to work on the matter.

To counter the threat, the Countess of Niebla and the Duke's kin, Don Pedro de Guzmán, first Count of Olivares, and Don Antonio de Guzmán, Marquis of Ayamonte, sought influence at court through an alliance with Ruy Gómez de Silva, Prince of Eboli and the King's closest and most trusted minister. It was Ruy Gómez that the King had sent to Spain to find money after he had declared bankruptcy in 1557.

They proposed to the Prince that the young Duke of Medina Sidonia marry his daughter Doña Ana de Silva y Mendoza, then aged five. Eboli accepted.

Eboli was the ambitious scion of middling Portuguese nobility and had come to Spain as a page to the Empress Isabel, Philip II's mother. He early won Philip's favor, and Philip arranged Ruy Gómez's marriage to Doña Ana de Mendoza, the heiress of Don Diego de Mendoza, Prince of Mélito and Duke of Francavilla, a member of Castile's extensive Mendoza clan; he also made him Prince of Eboli in Naples, Duke of Pastrana in Castile, and Grandee of Spain. The influence of Eboli with the King was so pronounced that people called him Rey (King) Gómez.

Eboli recognized the advantage of adding Spain's richest grandee and head of the house of Guzmán to his network of allies. The marriage, he admitted to the Sieur de Fourquevaux, Ambassador of France, would benefit him greatly.[45] Eboli needed all the help he could enlist in his ongoing rivalry for influence at court with the Duke of Alba, head of the powerful House of Toledo. Alba had served Charles V as a soldier and statesman and acted as leader of the many senior ministers who continued to serve Philip. Philip respected Alba but found him often presumptuous and overbearing. He preferred to work through Eboli, to whom he gave considerable authority in matters of diplomacy, administration, and finance. Alba and Eboli differed most strongly over the government of the Netherlands, and for the rest each did all he could for his kin, clients, and allies in matters of royal patronage and ecclesiastical preferment.

The Duke of Medina Sidonia counted many kinsmen among the grandees and titled nobles of Spain, whose weight could be added to Eboli's side of the scale. While the Andalusian Guzmáns were not rivals of Alba's Toledo clan, the sixth Duke of Medina Sidonia had been involved in an acrimonious personal dispute with Alba at Salamanca on the occasion of Philip II's first marriage. But the Countess of Niebla's Zúñiga family were historic rivals of the Toledo, whose holdings bordered those of the two Zúñiga grandees, the Duke of Béjar and the Count of Miranda.

In June 1566 the Countess of Niebla took her son, aged sixteen, to court, where the contract for his marriage to Doña Ana de Silva was signed. The dowry Doña Ana brought with her was 100,000 ducats "in gold," a standard figure among the great families of Castile. The sum was met by various devices, including a *juro* (government bond) held against the alcabalas of Jerez, which paid an annuity of 2,500 ducats.[46] It was not until 1568, when Doña Ana reached the age of consent, seven, that she signed the contract.

At court Medina Sidonia did homage in July to Don Carlos, the ill-fated heir to the throne, then in August the Countess and Eboli combined forces to complain to Cardinal Espinosa, President of the Royal Council of Castile and chief architect of Crown fiscal policy, about how that policy threatened the Duke's rights.[47] The Countess accused the Crown of trying to seize assets "down to the tunafish" which the Duke's ancestors had won when they conquered their lands from the Moors. A day after the Countess addressed the Cardinal, Eboli reiterated her complaint and stated that he had the King's approval to participate in the Royal Council's deliberations to insure that the interests of the Duke and his vassals would be considered along with those of His Majesty.

The outcome was that Medina Sidonia retained control of his customs house, his salinas, and his tunny fishery. The worth of the Eboli match was clear, for so long as the Prince lived.

Medina Sidonia was nineteen when he next needed Eboli's good offices in a dispute with citizens of the city of Medina Sidonia over the provision of *lanzas* (armed horsemen) to serve in the Kingdom of Granada, where at the end of 1568 aggrieved Moriscos rose in rebellion. To subdue the revolt, motley forces took the field under the Marquis of Mondéjar, Captain General of Granada, and the Marquis of los Velez. Over the contentious marquises, Philip II placed his twenty-one-year-old half-brother, Don Juan of Austria. As the revolt spread, Don Juan had to find more men in a Spain stripped of able-bodied recruits and available veterans by the demands of the Netherlands revolt. Militiamen were mustered, and the feudal obligation of nobles and prelates to provide a set number of lanzas was invoked.

Medina Sidonia received orders to alert the militiamen of his estates to be ready to march to the defense of Gibraltar or Cádiz. Reports received in Spain of ship movements in Algiers convinced Madrid that the Turks planned to land men and supplies to support the Moriscos. It was believed that the Moriscos had been encouraged to rebel by the Turks and Algerians with promises of aid.[48] Memories of the Turkish attack on Gibraltar in 1540 were still vivid. At the head of a hundred horsemen, Medina Sidonia himself patrolled the coast.

From Granada Don Juan wrote Medina Sidonia, addressing him as *Vuestra Merced* (Your Grace), a term used in Spain for ordinary gentlemen, rather than *Vuestra Excelencia*, then used for grandees. He begged him to arm and send to Granada all the men on horse and foot he could and to provide for their pay.[49]

The answer, which the Duke's mother likely directed, informed Don Juan that the ducal house provided and paid for eighty lanzas on such occasions and reminded him that men had to remain for the defense of Gibraltar and Cádiz. A copy was sent to Eboli in Madrid. Don Juan replied by thanking "Your Excellency" for clarifying matters. The eighty lanzas soon reached Granada.

The eighty did not include people from the city of Medina Sidonia, which refused to contribute its share. The Duke soon had the responsible civic leaders tried, convicted, and imprisoned by a local court that functioned under his jurisdiction. The imprisoned men, whom the Duke identified as troublemakers, appealed their case to the Royal Chancellery of Granada, "where some have relatives." At the same time they made Don Juan a direct offer of sixty lanzas.

Their maneuver succeeded. The Chancellery assumed jurisdiction over the case and ordered the imprisoned men released and their horses returned to them. Don Juan accepted their offer of sixty lanzas. Seemingly vindicated, they sent to Sanlúcar a messenger who, not finding the Duke, who was away on patrol, accosted the Countess of Niebla "coming from Mass in the midst of a crowd" and gave her the news.

In his response to Don Juan, Medina Sidonia expressed outrage at the acceptance of an offer made by "rebels in disloyal leagues." He volunteered to provide the sixty additional lanzas if he were granted the necessary authority and given the names of those who had been willing to pay for them. At the same time, he sent a full report to the King, via the hands of Eboli.

The report is interesting for what it reveals of the attitude of the Duke and his mother about government. They regarded themselves as virtuous aristocrats and the factious civic leaders as representatives of selfish interests. Their sentiments seem well expressed by Carranza in a dedication to the Duke: "The gentleman is worthless in this century. To be honored most, be seen as richest; the sway of Señor Merchandise."[50] If the city's offer were accepted, the Duke and Countess argued, it would encourage further disobedience among the Duke's vassals, and the city government would pass from the control of the Duke and his councilors to private persons, which would overturn the proper order of things. "These private persons by devious means would soon exempt themselves from the duty to serve Your Majesty as men of means, and toss the burden onto the poor and those excused by law."

They achieved their purpose. Don Juan agreed not to accept the city's sixty lanzas, and the King transferred the case from the Chancellery of Granada to the Council of War in Madrid. The council, whose members were nobles, voted in the Duke's favor and for the time being settled the matter.[51]

The next spring the Morisco revolt flared briefly in the Sierra de Ronda and threatened estates belonging to Medina Sidonia and his neighbor the Duke of Arcos, on which some ten thousand Moriscos lived and worked.[52] Rumor that they were about to join the revolt reached Seville, where the two dukes were attending the King on his progress through Andalusia. Medina Sidonia and Arcos hurried to placate their Morisco vassals, who protested their loyalty but complained of the depredations of unruly soldiery.

In the expulsion of Moriscos from Andalusia and their dispersal throughout the central parts of Spain that followed the suppression of the rebellion, Medina Sidonia seems to have had only limited success in preventing the expulsion of Moriscos from his estates. The population figures for his towns in the Sierra de Ronda in 1587 show only thirty vecinos for Benarraba and sixteen for Algotocín.

The marriage of the Duke with Doña Ana de Silva was celebrated in Madrid on 4 November 1574, a little over a year after the death of her father, the Prince of Eboli. The bride was thirteen. Because it was customary to wait until the bride was fully mature before attempting to have children, their first was not born until January 1579. He was Juan Manuel, the future eighth Duke. Eight other children of the fourteen born to the Duchess survived and were well placed, through marriage, service to the Crown, and preferment in the church.[53]

The mature Doña Ana appears to have been an attractive and strong-willed woman, in these regards taking after her mother, the Princess of Eboli. She seems not to have displayed her mother's mercurial temperament or interest in intrigue. Medina Sidonia's character, moreover, seems much like that of her father, the Prince of Eboli, who was known for his firm but gentle manner. The gossip chroniclers claimed that the Duke, who had enjoyed youthful flings and sired a bastard, fell utterly in love with her and proved a dutiful husband.[54] Until her death in 1610 she seems to have played an important and influential role in his life, albeit one about which we have scant detail. Her mother's family would prove to be another matter.

About the life of the ducal family at Sanlúcar the literature and documents say little. There are occasional references to health, births, and deaths that carry the suggestion of a closely knit family. In the traditions of the house, piety and a sound education were certainly stressed for both sons and daughters. In his history of the House of Silva, Salazar y Castro praises the merits of the daughter Doña Leonor de Guzmán, who married the third Duke of Pastrana.[55] Most of her brothers went on to distinguished careers of service.

✳ CHAPTER TWO ✳

A Career of Service

WHEN Medina Sidonia was in Madrid for his wedding to Doña Ana de Silva y Mendoza late in 1574, he used the occasion to seek some important and honorable office. Aged twenty-five, he was described as a well-knit man, shorter than average in height, a superb horseman, and expert in jousting with *cañas*, light Moorish lances.[1] What he looked like is not clear: the only certain portrait dates from his old age and shows that he had a broad, high forehead, penetrating eyes, and a long, straight nose.[2]

The grandees and titled nobles of Spain who sought to serve their sovereign found in the Habsburg Monarchy an abundance of great offices at home and abroad that fulfilled their ambitions and appealed to their chivalric ideals, nurtured on Castiglione's *Book of the Courtier* (translated into Spanish by the poet Juan Boscán and published in 1534) and romances of knight-errantry. Many nobles who served the Crown were related to Medina Sidonia; his uncle, the Marquis of Ayamonte, had just been appointed Governor General of Milan.

It would not have been unusual for Medina Sidonia, as head of a great house, to remain the big man of his region and leave service at court or abroad to kinsmen of lesser station. Many heads of great houses did, including the sixth Duke of Medina Sidonia, and contented themselves with only an occasional campaign or embassy, if that. Those who served, most famously the third Duke of Alba, complained constantly that their service was bankrupting them because the Crown proved forever remiss in repaying expenses paid out of pocket or against their own credit.[3] Nonetheless Medina Sidonia joined those who chose to be active in the royal service. He approached the Junta de Armadas y

19

Galeras about taking the *asiento* (contract) for the administration of the galley squadron of Spain.

Fighting wars on two fronts, in the Netherlands and in the Mediterranean, Philip II was close to bankruptcy and desperate to find means of maintaining his armed forces. Many war councillors argued that turning the administration of the galley squadron over to a private contractor was both more economical and more efficient than leaving it under royal officials.[4] In operations the galleys would come under the King's commanders, and in practice, those who contracted for the galleys were the same men.

The asiento system had a long history in Spain, which had little tradition of a royal navy. When Castilian or Aragonese kings had needed an armada, they hired one. In the Mediterranean, where war and piracy were endemic during the sixteenth century, galley contracting had become a big business. Members of the Mendoza, Bazán, and Toledo families in Spain made careers of it. Genoese, with the Doria family heading the pack, also leased galleys by contract to the Spanish Crown.

Through an asiento Medina Sidonia would receive a set sum per galley, from which he had to maintain and provision the vessel and make a small profit. To make matters easier, he would be exempted from many taxes and customs duties. Supposedly he would be more concerned with economies than royal officials who drew salaries and seemed, people believed, less concerned with costs and more susceptible to bribery. Opponents of the asiento system feared that contractors would cut corners and endanger the galleys or avoid battle to avoid losses. This latter charge was repeatedly hurled at the Genoese Dorias.

The galley squadron of Spain under debate in 1574 had been built after twenty-five galleys under asiento to Juan de Mendoza foundered in 1562 in a freak winter storm near Málaga. Put together directly by the Crown and administered by royal officials, the squadron had been commanded first by Don García de Toledo and since 1568 by Don Juan of Austria, Captain-General of the [Mediterranean] Sea. In 1574 it numbered on paper forty galleys, of which the *capitana real* (royal flagship) and a dozen others had been with Don Juan at Lepanto.

Vying with Medina Sidonia for the contract were the Marquis of Estepa and the Marquis of Comares, of the illustrious Fernández de Córdoba family and heir to the Duke of Cardona. Both had experience of war but neither had Medina Sidonia's wealth. The council debated letting the asiento to Medina Sidonia at the low figure of 6,000 ducats per galley, stipulating forty galleys, but they divided over the Duke's demand for precedence in the squadron in the absence of Don Juan.[5] In effect he expected the lieutenant-generalship. The squadron's lieutenant general, Don Luis de Requesens, had become Governor General of the Netherlands in 1573. Both the Duke of Alba and the Duke of Francavilla, grandfather of Medina Sidonia's wife, thought that neither the Crown nor Medina Sidonia would benefit by the proposed arrangements.

Philip II, reviewing the minutes of the junta's discussions, decided to make no commitment and added, "I am not sure that the time is right, or that the Duke is ready." Negotiations continued after Medina Sidonia returned to Sanlúcar, and the sum per galley rose to 6,500 ducats.[6] The Duke found 6,500 acceptable but complained to the Marquis of Auñón, Treasurer General, that given the contract's terms, "it will not amount to 4,000." Only "the desire to serve His Majesty in this business" had led him to agree to 6,500, "when 9,000 is needed to keep one up."[7]

The difference between the two figures the Crown's agents assumed he would make up by exploiting the privileges the asiento allowed him, such as buying supplies cheaper abroad and importing them duty free, provisioning the galleys from his estates, and using the labor of the galleys' slaves and convicts on his own properties when the galleys were laid up for the winter.

More bothersome to the Duke than the issue of money was the continuing failure to grant him the status he wanted in the absence of Don Juan. "They have ignored it," he wrote, "as though they were handing this charge to some rich man. This is not a matter that permits dispute."

As weeks passed without a decision, the Duke decided to enlist the President of the Council of the Indies on his side. The galleys, he claimed, would be stationed in Cadiz Bay, bring money to Seville and protect the Indies flotas. Because the asiento would take effect in October 1575, he wanted all to be ready.[8]

Early in 1575 Don Juan arrived at court from Naples, disgruntled by the loss of Tunis the preceding autumn, for which he blamed the King's chaotic finances that denied him an adequate fleet. Medina Sidonia appealed to Don Juan directly, and Don Juan seemed favorably disposed until others close to him raised the old objections, of the Duke's lack of experience and demands for precedence, and the desirability of administering the galleys by asiento. The Lepanto veteran Don Juan de Cardona—a kinsman of the Marquis of Comares—wrote to Don Juan that he had "heard around the court that certain young gentlemen were seeking to take over the galleys," which, he insisted, should only be contracted to their own generals, veteran seamen with combat experience.[9]

Faced with continuing procrastination on the part of the Council of War, Medina Sidonia decided to abandon active pursuit of the asiento, though he asked his cousin Don Enrique de Guzmán, Count of Olivares, who was active at court, to keep track of the matter.[10] Nothing came of it, and the galleys of Spain continued under royal administration.

Back at Sanlúcar Medina Sidonia took an increasing interest in the shipping entering and leaving the Guadalquivir, above all the flotas that assembled annually for the voyage to New Spain and Tierra Firme, and did what he could to assist their sailing. Years later he claimed that the King, during his visit to Seville in 1570, had requested that he do this.[11]

He also paid more heed to events across the Strait of Gibraltar in Morocco, whose independence was threatened by Turkish-dominated Algiers. In the spring of 1576 Abd al-Malik, who claimed his late brother's Moroccan throne, invaded Morocco with Turkish aid and overthrew the government of his nephew, Sharif Muhammad el-Motawakkil. The deposed Sharif fled the country and sought support in Spain and Portugal. On the coast of Andalusia opposite Morocco the local militia stood to arms, and Madrid sent engineers to inspect Gibraltar and Cádiz, which the aged hero Don García de Toledo claimed were virtually defenseless.

Medina Sidonia ordered the muster of the militiamen of his estates. From the corregidor of Jimena, which overlooks Gibraltar, he received a report he found unsatisfactory.[12] In response, he ordered the corregidor, the *alcaide* (castellan), and the captain of infantry to select four good men "zealous for the public welfare," who knew all the vecinos and their sons, aged eighteen and older, and to hold a second muster. As the town crier called the roll, the householders were to form units of twenty on horse or on foot and in accordance with the weapons they brought: lances, firearms, or crossbows. Each was to declare under oath what sons he had who were over eighteen and see that such sons were armed in accordance with their station (which was determined by the worth of the household). The four good men moreover had to make sure that the grown sons of female heads of households also mustered with the weapons they were expected to carry.

In defending the thinly populated coast, horsemen were especially needed. They were to go armed and were not permitted to leave the vicinity for more than a day until after the end of September, when autumn weather reduced the threat of corsair attack. The Duke ordered his corregidor to be generous in extending the privileges of *caballeros* to all who served on horseback, even if they lacked firearms. Mounted men with firearms in addition to lance, sword, and buckler were known as *caballeros de cuantía*; those without as *caballeros de gracia*. Their privileges included exemption from quartering troops and freedom from having goods sequestered during civil suits.

To insure that all required to serve in the militia bore the proper arms, the Duke offered a bounty to those who enrolled recalcitrant householders or their sons and a stiff fine of 2,000 maravedís (about 5 ducats, or three months' wages for a farmhand) for convicted shirkers. Half the sum went to the Duke, the rest was divided between the sentencing judge and the informer. To encourage the possession of firearms and good marksmanship among the militiamen, Medina Sidonia conceded to them free hunting privileges on Sundays and holidays. The men of Jimena, he concluded, "must be ready to march wherever necessary."

Across the strait from Jimena the new Sharif of Morocco, Abd al-Malik, aided by his brother Ahmed, turned his attention to consolidating his power in Fez and Marrakech. Though he accepted Turkish assistance, the political and religious authority of the Moroccan sharifs he wielded rested on a tradition that extended back to the Prophet and was incompatible with subjection to the Ottoman Sultan. To keep his independence, the Sharif, who spoke both Spanish and Italian, needed support from Spain. What he feared immediately was that Spain and Portugal might be tempted to deal with his nephew, the deposed Muhammad el-Motawakkil. He wanted his rival handed over to his custody. Medina Sidonia followed closely the Sharif's maneuvers, and in April 1577 he suggested to Madrid ways to negotiate with the Sharif to achieve the expulsion of the Turks from Barbary.[13]

Philip, in the process of seeking a truce with the Ottoman sultan, had to proceed cautiously. He refused to receive the deposed Sharif, but his nephew, King Sebastian of Portugal, welcomed him and promised support. Dom Sebastian wanted to recover the fortresses Portugal once possessed along the Moroccan coast but lost after 1540. Philip met with the Portuguese King at Christmastide 1577 but failed to dissuade him from his determination. Rather, he reluctantly agreed to provide Sebastian with a contingent of Castilian volunteers for his expedition.

In June 1578 Medina Sidonia welcomed Dom Sebastian at Cádiz. The King had sailed from Lisbon aboard a fleet that carried an expeditionary force of seventeen thousand men of mixed quality, bound for Morocco. The fleet anchored in Cadiz Bay to embark the promised Castilian volunteers. While they waited for the volunteers Medina Sidonia staged for Dom Sebastian lavish entertainments, including bullfights and jousts, on which he spent over 30,000 ducats.[14] When after eight days the volunteers had not arrived, the Portuguese armada weighed anchor.

Six weeks later, on 8 August, news reached Medina Sidonia from Morocco that Dom Sebastian had been defeated and his army almost annihilated in battle four days before at Alcazarquivir. After some hope that Dom Sebastian had survived, it became clear that he had fallen.[15] Captive Portuguese nobles identified the body. The reigning Sharif Abd al-Malik had also perished, along with Muhammad el-Motawakkil, his rival. The Sharif's brother Ahmed, acclaimed on the battlefield al-Mansour (the Victorious), became Sharif of Morocco. Barely a hundred survivors of Sebastian's army reached the safety of the coast, where the Portuguese fleet was anchored. All other survivors were captives, held for ransom or destined for slavery.

Medina Sidonia put on the alert the two thousand Castilian volunteers who had reached Cádiz too late to join Dom Sebastian, while the Spanish galley squadron under the Marquis of Santa Cruz at Gibraltar prepared to cross the strait to assist in the defense of the Portuguese strongholds of Ceuta, Tangier, and Arzila in case they were attacked. The Duke soon embarked the two thousand men in the galleys he once aspired to take by asiento.

While he assisted Santa Cruz and attended to Andalusia's defenses he also became involved in ransoming Portuguese nobles who had survived Alcazarquivir. Chief among these was his kinsman ten-year-old Dom Theodosio, Duke of Barcelos, eldest son of the Duke of Braganza. Braganza, Constable of Portugal, was in poor health and allowed his heir to accompany King Sebastian to Morocco in his place. A month after the battle, Medina Sidonia ordered his warden of Zahara to assist those on their way to negotiate Barcelos's ransom, and a year later requested his treasurer of Niebla to release funds to aid Barcelos's return.[16] According to the Prince of Parma's agent in Madrid, Medina Sidonia also helped Dom António, Prior of Crato, win his freedom, though Dom António, on his return to Lisbon, claimed he had escaped.[17]

Both ransoms would have their repercussion in the succession to the Portuguese Crown. Dom Sebastian died unmarried and without offspring, and the Crown of Portugal passed to his great uncle the Cardinal Henry, the last surviving son of King Manuel the Fortunate. The King-Cardinal was aged sixty-six, not in the best of health, and bound by vows of celibacy. Of the several claimants who awaited his death, none was more determined or more powerful than Philip II of Spain. He rested his rights on the fact that he was the eldest male descendant of King Manuel through his mother, Isabel of Portugal, Dom Manuel's eldest daughter. Barcelos's mother, Duchess of Braganza Doña Catalina, also raised a claim to the Portuguese Crown as grand-daughter of King Manuel through her father, the Infante Dom Duarte; and Dom António raised his own claim as son, albeit illegitimate, of the Infante Dom Luis.[18]

Philip was at first hopeful that the King-Cardinal would favor him over the Duchess of Braganza or Dom António, Prior of Crato. The Duchess's husband was inept and unpopular, and the Prior, though popular, was of illegitimate birth and allegedly tainted blood because his mother was a *conversa*, descended from Jews who had converted to Christianity. The King-Cardinal detested the Prior and, when the Prior claimed that his parents had eventually married, convened a special tribunal that reasserted the Prior's bastardy.

To the King-Cardinal Philip sent a special envoy, Don Cristóbal de Moura. Portuguese by birth, Moura had come to Spain in 1554 with Philip's sister Doña Juana, Dom Sebastian's mother, after she was wid-owed. He carried a list sent by Spain's envoy in Morocco of captured Portuguese *fidalgos* (gentlemen) and the ransoms demanded for them by Sharif Ahmed al-Mansour. Philip promised to do all he could to help with the ransoms, for which he expected the fidalgos' gratitude and support.

The Duke of Medina Sidonia had views of his own about how to proceed with the Portuguese and in late October sought an interview with Philip. Through his private secretary, Mateo Vázquez, Philip sug-gested that the Duke confide his thoughts to writing, though if the Duke were in the neighborhood, "it would be appropriate to hear you in person."[19] He thanked the Duke for his condolences on the death of Don Juan of Austria (1 October 1578), which had thrown the court into a state of confusion and likely made the King, in mourning for his brother, less than eager to stage the sort of interview a grandee felt his due.

In the spring of 1579 a new embassy, this one headed by the Duke of Osuna, Medina Sidonia's uncle, took the road from Madrid to Lisbon. Osuna's sister was wife of the Portuguese Duke of Aveiro, missing after the Battle of Alcazarquivir and presumed dead. Osuna's first report carried the disturbing news that the King-Cardinal seemed inclined to favor the Duchess of Braganza.

In Madrid Philip II's councillors met to prepare for the eventuality of war, and the King summoned from Rome Cardinal Granvelle, a distinguished Burgundian statesman who had long served Habsburg interests, to give firm direction to the Monarchy's government. Orders were sent to the King's viceroys and governors in Italy to bring their *tercios* and *coronellas* (Spanish and Italian regiments) of infantry up to full strength and assemble shipping to embark them for Spain. The plan was for the army to mass at Badajoz in Extremadura and march straight for Lisbon.

While the army marched overland, the armada would attack Lisbon from the sea. Along the Cantabrian coast of Spain naval contractors outfitted ships for combat and in Cadiz Bay the Marquis of Santa Cruz formed a large armada of galleys and greatships that would be augmented by vessels arriving from Italy. Medina Sidonia was not on the best of terms with Santa Cruz, though the two cooperated when necessary. The Council of War had to settle a dispute over precedence in saluting between the young grandee and the Marquis by instructing the Marquis to fly the royal standard rather than his personal flag when entering Sanlúcar, "to avoid inconveniences."[20]

Because of concern that the King-Cardinal might die before Philip's regular forces had concentrated, orders were dispatched to the Castilian lords, prelates, and towns along the Portuguese border to alert their lanzas and militias and be ready to march. The supervision of these preparations in Andalusia was assigned to Medina Sidonia. His estates and the city of Seville provided most of the men.

By royal order the Duke raised in May six thousand infantry and over five hundred horsemen from his estates and moved them toward the Portuguese frontier.[21] Most of the men had little experience beyond holiday drills and occasional patrol duty along the coast, but some of their officers and sergeants were grizzled veterans of Spain's imperial wars. The Duke, assisted by his brother-in-law, the Marquis of Gibraleón, established his headquarters in Ayamonte, a town that belonged to his uncle the Marquis of Ayamonte, Governor General of

Milan. Facing Medina Sidonia in the Portuguese Algarve were an estimated eighteen thousand militiamen.

Osuna and Moura expressed to Philip their fear that if the King-Cardinal died and Medina Sidonia invaded the Algarve before Spain's principal land and sea forces were ready, he would be repulsed and "reputation could be lost, which at the outset could be of great harm."[22] Philip assured them that he would order Medina Sidonia's small army across the border only if a majority of the Portuguese demonstrated their support of his rights.

To determine the strength of Philip's support in the Algarve, Medina Sidonia sent agents across the frontier. They found that people everywhere favored Philip II. Of the twelve hundred vecinos of Serpa they reported that "almost everybody says he will support none other but the King of Castile, and that all think so badly of the Duke of Braganza that it becomes tiresome to hear it."[23] At the same time Medina Sidonia himself sounded out the Duchess of Braganza and the Prior of Crato and tried to persuade them to accept Philip's succession.

At the beginning of August Medina Sidonia was stunned to learn through a personal letter from the King of the arrests on 28 July of the Princess of Eboli, the Duke's mother-in-law, and Antonio Pérez, the royal secretary who dealt with the Portuguese correspondence.[24] According to the King, she had been meddling in the affairs of Pérez and Mateo Vázquez, the King's private secretary, and had refused to heed the royal confessor, Padre Chaves, when he asked her to desist.

Preparing his response, Medina Sidonia admitted the distress he felt. With some protest that punishment for the sins of parents ought fall on the children, he urged the King to pardon her for activities that seemed the fault of her sex and send her home to her estates at Pastrana. He understood that the King had to deal rigorously with the matter, but having done so, he should proceed with leniency. "She was not born to be a prisoner and oppressed, and it might endanger her health and even her soul."[25] For the King the matter was more serious than the Duke at first seemed to believe. The Princess was confined to the small Torre de Pinto, some three leagues from Madrid.

The reasons for the arrests of Pérez and the Princess have excited wild speculation ever since. Whatever Medina Sidonia learned, he never committed anything specific to writing. Current were rumors about a love triangle involving the Princess, the King, and Pérez and about secret affairs of state. Feeding the scandal was the murder by Pérez's henchmen in 1578 of Juan de Escobedo, secretary to Don Juan of

Austria. Few made sense of the murder, and tales spread that Escobedo had found Pérez and the Princess in lascivious embrace and threatened to tell the King.[26] Modern scholars discount any affair between La Eboli and the King, and some doubt that her relations with Pérez went beyond her fascination with intrigue and power.

All Madrid knew that Pérez was involved in a struggle for influence with Mateo Vázquez, a pious, obsequious priest who was perceived as the chief instrument of Pérez's downfall and Eboli's arrest. Pérez served as leading spokesman for the faction previously headed by his late patron, the Prince of Eboli, in continued opposition to Alba's faction. Vázquez was associated with what might be called a faction of bureaucrats committed to the increase of royal power and the rule of royal law as opposed to privilege; and more concerned with the affairs of Spain than Habsburg interests abroad. Against Pérez, Vázquez was willing to work with the Duke of Alba's faction, though Alba himself had been banished from court for acting in a family matter contrary to the King's will. Pérez and the Princess, implacable foes of Alba, had played an active part in Alba's disgrace.

But at the bottom of the mystery were affairs of state, which none dared mention save in the vaguest terms until after 1591, when Pérez escaped prison and broadcast charges against the King and his enemies at court. How the Princess of Eboli was implicated remains uncertain, but most probably as a vociferous supporter of Pérez, who could arrange to have Vázquez intimidated by threats of bodily harm or even death, and for obtaining state secrets about Portugal from Pérez as part of her scheme to marry a son or daughter to a daughter or the son of the Duchess of Braganza. The Princess had on her payroll several bravos, and Medina Sidonia found out that her kinsman the Marquis of La Favara had threatened to "do harm to Vázquez."[27]

Referring to her scheme for a marriage alliance with the House of Braganza, a royal official in a memorandum to Vázquez described her as "Jezebel" and hinted that she had coaxed information from Pérez that would aid her in her dealings.[28] According to a report sent to Cardinal Farnese in Rome, she was fishing for a marriage of her younger daughter to the Duke of Barcelos.[29]

What did Medina Sidonia know about this? He corresponded with the Duke and Duchess of Braganza about the ransom of the Duke of Barcelos from Morocco and to persuade them to accept Philip II's claims. He kept the King informed about what he did. Curiously, nothing about La Eboli's marriage designs appears in any of his surviving correspondence.

About Barcelos, now aged eleven, Medina Sidonia received a letter from Philip in September 1579 which read, "The Sharif, in deference to me, has graciously conceded liberty to the Duke."[30] Pedro Venegas de Córdoba, Philip's envoy to Fez, had orders to bring Barcelos to Sanlúcar and thence to court. The whole matter had to be treated with careful dissimulation, the King warned Medina Sidonia, "lest some Portuguese put doubts into his head that he might be detained, . . . and advise him to flee," and because there was "no other guarantee than the word of a Moor."

At the same time Barcelos wrote Medina Sidonia that he would soon be freed, while agents of the Duke of Braganza informed him that 400,000 ducats had been spent in the ransom of Barcelos and eighty Portuguese fidalgos.[31] Aware of the eighty fidalgos and worried about the failing health of the King-Cardinal, Philip instructed Medina Sidonia to separate Barcelos "from that multitude that comes with him" and keep him entertained.[32]

Early in November Barcelos reached Fez from Marrakech, escorted by Venegas de Córdoba. Braganza complained of the close watch kept on his son as unbefitting the nephew of a king and noted, "I have understood from some captive fidalgos that [Venegas] is sleeping in the same chamber."[33] He and the Duchess accused Philip of deliberately delaying Barcelos's homeward journey. Philip denied it and expressed to Medina Sidonia his fear that the delay was "some artifice of the Sharif."[34] He wanted Barcelos free and safe, he insisted, "as though he were my own son," and asked Medina Sidonia to persuade Braganza of his good intentions.

Barcelos and his party arrived at Sanlúcar late in January 1580, after a voyage from Tetuan to Gibraltar aboard a galley dispatched by Santa Cruz. Already the Portuguese Cortes were in session and all expected the King-Cardinal to name his choice of successor at any time. Philip's instructions to Medina Sidonia about what should be done with Barcelos varied almost daily in light of developments in Portugal. One day he would issue an order to "detain him artfully and gently . . . so that it does not seem a trick or cause resentment," the next, to let Barcelos leave at will.[35]

Regarding the fidalgos, Philip urged Medina Sidonia to persuade them to accept his claim to the Portuguese Crown. "Otherwise," he stated, "there will be war. . . . I shall give much to avoid rupture, which would upset me greatly, for the damages and inconveniences that might follow to these kingdoms and that, and even to the rest of Christendom."

Medina Sidonia entertained Barcelos well, and the boy seemed in no rush to depart. But when news came at the beginning of February of the King-Cardinal's death, Medina Sidonia had to detain him. Braganza suspected as much and angrily wrote to Medina Sidonia about his son's detention "with fiestas when all should have been in mourning for the King-Cardinal."[36]

"Being a relation and servant of Your Excellency," Medina Sidonia answered, "I cannot help being sorry. . . . I have spent in his ransom 50,000 ducats." He admitted the fiestas but insisted they had stopped on arrival of the news of the King-Cardinal's death. Barcelos, he claimed, "has enjoyed himself so in this house, and we with him, that it gives us grief to let him go so soon. . . . Let Doña Catalina know that he is here with me. . . . I excuse myself for acting thus."[37]

The Duchess Catalina's reaction to the Barcelos affair has been reported by the contemporary historian Luis Cabrera de Córdoba: "With an agitated voice she said that she would rather see him in the power of the Turk, for then she could ransom him for cash, rather than in that of the King of Castile."[38] Barcelos departed Sanlúcar, well attended, early in March. Medina Sidonia rode with him to the frontier. On the fifteenth he reached Almerim and the arms of his parents.

The death of the King-Cardinal had cast the sessions of the Cortes meeting at Almerim into confusion. After weeks of wrangling, the board of five governors of the kingdom established by the King-Cardinal's will was able to dissolve the Cortes with promises to summon another to determine the succession. The Duchess of Braganza begged Philip "as a Christian prince" to back her candidacy, though she knew he would not, and sent agents to Medina Sidonia and Don Rodrigo de Castro, Bishop of Cuenca, her husband's uncle, to seek the best settlement possible from the Spanish King. The number of her active supporters was small: nobles traditionally loyal to the House of Braganza and the Jesuits, who distrusted Philip II and Dom António equally.

Dom António found broad popular support and fashioned a party based on a few noble friends, such as the Count of Vimioso, the smaller merchants, and the conversos. The Mendicant Friars inclined toward the Prior, whereas the higher clergy favored Philip of Spain. From Pope Gregory XIII, no friend of Spain, the Prior obtained a brief that permitted the case of his illegitimacy to be reheard. The Pope claimed that the right to settle the Portuguese succession was his and sent a legate to Spain to restrain Philip II from making war.

Philip II could count as adherents a majority of the nobility, many of whom owed him their ransoms from Morocco, the high clergy, and the big merchants, who had commercial ties with Seville and Antwerp. While Moura and Osuna in Portugal worked hard with promises and gifts to gain support for their master, Philip himself pressed ahead with his invasion plans and in March 1580 journeyed to the monastery of Guadalupe to be near the Portuguese frontier. Some talked of Medina Sidonia for the command of the army assembling at Badajoz, but Cardinal Granvelle and the Council of War persuaded the King to recall the Duke of Alba from banishment and give the command to him.

Medina Sidonia in Andalusia had been watching the army grow as ships brought veterans from Italy. On Christmas Day 1579, Marcelo Doria's Genoese galleys had disembarked twenty-five hundred Spaniards of the tercio of Pedro Zapata at Gibraltar, while into Cadiz Bay sailed galleys and greatships from Naples and La Spezia bringing three thousand Italian soldiers, five thousand Germans, and twenty-five hundred more Spaniards. The Marquis of Santa Cruz counted nearly eighty galleys and over two dozen greatships at Gibraltar and Puerto Santa Maria. In the ports of Galicia, Asturias, and the Basque country more ships were under way, commanded by Don Pedro de Valdés and Juan Martínez de Recalde. Some four thousand infantry assembled near La Coruña ready to embark.

For the anticipated campaign Medina Sidonia recalled the men he had mobilized in 1579 and soon mustered well over four hundred horse and four thousand infantry. The King granted him license to take a census of incomes and goods in his estates in order to raise 50,000 ducats for the maintenance of border forts.[39] Along the river Guadiana up to Mertola a flotilla of twelve *bergantinas* (small vessels of sail and oar) assembled by the Duke patrolled. Other men recruited for the King's service by the prelates, lords, and towns of Andalusia were put under Medina Sidonia's command and marched toward the frontiers. By royal order their banners bore not the arms of Philip II or Portugal, but rather images of the Virgin and saints.

At the Duke's request, the King dispatched veteran officers to assist him. Two whom he sent, Commendador Francisco de Valencia and Maestre de Campo Pedro de Padilla, became the Duke's chief aides at his headquarters at Ayamonte and helped him unravel complications in the levy of men and drill them for the campaign to come. Not all had complied with the order to levy men, and many who did offered inadequate supplies and pay. A second order was sent to the Count of Castellar, "so that it is not thought that some are being excused for some reason, or just because they did not respond."[40] In some cases the reasons for being excused were compelling. Medina Sidonia's brother-in-law Gibraleón argued that his estates, which lay on the coast and were impoverished, were constantly harassed by Moorish corsairs and he needed all the men he had to defend them. Quite different was the problem of Seville, which offered to pay its companies double the customary rate. The Duke feared men would desert companies already formed to enlist in Seville's. Seville was ordered not to pay double and to suspend recruiting until the companies already enlisted had marched out.

In addition to finding men for his invasion army, Medina Sidonia had to assist the Marquis of Santa Cruz in finding crewmen, soldiers, and rowers for the galleys. In maritime districts "volunteer" oarsmen called *buenaboya* could be levied, but only with great difficulty. Men avoided the service and fled inland; recruiters resorted to press gangs. Aboard the galleys the buenaboya were chained to the benches like the convicts and slaves to prevent their deserting. For money and supplies Medina Sidonia depended on the efficient Factor of Seville's Casa de Contratación, Francisco Duarte, who provisioned the annual flotas to the Indies.

In mid-April Medina Sidonia, accompanied by his eighteen-year-old brother-in-law, the Duke of Pastrana, with him for the campaign, left his post for a fortnight and rode to Guadalupe to see the King and urge that the Princess of Eboli be allowed to return to her palace in Pastrana. She had been moved already to more capacious and comfortable quarters at Santorcaz, close by her estates, but remained under strict guard. Medina Sidonia persuaded the King to relax the guard and allow her to receive her children and oversee the business of her estates. A former official of the late Prince of Eboli was permitted to assist her.

When Medina Sidonia returned to Andalusia, he resumed organizing his armed force and continued his diplomatic dealings across the frontier. His connections in Elvas assured him that they would deliver that border town for Philip of Spain, assuring Alba's army easy entrance to Portugal. From the Duke and Duchess of Braganza he received another agent, sent to confer with him about their situation. He decided to send the man to court to speak confidentially with Secretary Zayas.[41]

At the end of May the five governors of the kingdom provided by the King-Cardinal's will reassembled the Portuguese Cortes at Almerim but then, faced with mounting tensions, withdrew to Setúbal while the Cortes broke into factions. Dom António's supporters convened in Santarem. On 18 June several companies of Castilian troops crossed the frontier and occupied Elvas, whose Governor declared for Philip II as anticipated.

News of the occupation created consternation throughout Portugal. Dom António and his people seized Santarem, then rode hard for Lisbon, where they occupied the royal arsenals and treasury as crowds cheered. The Count of Vimioso took possession of Setúbal and forced the flight of three of the five governors of the kingdom, who sailed in a Sardinian caravel for Andalusia.

Dom António sought the support of the Duke and Duchess of Braganza with promises to remain unmarried (though he had two illegitimate sons) and designate Barcelos as his heir. The Duke and Duchess spurned his offer and retired to their estates at Vila Viçosa to see what would happen. Their agents pressed Philip II for favors in return for their acceptance of his succession.

Philip II moved his court to Badajoz, where he reviewed his army. The Duke of Alba paraded before the royal reviewing stand regular soldiers of Spanish, Italian, and German nationality and militiamen mustered by the towns, prelates, and señores of the border provinces. Then, at the urging of Moura, who had barely escaped Setúbal alive, the army poured across the frontier into Portugal, already racked with disorders and in 1580 plagued by disease.

At Ayamonte Medina Sidonia received orders to march. He reviewed his forces and complained to the King that apart from Seville and his kinsman the Marquis of Ayamonte he had received little cooperation from the rest of Andalusia in providing men. There were limits to the Duke's influence in his own province.

As he prepared to cross into the Algarve, the Sardinian caravel from Setúbal with the three Portuguese Governors and several refugee noblemen, all friends of his, dropped anchor in the Guadiana. They joined Medina Sidonia's expedition.

From Cádiz Santa Cruz's armada, which now consisted of eighty-seven galleys and thirty ships, weighed anchor and coasted north. On reaching Ayamonte, Santa Cruz and his chief subordinates, including

Don Juan de Cardona, Captain General of the Neapolitan galleys, came ashore for a council of war with Medina Sidonia and his people. Medina Sidonia wanted the armada to assist him in the conquest of the Algarve. It was a matter of time, since plans called for Santa Cruz and his armada to "join hands" with Alba and his army to surprise Lisbon from the sea.

Medina Sidonia and Santa Cruz agreed that the armada should be kept together in massive strength and that no part should be detached to secure the Azores, which would have to wait. The armada would assist Medina Sidonia in the conquest of the Algarve, since it would take Alba several weeks to reach Setúbal. With the Algarve in hand, Santa Cruz would round Cape St. Vincent for his rendezvous with Alba.

On 11 July the armada stood off Faro, while Medina Sidonia and his forces approached overland. Faro's governor, softened by diplomacy, surrendered without a fight. The governors of Vila Nova de Portimão and Lagos followed suit, persuaded by Antonio de Castro, a Portuguese emigré from Setúbal. Soon afterward Sagres surrendered, and before July had run out the Algarve was conquered. The three governors of the kingdom who had fled Setúbal established themselves under Medina Sidonia's tutelage at Castro Marim and issued an edict outlawing the Prior of Crato and the "rebels and malcontents" who rallied to him.[42]

Santa Cruz rounded Cape St. Vincent with the armada and headed north, and Medina Sidonia turned his forces inland. Before the end of August he received the surrender of Almodovar, Ourique, Beja, Serpa, and Moura. Philip wrote to thank the Duke for "the cities, towns and places that through your industry and diligence have been subjected and come over peacefully to my obedience."[43] He also sent Medina Sidonia a long, detailed relation of the taking of Lisbon by Alba and Santa Cruz by a brilliantly conceived and conducted amphibious operation.

Medina Sidonia decided to take advantage of the King's gratitude to obtain further concessions in the arrest of the Princess of Eboli. He sent Pastrana in person to Philip at Badajoz to make full report of the conquest of the Algarve and to seek once more his mother's transfer to her own palace in Pastrana. Her health was not good, and they hoped that greater freedom might prove a cure. The King remained unmoved.

Medina Sidonia returned in early September to Sanlúcar, where, in accord with royal orders, he sent the corregidores of Jerez, Cádiz, and

Gibraltar to receive the surrender of the Portuguese North African presidios of Ceuta, Arzila, Tangier, and Mazagan.

Fighting in northern Portugal persisted until November. Dom António escaped the defeat at Lisbon, rallied his people at Oporto, and tried to build support for his cause by methods that mixed terror and persuasion. Alba's chief lieutenant, Don Sancho Dávila, led a flying column north and shattered the motley force Dom António had mustered. Once more Dom António escaped. He went into hiding and traveled furtively round the country, still hoping to find support and raise the populace against the King of Spain.

Medina Sidonia received from the King of Spain offer of the Governor Generalship of Milan. He had made a favorable impression on the King, appeared willing to serve the Crown, and Milan seemed a fitting honor. From Madrid Cardinal Granvelle wrote Medina Sidonia to admit that he had recommended the offer and urged him to accept it promptly. The office had been vacated by the death that summer of his uncle the Marquis of Ayamonte.[44] Customarily held by a Spanish or Italian nobleman of high station, it was temporarily filled by the castellan Don Sancho de Padilla.

In separate letters Medina Sidonia learned of the problems he would face. Jurisdictional disputes between Philip, who ruled Milan as hereditary Duke, and Archbishop Charles Borromeo remained unsettled. Duke Emmanuel Philibert of Savoy, a faithful supporter of Habsburg interests, had died that August, and his son and successor Charles Emmanuel sought a Spanish marriage. There were also secret negotiations in progress over the surrender of strategic places in the independent marquisate of Saluzzo south of Turin, which was dominated by France and coveted by Savoy.

Medina Sidonia accepted the office, for which he received Granvelle's thanks, and began to put his affairs in order for the journey. Then at Badajoz in October the King and Queen fell gravely ill to an epidemic of influenza raging through Spain and Portugal, and the Queen, still weak from having given birth to a daughter that spring, died. Business came to a standstill till the end of the year.

Only in December did Philip II, his health recovered, formally enter Portugal and establish his court at Elvas, where he received the homage of the Duke of Braganza and his son Barcelos. In February Medina Sidonia arrived at court to discuss Milan. He impressed the King, who was beginning to show the doubts about the younger generation often found in the older. He wrote to Granvelle, "I expect that the Duke of Medina Sidonia, who is here now, will do well in Milan. Although he is young, he seems prudent and of good parts. Given the few persons available. . . I believe he will not be bad."[45]

Even as Medina Sidonia discussed Milan with the King, rumors began to circulate that he did not want the post. "It is understood," ran a report from the French Ambassador, "that the Duke of Medina should like to remain in Portugal, or hungers for Naples, but not to go to Milan. This, according to some is to spite the appointment to Naples of the Duke of Osuna, though some say Milan is better."[46] Whatever the rumors, Medina Sidonia proceeded as though he were going.

At Elvas he did raise again the matter of the Princess of Eboli. He had heard that Antonio Pérez, whose confinement in Madrid had been relaxed, had visited her in Santorcaz. The hotheaded Pastrana was outraged and loudly denounced both, threatening to kill Pérez. Medina Sidonia argued that it would be better if she were farther away from Madrid, in Pastrana, where he at last persuaded the King to allow her to go. He accompanied her to Pastrana and saw her settled in her own palace. He explained to her in person the terms of her confinement.

From Pastrana Medina Sidonia returned to Sanlúcar, where he arrived on 23 March. To Mateo Vázquez he wrote a note about Eboli's problems and asked for the return of a chronicle of the deeds of his ancestors he had sent the secretary in support of his quest for the office of Captain General of Andalusia.[47] Given his experience of the Portuguese campaign, he wanted to increase his authority, and likely he sought an honorable alternative to Milan. He hinted at his reluctance to go to Milan, though he pushed ahead with his preparations for the journey with his wife, their two-year-old son, and the ducal household.

From Elvas the court proceeded to Thomar, where Philip had convoked the Portuguese Cortes to acclaim him King of Portugal. On 15 May the Duke arrived to receive from the King's hands the Collar of the Golden Fleece. He was further briefed on Milan and given the ciphers he would need to communicate confidential material.

The King also put him in charge of efforts to track down and apprehend the outlawed Dom António, who remained at large and threatened to stir up trouble. On taking up the charge, Medina Sidonia insisted that the effort be kept secret: there were many Portuguese who could not be trusted, including members of Portugal's Council of State.[48]

For the search Medina Sidonia divided Portugal into districts. In each, a reliable Portuguese captain or carefully selected Castilian would direct the hunt for the fugitive. He insisted that those who participated should be well rewarded and assured protection for their lives and households.

Late in May a leading accomplice of Dom António was captured near Alcácer do Sal and revealed that Dom António was in communication with the Queen Mother of France and planned to flee by sea. Galleys scouted the coast and inlets from Lisbon to Faro. On 1 June Dom António's confessor was taken and admitted that the fugitive had been in hiding between Sesimbra, Arrabida, and Setúbal; he had no doubt that Dom António and his companions had already embarked in a French ship.

If Dom António had sailed for the Azores, where he had support, Medina Sidonia surmised, a Spanish armada would have to be sent after him. He was not sure that the Portuguese fleet of galleons, which he found superior to Spain's, would prove reliable. If, however, Dom António had fled to France, Medina Sidonia from Milan would "seek his trail and get rid of him by whatever means should be easiest."[49]

With Dom António fled from Portugal and Philip II securely on its throne, the Duke of Medina Sidonia, the Collar of the Golden Fleece round his neck, headed again for Sanlúcar. The galleys of the Sicilian squadron, commanded by Don Alonso de Leyva, were ordered to carry him and his household to Italy, when they sailed in the summer. Related by marriage, Leyva and Medina Sidonia would serve together in a number of different capacities prior to the armada campaign of 1588, in which Leyva would be designated as Medina Sidonia's replacement.

✳ CHAPTER THREE ✳

Captain General without Title

B EFORE he left court, Medina Sidonia had hinted that he would prefer not to become Governor General of Milan, which ordinarily included the Captaincy General of Lombardy, but wished instead to serve as Captain General of Andalusia. He wanted to remain close to home because the health of his mother, the Countess of Niebla, was failing, and he would have to take full charge of managing his estates. Also he knew that in 1583 the Almojarifazgo Mayor of Seville, which included his customs house of Sanlúcar, was due for its decennial renegotiation and likely wished to be at hand to protect his interests.

Barely had he returned to Sanlúcar to resume, however reluctantly, preparation for his journey to Milan when he received an order from the King "to suspend for now" the journey and organize an expedition to occupy the Moroccan port of Larache.[1] In the sixteenth century Larache's harbor, formed by the estuary of the Wadi Loukkos, served as an anchorage for coasting vessels and often as a lair for corsairs. Its fort was half in ruins but it could be repaired and the harbor improved, which would make Larache a serious threat to shipping in the Gulf of Cadiz or, if it were in the hands of Spain, an asset for the gulf's security. Dom Sebastian had meant to take Larache by assault from land and sea when his army was trapped en route and annihilated at Alcazarquivir. In the months after the disaster, Santa Cruz and Philip II had considered taking Larache by surprise but were distracted by developments in Portugal.

The new Moroccan Sharif, Ahmed al-Mansour, however, was less worried about Philip II than about the Ottoman Turks. He was determined to keep his independence and continue the policy of his dynasty, the expansion of Moroccan power southward over the West African Sudan. He had no intention of being a client of the Sultan and servant of the Turks' Mediterranean interests.

Rumors were rife early in 1581 that Eulj Ali, the Ottoman Beylerbey of Algiers, had decided to subject Morocco to direct Turkish rule. His lieutenant Ramadan Pasha collected twenty-three galleys in Algiers, purportedly to seize Tetuan and Larache, while an Algerian army spearheaded by Janissaries would advance from Tlemcen to capture Fez. Eulj Ali himself planned to sail west in support of these operations with sixty galleys from Constantinople.

The alarm this news created at Philip II's court was sufficient to keep Santa Cruz and the bulk of his armada in Iberian waters. Therefore only a few warships and troops under Pedro de Valdés could be spared to sail for the Azores, which had sided with Dom António and received reinforcements from France. Valdés failed to subject the Azores. The Mediterranean for the moment had taken precedence over the Atlantic.

The Sharif appeared as alarmed as the King of Spain about the threat of Eulj Ali and turned to him for support. Philip II proved forthcoming and informed his envoy, Captain Pedro Venegas de Córdoba, to tell the Sharif that his price was the delivery of Larache. To impress on the Sharif the urgency of the matter, he forwarded news that thirty galleys had already sailed from Constantinople to join Ramadan Pasha. He moreover instructed Venegas to remind the Sharif that two Moroccan princes with claims on his throne remained in exile in Lisbon and to add that Mulai Daoud, a rebel against the Sharif, had sent agents to Lisbon in search of backing. Philip protested that he preferred the friendship of the Sharif and confided to Venegas that he would consider ceding the less valuable Portuguese citadel of Arzila to him if something were demanded in compensation for Larache.[2]

At the end of June Philip learned from a month-old dispatch sent by Venegas that the Sharif had agreed to cede Larache without delay. Philip had feared he would prolong negotiations through the summer until the Turkish threat had evaporated. At this point he ordered Medina Sidonia to suspend temporarily his departure for Milan and raise forthwith on his estates eight hundred to one thousand men for the occupation of Larache. To carry the Duke and his men to Morocco the King ordered the ten galleys of the squadron of Sicily to stand by in Cadiz Bay. The squadron's general, Don Alonso de

Leyva, was in Barcelona; in command was his brother Don Pedro.

The scale of the enterprise grew rapidly, and fresh operations orders were issued that covered every detail from the men's equipment to their food, clothing, and pay. Medina Sidonia soon had under his command two thousand infantry and seventeen galleys. The Factor Francisco Duarte was authorized to disburse 30,000 ducats to meet expenses, and Don Francés de Alava, Captain General of the Artillery, arranged for the issuance of muskets, arquebuses, pikes, and other munitions from the royal arsenals of Cádiz and Málaga.

Medina Sidonia hastened to have all ready to get under way on receipt of word from Venegas in Morocco. He visited the preparations at Gibraltar and inspected the galleys in Cadiz Bay. The Sicilian squadron he found in poor condition and unable to make effective response to a rash of corsair raids along the coast led by the redoubtable corsair chief Murad Reis, who used Larache as a haven. When the Duke, royal order in hand, and Don Pedro de Leyva sought the munitions needed by the galleys from the Cádiz arsenal, its warden proved cantankerous and they had to use force to secure them.[3]

Medina Sidonia had to recruit most of his men from his own estates, as he had when he organized the invasion of the Algarve. The other señores and the towns ignored his requests for people and arms or responded grudgingly and by halves, despite the King's orders. In Cádiz, the corregidor's compliance with a royal order to assign one hundred arquebusiers of the garrison to Medina Sidonia's force led to a riot instigated by the chief city councillor, Pedro del Castillo. Medina Sidonia once more suggested to allies at court that the King should confer on him the authority of a Captain General and sent Mateo Vázquez a copy of Ferdinand and Isabella's appointment of the third Duke of Medina Sidonia as Captain General of Andalusia.[4]

August came and Medina Sidonia waited expectantly. Venegas's letters from Marrakech dated in mid-June claimed the Sharif had to await his son Mulai Muhammad ech Sheik to make delivery but promised speedy resolution of the matter. About the Turkish threat the Sharif had changed his mind and claimed Eulj Ali had no designs on Morocco. The delivery of Larache would be a demonstration of friendship for Spain.

In Spain Eulj Ali's imminent coming was taken more seriously. The repaired galleys swept the Gulf of Cadiz searching for corsairs and awaited the return of the treasure fleets. The corsairs avoided the sweep and struck the Portuguese fishing village of Vila Nova de Milfontes, well north of Cape St. Vincent.

On land new captains arrived and the tempo of recruiting increased further. Some fourteen hundred men had to be found to reinforce the North African presidios of Ceuta, Tangier, and Arzila, and others for fleets bound for the New World. Once more Medina Sidonia confronted the Andalusian señores and towns with royal orders that authorized him to raise the needed people. The Duke of Alcalá de los Gazules responded by demanding a special explanation from the King.[5] To assist Medina Sidonia with the men recruited the King assigned as Maestre de Campo the veteran captain Antonio Moreno, who arrived at Sanlúcar early in September.

Already there and fretting was the Marquis of La Favara, Don Lorenzo Téllez de Silva, the late Prince of Eboli's bold but unruly cousin, who had begged license of the King to join the expedition. Soon after his arrival an angry quarrel erupted between him and Medina Sidonia. The two had gone to Gibraltar, where at table with a large crowd La Favara challenged two Portuguese to admit they secretly favored Dom António as king.[6] Both insisted that they thanked God for the king they had, Philip of Spain. La Favara loudly asserted that Dom António was their king and that they knew it in their hearts. Medina Sidonia rose from the table as though he would kill La Favara and furiously denounced him. Swiftly others intervened to keep the Duke and Marquis apart. The Duke lost no time in protesting La Favara's presence and behavior to the King. The King apologized that La Favara had been insistent about joining the Larache expedition and hoped that something worthwhile might be found for him to do, although he did agree that it might be best if La Favara could be persuaded to return to his estates in Sicily.[7]

Medina Sidonia's irritation with La Favara joined his frustration that nothing was happening about Larache. He wrote to Venegas that he feared a double cross. "You are dealing with people who are quite astute and changeable, of a nature different from ours. . . . Stick to the business and keep your eyes open. . . . The loss of me and the armada would be less important than the consequent loss of reputation to His Majesty."[8] The King too appeared frustrated, and to assist Venegas in his negotiations with the Sharif he sent the Arabist Diego Marín, a priest. The Sharif's promises had been couched in vague terms that perhaps Venegas did not fully grasp. Marín brought with him an offer to surrender the Portuguese fort of Mazagan on the Moroccan coast to the Sharif when Larache was delivered to Spain. (At some point, the King decided to abandon Mazagan, further down the coast, rather than Arzila, which lies between Larache and Tangier.)

Apart from their frustration over Larache, both Duke and King were becoming increasingly anxious about the arrival of the treasure fleet from the New World. There were rumors that English pirates lurked in the Azores and fears that Eulj Ali would come through the strait with his fleet from Algiers. In late August the Duke dispatched five caravels to find the flota and make sure its commanders were alert to the possible dangers ahead. Early in September seventeen galleys from Cadiz Bay sortied under the command of the Lepanto veteran Rodrigo de Benavides and awaited the flota off Cape St. Vincent. Then on 15 September the ships from Tierra Firme and four vessels from New Spain entered the estuary of the Guadalquivir, escorted by galleys. "In them are 2,300,000 ducats," Medina Sidonia wrote the King, "and as I write I can see thirty-four ships."[9] The next day he reported that the remaining ships had anchored safely.

During the same weeks that Medina Sidonia was organizing the Larache expedition he became embroiled in the preparations of the armada *del estrecho de Magallanes*, ordered to sail to the Strait of Magellan to built forts approved by a junta that met in Lisbon in March. The junta's purpose was to discuss the government and defense of Spain's Indies.

Medina Sidonia, who had come to be regarded as an expert on such matters, was among the junta's members. The others included Alba, Santa Cruz, and representatives of the Council of the Indies and Seville's Casa de Contratación.[10] The weakness of Spain's defenses in the Caribbean had been demonstrated by French and English pirates, and Francis Drake had revealed during his 1577–1580 round-the-world voyage the vulnerability of the South Sea, as the Pacific was then known. In dealing with the problems, Medina Sidonia and Santa Cruz had the most to say.

To block access to the South Sea, the junta approved a plan proposed by Pedro Sarmiento de Gamboa to build forts in the Strait of Magellan. "Though some say there is another passage further south," Medina Sidonia commented, mistakenly, "I doubt it." The South Sea ports that Drake had menaced ought to be fortified, he insisted, and the Viceroy of Peru should outfit several *fregatas*, which employed sail but could be rowed, for patrol duty. No one wanted to hear again—as they had when Drake plundered a ship off the Peruvian coast in 1579—of an inadequately armed and unescorted vessel laden with treasure being taken.

Other issues were discussed in the same meetings. A plan to assign four galleys to Santo Domingo, two to Florida, and two to the South Sea was opposed by both Medina Sidonia and Santa Cruz. Galleys, Medina Sidonia argued, were unfit for the high seas and cost too much to operate. He suggested instead that two fregatas be stationed at Havana to patrol the Florida coast, and a squadron of ten *galeoncetes* (small galleons) operate from Cartagena de Indias for the security of the Caribbean. He believed that a proposed chain of forts along the Florida coast made no sense; he preferred a few lookout stations, backed by an adequate armada.

About the Indies flotas, Medina Sidonia spoke from firsthand knowledge. Since boyhood he had watched their annual assemblies in the estuary of the Guadalquivir and in Cadiz Bay, and in 1570 the King had asked him, so he stated in his old age, to assist in their preparation.[11] The merchantmen ought to sail only in convoy, he stated, escorted by two galleons and two fregatas. All vessels should carry bronze, not cast-iron, guns; like most of his era, he did not trust cast-iron artillery. Merchant ships not properly armed should be assessed a higher tax than those that were.

The armada anchored at Sanlúcar and bound for the Strait of Magellan was not a merchant flota, but rather was assembled for a royal expedition to build Sarmiento's forts and populate a colony. Lending a hand to its preparations, Medina Sidonia found that dissension, delays, and a shortage of cables, among other things, gripped what he described as "this sad armada."[12] Its general, Diego Flores de Valdés, whom the Duke found weak and indifferent, barely spoke to Sarmiento, who was second in command. Juan Delgado, Secretary to the Council of War, was pleased when he learned that the Duke had intervened and progress was being made. "The best remedy would be his diligence, in case he remains there some days," Delgado informed the King in a memorandum dated 14 June, soon after the Duke had returned to Sanlúcar and before the matter of Larache came up.[13] The King, with Milan in mind, scribbled in the margin, "So you say, although he is needed very much where he is going."

The armada del estrecho consisted of twenty-three ships and had by the beginning of September cost 84,427 ducats charged to various royal accounts or borrowed in Seville.[14] Manning the ships were 670 sailors and ordered to board them were 1,332 soldiers. In addition to soldiers and crew some 600 settlers bound for Chile and 100 bound for the Strait awaited embarkation. Many of the soldiers tried to desert and join other units being mustered to serve in the galleys or for the Larache expedition. Medina Sidonia finally had them put aboard the ships, explaining that it was easier to replenish what they would eat and drink than to replace them.

On 27 and 28 September the armada weighed anchor and, assisted by galleys, crossed the bar of Sanlúcar and headed for the open sea. Two days later the weather turned "fresh," and the Duke began to worry. At the beginning of October nineteen of its ships, battered by storm, had found haven in Cadiz Bay. Four others had been driven aground and wrecked. Some blamed Medina Sidonia for ordering the armada to sea against the judgment of its officers, but records of the council meetings on board show that a majority of the officers, under pressure or not, had voted to sail when they did.

The armada did not weigh anchor again till December and, dogged by hard luck, got no further than Rio de Janeiro. After operating for two seasons in Brazilian waters, Diego Flores returned to Spain in 1584. Sarmiento pressed on to the strait, where he started to build his ill-starred forts. In 1587 Medina Sidonia was asked for advice about how to rescue the few survivors. By then he had changed his mind about the strait as the sole passage to the South Sea and come to suspect that open water lay south of Tierra del Fuego.[15]

Medina Sidonia did not become as involved with the armada del estrecho when it was anchored at Cádiz as he had when it stood in the roads of Sanlúcar. For the remainder of the autumn he expended all his efforts on the Larache expedition. The number of men under his orders reached almost five thousand, and his galleys were ready. And he saw in Cadiz Bay more ships and men, returned from the Azores and the Indies.

While awaiting word to sail for Larache, Medina Sidonia learned from a long relation received in October what had happened in Algiers, the root of both Philip II's and the Sharif's anxieties, on which the whole Larache business hung. The Ottoman Beylerbey Eulj Ali, with fewer men and galleys than expected, had reached Algiers early in September, where he found that the corsair captains were restless and unruly (they resented the Sultan's truce with the King of Spain and the shift in direction of Ottoman policy from the Mediterranean to the Caucasian war with Persia, which Eulj Ali himself did not appreciate). The Beylerbey endeavored to placate the corsairs and strengthened his tenuous grip on Algiers's government by placing trusted lieutenants in key posts. At the same time he sent Ramadan Pasha with a half dozen galleys to make certain of Tunis and Tripoli. To lull the Sharif of Morocco he sent to Fez an embassy bearing gifts and promises of friendship. He had achieved little when he was summoned by the Sultan to Constantinople and sailed east. That he would never return west was at the time unknown and until his death in 1586 there was concern every summer in Spain about his intentions.

Eulj Ali's departure and the tensions in Algiers gave Medina Sidonia new ideas about how to employ his men and galleys, along with the other ships and men congregated in Cadiz Bay. To Secretary Gabriel de Zayas, who was handling the diplomatic correspondence concerning Morocco, he broached the proposition that he and his force, augmented by the other ships and men available, surprise and capture Algiers.

Zayas responded enthusiastically and informed the Duke that he would approach the King about it when the occasion warranted. "If His Majesty would commit the enterprise to Your Excellency, all Spain would freely follow. With that city, he would control the affairs of Africa and no longer stand in fear of it, since it would become an open highway for Spain, with the sea for a moat."[16] There was even talk at court that Medina Sidonia would get the appointment of Captain General of the Sea, vacant since Don Juan of Austria's death.[17] Nothing came of the plan to seize Algiers, and the bruited appointment eventually went to Gian Andrea Doria. In the same weeks, all concerned had become exasperated with the Sharif's continued delays over Larache and began to hint that if he did not deliver it forthwith, Spain had the power to seize it.

Whether the goal was Larache or Algiers, Medina Sidonia decided he wanted the assistance of a veteran general and requested that the King appoint Sancho Dávila, Alba's chief lieutenant in the Low Countries and Portugal, to serve under him.[18] Almost sixty years old, Dávila had just secured the post of Captain General of the Coast of Granada. He protested to Alba that he did not wish to serve under Medina Sidonia, and while he did not say as much in writing, he most likely considered the idea humiliating. Alba proved understanding but suggested to Dávila that he consider serving Medina Sidonia as an adviser, without coming under his orders. The King thought that Dávila might yet inspect Larache after its occupation, but Dávila insisted on proceeding to Granada, though he did agree to send Medina Sidonia his advice when it was needed.

On learning of what had transpired at court, Medina Sidonia felt that his authority had not been accorded sufficient respect by Alba and complained about it to Zayas. Zayas tried to smooth his ruffled feathers. "Believe me, Your Excellency, the Duke [of Alba] loves and esteems you like his own son. Whoever gives Your Excellency contrary views must have ruinous intent and the spirit to sow discord."[19] It bothered Medina Sidonia that he did not enjoy the respect of Spain's military and naval professionals that Alba did. But Alba had run off to the wars at age sixteen, before he succeeded to his titles and estates, and at least figuratively had worked his way up through the ranks before he assumed high command and compiled one of the most distinguished military records of the era. Medina Sidonia was Duke and Grandee at nine years old, and when he came of age to serve his King he sought immediately to become in effect Lieutenant General of the Spanish galleys. In 1580 he commanded a small army in the invasion of Portugal, by virtue of his station and landholdings as much for his willingness to serve and contribute to the costs, his complaints notwithstanding. But the suggestion raised at court that he be given overall command of the invasion of Portugal had been given short shrift by the Council of War because of his lack of experience. His subsequent conquest of the Algarve provided him some, but that chiefly in matters of logistics. He had acquired none in combat.

Very different was the case of his headstrong brother-in-law Pastrana, who did briefly "trail a pike" in Flanders before becoming a distinguished if impetuous cavalry commander. But Pastrana was the bizarre and erratic heir of the equally bizarre and erratic Princess of Eboli and inherited few traditional responsibilities to compare with those that came with being Duke of Medina Sidonia. Pastrana's title was new, his mother was still alive, and his estates were in effect looked after by agents approved by the Crown. He was free to play knight-errant, and his errantries would for a time compound his brother-in-law's other worries.

Pastrana had been with his mother at Pastrana that summer of 1581, and there was talk that he would journey with his sister the Duchess and Medina Sidonia to Milan. But in September he left home abruptly after a quarrel with his mother and appeared at Don Alonso de Leyva's house in Madrid. He complained openly that she had resumed relations with Pérez, who was ruling her life and ruining his inheritance. The Admiral of Castile retorted that he should not speak so of his mother and threatened to thrash him if he persisted.

Medina Sidonia had already suggested that Pastrana join him for the Larache expedition before making the journey to Milan. He quickly obtained the King's approval. In November the nineteen-year-old arrived in Sanlúcar, where he tried to make peace between his cousin La Favara and Medina Sidonia. La Favara managed to outrage both dukes by showing them a small portrait of the King he wore round his neck and cursed and hit when the King displeased him. He revealed that he had cut off the portrait's nose when the King had suggested that he return to Sicily.

La Favara roamed Sanlúcar with a gang of armed bravos, lived uproariously and threatened mayhem against any who crossed him, setting a bad example for Pastrana, which Pastrana in fact was prone to emulate. To Medina Sidonia's relief, La Favara finally departed from Sanlúcar in January to join the expedition being prepared in Lisbon to conquer the Azores.

Medina Sidonia gave the restless Pastrana a company of his own to command. Pastrana was soon in trouble. He threatened an *alférez* (ensign bearer) that he would have his nose cut off but then apparently relented. Shortly afterward in Sanlúcar, twelve of his soldiers assaulted a passerby and brutally slashed his nose with swords. Their leader told the victim that the Duke of Pastrana had ordered him to kill him. Medina Sidonia had the leading culprit arrested, tried, and sentenced to have his head cut off. (The sentence, handed down by a seigneurial court, automatically went to a higher court for review.) Whether or not Pastrana had instigated the deed, he was not charged, though it made him a subject of scandal.

Pastrana came and went between Sanlúcar and Seville with cavalcades of hangers-on at all hours of the day and night, causing Medina Sidonia headaches and costing him money. In July 1582 Medina Sidonia at last wrote Vázquez in exasperation and begged him to have the King order Pastrana home to his mother, who in the meantime had tempered her behavior to comply better with the terms of her confinement.

Before Pastrana came to Sanlúcar, Medina Sidonia had decided to write bluntly to the King's secretaries, Mateo Vázquez and Gabriel de Zayas, that he wished to be relieved of the appointment to Milan. They knew of his difficulties with Larache, of the poor health of his mother, and of his own ailments. Both proved sympathetic but reluctant to raise the matter with the King.

In January 1582 the Duke sent his chaplain and confessor, Fray

Vicente de Herrera, to Lisbon to speak about Milan directly with the King. He did not wish to avoid service, he wanted it known, but asked rather to serve the King closer to home. Mateo Vázquez arranged for Fray Vicente's audience and supported the Duke's request for the withdrawal of the appointment. The King agreed. Vázquez informed the Duke of the decision and told him further that he was already seeking another important position for him. He hinted that the Duke might act as lieutenant to the Cardinal-Archduke Albert, the king's nephew, who was likely to become Viceroy of Portugal. Because Albert was a cleric (though not ordained a priest), the Captaincy General of Portugal would be given to a layman.

When Cardinal Granvelle in Madrid learned that the King had granted the Duke's request to be relieved of the appointment to Milan, he proved less agreeable. "It is a shameful and insupportable thing," he wrote to the Duchess of Parma, "and cost the King no little reputation."[20] The King concealed whatever feelings he had about it.

While Medina Sidonia worked to be relieved of his appointment to Milan, Larache remained in the Sharif's possession, though the Sharif insisted to Venegas and Diego Marín that its surrender was close at hand. In return he suggested that Spain assist him to conquer Tlemcen. Granvelle, viewing the situation from Madrid, described the whole negotiation as "treating with fables."[21] Yet, in case the negotiation proved real, Medina Sidonia in Sanlúcar did what he could to keep the forces he had collected from completely disintegrating during the winter.

Philip II, while more sanguine than Granvelle about Larache, gave priority to the conquest of the Azores. Medina Sidonia, on learning that part of the expedition might be outfitted at La Coruña, recommended that it be prepared instead in Andalusia. Andalusia, he argued, was accustomed to fitting out the two annual flotas bound for the Indies and could provide the armada with the necessary materials and manpower, from which La Coruña was remote. The rest of the expedition would be outfitted in Lisbon, though it remained unhealthy and many around the King had little confidence in the enthusiasm of the Portuguese for the enterprise.

His recommendation accepted, Medina Sidonia was soon dutifully assisting the Marquis of Santa Cruz, in command of the expedition, to provision and man the ships assembled at Cádiz. Despite their cooperation during the Algarve campaign, the two were soon at odds, and

Medina Sidonia felt that the Marquis did not duly appreciate his assistance. When the two had been together in Lisbon the year before, an informant of the French ambassador spotted Medina Sidonia with the Marquis riding through Lisbon's streets in a hired carriage and reported that the Duke wore an Andalusian cape of coarse cloth and was accompanied by only one servant in order to subject the Marquis to the mockery of the Portuguese.[22] The episode is curious: perhaps Medina Sidonia wished to maintain his popularity in Portugal by subtly embarrassing the Marquis, who was generally hated there. Whatever the case, Mateo Vázquez had to write Medina Sidonia to assure him that the King would inform Santa Cruz of his pleasure with Medina Sidonia's services.[23]

Medina Sidonia's activities raised again problems with Cádiz and caused a division on its city council. The Corregidor Alarcón complained to the King that two town councillors favored by the Duke were out to get him, and he lived in fear of his life. He had been insulted and threatened by soldiers who served under the Duke's orders.[24]

The Duke, as he assisted with the preparation of Santa Cruz's armada, saw his own force which stood by for the occupation of Larache reduced to six companies. Yet from Morocco Diego Marín, who had largely taken over the negotiations from Venegas, sent a stream of dispatches that kept up hope for Larache's prompt surrender. To be closer to Larache, Venegas went from Fez to Tangier, and Medina Sidonia decided to send Alférez Juan de Larea and the engineer Juan Mateo, both disguised as ordinary seamen, to reconnoiter Larache's forts.

Santa Cruz returned to Lisbon and left Juan Martínez de Recalde, who would serve as *Almirante General* in the 1588 armada, in charge of the ships in Cádiz. Recalde sailed in July. Twelve galleys of the squadron of Spain, under Don Francisco de Benavides, plus the Sicilian galleys, remained in the Strait of Gibraltar in case Eulj Ali sailed west again. Don Alonso de Leyva had arrived to resume command of the Sicilian galleys, which continued to be at Medina Sidonia's disposal for Larache. At Conil, where Medina Sidonia was supervising his almadraba, he and Leyva discussed the expedition at length.[25]

On 25 July, the feast of Spain's patron St. James, the Duke did board Leyva's galleys, not with the intention of occupying Larache but rather to transport from Ceuta to Faro the body of Dom Sebastian, which the Sharif had already delivered. The Bishop of the Algarve received on 5

August the damask-draped coffin, which was carried in state for burial in the monastery of Belem on the outskirts of Lisbon. With the cortege went the Duke of Pastrana, no doubt to Medina Sidonia's relief. Don Alonso de Leyva went also, leaving his brother Don Pedro again in command of the Sicilian galleys.

From Faro Medina Sidonia decided to travel overland by horse to Sanlúcar because contrary easterlies prevented his return by sea. He stopped at Gibraleón to visit his sister, the Marquesa, and console her on the death of a daughter. As he neared Sanlúcar, his horse stumbled and fell on top of him, fracturing his leg in two places. He had with him only one servant, who did what he could for the injured leg. The Duke admitted he felt abandoned by God, but help arrived and he was borne the last league to Sanlúcar in a litter. Attending physicians assured him the leg would mend well, without deformity.[26]

Returned to his own palace, in bed and in pain, he looked at the correspondence awaiting his attention, which included the news from the Azores that Santa Cruz's armada had smashed the fleet of the French and Portuguese supporters of Dom António. After reviewing Diego Marín's dispatches from Morocco and the replies from Lisbon about Larache he gave way to an outburst of anger and pent-up frustration.[27] "We are all tired of waiting," he wrote the King. "I have not gone out of my house for a year other than to work on this deal offered by the Sharif, which comes to nought. Good will turns to hate. In spite of our victories and power, there have been so many delays and extensions that I cannot go on hoping. I am sorry, but I must raise my hand to it. Only Your Majesty has not been able to persuade yourself that a king such as the Sharif has no honor."

He complained about Marín and urged the King to consider using Santa Cruz's victorious armada to force the issue if the Sharif did not fulfill his promise to surrender Larache. He had told Marín "to put fear" into the Sharif and demand that he fix a date for Larache's delivery. "If Marín does not answer me within fifteen days about this business, which I believe will drag on forever," the Duke concluded, "for the love of God I am getting out of it." Four days later he wrote Zayas to urge that Diego Marín be replaced by "someone of intelligence and credit, to bring an end to this business," and referred him to what he had written the King.[28]

The Duke could not get out of it. The same day he wrote Zayas his scouts Larea and Mateo arrived from Morocco with new word from Marín. They had been caught there, but the Sharif released them, though he used their spying as an excuse for further procrastination in the delivery of Larache. Nonetheless, Larea informed Medina Sidonia, Marín remained convinced that delivery was at hand. The Duke found Larea's report believable and wrote Marín to apologize for the unkind words he had written of him.[29] He ordered his troops to reassemble and asked for more galleys. The King assigned Benavides's dozen Spanish galleys to join the nine available Sicilians for the Larache expedition. He authorized the Duke moreover to provide "gifts" of money to the Sharif's agents and to liberate if requested enslaved Moroccans from Spanish rowing benches, "so long as none was a *Reis* (corsair captain), but only men of no account."[30]

To the King, Medina Sidonia reported at the end of August that he had over twelve hundred men, including one hundred and fifty of the expected six hundred from Seville.[31] He asked that several companies that had returned from the Azores and were at Cádiz be added, because he planned to put one thousand men into Larache and four hundred into its fort, while six hundred remained aboard the galleys. He proposed to lead the expedition in person. The King approved with the proviso that the Duke, whose broken leg was still healing, would "in nothing so much serve me as in guarding your life and your health."[32]

A muster report given the Duke by one of his veteran officers described the forces he would lead and made clear why he wanted the companies from Cádiz: "They have all the shortcomings possible, such as little experience and poor attitude. . . . Some are sick, some poorly clad, and all are tired of bad treatment. Not all of their captains are the sort I prefer for the service of His Majesty, the glory of Your Excellency and my own honor. I have more hope for the sergeants."[33]

The muster detailed their needs. Seven hundred men were in rags and needed suits and shoes. A chaplain was required, with a tent and altar for a field church; also needed was a hospital tent with one hundred mattresses and three hundred sets of sheets and blankets. The men lacked armor: corselets and morions were on order from Málaga, but they were rusty and required cleaning. Of the firearms, three hundred were "ruins"; powder, shot, and matchcord were lacking. Required at once were seven hundred pikes, two hundred muskets, and one thousand arquebuses. Because the plans Larea and Mateo had brought back revealed that both Larache's fort and town walls were crumbling, six hundred sappers would have to be found to repair them. For everything the "good will of Seville" was vital. Medina Sidonia knew that well and succeeded the next year in purchasing for 16,000 ducats the office of Alférez Mayor of Seville, a key post in the city's militia. He explained to Mateo Vázquez that he had bought it "in order to serve His Majesty."[34]

As autumn approached, the Duke asked for some big sailing ships to help ferry the men and their stores to Larache. He considered the coast of Morocco treacherous for galleys in autumn and winter. Although he admitted that the Spanish galleys could carry a good number of troops, the tired Sicilians "cannot carry enough to man a barricade."[35] Three greatships, plus six more galleys and six hundred veterans were soon added to the assembled force.

By the end of September, Medina Sidonia was out of bed, though not able to use the leg he had fractured. The Duchess during the same month had taken to her bed to give birth to a son.

Medina Sidonia now counted for his expedition over two thousand soldiers and sappers, with twenty-seven galleys and three greatships and their crews, which he kept on the alert. He also prepared to evacuate the Portuguese garrison of Mazagan, which had been promised to the Sharif, and its Christian population, which was found to be more numerous than expected. He had suspicions about the loyalty of Dom Francisco de Almeida, its governor, but was reassured by the King that Almeida was reliable.

However, Marín's constant dispatches full of hope and reassurances, which arrived during October and November, proved vain. By December most of the men and galleys assigned to Medina Sidonia for Larache had been detached for other operations. Of these, chief was the planned conquest of the Azores, to which the best men were assigned. Santa Cruz's victory at San Miguel in 1582 had been at sea; he had not been able to follow through with landings. Don Alonso de Leyva and his brother Don Pedro commenced the return voyage of their squadron to Sicily.

Medina Sidonia wanted to visit Madrid and Pastrana at Christmas but was refused licence by the King, "lest the Sharif judge it as a lack of hope."[36] With a thousand men and four Spanish galleys the Duke whiled away the winter in Andalusia. On 24 April 1583 the King ordered what remained of the Larache expedition, five hundred Spaniards and five hundred Italians, to march for Lisbon to board the armada making reading to sail for the Azores.

Cardinal Granvelle desired to drop the whole matter. "They have mocked us so many times," he wrote to Don Juan de Idiáquez, whose star was in the ascendant with the King, "that we cannot hold hope that they are going to give it to us. On account of Flanders, we should forget it.[37] To Margaret of Parma Granvelle admitted, "Larache can be taken any time . . . but I do not think it can be sustained, where so many Moors, Arabs and Turks can come in large numbers to retake it. . . . I have complained loudly about the unbelievable expenses which have been put into it for two years, in hope that the Sharif would place it voluntarily into our hands."[38]

Medina Sidonia kept his eye on Larache and developments in Morocco but found more to concern him at home. In 1583 the Crown renegotiated the administration of the Almojarifazgo Mayor of Seville, and control of the lucrative Sanlúcar customs house was wrenched from the Duke's hands, although not without protest. The Duke, who did not receive high office in Portugal as he had hoped, now sought office in Madrid, where Philip II had returned that spring. He made it clear to Antonio de Eraso, Secretary to the Council of the Indies, and to Mateo Vázquez, that he would like the office of President of the Council of the Indies, which was vacant. His experience with the Indies flotas and Seville coupled with his station, he believed, suited him for the post. He complained to Mateo Vázquez that corruption stretched from Peru and Mexico through Seville right up to the council itself, and he included those who administered the Almojarifazgo Mayor and the Royal Assistant of Seville, who supported them.[39] He challenged the appointment of the Royal Assistant, the Count of Villardompardo, to the Viceroyalty of Peru and proposed instead his uncle, the Marquis of Villamanrique.[40] But the King found no cause to replace Villardompardo, though he did accept Medina Sidonia's recommendation of Villamanrique and appointed him to the Viceroyalty of New Spain.

In response that summer to allegations regarding widespread smuggling that involved the generals and admirals of flotas, the King had already ordered Medina Sidonia to do what he could to stop it. Given his efforts to interdict smuggling, his complaints to court about so many people who were involved in the commerce and government of the Indies, and his fight to keep his customs house, Medina Sidonia likely generated as much opposition to his candidacy as support for it.

Mateo Vázquez claimed to support it and sent the Duke a letter studded with Latin phrases he knew the Duke would appreciate, in which he unctuously expressed his belief that what Medina Sidonia had proposed, a grandee in the Presidency of the Council of the Indies, would be a good thing.[41] Vázquez and the Duke always expressed a good deal of mutual admiration, which seems sincere enough, but each expected something of the other. Vázquez was endlessly seeking advantage for his extended family, and the Duke with his wealth and his influence in Andalusia did what he could for him. The Duke, like everyone else, knew that no one was closer to the King than Vázquez, the King's personal "arch-secretary," and there was no better way to reach the King's ear than through him. But Vázquez was always cautious, and save for a few occasions, such as the matter of Antonio Pérez, never seems to have forced matters.[42]

In 1584 the Presidency of the Indies was settled on a *letrado* (one trained in law), Hernando de Vega, in line with custom and the habits of the bureaucracy as much as anything else. The office had long been held by letrados, who were accustomed to the routine of administration. Some were younger sons of great houses, but most were men of the lower or middling nobility. Of substantial family, Vega eventually became Bishop of Córdoba. During the reign of Philip II, most of the few titled nobles who held presidencies were resident at court or lived in the environs of Madrid, and their estates were close by.

Vázquez, on the same day he claimed it a good idea to make a grandee President of the Indies, took up in a second note another of Medina Sidonia's concerns, the Duke of Pastrana, his troubles, and the difficulties in finding him an acceptable bride. Already Pastrana's younger brother, the Duke of Francavilla, was causing scandal by ignoring his new wife. Discussing the need to find "remedy for that entire house and most noble family," Vázquez launched into a long-winded essay on proper child-rearing for scions of the nobility.[43] "Oh, *señor*, how important it is that children, especially those who must succeed to great houses and estates, be raised with extreme vigilance and care. Their parents cannot rest content with having appointed governors, however carefully chosen. . . . Many things in this world go from bad to worse if parents do not continually watch over their children and their governors, with sage love and prudence." The aim of a proper upbringing for noble children was for them to grow up "virtuous, intelligent and prudent," capable of assuming "great offices and ministries in which to serve God, the King and the public good." These were aims with which Medina Sidonia concurred and which he strove to fulfill.

The King separately advised Medina Sidonia that he would ensure that justice was done in Pastrana's case and saw no need for Medina Sidonia to come to court to discuss the matter with him. "What you are doing there in my service does not now permit your absence; I have much confidence in you."[44]

It was not until the end of 1583 that Medina Sidonia journeyed to Madrid and Pastrana. When he returned to Sanlúcar, he returned to his routine. While he managed his estates, he continued to supervise the sailing and return of fleets bound for the Indies and observe developments in Morocco and Barbary. About all he corresponded with Madrid and offered advice.

Talk about occupying Larache persisted, but nothing happened except that the Sharif made Philip II a gift of ostriches. Medina Sidonia shipped them to the King's zoo at Aranjuez, where they arrived safely.[45] Venegas returned to Spain; another took his place in Morocco but lacked his credentials. Marín remained as Spain's chief voice in Fez.

For Medina Sidonia, the dissolution of the Larache expedition had removed any pressing need for the King to bestow on him the Captaincy General of Andalusia he sought. It can only be guessed that the King, given his knowledge of history and of the past conduct of the nobility, preferred not to enlarge the authority of his mightiest subjects; and being aware of the traditional tensions between Medina Sidonia and the other powers of Andalusia, both señores and towns, he probably hoped to keep everybody more or less content by making no major change in the existing arrangements. Such a policy had so far proved adequate.

✳ CHAPTER FOUR ✳

War Comes to Andalusia

I N the late summer of 1585 rumor reached Andalusia that Sir Francis Drake was outfitting a fleet that might attack Spain. Medina Sidonia was following the tiresome negotiations with the Sharif of Morocco to keep him from allying with the Turk, while the Spanish galleys patrolled the coast against the coming of Eulj Ali, reported to be at sea with a hundred Ottoman galleys. At Sanlúcar eight new Vizcayan galleons were being outfitted in the Guadalquivir for the reconstituted Armada de la Guarda de la Carrera de las Indias (Armada of the Guard of the Route to the Indies), which protected the treasure fleets. About their designated commander, Juan Martínez de Recalde, Medina Sidonia wrote Mateo Vázquez that it was well "such a subject was not left idle. . . . I am of the opinion that for maritime affairs, no one will serve His Majesty better in the galleons."[1]

Because the galleons were not yet ready for sea everybody became fearful for the safety of the flotas due to arrive at any time from New Spain and Tierra Firme. The new chief of the Spanish galleys, Don Martín de Padilla, Adelantado Mayor of Castile,[2] took his squadron out to Cape St. Vincent, and in Lisbon the Marquis of Santa Cruz struggled to reassemble an oceangoing armada.

The possibility that Drake might attack Spain was the immediate result of the embargo that Philip II, who was in Aragon, declared in May against all English shipping in Spanish ports. His principal aim was to persuade Queen Elizabeth I of England to cease her negotiations with the States General of the United Netherlands, who were regarded in Spain as an assemblage of rebels and heretics. In Sanlúcar as elsewhere in the peninsula English merchant vessels were detained.

What Medina Sidonia thought about the embargo is not clear. Sanlúcar did a brisk business with England: in 1578 it was reported that of 246 foreign ships calling in Sanlúcar, 93 were English, "among them two Irish."[3] The French ambassador reported in August that most of the detained ships had been released because of the outcry against the embargo.[4]

Elizabeth did not cease negotiations with the States General and in August signed with them the Treaty of Nonsuch. She agreed to aid them in their rebellion against Philip II and, as security for a loan she made them, occupied with English troops the ports of Flushing in Zeeland and Brielle in Holland, both part of Philip's inheritance. A growing enmity rooted in religious difference and exacerbated by English piracy against the shipping of Philip's subjects and raids against his overseas possessions rushed toward open war between Elizabeth and Philip, a war each had for a long time tried to avoid, but which the Queen certainly and Philip most likely had come to believe was inevitable.[5]

When news of the embargo reached England, Drake's fleet, in which the Queen had invested ships and money, was being outfitted at Plymouth "for the annoyance of the King of Spain" by a raid into the Caribbean. Drake received a new commission to sail for Spain and attempt to force the release of embargoed English merchantmen. His fleet weighed anchor in late September and on 7 October appeared in Vigo Bay. He found the embargo in effect lifted, so he took on stores and water (with the forced cooperation of Vigo's Governor), liberated some English seamen who had been jailed, seized the cathedral's treasury, which the Spaniards had tried to spirit away, and resumed his voyage. When report of Drake's attack on Vigo reached Philip in Aragon, following news of Nonsuch and other belligerent acts, Philip decided to resume planning for the invasion of England, the great enterprise he had long been urged to undertake. He wrote Pope Sixtus V and the Grand Duke of Tuscany, two advocates of the enterprise, about the difficulties and costs and solicited their aid.[6]

By the time Medina Sidonia learned that Drake was at Vigo, both treasure flotas had safely anchored in the roads of Sanlúcar. Drake did not attempt Cádiz or Sanlúcar but proceeded south to raid the Cape Verde Islands and then headed across the Atlantic. "He is Master of the Sea," wrote the Venetian Ambassador to Spain, Vincenzo Gradenigo, "and finds no hindrance to the development of his designs."[7] He described the Spaniards' difficulties and attributed their slow response to a lack of adequate organization in Seville and Lisbon and to their "national character," all of which was complicated by "the King's determination to see, to understand and to deal with every point. . . . the source of constant delays."

Early in 1586 the King summoned Medina Sidonia to court to discuss the situation. Gradenigo described him as "a gentleman of royal blood and very rich . . . considered by everyone . . . diligent and prudent. Those who know think he is to be of the Council of State and General of the Spaniards."[8] Whether by this he meant general of a Spanish squadron or of the embarked Spanish troops is not clear and did not matter. He soon after wrote that Medina Sidonia's presence in the armada was "incompatible with that of the Marquis of Santa Cruz."[9]

Santa Cruz was Captain General of the Ocean-Sea, which gave him command of all of Philip's naval forces in the Atlantic, and Captain General of Portugal, which gave him necessary authority for the manning and victualing of his armada, which was based in Lisbon harbor. He had also been made a Grandee of Spain in 1583.

When Medina Sidonia arrived at court in Aranjuez late in March he had a personal interview with the King, who had returned from Aragon and Valencia; then he met in Madrid with Don Juan de Idiáquez, Secretary of State and War Councilor, to discuss the war with England. Idiáquez was in the course of consolidating his position as one of Philip's two principal ministers—the other was Don Cristóbal de Moura. Idiáquez became the King's chief adviser on foreign policy and the Enterprise of England and enjoyed the support of Cardinal Granvelle, an old advocate of invasion. Granvelle's own authority with the King was on the wane, in part because he promoted the appointment of Gian Andrea Doria rather than Santa Cruz to be Captain General of the [Mediterranean] Sea and thus earned the enmity of what might be called Spain's professional military establishment.

In 1586 the establishment's leaders were Santa Cruz for naval affairs and Don Hernando de Toledo, Grand Prior of Castile, for land matters. Toledo was the Duke of Alba's natural son and true heir to his father's talents. He and several other veteran officers joined the Council of War in 1586 and 1587, but their agenda was largely determined by Idiáquez.[10]

Idiáquez, like Granvelle, was often at odds with them and their fellows and chose when it suited him to seek expert advice from others. He sought the advice Medina Sidonia was ready to offer, not only because it was sound, but also, it would seem, because Medina Sidonia was not an accepted member of the establishment dominated by Toledo and Santa Cruz.

In the midst of the meetings between Medina Sidonia and Idiáquez news arrived that Drake had captured Santo Domingo, destroyed part of the town, and forced its inhabitants to pay him ransom. From the Escorial, where the King had gone for Easter, Moura wrote the Duke in secrecy and haste to ask about the eight galleons being outfitted in the Guadalquivir and how soon they might sail "to repair the damage which the fleet of the corsair has done."[11] At the same time orders were sent to Santa Cruz in Lisbon to prepare his armada to intercept Drake or even "punish" the English "in their own homes."[12]

When at the end of April Medina Sidonia left court, he carried a commission to raise six to eight thousand troops for Santa Cruz's armada, though all admitted that it was unlikely the armada would be ready to sail before the first week of July.

The King wrote the nobles and towns of Andalusia about what the English had done to Santo Domingo, "without mentioning other robberies at sea," and commanded them to follow the Duke's orders, "because he is carrying out my orders."[13] The Duke found their response heartening but informed the King that to pay their men, some towns wanted to levy a tax on foodstuffs. The King answered that such a tax would "not be convenient . . . for we shall not tax the poor in this manner."[14]

Medina Sidonia soon had a Maestre de Campo, Agustín Mejía, to drill the new recruits and make soldiers of them, and turned his attention again to the Armada of the Guard, which had left the Guadalquivir and anchored in Cadiz Bay. Now under the veteran Asturian seaman Alvaro Flores de Quiñones, who replaced Recalde, the eight galleons joined another galleon owned by Santa Cruz and eleven armed merchantmen to form a potent armada to sail to the Indies and fetch the annual treasure from Cartagena and Nombre de Dios. Aboard were forty-five hundred men. At Havana Quiñones would rendezvous with the flota from New Spain and escort it back to Spain.

But some feared Quiñones's armada was not yet strong enough to risk the voyage and believed that it ought to wait until Santa Cruz was ready before sailing. Quiñones disagreed. Medina Sidonia was ordered to decide whether Quiñones should proceed to the Indies or wait for Santa Cruz. In a postscript to the order, the King added in his own hand that the Duke should also investigate reports of smuggling in the armada.[15]

Medina Sidonia decided that Quiñones's armada had the strength to risk the voyage, and on 30 May it weighed anchor. He found sufficient evidence of smuggling that orders were sent to the President of the Audiencia of Quito to make a *visita* (inquiry) to investigate the armada when it lay anchored at Cartagena. There had been too little time to do so in Spain.

The troops the Duke raised in Andalusia to march to Lisbon were kept in their hometowns "to prevent disorder," since the armada was not yet ready for them, and the Duke turned his attentions to six galleys assigned to the defense of Caribbean ports,[16] and the annual flotas bound for New Spain and Tierra Firme. Ideally the New Spain flota sailed in May and the Tierra Firme flota in August. It was already June. To a query from court about whether it would be safer to combine the two flotas, the Duke responded that the New Spain flota was almost ready and should sail when it was able, rather than wait on the other.[17]

Manning the two flotas proved to be the biggest problem since so many men had sailed aboard Quiñones's armada. Forced by necessity Medina Sidonia authorized Portuguese, Flemish, Ragusan, and Italian sailors, legally not permitted to sail to Spain's Indies, to sign aboard the flotas.[18] He also allowed soldiers to sail who could not afford to post the required cash guarantee that they would return, and mariners who had some skill at navigation but had not yet passed their pilot's examination to serve as pilots.

At the end of June the New Spain flota had been inspected and stood ready to weigh anchor when a storm struck: "The most contrary and unseasonable that I have ever seen," Medina Sidonia complained.[19] Neither the flota nor the dispatch vessels detailed to follow Quiñones's galleons dared leave port.

Running before the storm, a vessel from the Indies dropped anchor in the Guadalquivir. It brought news that Drake had forced the harbor of Cartagena de Indias, destroyed the two galleys assigned to its defense, and sacked the town. Medina Sidonia expressed surprise and anger that the galleys had failed to do what they, in conjunction with forts, could do well, cover a narrow harbor entrance. They were lost, he wrote the King, "through the fault of their general, according to accounts received here. It would have been impossible for the English to enter Cartagena had the galleys defended the port. I shall send Your Majesty a report; since there was culpability, it should be punished."[20]

The King had already received the news. He commanded Medina Sidonia to dispatch orders to Quiñones to collect all available ships in the Caribbean, including those that would come with the New Spain flota, and form an armada strong enough to drive Drake from the

Indies. Quiñones was not to pursue Drake back across the Atlantic, since "his punishment still remains with the Marquis of Santa Cruz and his armada."[21] In a separate note to Medina Sidonia, Idiáquez added, "The English sting us much; perhaps God permits it thus for something better."[22]

On 12 July Medina Sidonia watched the ships of the New Spain flota begin to warp over the bar into the open waters of the Gulf of Cadiz, where they were joined by another thirteen ships that had sailed from Cadiz Bay and four of the six galleys. Medina Sidonia had worked hard to reinforce the galleys for the high seas, but he was never enthusiastic about galleys in the Caribbean.[23] Six days later the flota and galleys had disappeared over the horizon.

Medina Sidonia turned to a new task assigned him by the King, supervision of an experiment proposed by a Genoese for the safe distillation of fresh water from seawater. He decided, after Miguel de Eraso, General of the Tierra Firme flota, had observed the experiment aboard a ship anchored at Bonanza, that it was too dangerous for shipboard use because of the heat required but thought it suitable for use ashore.[24]

In August a squadron of Santa Cruz's armada put to sea from Lisbon, followed a few weeks later by the armada of Vizcaya, commanded by Juan Martínez de Recalde. Recalde's squadron sailed for the Azores to meet the returning treasure flotas and escort them to Spain. An English squadron under John Hawkins that had covered the Channel when the Spaniards first ventured to sea also sailed for Azores, in hope of intercepting and taking the flotas.

In Spain all concerned became anxious about the safety of the flota returning from New Spain, which had left Havana on 19 August, and more so when Recalde returned from the Azores at the beginning of October without it. Medina Sidonia assisted the Adelantado Mayor in bringing the Spanish galley squadron, about to be laid up for winter, back to full strength in men and munitions so that it might cover their return. The outbound Tierra Firme fleet at last sailed on 22 October. Medina Sidonia went without sleep the night before, attending to final details. A fortnight later the returning flota passed under Cape St. Vincent and on 5 November entered the safety of Cadiz Bay and the Guadalquivir. Hawkins's fleet followed in hot pursuit and managed to pick off a fat straggler. "The news of its arrival," Idiáquez wrote the Duke soon afterward from court, "removes much care from everybody."[25]

Idiáquez already had before him the apt opinions he had solicited from Medina Sidonia about the defense of Portugal from English attack.[26] After making recommendations in some detail about garrisoning presidios and stationing reserves, the Duke urged that Santa Cruz's and Recalde's separate armadas be combined into one and insisted that it be maintained in a state of readiness. He had watched for most of 1586 the sluggish performances in Lisbon and Vizcaya and Spain's inability to respond to Drake's assault on the Caribbean. "For whatever might occur in Portugal as well to respond anywhere else the English sail with their fleet, because time is essential for success, it would be most unfortunate for us if after the damage was done we had to form an armada, which perforce takes much time. The present situation demands that His Majesty have ready a powerful fleet, and when that is known in England, it will put a brake to them so that the force upon which that Kingdom depends, its fleet, dare not go far away. This," he concluded, "is how it appears to me, but I defer in all to better opinions." What Medina Sidonia advocated was a permanent armada, not an armada that had to be scraped together for each emergency, as had always been the case.

Through the autumn and into winter the Duke continued to supervise maritime activities in Andalusia and report on them to court. The King reiterated the declared embargo against English shipping and goods and passed to the Duke complaints about the vagaries of its enforcement at Sanlúcar. The Duke did secure the release to the owners of merchandise in custody that had arrived in Spain before May 1585, when the embargo was first declared.

The King in the meantime decided to spring a limited embargo against ships and goods from the rebel provinces of Holland and Zeeland. He had long been hesitant, he insisted, to declare a general embargo against Hollanders and Zeelanders, whom he regarded as his subjects. The rebellion he saw as the work of a minority of heretics and malcontents, who had coerced the loyal population into submission, and he hoped that the benefits of continued commerce with Spain might persuade the merchants and shippers to overthrow the rebel government and return to his obedience.

The limited embargo added threat to persuasion: the ships of those suspected to be active in the rebellion or of heresy were to be seized. At Sanlúcar, Medina Sidonia was responsible for the seizure of those ships from northern waters, generically described as *urcas* (hulks) or easterlings, owned or commanded by "rebels and heretics."

At first the Duke's investigation yielded insufficient evidence for the purpose, until a Genoese who knew the Low Countries well began to point the finger at rebel hulks. He explained that their owners and masters had ways of obtaining licenses in the ports of the Empire, Denmark, and Norway to avoid the risk of having their ships and goods seized in Spain. One accused Dutch master testified that he was Catholic and loyal, but that his life and property, and even the lives of his family, were forfeit should he admit the truth.[27]

Yet by March, the Duke had legally detained only five or six ships. The rest, from Emden, Danzig, Copenhagen, Hamburg, and other northern ports, were released. In the margin of a letter to Medina Sidonia, the King noted that the embargo of Dutch as well as English ships had served the purpose of making all understand that the same prohibitions applied to both.[28] He praised the Duke for the prompt release of two ships from Ireland and stressed that no Irish ships be detained or "suffer any vexation." In his war with England he wanted the friendship of the Irish.

In all the embargo eventually netted some sixteen vessels, around which lawsuits quickly developed. The whole problem was intensified when the embargo was extended in August to Dutch goods, regardless of where the carrier was from. Medina Sidonia quickly reported that it was virtually impossible to distinguish goods from Holland and Zeeland from other goods arriving from northern Europe.

With the masters of eleven of the arrested hulks Medina Sidonia arranged for contracts to be made for the shipment of much-needed salt to Flanders through the dangerous waters of the Channel. Of those that remained, a couple of the best were assigned to the armada and the rest sold with licence to be used in the Indies but never to return.

While Medina Sidonia kept busy in Andalusia, at court plans for an invasion of England were studied and began taking shape. During the autumn of 1586, a small junta that included Idiáquez, Moura, and Don Juan de Zúñiga, a senior statesman who had long served Philip II as Ambassador to Rome, sorted through proposals submitted by Santa Cruz and Alexander Farnese, the King's nephew, Duke of Parma and Governor General of the Netherlands.

In a meticulously detailed relation Santa Cruz proposed an armada of 150 galleons and greatships, 6 galleasses, 50 galleys, 40 hulks, 320 small craft, and 200 landing barges.[29] Ships' crews, soldiers, and rowers would number over 30,000, and the invasion army would include 55,000

Spanish, Italian, and German infantry, 1,200 cavalry, and over 4,000 sappers, muleteers, and gunners. He preferred landing first in Ireland and then invading England if the Queen refused to come to terms. He calculated that the operating costs of ships, the pay of the men, and expenses for foodstuffs and munitions for an eight-month campaigning season would come to some 3,801,288 ducats. Not included were the basic costs of the ships and their guns.

The Duke of Parma suggested that he might launch an army of 35,000 men directly against England in a swarm of small to medium size vessels collected in the estuaries and ports of the Low Countries.[30] Required were easterly winds, which would hinder the English naval response, superb organization, speed, and great secrecy. While the required combination of circumstances seems farfetched, when Parma proposed his plan the Queen's navy appeared to be ill-prepared for war, and relations between the English and Dutch already showed serious strains. Parma believed that his massing of men, ships, and barges could be disguised as an attack on Zeeland. If secrecy could not be kept, Parma added, the armada from Spain that Philip ought to possess to be "lord of the sea" could open the way for the invasion flotilla.

In Madrid the two plans were gradually combined. What Santa Cruz proposed seemed too costly and required more men and ships than could likely be assembled, and what Parma proposed seemed too risky. It remained possible that Santa Cruz with a smaller armada might land an army in Ireland, or use the armada to cover the crossing of Parma's army from Flanders to England, as Parma had suggested might prove necessary.

Idiáquez, with the close assistance of Moura, became the King's chief manager of the Enterprise as it took final shape. Both Granvelle and Zúñiga, the last of the elder statesmen at the court of Philip II, died at the end of 1586.

To make available the ships Santa Cruz would need, Idiáquez believed that the New Spain flota of 1587 should not sail and that the armada of Alvaro Quiñones ought to be held in Iberian waters when it returned from the Indies. He wrote to Medina Sidonia to seek his opinion. Medina Sidonia responded bluntly that the flotas ought to sail every year, "because on the communication between the two worlds depends the wealth and power we need here. The English and others not subject to His Majesty use all possible means to break this communication because they know that it is the source of the King's power, which they fear. Rather than halt the sailing of the flota, its prompt dispatch should be encouraged."[31] The Duke suggested that four stout ships currently in Cadiz Bay might join the armada, but the other ships of the New Spain fleet were not as strong and might be lost in a hard campaign, which would hit the King with the cost of reimbursing the owners. Moreover, he added, their guns were of iron and thus not considered entirely trustworthy.

Quiñones's armada, the Duke believed, ought to be careened, refitted, and sent back to the Indies, where "the present state of things obliges us to keep an armada . . . until the affairs of England take a different turn." It could pick up the Tierra Firme treasure of 1588 and escort the New Spain flota back to Spain.

In response Idiáquez admitted that Medina Sidonia's points were well-taken, "given what until now you have understood." However the King now wished that the Duke know his latest thoughts. The English had taken over Holland and Zeeland and "infest the Indies and the Mediterranean; defensive measures will no longer suffice. He must set fire to their house . . . to draw them home." An attack either directly on England or by way of Ireland seemed the solution to both the English menace and the revolt of the Low Countries, "that voracious monster that consumes the men and treasure of Spain." For this purpose the most powerful armada possible was needed. He asked the Duke to reconsider what he had previously proposed.[32]

Medina Sidonia answered promptly. "When I was in Madrid last year, I heard some persons discussing what Your Grace [*Vuestra Merced*, the root of the polite *Usted* in modern Spanish][33] now proposes to me, of putting foot in Ireland and from it, or by passing directly, going against its neighbor. . . . Indeed it is a matter to which I have given many hours. . . . It may provide the means to subdue that 'voracious monster,' as Your Grace put it." Medina Sidonia emphasized the strength the English enjoyed at sea and the naval support they would likely gain from Holland, Zeeland, La Rochelle, "and other parts as yet unsuspected." He stressed that "His Majesty's armada must sail very much superior to whatever they might muster."[34]

He admitted that his previous proposal had been made "blindly," then spelled out his new ideas. According to what he knew, and he knew much, the armada at Lisbon consisted of twelve Portuguese galleons, eight greatships of Recalde's Vizcayan squadron, and a galleon belonging to the Grand Duke of Tuscany that Santa Cruz had pressed into service. Designated to join Santa Cruz were four stout ships from Cádiz and Seville that he had recommended, ten heavy ships coming from Vizcaya,[35] six galleasses under way from Naples,[36] and twenty light, swift pataches and zabras. This armada, he believed, was sufficient, but to conceal its true purpose, report should be made that it would escort the Indies flotas.

To carry infantry and munitions for the landing in Ireland the Duke suggested that thirty sturdy, well-armed hulks be hired in the ports of Andalusia. Because the voyage was short, enough infantry could be carried for both the landing and the defense of the ships. To assist with the landings he urged that eight galleys sail with the armada. About Irish ports, he stated that he had been seeking what information he could without raising too much suspicion. He persisted in his conviction that the New Spain flota should sail on schedule, because "the greatness of His Majesty is such that he can form an armada and not have to disturb the ordinary trade and commerce of the Indies." In all the Duke stressed the need for due haste.

Regarding the New Spain flota the Duke was overruled. Orders were issued that it not sail, although the Duke was to keep the matter secret and to proceed as normal with the flota's preparation. What the King now wanted was an alternate plan for the recovery of the New World treasure for 1588.

Medina Sidonia acknowledged in response that sending an armada of twenty-five or thirty galleons for the treasure might prove inadequate, given reports that Drake was assembling a fleet of sixty ships to sail for the Caribbean.[37] It would also cost over a half-million ducats. Better, he argued, would be twelve swift brigantines, light, sturdy craft of sixty *toneladas* (tons burden) propelled by both sail and oar, that could fetch the treasure "at little cost and in great safety." He suggested that suitably well manned and well gunned vessels be built in Vizcaya, with great secrecy. At the same time it would be bruited that thirty galleons would fetch the treasure, so that everybody would confidently consign large quantities of gold and silver for dispatch to Spain. To reinforce his argument, he reminded the King that Pedro Menéndez de Avilés, Spain's chief midcentury maritime strategist, had done the same in 1557 and 1558 to send treasure through the pirate-infested Channel during the war with France.

The King accepted the Duke's intelligent recommendation and issued the necessary orders for building vessels and collecting others and informed the viceroys in the Indies of his decision. In 1588, and again in 1589, 1590, and 1591, the use of small, swift vessels, as proposed by Medina Sidonia, was followed to bring the annual treasure haul safely to Spain through the gauntlet of lurking English squadrons.

A month after he sent the proposal for fetching the treasure to the King, Medina Sidonia was at Sanlúcar attending the Duchess following the birth of a daughter. At ten in the evening of 29 April, three days after her birth, he received report that the English fleet he understood Drake was preparing for a foray into the Caribbean had appeared that afternoon at the entrance to Cadiz Bay. Immediately he dispatched orders to the neighboring señores and towns, commanding them to assemble their militia companies and march them to Cadiz Bay, then himself hastened on horseback to Puerto Santa Maria accompanied by four retainers.

Over a month earlier he had issued detailed instructions for the defense of the region to the local militia, posted watches along the coast and signalers on hilltops, and inspected local fortifications. To each company he assigned a destination and a task either for the defense of Cádiz and its bay, for the defense of Gibraltar, or for the defense of the smaller ports between the Guadalquivir and the Guadiana. In Sanlúcar, his militia was well drilled and well equipped, and sturdy bulwarks covered with cross fire the mouth of the Guadalquivir. The bulwark on the Sanlúcar side held a large bastard culverin, two full cannon, and two demiculverins; the bulwark on the far shore held three demiculverins. In the castle of Sanlúcar were twelve guns, which included two bastard culverins whose shot reached the far bank of the river, over a mile away. About the forts defending Cadiz Bay he complained to the court that too few guns were available and that too many of them were "old and in ruins."[38]

In Cadiz Bay on 29 April some three score merchant ships of all sizes, from Iberian, northern, and Mediterranean ports, rode at anchor while small craft plied round them. A large galleon that belonged to the Marquis of Santa Cruz had not yet been equipped with guns. The only armed warships were nine galleys of the Spanish squadron and a hired galliot, temporarily under Don Pedro de Acuña. The squadron's general, the Adelantado of Castile, was at Málaga. Medina Sidonia had been assisting Acuña to find men and munitions for the galleys, which were short of both.

Drake's attack caught Cádiz wholly by surprise. No one had worried at first about the two dozen or so sail spotted eight leagues at sea around midday. With rising afternoon breezes the ships neared the harbor mouth, and a galley and galliot put out to investigate. Juan Martínez de Recalde's Vizcayan squadron was expected. The

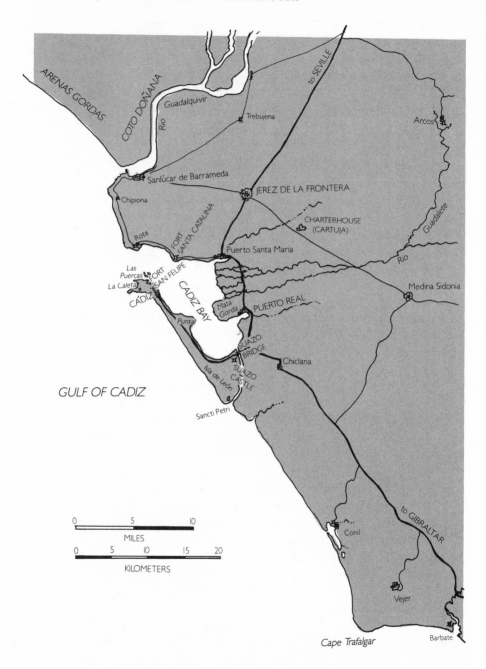

Map 2. Cádiz, Sanlúcar, and vicinity in the late sixteenth century.

galley and galliot had not charged their gun batteries.

When Drake's flagship opened fire, the galley and galliot turned tail and beat a hasty retreat, responding only with musketry. A shot damaged the galliot's battery and killed several men. Under Cádiz's walls the pair joined five other galleys that Acuña arrayed stern-to so their batteries faced the advancing English. Acuña soon learned that the English guns outranged his. Later that evening the galliot darted to Puerto Santa María with the news from Cádiz.

In the city panic struck. People swarmed to the safety of the old castle, and some two dozen women and children were trampled to death in the press. Men hurried to fetch their weapons, and in plazas ragged militia companies formed as the tocsin rang out.

Drake and his fleet surged into Cadiz Bay. Medina Sidonia claimed that Drake had twenty-two ships, of which five or six were large and the rest medium to small. A stout Genoese vessel fought back, but many of the bigger merchantmen, unprepared for a fight, were abandoned by their crews. Some ships escaped to the inner bay, while small craft scurried for shelter in the shallows of the landward shore or the protected harbor of Puerto Santa María. English shot soon had the Genoese sinking, and as night fell Drake was master of the outer bay. The English took to small craft and began to plunder the abandoned ships. A few they seized as prizes; the rest, when their cargoes had been looted, were set afire.

The galleys ventured out shooting in a vain effort to drive the English off, but the far more numerous English guns kept them always at a distance. Four of the galleys skirted the English fleet and assaulted a stray pinnace, which put up a stiff fight before being sunk. They took five English survivors captive and made the safety of Puerto Santa María, where they embarked more men and munitions.

By the time Medina Sidonia reached Puerto Santa María, the predawn sky was illuminated by blazing ships. He found the Puerto prepared to defend itself. With daybreak he continued around the bay and at sunup reached the Suazo Bridge, which spanned the shallow Rio Sancti Petri and connected the mainland with Cádiz. A bulwark that guarded the bridge had been equipped with two good cannon, and offshore stood two galleys that had been loading stores when the English attacked. Militiamen from the Duke's town of Chiclana had taken their positions to defend the bridge and were digging trenches and building barricades. They were raw men and their officers worried about how well they would conduct themselves in a stand-up fight with the English.

Already men on horse and foot had gone on toward Cádiz, which sits at the end of a long spit of land. Medina Sidonia followed, leading a large contingent of horse and foot from Jerez, a city known for its loyalty to Medina Sidonia's historic rival, the Duke of Arcos. He positioned men along the shore as he went and entered Cádiz at eleven Thursday morning. He conferred with its corregidor, Juan de la Vega, and Don Pedro de Acuña of the galleys, then spent the day supervising the organization of the city's defenses. Guns were hauled from bulwarks facing the sea and placed to fire at the English ships.

Drake had led most of his fleet toward the inner bay, where the ships that had escaped him huddled. To hinder him, Medina Sidonia ordered two big bronze guns tugged to the promontory of Puntal, which defined on the west the separation of lower from upper Cadiz Bay. Because of the shoals and shallows of the upper bay, Drake lowered skiffs and launches from his big ships to renew his attack on Spanish shipping. He set fire to Santa Cruz's galleon and a few other vessels, but gunfire from shore and the two Spanish galleys from the Rio Sancti Petri proved effective in limiting his movements.

The bronze guns at Puntal damaged the English galleon *Golden Lion*, which had to be taken under tow. Six of Acuña's galleys emerged from their havens to the attack but did no harm to her before other English ships came to her rescue and forced the galleys to withdraw. During the night report that the English were approaching Puntal in launches brought Medina Sidonia at the head of several hundred horsemen to meet the threatened landing. From Cádiz small craft filled with pitch and fired were set adrift toward the English fleet but were fended off.

At dawn a freshening offshore breeze filled the English sails. By midmorning Drake's fleet, laden with booty and towing prizes, had left smoke-shrouded Cadiz Bay on a westerly course. Medina Sidonia reported that Drake had destroyed or taken twenty-four ships.[39] At a safe distance Acuña's galleys trailed the English fleet while on shore the eight thousand Andalusian militiamen who had rallied to the defense of Cádiz watched helplessly.

Medina Sidonia made ready two swift caravels, each under a veteran naval officer, and sent them off to shadow Drake and report his movements. At the same time he sent a warning vessel to the Canaries and dispatched across the Atlantic a fast ship of his own, which reached Cartagena de Indias in a record twenty-seven days with dispatches to alert Alvaro Flores de Quiñones, in command of the treasure galleons due to return to Spain, and the New World viceroys and governors to the threat posed by Drake's fleet.

News of Drake's attack on Cadiz Bay reached the King at Aranjuez on 2 May, even as Don Juan de Idiáquez was about to post warning to the Duke that Drake had left Plymouth and was at sea. When report came from Medina Sidonia about his response to Drake's attack and his consequent dispatch of warning vessels, the King answered with praise and approval. The Venetian ambassador noted that the King would reward the Duke by creating him "Captain General of Andalusia, Granada and Murcia, an honorable office which the Duke had long desired," and added with an Italian touch that "the fact will greatly annoy the Duke of Osuna, his rival."[40]

Drake in the meantime rounded Cape St. Vincent and headed north, hoping to intercept Juan Martínez de Recalde's Vizcayans. He was too late: Recalde had been warned and made the safety of Lisbon harbor. His prize escaped, Drake returned to the waters of Cape St. Vincent and put himself athwart the sea route from Cádiz to Lisbon. After his attempt to seize Lagos failed, Drake landed his men at the smaller port of Sagres further west and overpowered the defenders of its castle. Medina Sidonia soon learned from his caravels that Drake was again in Andalusian waters.

With Drake at Cape St. Vincent, Medina Sidonia took the opportunity to impress on the King and Idiáquez the weakness of the defenses of Cádiz and Andalusia.[41] He sent to court two Cádiz town councilmen to appeal to the King, who told them, according to Cabrera de Córdoba, that they should look to their own defenses, while he would protect them with his armada.[42] Nonetheless, he sent military engineers to Cádiz to inspect its fortifications and submit plans for their improvement.[43] More immediately, he stepped up the tempo of preparations for Santa Cruz's armada and the Enterprise of England.

In May 1587 his armada seemed able to do little. At Cadiz Bay the Adelantado of Castile, recuperating from a fall from a horse, arrived from Málaga and took charge of his galleys. He ventured along the coast of the Algarve as far as Lagos but hesitated to close with Drake's bigger and better-armed ships. In Lisbon, the Marquis of Santa Cruz had to depend on the galleys commanded by his brother, Don Alonso de Bazán, to cover the entrance to the Tagus when Drake tested Lisbon's defenses in mid-May. Santa Cruz's galleons remained short of crews and munitions. Never popular in Lisbon, he seems to have suffered from less than enthusiastic cooperation by the Portuguese factors on whom he depended for the maintenance and provisioning of his armada.

Much of what Santa Cruz needed would have to be provided from Andalusia, where in response to new orders from court Medina Sidonia recruited 5,200 men.[44] Seville and the other towns and the señores, angered by the raid on Cádiz, responded enthusiastically. Of the 5,200, 2,200 were ordered to Lisbon but were held back by Medina Sidonia. Drake's presence at Sagres blocked their transport by sea, and he feared they might desert if marched overland.

More ships for the armada were also sought in Andalusia. Medina Sidonia received the King's authority to embargo for the royal service suitable vessels from the flota of New Spain that had been canceled. He selected fifteen, for which the King released 14,000 ducats to outfit and arm them and 20,000 for the soldiery who would sail on board.[45]

At the same time, six ships expected in Cadiz Bay from Sicily, with Diego Pimentel's veteran tercio of infantry aboard, had put in at Gibraltar on the news that Drake was near Cádiz. Medina Sidonia hurried to Gibraltar to inspect the tercio and arrange for their transport in the Adelantado's galleys to Ayamonte. "It should be safe," he explained to the King, "because it is supposed Drake has other designs."[46] From Ayamonte he intended the men to travel by barge up the Guadiana to Mertola and thence march overland to Lisbon.

As the Duke and the Adelantado discussed the troop movement, both came to the conclusion that they had available in the Andalusian ports enough ships and the men to form a potent armada. They counted the fifteen greatships pressed into service, twenty-seven hired hulks, the six ships from Sicily, plus smaller vessels and ten galleys, and seven thousand infantry. Moreover, they expected the arrival at any moment of four galleasses and two greatships with the tercio of Don Alonso de Luzón from Naples. In a letter dated 30 May they proposed to the King that he authorize the Adelantado to sail with the Andalusian armada for Lisbon and in route attack Drake if he were still at Sagres.[47]

The King was ill and business lay in the hands of Idiáquez and Moura, but important matters still needed the King's approval. The letter reached him on the road from Aranjuez to Madrid. He approved the plan submitted by Medina Sidonia and the Adelantado at once but insisted that the Adelantado and the Andalusian armada not sail before the Neapolitan galleasses and ships had joined.[48] The Neapolitans carried extra artillery that could be mounted on board the pressed hulks. He moreover commanded that the Andalusian armada not go in pursuit of Drake had he departed Sagres and put out to sea, but rather proceed directly to Lisbon. The King and his two closest advisers meant to take no risks in preparing the Enterprise of England.

In a separate note, Idiáquez complimented the Duke on his initiative, then expressed his concern about the loading of powder consigned for delivery to Lisbon: "Does not the Adelantado think it wiser that the powder travel in the hulks to Lisbon, rather than in fighting ships which may have to close with the enemy?"[49]

By the time Medina Sidonia and the Adelantado received the King's guarded approval of their plan, they had learned that Drake had sailed from Sagres and was headed for the Azores to await the treasure fleets. It became urgent that Santa Cruz pursue him.

Medina Sidonia went back to recruiting men, not only to meet the insatiable demands of the armada, but also to fill the request of the Viceroy of Sicily for people to replace those who had come to Spain in Pimentel's tercio. The Duke's complaints to the court illustrate afresh some of the problems he routinely faced and how recruiting was in fact accomplished: "Seville, Arcos and Jerez have been allowed to appoint their own officers; the Adelantado and the Marquis [of Santa Cruz] will not accept those I have sent with the companies which they embarked; and now twenty-two captains and alféreces have arrived here with *cédulas* [sealed orders] from Your Majesty that they be given companies in this Andalusia. Here there are captains who have served Your Majesty for many years, like Don Luis de Carvajal, as an alférez in Flanders and Italy, Pedro Guajardo de Aguilar, in the wars of Granada and Portugal, and others of such merit."[50] The Duke continued by stating that he would refuse to give the newly arrived officers companies until he had taken up the matter with the King. The local officers who had recruited the companies had used "their relatives, friends, acquaintances and *compadres*—to use the term of this region [it best translates 'pals']—without whose diligence the tercio could not be embarked." If the King insisted on appointing new officers, the Duke concluded, it would be best to make the change after the local officers had got the men aboard ship.

Another fresh arrival with a commission from the King was Don Alonso de Leyva, former general of the galleys of Sicily and swashbuckling idol of the Duke of Pastrana. Pastrana did not come to Sanlúcar with him but went instead to Flanders, where he joined Parma's invasion army.

About Leyva, as about Pastrana, Medina Sidonia always had mixed feelings, but Leyva as an officer was serious and hardworking. His initial instructions were to supervise the loading of the ships in the Andalusian ports. Useful in this task was his relationship to Francisco Duarte, who was married to his sister. In all he was to cooperate closely with Medina Sidonia and the Adelantado and report back to the King. Leyva, who was fishing for high command in the armada, had his foot in the door.

Medina Sidonia, the Adelantado, and Leyva had the Andalusian armada ready to sail by mid-June and waited only for the galleasses and ships from Naples, which were reported to be at Málaga. Pimentel's tercio of 1,500 sailed ahead to Mertola and marched for Lisbon while 4,600 infantry recruited in Andalusia boarded the Adelantado's armada in Cadiz Bay. Another 350 men were reserved for the garrison of Cádiz.[51]

On 5 July the King finally tired of having the Andalusian armada wait for the squadron from Naples and shot off orders to Medina Sidonia, the Adelantado, and Leyva that the Andalusians should weigh anchor for Lisbon.[52] The Adelantado was put in overall command till he met the Marquis of Santa Cruz off Cape St. Vincent or at Lisbon. He would then transfer command of his ships and urcas to the Marquis and return to Andalusia with his galleys to guard the Strait of Gibraltar. Under the Adelantado, Diego de Alcega, a veteran of the Indies route, commanded the fifteen great ships and ten smaller zabras and pataches for the voyage to Lisbon, and Leyva commanded the hulks and the six Sicilian ships. Both officers were to remain with Santa Cruz.

On 12 July the Andalusian armada put to sea from Cadiz Bay and Sanlúcar and headed toward Cape St. Vincent, where contrary weather checked its progress. Orders followed for Alcega with his twenty-five vessels to sail in the wake of Santa Cruz's armada to the Azores but were countermanded when news from England reported that another powerful English flotilla had put to sea. About every expedition that sailed from England rumor claimed that the Prior Dom António rode aboard to raise Portugal in revolt against King Philip.

Santa Cruz's armada cleared the Tagus on 14 July and steered for the Azores to meet the returning treasure flotas and escort them safely to Spain. At the end of July the Andalusian armada entered the Tagus, where the Adelantado relinquished command to Leyva and returned with his galleys to Cádiz. The tardy Neapolitan squadron reached Cádiz the same month towing an English prize,[53] then continued to Lisbon.

Having seen the Neapolitans off, Medina Sidonia returned to the business of recruiting men and waited for the treasure flotas to return. He knew that Drake had sailed to the Azores in search of them and that Santa Cruz had followed in order to frustrate Drake's designs and escort them to Spain in safety.

✳ CHAPTER FIVE ✳

Command of the Armada

FOR Medina Sidonia, King, and court the most urgent concern in the late summer of 1587 had become the safe return of the treasure fleets, upon which the King waited to pay his creditors and cover the mounting cost of the Enterprise of England. On 21 August a caravel sent by Quiñones as his galleons and treasure flota cleared the Bahamas Passage reached Sanlúcar. Medina Sidonia forwarded to court Quiñones's dispatches and added in a letter of his own that the fleet carried "more than sixteen millions, the greatest treasure that has entered these kingdoms in one sum from the Indies."[1] He also urged the King to heed a report from the Viceroy of Peru that the English had found a navigable passage south of the Strait of Magellan.[2]

Medina Sidonia at the same time tended to the defense of the coast of Andalusia, "in case," as the King put it, "the government of Algiers wants to molest it."[3] He assisted the Adelantado in adding to his squadron galleys that had been laid up and reviewed plans for the fortification of Cádiz and its environs drawn up by Tiburcio Espanoqui, an Italian engineer sent from court.[4] The King was particularly concerned about how to raise the necessary money.

The Duke could neither ignore the affairs of Morocco, where an English embassy had been active there since late 1585 seeking havens for English ships and markets for their merchandise and encouraging the Sharif to join an alliance against Spain that would include the Dutch and the Turk.[5]

As September drew to an end, raging storms whipped the waters of the Gulf of Cadiz and pounded the shores of Andalusia. On 27 September Medina Sidonia saw the tattered sails of the Indies galleons and flota heave into view beyond the bar of the Guadalquivir. He hastily sent warning to the ships to stand clear until he could organize their recovery. Small craft warped some over the bar; others headed for Cadiz Bay. From a foundering galleon he arranged for the salvage of the treasure, and he sent the Adelantado out with the galleys to aid stragglers seeking their way along the coast of the Algarve and the Arenas Gordas.[6]

The Crown laid heavy hand on the treasure and men arrived from the Indies. Three judges from the Chancellery of Granada and the Marquis of Auñón, Treasurer General, visited the merchantmen and levied all possible taxes and assessments on both ships and goods.[7] Unwilling merchants were coerced into asientos with the Crown or forced to purchase unwanted juros and offices.

The three thousand men of Juan de Tejeda's tercio who provided the infantry for Quiñones's galleons were transferred to the Adelantado's galleys for the voyage to Ayamonte, the barge trip to Mertola, and the march to Lisbon and the armada. Medina Sidonia reported that the men were hungry, sick, and in rags and received authority from the King to spend 20,000 ducats to clothe and reequip them.[8]

In mid-October, Medina Sidonia himself departed from Andalusia and journeyed to Madrid on state and private business. According to the Venetian ambassador he had been summoned to court and would be "made a member of the secret council and appointed to other posts."[9]

The armada that had escorted the treasure fleets from the Azores Santa Cruz took from Cape St. Vincent back to Lisbon. All hoped that he would quickly reprovision it, make such repairs as were necessary, embark the waiting tercios, and execute the plan for the Enterprise of England. Don Alonso de Leyva reportedly had the greatships, hulks, zabras and pataches of the Andalusian armada, and the galleasses and ships from Italy ready to weigh anchor, while Miguel de Oquendo's Guipuzcoan squadron of eight greatships and four pataches only awaited orders to put to sea from La Coruña and meet Santa Cruz off Cape Finisterre.

The revised plan for the Enterprise approved by the King in September 1587 called for Santa Cruz's armada to sail directly against England. At court he and Idiáquez had been sufficiently impressed by the Duke of Parma's reported success in mobilizing an armada of light vessels along the Flemish coast and in the estuary of the Scheldt that they decided to scrap the alternative plan they had discussed with Santa

Cruz during the summer. That plan provided that Santa Cruz's armada should land an army in Ireland late in 1587 and support it through the winter; in 1588 England would be invaded from both Ireland and the Low Countries.[10] As the King and Idiáquez reflected on it, they came to fear that the army might become bogged down, and with the armada committed to its support, the English fleet would remain free to strike again into the Caribbean or against the Iberian Peninsula. They had also heard that the Queen was trying to recruit German veterans to augment the forces defending her coasts.

According to the revised plan, the Duke of Parma would provide thirty to forty thousand men and their transport, and the armada would bring him six thousand more, all Spaniards, of whom Parma claimed he had too few, with their artillery and impedimenta. Santa Cruz would force the Channel with the armada, stand off Margate, and cover Parma's crossing, providing such support for the invasion as needed.

But Santa Cruz shocked everybody when he announced on his return to Lisbon in October that his armada could not sail at once to carry out the Enterprise because of storm damages suffered on the return from the Azores. He promised to do "all that is humanly possible to do" to sail early in November.[11] At once the complaints that the Marquis had long been remiss in the preparation of the armada for the Enterprise resurfaced. The King, while praising Santa Cruz for his services, heeded the complaints and ordered his Viceroy, the Cardinal-Archduke Albert, to conduct an inspection of the armada. Albert assigned Leyva and Luis César, the Portuguese Provisioner General of Armadas, to the task. After his inspection, Leyva claimed that the armada could sail and wrote to Madrid that if Santa Cruz would not carry out the Enterprise, he, Leyva, would. Leyva could afford to be brash, Cabrera de Córdoba later wryly noted, because he had "less fame and fortune to risk" than did Santa Cruz.[12]

Santa Cruz retorted that the weather was bad and the season late, too many ships were scarcely seaworthy, and he was not certain that Oquendo's squadron could be relied on to join in time. With Oquendo's ships, he had only thirty-eight that dared venture the voyage, and they were short of seamen and gunners. He continued to promise that he would do everything possible to sail.[13] The King believed he could raise the number to forty-five or forty-eight but admitted the late season might force them to revive the plan to land troops in Ireland.

When the Duke of Medina Sidonia arrived in Madrid he found the court embroiled in argument over the conflicting claims of Leyva and the Marquis. Summoned to testify before the Council of War, he sided with Santa Cruz and argued that to sail so late in the season risked disaster.[14] The most prominent member of the council, Don Hernando de Toledo, was of the same opinion. When new reports of bad weather, damages, and other difficulties were received from Lisbon, the armada's sailing date was repeatedly postponed. The earliest possible came to be set at 15 February 1588.[15]

Medina Sidonia also discussed at court the limited embargo declared against the ships and goods of Holland and Zeeland, the defenses of Andalusia, and the recovery of the 1588 treasure from the Indies. To fetch the treasure it was decided to take Alvaro Flores de Quiñones from the Guard Armada anchored at Sanlúcar and put him in command of a dozen or so pataches and zabras to be assembled in secrecy at Medina Sidonia's town of Huelva.

Cabrera de Córdoba offered another reason why Medina Sidonia journeyed to court: his concern that the efforts of his uncle, the Duke of Osuna, to gain appointment to the Council of State and the office of Majordomo to the King might bear fruit, while he garnered nothing.[16] He did not need to worry. Osuna was politely turned down, for reason of his poor health, while the King approved Medina Sidonia for the office he had long sought, the Captaincy General of the Coast of Andalusia. The commission, dated 8 January 1588,[17] gave definition to the authority he had exercised almost constantly for ten years under a variety of royal warrants and orders. The coast of Andalusia was understood to encompass the coast from the Rio Guadiana to the border of the Kingdom of Granada, and inland for a distance of twenty leagues. The region demarked coincided to a large degree with the province called the Kingdom of Seville. The commission enjoined all señores and royal and municipal authorities in the region to cooperate with the Duke in matters regarding the militia and maintenance of local defenses, and all those who came under his command to obey his orders. He was to enjoy the same honors and perquisites that all other Captain Generals did.[18]

When Medina Sidonia returned to Sanlúcar he found the galleons of the Guard Armada sitting in the Guadalquivir across the tidal flats and beaches that bordered the town, being outfitted for sea under the supervision of Antonio Guevara, provisioner of the galleys. Though it was widely believed they would sail to the Indies in the spring, the Duke knew they would be sent to Lisbon to join Santa Cruz. He had admitted to the Council of War that they were fine ships and would enhance the armada's strength. But if the merchants of Cádiz and Seville, whose credit made their arming possible, and the men who manned them thought the galleons would not go to the Indies, the credit would dry up and the men would desert.

With the galleons in Guevara's competent hands, Medina Sidonia turned to the defense of the coast, for which he now had the King's commission. He informed the señores and towns that the region would be vulnerable to attack because the King's armada would not be at hand and ordered them to tend to their defenses. To Madrid he complained that the construction of galleys should be hurried and asked why the Genoese galleys might not guard the strait.[19] Four Spanish galleys from Puerto Santa María had been assigned to sail to Lisbon when approval had been granted for four galleys there to join the armada.

In mid-February, while preparing the defenses of the coast, the Duke received from Idiáquez a letter that informed him that the Marquis of Santa Cruz was ill, little hope was held for his life, and "the King had put his eyes on you" for command of the armada assembled in Lisbon harbor and due to sail.[20]

Medina Sidonia responded with a long demurral:[21]

> Your Grace wrote, by order of His Majesty . . . that the Marquis of Santa Cruz is ill and little hope is held for his life, and of the need there for his person because the armada is far enough along that it can sail by the middle of this month, and for a thousand reasons the delay of its departure cannot be allowed. And that His Majesty has put his eyes on me, to entrust me with this campaign and that I undertake it, for the great service to God and His Majesty expected of this Enterprise which it must effect, by joining hands with the Duke of Parma and the forces he brings; and both of us turning against England. And that I go in the armada being outfitted here to join the armada in Lisbon, and follow and obey his orders.
>
> Responding to all of this, I first kiss the royal hands and feet of His Majesty for putting his hand on me for so great a matter, which I should like to have the parts and strength necessary to fulfill. . . . But, señor, I do not have the health to embark and I know from what little experience I have of the sea that I get seasick, for I am rheumatic.
>
> Moreover Your Grace knows that I am in such necessity that I had to go to Madrid to borrow. My House owes 900,000 ducats

and thus I have not a *real* to spend in the campaign.

Besides this, neither conscience nor duty permits me to accept this charge, for it is not right that the command of so great a war-machine and so important an enterprise be taken by one who has neither experience of the sea nor of war, for I have never seen war nor engaged in it. Thus, señor, for the service of His Majesty and the love that I bear him, I tell this to Your Grace so that it may be reported that I am without ability, health or strength for this campaign, and without fortune. Any one of these things would be disqualifying: how much more so when all combine, as they do in me at present.

Moreover, I would join the armada knowing nothing of it, nor of the persons in it, nor the plans for it; nothing of the news of England or of its ports, or of the correspondence which the Marquis has conducted during the years this has been dealt with. I would be going blind, even had I much experience, putting myself into matters in mid-course on such short notice.

Thus, señor, all the reasons I offer are so strong and appropriate to the royal service of His Majesty that for them I shall not attempt to make the voyage. I have no doubt that I shall give a bad account of myself, going blindly, being guided by the experience and opinions of others, knowing neither what is good nor what is bad, not knowing who wishes to deceive or ruin me.

His Majesty has someone with experience, who would be able to serve in this voyage with the councillors the Marquis had, and I say in good conscience that he should entrust it to the Adelantado Mayor of Castile. He can put out with the armada that is here and join that of Lisbon. I am certain that the Adelantado will be aided by Our Lord, for he is a good Christian and a friend of what is right. He has much knowledge of the sea and was in the Naval Battle [Lepanto], and has experience on land.

This is my answer to Your Grace, in all the frankness and honesty it deserves. . . . Thus if His Majesty, in his greatness, wishes to do me a favor, I humbly supplicate that he not entrust me with something of which I cannot give good account, because I do not understand it, I have not the health for the sea, nor fortune to spend on it.

Why did Medina Sidonia phrase his response to Idiáquez in this self-disparaging manner, especially since Idiáquez knew that Medina Sidonia was hardly ignorant regarding the armada, its personnel, and the general plan for the Enterprise? When the King read the letter, he attributed Medina Sidonia's refusal to "modesty."[22] Castiglione in *The*

Courtier recommended that an honor at first ought to be declined, though not so strongly that the bestower might withdraw it.

What seems certain is that Medina Sidonia did not want command of the armada and hoped the bestower would withdraw it. He sent a second letter dated 18 February in the wake of his first that could only have been more adamant in its refusal of the post and desperate in its tone. Idiáquez and Moura read it and suppressed it:

> We have not dared give account of what you wrote to His Majesty. For the love of God, Your Lordship, consider the reasons we wrote you in our last, the office you are refusing, and at what a time, and look at what things are coming to. Do not bother us with fears about the success of the armada: in such a cause God will assure a good outcome. Because the appointment to which God and the King call Your Lordship is so important, you ought to show more spirit. To preserve the reputation and opinion which today the world has of your valor and prudence, which would all be hazarded if it were known what you wrote (which we shall keep secret), it is important that you step forward with the determination expected of Your Lordship. May God enlighten and protect you.[23]

Medina Sidonia's second letter, which has not been found if it still exists, most likely offered further reasons for his effort to refuse the armada command. What he confided to Idiáquez and Moura is perhaps what appears in a letter he wrote to the King four months after he took the command, when a storm forced the armada to seek port at La Coruña less than three weeks after its departure from Lisbon. In the letter he admitted it was the storm and the damage it had done the armada that had given him doubts about the will of God in so apparently just a cause and made him decide to reveal why he had attempted to refuse the post but had hesitated to tell the King earlier.[24] He believed that the armada Spain had assembled was inadequate for the defeat and conquest of a kingdom so large as England, which would moreover be supported by neighbors. He added that he understood matters would be made easier for the King by the *negocio* (business or negotiation) some understood, who only looked to his service without other ends. The negocio he referred to was probably the negotiation to seek terms for peace held in Flanders between Parma and an English delegation in Flanders.[25]

About the other, better-known reasons for his refusal of the post, there seems no doubt that he was sincere. Regarding his health, he did suffer from rheumatism and gout, although he was hardly alone in this.

His seasickness was another matter. He did not mention it when he was younger and wanted to take over the Spanish galleys, although in February 1588 he was over thirteen years older than he had been when he sought command of the galleys. A tendency to seasickness may have come with aging and his other ailments, and it certainly can be disabling.

He knew that his competence in maritime and military matters was largely logistical. He had a knack of getting hard work from provisioners and others concerned with outfitting fleets, and he proved effective in raising men for service, though much of the burden always fell on his own estates. His campaign in the Algarve had been a promenade and he had never come under fire.

His debts were heavy but not uncommon for a grandee. His heir, however, was only eight years old, and the Duchess Doña Ana seems to have had little more ability at estate management than did her mother. When Medina Sidonia eventually accepted the armada command he begged for and received assurance from the King that his sons would be provided for.[26] Doña Ana, according to the gossip chroniclers of the time, had urged him not to accept the command, claiming that it was "enough to be Duke of Medina."[27] Fray Juan de Victoria, a chaplain at court, reported that the Duchess said to her friends that the Duke was good around the house, but he would better leave men in doubt about his talents outside it. But Victoria is hardly a reliable witness, and it must remain doubtful what the Duchess Doña Ana thought and said. Medina Sidonia did, when he assumed the armada command, raise again with the King the matter of clemency for her mother, the Princess of Eboli.[28]

Medina Sidonia's express reasons, coupled with his convictions that the armada was inadequate and thus likely doomed to defeat in battle and that negotiations were the best means of dealing with the King's differences with England, seem quite sufficient to explain his determination to decline the command.

The chief puzzle that remains is not why Medina Sidonia attempted to refuse command of the armada, but rather why Philip II made the appointment in the first place. Once the appointment was made the King would be understandably reluctant to withdraw it despite the Duke's attempt to refuse it. The news of the choice was known at court before the Duke had received Idiáquez's letter in Sanlúcar, and report of it had been sent to Lisbon and Brussels.[29] It would have cost the King "reputation," as was said then, to withdraw the appointment, undermined confidence in the armada, and weakened the awesome impression the armada was expected to make upon England, the Dutch rebels, and the world. It was moreover common knowledge that a half-dozen years earlier the King had withdrawn the Duke's appointment to the Governor-Generalship of Milan at the Duke's request, after the Duke had accepted the office but not yet taken it up.

In searching for reasons to explain the choice of Medina Sidonia, one needs to begin by probing Philip's mind during these months. Philip was halfway through his sixtieth year in the winter of 1587/88 and often in poor health. His surviving heir, Prince Philip, was aged nine. The King seemed almost desperately determined to end quickly what had become the great issue of his reign, the revolt of the Netherlands, the birthplace of his father. He regarded the armada campaign as the solution to all his problems. As Idiáquez put it, "All the wars and enterprises have come down to this one campaign at sea."[30]

The last of Philip's councillors who had also served the Emperor, Cardinal Granvelle, had died in 1586, and the other chief ministers of the early years of Philip's own reign were likewise dead.[31] The only important adviser on matters of state and war who was close to his own age, the Duke of Alba's natural son Don Hernando de Toledo, Philip kept at arm's length, as he had Alba. His new top advisers, Idiáquez and Moura, were each a dozen or so years younger than the King. Looking over his court and the new generation of grandees apparently gave him little confidence or comfort. His sentiment was likely caught accurately by the French Ambassador Longlée when he wrote concerning Medina Sidonia's appointment, "It is seen here that there is a lack of ministers for the conduct of affairs."[32] This sentiment was rudely challenged shortly after Philip's death by the Adelantado, then commanding the armada, who exclaimed, "Now all shall see what Spaniards are worth, with a free hand, no longer subject to one brain that thought it knew all there was to know and treated everyone else like a blockhead."[33]

The unsettling news that Santa Cruz was ill and dying reached Madrid sometime late on 11 February, following more than a week's worth of dispatches concerning his failing health.[34] Thus instead of hoping that the armada would weigh anchor as expected on 15 February, Philip found himself searching for Santa Cruz's replacement. His choice apparently was made in consultation with Idiáquez and Moura alone. On the Simancas draft of Idiáquez's letter of 11 February, the King wrote, "I have entrusted Don Juan de Idiáquez to write on my behalf."[35]

Philip respected Medina Sidonia as an adviser on imperial and maritime strategy and would hardly forget that he had once sought service at sea. Philip knew that Medina Sidonia played a significant part in the annexation of Portugal and that Granvelle had believed him capable of assuming the government of Milan. He knew him as an organizer of royal forces in Andalusia and as knowledgeable in the affairs of North Africa; as familiar with the organization and preparation of Indies flotas and armadas, and as one who, unlike Santa Cruz, had useful connections in Portugal where the armada was outfitting. Getting the armada to sea without further delay had become Philip's overriding concern.

Also Philip knew Medina Sidonia personally; the Duke's wife was the daughter of the Prince of Eboli, with whom he had been as close as he ever was to any man, and of the Princess, whom he had known in happier days before she crossed him. He knew Medina Sidonia as gracious and well-educated, humane, and devout in religion. And he knew that the Duke was a grandee in whose veins flowed the blood of Ferdinand the Catholic and kings of Castile and Portugal, blood the King shared, in an age when blood was believed to determine qualities of character. The King had more confidence in Medina Sidonia than Medina Sidonia seemed to have in himself.

Idiáquez, like the King, seemed confident in the Duke for much the same reasons, and he had come to regard the Duke as one who took his side in court politics. Moura likely concurred and certainly appreciated the influence Medina Sidonia enjoyed in Portugal, which was so important to the success of the armada. Mateo Vázquez, the "Arch-Secretary," also thought well of Medina Sidonia, though he was probably too self-effacing to attempt to influence any decision about the command of the armada. His favorable regard for the Duke, however, was of no harm.

When news of the King's choice became known at court, there was chiefly praise but also a few reservations. Longlée wrote to Henri III of France, "He is rich and a man of affairs, and though he has never held command at sea, still he is one of the most capable subjects they have."[36] The Venetian Ambassador Lippomano's report has been quoted before, though it seems worth repeating the phrase "all other appointments posed greater difficulties."[37]

Who was "capable" of filling the post was hardly the chief question that faced Philip, Idiáquez, and Moura, since there were several dozen qualified persons available who had commanded squadrons of the armada, Indies flotas, or both. The problem was to find a capable person who posed the fewest "difficulties" and had sufficient prestige to rise above the envies and rivalries rife in the armada, who was in favor at court, had useful connections and the fewest enemies.

Prestige did not rest solely on noble rank, although rank was part of the equation. In the Spanish service not only grandees and titled nobles held high command, but also their younger sons and close kin, known as *segundones*, who ranked as untitled señores and were often *comendadores* (knight-commanders) or *caballeros* (knights) in the Military Orders. The Marquis of Santa Cruz had followed the naval career of his father, a señor and caballero whose forebears had come from Navarre to make their fortune in Granada. Santa Cruz received his title only in 1569 and was made a grandee in 1583, after his victories in the Azores. Don García de Toledo, who was Captain General of the Sea in 1564–68 was a segundón who did not become Marquis of Villafranca until 1569. Don Alonso de Leyva, who was designated in April 1588 to replace Medina Sidonia if something happened to him, was the eldest son of a señor and caballero who capped a long career of war with the office of Viceroy of Navarre, which he soon claimed he could not afford.[38] Medina Sidonia's rank as a grandee of Spain was certainly no hindrance, but hardly a prerequisite or even the chief reason for his appointment.

Had members of the Council of War other than Idiáquez and Moura been asked about the appointment, they most likely would have recommended Don Hernando de Toledo, Grand Prior of Castile and León in the Military Order of St. John of Jerusalem. His name was mentioned at court, and Miguel de Oquendo, general of the Guipuzcoan squadron and the armada's vanguard, recommended him.[39] As Grand Prior, Toledo ranked as a grandee of Spain. Sixty years old, he had chiefly commanded troops on land but had served briefly at sea and in 1570 escorted Ana of Austria aboard the armada that brought her from Antwerp to her marriage with Philip II. It was said he suffered from seasickness, but that was hardly disqualifying; Medina Sidonia said the same about himself.

More important would have been his differences with Idiáquez and Moura. A year after the armada's defeat, Toledo and another Council of War member complained to the Venetian ambassador that "the opinion of Idiáquez and de Mora [*sic*], one of whom has never been out of Spain, and the other never in a campaign, is constantly preferred to their own and declared that things must go ill when all decisions are taken by the inexperienced."[40] Moreover, if Toledo's ideas on England were the same as those of the Duke of Alba, his father, he would have been against the Enterprise from the start.

An even more serious difficulty in the consideration of Don Hernando was the matter of his having to serve under the Duke of Parma. He had previously served in the Low Countries under his father, of whose government resentful memories still lingered. Though Don Hernando had been personally well regarded, he would not likely have been welcomed back; and with Parma he would probably have had major disagreements, as much about the conduct of government as about command.

Though Don Hernando's problems with Parma were potentially serious, it was said about almost every likely candidate that he would not willingly serve under Parma, though Parma was the King's nephew and in effect a sovereign duke in his own right. In addition to Don Hernando, the Venetian Ambassador Lippomano mentioned at various times Santa Cruz, Medina Sidonia, and others as unwilling to cooperate with Parma and claimed that the Pope thought the same.

Yet the young Duke of Pastrana, a grandee of Spain, journeyed to Flanders and served under him, as did many other Spanish nobles. Age and experience may have had something to do with it: Parma was forty-two, whereas Santa Cruz and Don Hernando were over sixty and were bearing arms before he was born. Pastrana in 1588 was twenty-six.

Also coloring service under Parma was something of a Hispano-Italian cultural and military rivalry that sometimes erupted into mutual antagonism.[41] It affected both Philip II's Mediterranean forces and Parma's Army of Flanders. Parma's top subordinates were chiefly Italian, as the Duke of Alba's had been chiefly Spanish.

To turn to the squadron generals of the armada in Lisbon, among them were known rivalries that precluded the selection of any one of them over his fellows. Santa Cruz had tried to promote his brother Don Alonso de Bazán, for whom he had obtained the rank of General of the Galley Squadron of Portugal. The other armada generals, all Atlantic veterans, seemed to regard Don Alonso as someone who had arrived in his brother's baggage and hardly a person to put over them. The Marquis had come from the Mediterranean to the Atlantic already trailing glory and had quickly proved his mettle in sailing ship armadas by his victories in the Azores; no such reputation attended Don Alonso. Only after his chief rivals were dead and Medina Sidonia retired did Don Alonso get the armada command, and then he lost it three years later after lackluster performances against the English.[42]

If the vanguard commander Oquendo proposed Toledo, Santa Cruz's second-in-command, Juan Martínez de Recalde, proposed himself. But Recalde, though a superb seaman and a man of proven bravery, had not compiled a very distinguished record during a long career. He headed in his own right the powerful Vizcayan squadron contracted for and assembled in Bilbao, where he was a leading nobleman and shipowner. He had fought the Sea Beggars in the waters of Holland and Zeeland in 1572, without much success, and in 1580 served in the Portuguese campaign under the command of Don Pedro de Valdés, who was also with the armada in Lisbon. In 1581 Recalde commanded a squadron in papal employ that ferried a battalion of Roman Catholic volunteers to an ill-fated landing in Ireland. In Santa Cruz's victory off San Miguel in the Azores in 1582, Recalde's squadron arrived too late to join the action, though Recalde was made a knight-commander of Santiago. He was married to a relative of Idiáquez.

Next in rank below Recalde was Don Pedro de Valdés, a difficult Asturian who had long commanded squadrons hired in the maritime towns that stretched along Castile's northern coast from Santander to Vigo. After playing a significant part in the conquest of Portugal, Valdés led in 1581 an expedition detailed to conquer the Azores, which had proclaimed for Dom António. The expedition failed and Valdés was court-martialed but acquitted. His forces had been too small for the task during a summer when Spain's main forces had braced for the expected attack by Eulj Ali's Ottoman fleet that never materialized.

While Don Pedro was facing court-martial, his distant cousin Diego Flores de Valdés, another contender for high command, acquired some renown for chasing pirates from the coast of Brazil only to have it tarnished by Pedro Sarmiento de Gamboa, who was captured by Walter Raleigh and accused Diego Flores of abandoning to its fate the expedition sent to the Straits of Magellan. Don Pedro de Valdés did not like his cousin, nor, for that matter, did anybody else. Medina Sidonia had nothing kind to say about him in 1581 when the expedition to the straits outfitted at Sanlúcar.

Diego Flores defended his actions and sought another command. His chief recommendation, apart from his long experience, was his knowledge of English waters, derived from the voyage of 1554 when he had sailed in the armada that carried then-Prince Philip to his marriage with Queen Mary Tudor. Commanding that armada was Pedro Menéndez de Avilés, the great midcentury naval commander, whose daughter married Don Pedro de Valdés. In early 1588, Diego Flores de

Valdés, now aged fifty-seven, got his chance. When Alvaro Flores de Quiñones was ordered to fetch the treasure from the Indies, Diego Flores obtained command of the galleons of the Armada of the Guard fitting out in the roads of Sanlúcar.

Diego Flores was content to get a squadron. Another officer considered, Don Alonso de Leyva, who began his career serving Don Juan of Austria, wanted the entire armada and volunteered to replace Santa Cruz. In so doing he made enemies among the other officers of the armada. He had come late to the Ocean-Armada, after he had relinquished the generalship of the Sicilian galleys to his brother Don Pedro. He briefly held command of the squadron formed in Andalusia after the Adelantado had brought it to Lisbon but was replaced by Don Pedro de Valdés when Santa Cruz returned from the Azores. Leyva left Lisbon for Madrid. He impressed the King, who in April 1588 secretly appointed him as Medina Sidonia's designated successor. He returned to the armada as an "adventurer," but in order to obtain a rank higher than any of its squadron generals, he acquired from the Count of Fuentes the office of Captain General of the Light Cavalry of Milan, which has caused many historians to regard him a cavalryman rather than a career officer with service on both land and sea, something hardly unknown in the sixteenth century. What counted was the rank of Captain General; of what mattered little. He was well connected through kinship and marriage to the Count of Chinchón, probably the third most important of Philip II's ministers in 1588, to the Mendoza family and other important Castilian families, and to Francisco Duarte.

Three other possible appointees were neither with the Lisbon armada nor at court in 1588. These were Don Pedro de Toledo, Marquis of Villafranca, Prince Doria, and the Adelantado of Castile. Villafranca, son of Don García de Toledo, had just taken command of the galleys of Naples and before him lay a distinguished career in the Mediterranean. Because his squadron stood in the front line against any menace from the Turks, there was probably no thought to post him in the Atlantic. Moreover, he was a Toledo, a protege of his kinsman Don Hernando.

Doria, apart from being needed in the Mediterranean, was unpopular in Spain and disqualified by being Italian from what was chiefly an Iberian production.

The Adelantado, Don Martín de Padilla, whom Medina Sidonia recommended, eventually took command of the armada in 1596, but in 1588 he was left to guard the Strait of Gibraltar. In retrospect there seem to be no major difficulties to his appointment, only the usual resentments of other officers. He carried the titles Count of Santa Gadea and Count of Buendía, Adelantado Mayor of Castile and Captain General of the Galleys of Spain. A tough fighting man, he had served the King for over thirty years on land and sea, in Flanders, in Portugal, but primarily in the Mediterranean. He had fought, as Medina Sidonia reminded Idiáquez, at Lepanto. Medina Sidonia also mentioned that the Adelantado was a good Christian and a friend of what was right: was this a pious formula or did the Duke perhaps think it necessary to add in order to offset the Adelantado's reputation for outspokenness and a fiery temper?

How the Adelantado fit in court politics is not clear, though to garner the galleys of Spain required some influence. At a later date his daughter married the heir of the Marquis of Denia, Philip III's favorite who became in 1599 Duke of Lerma. The Adelantado had been caught up in considerable litigation over his Buendía title, and when he received appointment as Captain General of the Galleys of Spain, he very likely ran afoul of its former holder, Santa Cruz, who had wanted it for his brother Don Alonso. Whatever may have been the case, he was apparently not given serious consideration as successor to Santa Cruz. None of the reports from court mention him. It may have been believed that he was needed to guard the Strait of Gibraltar or he may have simply been overlooked. When Medina Sidonia proposed his name, it was too late. The choice had been made and it had become public knowledge.

The first orders Philip II sent his new Captain General of the Ocean-Sea, before he had learned of his attempt to refuse the post, instructed him to sail to Lisbon aboard the galleons anchored in the Guadalquivir at Sanlúcar. If they were not yet ready to sail, Medina Sidonia was to travel at once overland to Lisbon. Philip soon learned that the galleons were not ready and that his new Captain General would journey to Lisbon on horseback. In a postscript to his letter of 20 February, which dismissed the Duke's objections to the appointment and stated that it was now public knowledge, Philip wrote, "I cannot but believe that this letter will find you closer to Lisbon than to Sanlúcar, since my confidence does not oblige you to less. Hope in God that with His aid what is desired and expected will be done by your hand."[43]

Medina Sidonia in fact was closer to Sanlúcar, which he did not leave till 27 February, accompanied by his confessor, Fray Diego Calahorrano, five pages, two gentlemen of his household, eight domestic servants, two footmen, and a caravan of nearly fifty horses and pack animals and their drivers, among them a Moor. On his way, Medina Sidonia obtained from his treasurer of the County of Niebla eleven chests of currency totaling nearly 8 million *maravedís*, or about 21,000 ducats.[44] He arrived in Lisbon on the Ides of March.

CHAPTER SIX

The Armada at Lisbon

WHEN Medina Sidonia arrived in Lisbon, the warden of his castle of Barbate had already prepared his residence. He was welcomed by his onetime hostage Dom Theodosio, who had succeeded to his father's title of Duke of Braganza. Young Braganza made him a present of a pair of horses.

Medina Sidonia immediately conducted an inspection of the armada, which the Cardinal-Archduke Albert, Viceroy of Portugal, and the Count of Fuentes, Captain General of Portugal, had been supervising. The ships collected in Lisbon harbor for the armada numbered forty-seven galleons and greatships, four galleasses, sixteen hulks, and twenty-two smaller vessels that included zabras, pataches, and pinnaces. Ten more galleons, four more greatships, and four galleys were, the Duke knew, scheduled to join them. Philip II was assembling a war machine of colossal size.[1] Only twice before had he massed so many men and ships, for the campaigns of the Holy League in 1571 and 1572, and for the conquest in 1580 of Portugal.

Philip's contribution to the Holy League included some eighty well-armed galleys, their crews and rowers, twenty greatships, and some twenty thousand soldiers, altogether perhaps forty thousand men. But much of the administration had been handled by Genoese contractors and the viceregal governments of Naples and Sicily. Only a small part of the force had been mobilized in Spain.

Spain, apart from mounting the annual Indies flotas, had mounted considerable naval expeditions on its north coast in 1554 to take Philip, then Prince, to England for his marriage to Mary Tudor; in 1572 to carry the Duke of Medinaceli to the Netherlands; and in 1574 for an assault on the Dutch rebels planned by Pedro Menéndez de Avilés that was aborted because of epidemic.[2] In 1580 war fleets that totaled well over one hundred greatships and galleys were mobilized in the Bay of Cadiz and Spain's north coast for the conquest of Portugal; and in 1581, 1582, and 1583, armadas were assembled to carry out the conquest of the Azores. Both the small expedition of 1581, numbering six vessels, and most of the big invasion armada of 1583, which included five galleons, two Tuscan galleasses, twelve galleys, thirty-one greatships, and forty-one smaller craft carrying over twelve thousand men and supplies for six months, had sailed from Lisbon. Thus, for the awesome task of getting both armada and embarked expeditionary force to sea, there was in both Spain and Portugal considerable experience.

Reflecting that available experience, Francisco Duarte, Factor of Seville's Casa de Contratación and the man most responsible for the annual sailings of Indies flotas, had come to Lisbon in 1587 to assist Luis César, Portuguese Provisioner General, whose job it was to supervise Portugal's armada of galleons and the yearly sailing of the India fleet. Overseeing the galleons and greatships designated for the armada that were still anchored at Sanlúcar and Cadiz Bay was Antonio de Guevara, a royal provisioner who often assisted Duarte. Medina Sidonia had worked with them all.

At first glance, most of the ships Medina Sidonia inspected were in need of only minor adjustments in guns, some few small repairs and modifications to superstructures and rigging, and the loading of last stores before being ready to sail.[3] The ships of the Andalusian squadron, he did admit, seemed short on both men and guns.

The armada that Medina Sidonia inspected was divided for administrative purposes into squadrons that on contemporary reports were often called armadas. The armada's constituent squadrons were named after the region where they had originally been assembled or whence their ships had come; or by ship-type. Between early January and the date the new Captain General submitted his report, some changes in organization had been made.[4] In his first report Medina Sidonia listed nine galleons and two zabras that belonged to the Crown of Portugal; ten greatships and four pataches of the armada of Vizcaya; nine greatships and four pataches of Guipúzcoa; seven greatships, two galleons, and a patache of the Andalusian squadron; a galleon that belonged to the Grand Duke of Tuscany and eight greatships that formed the Levantine squadron; sixteen hulks that formed the squadron of urcas, nineteen smaller vessels that on other lists form the squadron of pataches and zabras, and the four galleasses.

While most of the armada's ships were expected to fight, its principal warships were its galleons, galleasses, and galleys and the better-armed greatships, some virtually indistinguishable from galleons.

Galleons were sailing ships constructed from keel up as warships, though Spanish and Portuguese galleons had some cargo-carrying capacity and sufficient room for provisions needed for long voyages. While more maneuverable than medieval roundships or stubby nordic hulks, their ratios of overall length to maximum beam of around 3.25 : 1 and a ratio of keel to beam of around 2.5 : 1[5] hardly made them nimble or swift. Maneuverability was further sacrificed to massive forecastles, built to carry musketeers and light artillery, and tower over opponents' decks.[6] The rated tonnage of the Spanish and Portuguese galleons ranged from under 300 (these were sometimes called *galeoncetes*) to more than 1,000.[7] They had three or four masts—a foremast, mainmast, and one or two mizzen masts—and a bowsprit. The fore and main each bore two large square sails, the bowsprit one, and each mizzen a lateen sail. The maximum length of the biggest galleons from bowsprit to stern probably surpassed 150 feet, with a beam of close to 40. These drew 25 or more feet of water, and from the waterline to the highest point of their superstructure at the stern might be 35 feet.

The number of guns carried on board the twenty-two vessels of the armada routinely designated as galleons ranged from twenty to fifty. The bigger Portuguese galleons carried their main batteries of twenty-six to thirty guns on two gun decks; the seven Castilian galleons rated at 530 tons built for the Indies armada each had one gun-deck with a main battery of probably twelve guns of medium caliber.

Galleasses originated in the Mediterranean as the result of an effort to develop an oar-propelled warship that could carry a substantial battery of big guns in broadsides. Experiments were conducted from the 1530s onward and bore fruit at Lepanto, where the six Venetian galleasses played a significant part.[8] The Venetian galleasses of 1571 were converted from great merchant galleys, and although they sailed with the Holy League armada from Messina to the Gulf of Patras, in the battle they had to be towed into station. Whether the gun platforms were built above the rowing benches or some rowing benches were cleared to make room for the guns is not clear, but in addition to the big guns at the bow and stern, in each broadside were arrayed three heavy pieces that fired fourteen-, twenty-, and thirty-pound shot.[9] After Lepanto, Venice constructed several new galleasses from the keel up, and although they proved more maneuverable, they remained, in comparison to galleys, slow.

The four galleasses that sailed with the armada in 1588 and two others had been likewise built as warships for the armada of the Kingdom of Naples to designs by Santa Cruz and constructed and launched between 1580 and 1584.[10] Santa Cruz intended them to combine the sailing features of galleons, and the rowing potential of galleys, which could maneuver in battle without depending on wind conditions. To create such a three-masted vessel he had to make compromises in their draft that limited their abilities in rough seas. They had particular problems with their rudders. The galleasses carried some three hundred rowers each and probably had twenty-five oars to a side with six rowers to an oar in battle.[11] Though we lack plans—and the contemporary depictions of them are of uncertain value—we can guess that they were some 150 feet long, about 25 feet in beam, drew probably 8 feet of water, and weighed over 500 tons. They were among the most heavily armed vessels of the armada, with four to six full cannon, two or three demicannon, two to six demiculverins, six to nine *pedreros* (cannon firing stone shot), and a host of lighter pieces.[12]

The four galleys were lighter and swifter than the galleasses but also carried far fewer guns and barely half the number of men.[13] The war galleys of the Portuguese squadron from which the armada's four were assigned had been built for the galley squadron of Spain, were big as galleys went, and reinforced for Atlantic use. With hulls about 150 feet long and 20 feet wide, and drawing perhaps 4 feet of water, they probably displaced about 200 tons.[14] Each galley carried in a low gun-house at the prow a main battery that consisted of a big gun on the centerline and four smaller pieces flanking it, two to each side. The centerline gun might be a cannon or culverin that fired a ball of thirty pounds or more; the flanking pieces were usually demipedreros or sakers that fired balls that weighed in the nine- to twenty-pound range. Swivel guns firing shot of two to four pounds were arrayed along the sides and poop.

In battle at sea, Spanish commanders did not expect vulnerable galleys to risk gun duels with well-armed enemy sailing vessels, but rather to support their own warships and seek opportunities to strike at the enemy with minimum risk. The most important function of the armada's galleys would be to ferry troops and work close inshore in support of landing operations. Galleys had been particularly effective in the landing of Santa Cruz's expeditionary force on Terceira in 1583.

Both Santa Cruz and Medina Sidonia wanted more of them but were refused more than four because of the costs involved, because Madrid believed that Parma had collected a sufficient number of light craft and barges to ferry troops and conduct landing operations, and because the King's available galley forces were needed for the defense of the Mediterranean and the Strait of Gibraltar against both a feared Ottoman attack and the routine raids of Barbary corsairs.

Most of the galleons, all of the galleasses, and all of the galleys were the property of Philip II, built to royal specifications. The other galleons were pressed into service with the armada. One belonged to the Grand Duke of Tuscany and at least two others to private owners.

The armed greatships, designated on armada lists as *naos* or *naves*,[15] had been built to serve as merchant vessels, though the careers of many were spent in the royal service, contracted by their owners to serve as *capitanas* and *almirantas* of the Indies flotas, vessels which by law had to be big and well-gunned, or in the King's armadas in time of war. Among the armada's naos and naves there was a difference in design and construction between those built in Atlantic ports for more demanding Atlantic conditions and those built in Mediterranean ports, generically called Levanters.[16] The Atlantic-built ships were constructed of larger timbers and thus were sturdier and heavier in relation to their size. In sheer dimensions the most imposing vessels in the armada seem to have been the biggest Levanters, which also suffered proportionally far greater losses than did the Atlantic-built ships. Even before the campaign commenced Medina Sidonia had serious doubts about the Levanters' ability to navigate in ugly Atlantic weather, and his doubts were reinforced after storm drove the armada to port in early June, a bare fortnight after it had sailed from Lisbon.

Some twenty of the armada's ships were designated urcas, what in English are called hulks. The term *urca* was generic for merchantmen built in Hanseatic and other North Sea and Baltic ports. Medina Sidonia often referred to Hanseatic urcas as *esterlinas* (easterlings). Urcas were stout ships but generally less wieldy than naos and naves. Built to sail along European coastlines, some had made the voyage to the Indies. They were constructed with cargo capacity foremost in mind, and in the armada carried the horses and mules and much of the bulkier impedimenta of the landing force. The urca *San Pedro Mayor* served as hospital ship. While most urcas were assigned to Juan Gómez de Medina's *armada de Urcas*, two appear with other squadrons, *La Duquesa Santa Ana* with the Andalusian and *Doncella* with Oquendo's.

The armada's smaller vessels were sturdy zabras, Basque-built ships of about 100 tons, sometimes more, and patches (often equated with English pinnaces, though Spanish ships called *pinazas* do appear), small ships of 60 to 120 tons. These vessels were intended for various errands, such as scouting ahead of the main armada and carrying dispatches.

The guns the armada's vessels carried were a mixed lot and were not standardized (as they were later for naval artillery).[17] What armament most of the armada's ships carried remains a matter of conjecture, though the total number of guns aboard the ships was listed on various occasions. Because the powder charge weighed roughly two-thirds the weight of iron shot to be fired, and one-third for stone shot, the quantity of powder compared to the number of guns carried given for each ship provides some clue about which ships had the bigger guns.[18] For the galleasses there is a breakdown of the guns by type and an itemization of the number and weight of the cannon balls, though both iron and stone balls are lumped together. For two vessels taken by the English there is a precise inventory of the guns by type and weight, though not their shot, which the English utilized during the battles. More information about the armada's guns has been provided by the work of underwater archaeologists off the Irish shore.[19]

The underwater archaeologists have also raised questions about the carriages on which the armada's guns were mounted and worked. The English seem to have mounted their guns on carriages that had four trucks or small wheels, a carriage that eventually became standard for shipboard guns. The Spaniards seem to have used two-wheeled carriages, which may have been less effective for laying and servicing the guns.[20] Yet a century later the renowned French military engineer Sebastien Vauban designed a two-wheeled carriage for shipboard use.[21] Until guns' recoil was harnessed to bring them inboard after firing, sometime in the seventeenth century, it would seem to have made little difference.

The Duke of Medina Sidonia and the other armada commanders were not satisfied with the number and size of their guns or with the quantity of powder and shot available for the battle they might have to fight with the English, whose guns they regarded as superior in size and range to their own. The latest research suggests that they were correct and that all but a few of the armada's chief ships were decisively outgunned by the English.[22]

The Spanish guns used to batter hulls were cannons, which fired shot of thirty to fifty pounds, demicannons firing shot of fourteen to twenty-four pounds, *cañoncetes* firing eight- to twelve-pound balls, culverins that fired shot of around twenty-four pounds, demiculverins that fired ten- to fourteen-pound shot, and pedreros made to fire stone shot that ranged in size from ten to fifty pounds.[23] All were muzzle-loaded and most were made of bronze.

For use against masts, rigging and men, a host of smaller pieces, including bronze sakers and demisakers and *falconetes*, minions, and *esmeriles*, some of bronze and some of iron, studded the decks of warships. Their shot weighed in the four- to nine-pound range for the saker types, and from one to five pounds for the others, some of which were breechloaders.

Bronze culverins were the most potent of the big guns but were also huge, unwieldy, and costly. A Spanish culverin that fired a twenty-four-pound iron ball would have measured fifteen or more feet long and weighed some three tons.[24] The problems involved in mounting, working, and firing such a gun aboard ship with a thirty-five-foot beam can be well imagined. Culverins' potency came not from their barrel length, but from the confidence gunners had in their reliability. In black powder ballistics, after twelve calibers (the relation of bore diameter to length of bore), the increase in velocity imparted by the explosion of the charge begins to fall off, and after eighteen calibers there is no further increase.[25] The reliability of culverins had to do with the thickness of the metal round the bore and their greater weight in comparison to the size of shot fired. Gunners in theory might charge them with an amount of powder equal in weight to the shot fired, and certainly with more powder than they dared put in a cannon with less thickness of metal surrounding the bore.

As gun-founders became more experienced, the cannon types, which were lighter in weight than culverin types in relation to the size of the shot, became stronger; and because cannon were cheaper to make and not so long, they would become the dominant shipboard gun in the seventeenth century. A demicannon that fired a twenty-four-pound shot would have measured on the average around twelve feet in length and weighed around two to two and a half tons.[26]

Pedreros were lighter than cannon and designed to fire stone shot. Stone shot proved effective enough, but the labor required to produce round cannonballs of stone made them increasingly expensive and thus less desirable and less available.[27] To fire its stone projectile, a pedrero required only about half the weight of powder needed for an iron projectile of the same weight.

About the ranges of the guns estimates vary. The Venetians carried out and described tests of guns under optimal conditions on the Lido.[28] Culverins could project a large stone or iron ball two miles and more, but beyond five hundred yards accuracy rapidly fell off. In the armada campaign gunfire proved effective only at ranges of a hundred yards or less, particularly during the fight off Gravelines on 8 August. At a range of one hundred yards, a twenty-four-pound shot can penetrate oak planking two and more feet thick.[29]

After his first inspection of the armada's ships, Medina Sidonia soon discovered that the armada's shortcomings were far more serious than he had thought, and he informed the King that the date for its sailing would have to be delayed.[30] The chief shortage was manpower. The number of soldiers, the Duke admitted, fell well below what was planned: "Every one assures me that there are not 10,000 men here; others say not 9,000." The men he counted were likely of the tercios of Naples and Sicily, what remained of the tercio Santa Cruz had embarked in 1587, and companies available around Lisbon. Two other tercios that had wintered along Spain's western border—one under Francisco de Toledo and the other under Nicolás de Isla—had been ordered to Lisbon but had not yet arrived.

Skilled seamen were in even shorter supply than soldiers, and trained pilots were scarcer yet. A muster of seamen taken that January listed 5,054.[31] To find pilots, the Marquis of Cerralbo, Captain-General of Galicia and Asturias, was scouring Spain's north coast for men who knew the waters of the Bay of Biscay and the English Channel, while Medina Sidonia, before he left Andalusia, had sought there as many pilots as he could find.

A large part of the problem was desertion. The prospect of the armada campaign was daunting enough, but more immediately, the men had not been paid for three months.[32] The King authorized the Duke to make up for two missed paydays, one when the men embarked and the other when they were safely on board: "Otherwise some would remain ashore and desert."

By the time the armada was ready to sail, the Duke could muster some 19,000 soldiers. With much prodding by the Viceroy, Cardinal-Archduke Albert, 2,000 Portuguese were enlisted under Philip's banner, though Medina Sidonia admitted that he would be reluctant to use them in the landing force. The Spaniards available from Lisbon castle and elsewhere in Portugal formed a tercio under Don Agustín Mejía, while Toledo's and Isla's tercios did arrive from western Spain. And with the galleons and greatships that arrived in late April from Andalusia came another 2,500 infantry.

Increasing the number of seamen was far more difficult. Before Santa Cruz's death, the Count of Fuentes wrote to the King that "another 600 or 700 sailors" would prove an important addition to the sailors already aboard the Lisbon armada, though he admitted he believed the armada could sail without them.[33] From the moment he arrived in Lisbon, Medina Sidonia repeatedly complained to the King of "the great lack of mariners."

If to the 5,054 seamen mustered in Lisbon in January are added the 1,719 seamen who came aboard the vessels Diego Flores de Valdés brought from Andalusia, the 362 aboard the four galleys, the 151 aboard the two Levanters that do not appear until the 9 May roster, the sum is 7,286 men. The number broadcast in Lisbon in May was 8,050, a figure Medina Sidonia admitted to be inflated. When the armada, increased by nearly twenty caravels and feluccas and minus only a couple of vessels from the last Lisbon muster, prepared to sail from La Coruña and other northern ports in late July, 7,408 seamen were listed. This figure, putting aside the 8,050 and taking the 7,286 sum as more realistic, hardly represents successful recruiting, but rather little more than body replacement. The largest recorded success in finding seamen was a draft of 9 pilots and 100 men rounded up by the Corregidor of Santander.

How many of those listed as seamen were in fact experienced mariners able to handle the myriad details of sailing a ship is another matter. In a breakdown of the crews aboard the ships pressed into service in Andalusia in 1587, the categories listed are *oficiales de mar* (officers and petty officers), gunners, seamen, *grumetes* (ship's boys), and pages, primarily cabin attendants. About a third of the 1,292 people counted fell into the last two categories. To underline the problem of losses, chiefly to desertion, these same vessels listed 1,006 mariners aboard in May 1588.

The ratio of soldiers to sailors in the armada's fighting ships has usually struck later generations as top-heavy, even though 6,000 of the soldiers were designated for the invasion force. Medina Sidonia would certainly have preferred more seamen, though no fewer soldiers. In the royal galleons, the ratio was roughly two soldiers to one sailor, which makes sense at a time when boarding was a favored tactic. But in the Levantine squadron, the ratio was four soldiers for each sailor. Don

Alonso de Leyva's ship, nicknamed *La Rata*, listed in the Coruña muster 355 soldiers and 93 seamen; when Leyva's swashbuckling companions and their retainers were counted, *La Rata* likely carried such a swarm of landsmen that its crew could hardly move, save in the rigging. The Levanters and the northern urcas, most with foreign masters, had suffered seriously from desertion among their crews and had little luck finding more people in Spain and Portugal. The vessels pressed in Andalusian ports had a more balanced ratio, with three soldiers for each crew member. The ships' crews, who had signed on for the lucrative voyage to the Indies, were probably kept aboard by fear of losing license to sail to the Indies in the future.

Medina Sidonia worried about the ancient animosities that divided seamen and landlubberly soldiers and issued stern orders to forestall troubles: "Because it is of such great importance to the safety and success of this armada that there exist between soldiers and seamen co-operation and friendship, and that they get along so amicably that there neither will nor can be differences, uproars or scandals, I command that the law be laid down, that none carry a dagger or quarrel for any reason. . . . If any commotion occurs, he who caused it shall *ipso facto* be severely punished."[34] The Duke further ordered that the seamen be allotted quarters in the fore and stern castles, so that they might more easily and quickly reach their stations for tending ship. The order cannot have always been carried out. A memorial from Guipúzcoa to Medina Sidonia after the armada's return complained that soldiers and their officers forced seamen from their quarters and onto open decks.[35] Another problem Medina Sidonia recognized with soldiers aboard ship—to which he referred in a 1601 opinion—was that "they were not very clean."[36]

If ordinary seamen and soldiers seemed too few, the number of unemployed officers seeking commands and places was too great: "So many," Medina Sidonia wrote the King, "that I do not know how they can be utilized. . . . They come here each day; they are without pay, alféreces, sergeants and other officials, soldiers of many years service, and all beg that I give them places and opportunities. I can give them nothing, nor reward their services. I confess that it grieves me much, and more than they know. . . . When they come with their pleas, they leave with nothing but words, and go deceived about how little I have to offer."[37] The King proved sympathetic and allowed the Duke 2,000 ducats to engage many of them.

Not pleading for places with pay but gracing the warships of the armada as their birthright were noblemen from the greatest families in Spain, and others from Philip's dominions abroad and from allied states. They came with retinues of squires and servants and covered with an air of gallantry the grim and tawdry work of fitting out the armada and forcing bewildered commoners to do their duty to God and King.

The name of Don Alonso de Leyva, secretly designated by the King, as noted earlier, to be Medina Sidonia's successor, headed the list, followed by that of his cousin Don Antonio Luis de Leyva, Prince of Ascoli, purported to be a bastard son of the King.[38] Don Alonso de Leyva, who arrived in Lisbon in April with the rank of Captain General of the Light Cavalry of Milan, was appointed commander of 6,000 men who would join Parma's army. When the armada sailed, Leyva assumed a combat command; his cousin Ascoli rode in the flagship *San Martín* with the Duke and several of the Duke's kinsmen, including Don Bernardino de Velasco, a brother of the Constable of Castile, Don Luis de Córdoba, brother of the Marquis of Ayamonte, and Don Pedro de Zúñiga, son of the Marquis of Aguilafuente. Also on Medina Sidonia's quarterdeck were several other Andalusian noblemen and Don Pedro de Castro, nephew of the Archbishop of Seville. Medina Sidonia's cousin Don Juan Téllez Girón, Marquis of Peñafiel and son of the Duke of Osuna, sailed in the galleon *San Marcos*, which he in effect commanded during the campaign and usually kept beside *San Martín*.

Many of the army and navy officers who served alongside these scions of Spain's high nobility were also of the high and middling nobility. The Maestre de Campo General, Don Francisco de Bobadilla, was brother of the Count of Puñonrostro, to whose title he later succeeded, and married to Leyva's half-sister. The chief of the tercio of Sicily, Don Diego Pimentel, was the second son of the Marquis of Távara; he had joined the Duke of Alba's expedition to Portugal when he was scarcely twenty, and had before him a long and remarkable career in the Spanish empire. Don Francisco de Toledo, who commanded the tercio of Flanders, was brother of the Count of Orgaz.

Of the naval generals Don Hugo de Moncada, second son of the Count of Aytona, alone was of a titled family, but most of the others came from families of señores and caballeros. Recalde, Oquendo, and Bertendona were from the middling urban nobility of the Basque coast, where by custom few thought it necessary to affix 'don' to his name, even when a member of an order of knighthood. The Valdés cousins belonged to one of the chief families of Asturias.

Aboard the armada's ships, both officers and noble adventurers sought cabins suitable to their rank and station, and those who did not find them soon began to construct private compartments. The ship's masters and crews complained but were denied by the Captain General, who assured the King that the compartments were "so flimsy that they could be kicked down in a moment." Once the armada was under way, they were.

Compartments for noble adventurers and infantry officers hardly compared to the shortage of manpower and need for victuals and munitions among Medina Sidonia's worries. By dint of tireless effort and steady importuning he had his squadron generals hunt seamen, his infantry captains recruit troops, and his principal provisioners, Francisco Duarte, Luis César in Lisbon, and Antonio Guevara in Andalusia, find the stores, victuals, and munitions the armada needed. From the King he begged unceasingly for money, while the King relentlessly pressured him to get under way for the great Enterprise.

The Duke found that guns had often been placed hastily and sometimes carelessly aboard the vessels that had not been built to carry them and had to be repositioned. From some well-gunned ships guns were taken to reinforce others. The captain of *Nuestra Señora del Rosario* stated that the Duke had taken eight pieces from his ship.[39] Yet Don Pedro de Valdés, who rode in her, had already much augmented the number of guns she carried so that she was one of the heaviest gunned in the armada.[40] But for the armada as a whole, all agreed that still more guns were needed, more powder and more shot.

Even before the Duke's inspection, the Captain-General of the Artillery, Don Juan de Acuña Vela, and Don Alonso de Bazán had written about the shortage of guns. Oquendo's squadron needed sixty or seventy pieces, and the guns aboard most ships of the Andalusian squadron commanded by Don Pedro de Valdés, though plentiful, were too small.[41] The King authorized Medina Sidonia to buy the pieces Oquendo needed from foreign vessels anchored in Lisbon harbor, while Acuña Vela and the Council of War ordered castings in Lisbon and scoured the Iberian Peninsula for more guns, powder, and shot. In the margin of a note on the matter, Medina Sidonia wrote that the guns of the foreign ships, mostly German, were iron and not much good.[42] Yet by the time the armada was ready to sail, the Duke and Acuña Vela had added another 200 or 210 guns to what the ships already carried.[43]

Regarding powder, the Spanish commanders claimed that Santa Cruz's armada in the invasion of Terceira in 1583 had expended 180,000 pounds of powder in one day and all its guns had not fired. When Medina Sidonia arrived in Lisbon he found the armada had no more than 300,000 pounds for the planned campaign, a quantity he managed to increase to over a half million pounds. Of that, almost 400,000 was for the naval artillery.[44] This averages 152 pounds per gun and three pounds per shot, though in fact the distribution of powder favored the principal fighting ships. In the battles, much of the shot carried, an average of fifty per gun, was not fired.[45] Nonetheless, the amount of powder carried reinforces the argument that most of the armada's guns were light-shotted pieces.

In the midst of the feverish preparations for the armada's sailing, Alvaro Flores de Quiñones arrived in Lisbon to meet with Medina Sidonia to discuss the recovery of the 1588 treasure with the dozen to fourteen pataches he was secretly assembling at Huelva. He was to make the crossing nonstop, without touching at the Canaries. During a meeting on 11 April, with Recalde, Valdés, and Oquendo present, the discussion touched on the possibility of a northwest passage, by which one could sail from England to Japan. When Quiñones left for Huelva, he carried the Duke's orders for Antonio de Guevara to assist him and provide 320 sailors and 120 soldiers for his ships.[46]

By the latter part of April Medina Sidonia could write the King that all seemed about ready; he fixed 27 April as the date for sailing. On Sunday, 24 April, in a simple ceremony at the royal palace in Lisbon, he took his oath of office before the Viceroy, Cardinal-Archduke Albert, and several gentlemen of the viceregal suite. At six the following morning, the Feast of St. Mark the Evangelist, the ceremony of blessing and taking up the royal standard for the great Enterprise commenced.

In front of the palace Maestre de Campo Don Agustín Mejía mustered 650 arquebusiers, while the Count of Fuentes lined the street that led to the cathedral with men of the Lisbon garrison. Close to the quayside the Neapolitan galleasses took station and exchanged gun salutes with the Castillo San Jorge, high above the old town. The Cardinal-Archduke, with Medina Sidonia at his right hand, led the parade to the Seo de Lisboa, partway up the hill toward the castle. In the Seo the Archbishop of Lisbon celebrated Mass and blessed the royal standard, which the Cardinal-Archduke took up and handed to Medina Sidonia.

With Medina Sidonia's cousin Don Luis de Córdoba acting as standard bearer, the Viceroy and the Duke led a procession from the Seo to the Praça Rossio. There, at the convent of Santo Domingo, the

Duke and his chief officers received the Holy Sacrament. Monks then raised the Sacred Host for the blessing of the armada and led the procession, which wended along the quayside between the ranks of assembled troops. The sound of sacred chants blended with the music of trumpets, fifes, and drums. From the decks of the ships anchored in the Tagus, soldiers and sailors watched. When the armada had been blessed, the procession returned to the royal palace.

Medina Sidonia's hope of weighing anchor on 27 April did not materialize: new delays in loading troops and the onset of wicked weather froze the armada in Lisbon harbor. Diego Flores's squadron of galleons and greatships arrived from Andalusia short of seamen. He had made sail hastily on Good Friday and left behind men who had taken Easter furlough; they had to be rounded up and shipped after him to Lisbon.

While waiting for the weather to improve, Medina Sidonia tended to last-minute business. To Madrid he sent a final roster, dated 9 May 1588, of the armada's men, its ships with their tonnages, the number of guns, the quantity of shot and the amount of powder each carried, the victuals aboard, and the guns, munitions, and animals for the invasion force. By name were listed the naval generals, the royal officials, the maestres de campo, company commanders, and adventurers aboard the fleet.

The roster of what was dubbed the Felicíssima (Most Happy) Armada was printed, perhaps at Medina Sidonia's order, and copies were soon disseminated throughout Europe. While there could be little secrecy at Lisbon, the roster made easy the work of spies, and Philip II was upset with its publication.[47]

Heading the roster came the armada or squadron of Portugal, which consisted of ten galleons, nine that belonged to the Crown of Portugal, plus the Grand Duke of Tuscany's galleon *San Francesco*, which the Marquis of Santa Cruz had pressed into the service of Spain. Two zabras, both unusually large, were also attached to the squadron.

The galleons of the Armada of Portugal were regarded as the stoutest and best-armed in the armada, and the armada's ranking officers preferred them. Medina Sidonia rode in the capitana real, the royal flagship *San Martín*, which also served as capitana of the Portuguese squadron. *San Martín* had been Santa Cruz's flagship in the campaigns to the Azores and had fought at San Miguel.

The armada's *Almirante General*, Juan Martínez de Recalde, chose as his *almiranta general* the galleon *San Juan*, almiranta of the Portuguese squadron, rather than the capitana of his own Viscayan squadron. Medina Sidonia's cousin, the Marquis of Peñafiel, chose *San Marcos*, Maestre de Campo Don Francisco de Toledo, *San Felipe*, Maestre de Campo Don Agustín Mejía, *San Luis*, and Maestre de Campo Don Diego Pimentel, *San Mateo*, while the principal captains of the embarked Portuguese infantry took the remainder. In the campaign the Portuguese galleons did not all sail together, but rather each took its place in that part of the armada to which it was assigned for tactical purposes.

The Castilian squadron was formed of ten galleons, four greatships, and two pataches that Diego Flores de Valdés brought from Sanlúcar to Lisbon in late April. The greatships Medina Sidonia described as Levanters, though one, *Nuestra Señora de Begoña*, was probably built in Bilbao, unless there was confusion about the name.[48] Except for its capitana and almiranta, the squadron's galleons were smaller than the Portuguese galleons and many of the armada's greatships. Seven were rated at 530 tons and one was rated at 230. Solidly constructed for the purpose of escorting the Indies flotas and dealing with pirates, these galleons carried fewer guns than most of the Portuguese galleons and many of the armada's greatships.[49] Because they arrived so late, they carried few noble adventurers. Most had already been assigned places.

The armadas of Vizcaya and Guipúzcoa had been assembled, respectively, by Juan Martínez de Recalde at Bilbao and Miguel de Oquendo at San Sebastián from merchantmen that they had armed for the King's service. The ships of the two squadrons varied considerably in size. Most were built in the Basque country, though several, added to the squadrons from ships pressed at Lisbon or in Andalusia, were perhaps of Mediterranean rather than Atlantic construction.[50] The Vizcayan squadron counted a total of nine greatships, the galleon *Grangrín*, and four pataches; the Guipúzcoan, nine greatships, an urca, three pataches, and a pinnace.

Ten of the fifteen ships embargoed for service in Andalusia in 1587 formed what was named the Armada of Andalusia, which included eight greatships, a galleon, and an urca, plus two pataches. These were all vessels deemed fit to make the rigorous voyage to the Indies. Its general was Don Pedro de Valdés, whose capitana, the well-armed *Nuestra Señora del Rosario*, was rated at 1,150 tons and built as a flagship for the Indies flotas.

The Armada of Italy consisted of ten big, imposing Levanters hired or pressed from Venetian, Genoese, and Ragusan owners. Because of their size, they seem to have been loaded with additional guns, argua-bly more than was safe for their somewhat fragile build.[51] They proved popular with the noble adventurers, and Don Alonso de Leyva picked one, the *Rata Santa María Encoronada*, rated at 820 tons burden, to serve as his flagship. Maestre de Campo Don Alonso de Luzón sailed in the 1,100-ton *Trinidad Valencera*. In command of the Levanters was Don Martín de Bertendona, a Basque from Vizcaya.

Twenty-three of the hulks formed the *Armada de Urcas* under the veteran seaman Juan Gómez de Medina. Three small ships, thirteen pataches, and five zabras, rated as weighing between about 60 and 300 tons, formed an Armada of Pataches and Zabras, under the command of Don Antonio Hurtado de Mendoza, who sailed aboard a 300-ton capitana. The capitana and five other vessels carried between eight and a dozen guns worthy of note; some of the smallest carried two only or even none. The second biggest vessel, of 180 tons, was English-built, and a 150-tonner was Scottish.

The number of vessels listed on 9 May 1588 totaled 131, not includ-ing ten caravels and ten falúas, these last with six sailors each, which served as tenders and, according to a later muster, carried extra water. On paper at least, the armada carried rations of food, wine, and water for six months.

Of the nearly 30,000 men who would have to subsist on the victuals the armada carried, some 8,000 were reported as seamen and 2,000 more as rowers for the galleasses and galleys. The soldiers, who num-bered 19,295 according to the list, were organized in five tercios, each under a maestre de campo, two *banderas* of Portuguese reckoned to number 2,000 men under two captains, and over thirty other compa-nies. They served under the overall command of Don Francisco de Bobadilla, Maestre de Campo General, a veteran of the Azores campaigns.

As May wore on, the Felicíssima Armada with all its soldiers and crews embarked remained in the Tagus. The moored or anchored ves-sels stretched along the shore from Lisbon to Belem, while Medina Sidonia complained almost daily to Court about the contrary weather and expressed his fears that it remained easy for men to desert.

CHAPTER SEVEN

The Armada Campaign: Lisbon to the Channel

THE first days of May Medina Sidonia found the weather "as wretched as December,"[1] but on the eleventh Miguel de Oquendo felt it was improving. He requested permission to move the armada's vanguard to the Bay of Cascais, outside the mouth of the Tagus. Pleased that Medina Sidonia had accorded him the honor of leading the vanguard, a distinction he had also enjoyed under Santa Cruz, Oquendo wrote the King that Medina Sidonia "shows much understanding of everything and provides very well."[2] At sunset, Oquendo's squadron lay anchored off the fort of San João de Estoril.

The Duke had reviewed the King's instructions and issued all the necessary orders to the armada's captains. The King's orders referred the Duke to the basic plan of campaign, contained in his letter of 14 September 1587 to the Cardinal-Archduke Albert.[3] Though Philip admitted that delays had given their enemies more time to prepare, he remained confident that matters would turn out in their favor, through the intervention of God. Following the custom of the age, he proclaimed the war in God's cause and stressed that those who sailed in the armada should not risk God's wrath through blasphemies or sin.[4] In the instructions to the Duke that accompanied his commission of Captain General of the Ocean-Sea, the King had warned him to be particularly alert for heresies against Holy Mother Church, blasphemies, and the "nefarious sin," that bane of navies, sodomy.

Having dealt with God's will and the problem of sin, the King returned to the plan of campaign and reiterated that the armada would proceed to the waters off Margate and there assure the crossing of the

Duke of Parma. How Medina Sidonia and Parma would achieve this, he did not say. While he dealt with many matters in meticulous detail, he seems to have had the good sense to leave the conduct of war operations to his commanders on the spot. When Medina Sidonia entered the English Channel, he was to send trusted messengers ahead to alert Parma.

The King discussed then eventualities that might occur during the voyage from Spain. He emphasized that the armada should not seek battle before meeting Parma and fight only if forced to, though he admitted that if Drake, with his part of the English fleet, tried to prevent the armada from entering the Channel, the armada might have a good chance to defeat a divided enemy. Philip, who had been interested in the English navy when he was England's titular King,[5] believed that the Lord Admiral with his squadron would be in the Narrows.

For the day of battle, when and wherever it occurred, Philip admitted he could offer little advice, since what had to be done would depend on the circumstances. He repeated what Medina Sidonia had once written him about English tactics—that they would endeavor to keep their distance and use their guns at long range to batter the armada—and urged the Duke to be alert for the chance to close, grapple, and board. When the battle was won, the Duke was reminded to keep the armada together and not allow vessels to scatter in pursuit of booty. The Council of War had issued separate instructions about the distribution of prizes.

However, Philip stated, combat should be risked only if there were no other way to ensure Parma's passage across the Narrows. If there were no battle, six thousand troops from the armada were to join Parma's army ashore in England; if there had been, as many should be landed as could be spared after losses in shipboard infantry were replaced.

Once Parma and the men were safely ashore, the armada was to find anchorage in the Thames estuary and maintain secure passage between the beachhead and Flanders. From all this, it would appear that the King had little doubt that his armada would sweep all before it and corner the English fleet in the Thames estuary, making Parma's crossing a simple thing.

The King then proceeded to lecture Medina Sidonia on the subject of close and friendly cooperation between him and Parma. "There will be more than enough honor for you both." When Parma had gained his objectives in England, the King allowed that Medina Sidonia might

200 Statute Miles

300 Kilometers

FAROES

SHETLAND IS.

FAIR ISLE

22 Aug.

18 Aug.

23 Aug.–3 Sep.

ORKNEY IS.

NORWAY

SWEDEN

SÖDERMAN LAND

60⁰

55⁰

SCOTLAND

Edinburgh

Glasgow

NORTH

SEA

13 Aug.

DENMARK

BALTIC

SEA

11–13 September

IRELAND

Kinsale

ENGLAND

Bristol

London

Rostock

Lübeck

Hamburg

Emden

CAPE CLEAR

50⁰

Plymouth

10 Aug.

DUTCH REP

Amsterdam

HOLY ROMAN

OCEAN-SEA
(ATLANTIC)

29 July

31 July

3 Aug.

4 Aug.

6 Aug.

8 Aug.

Bruges

Dunkirk

Calais

Antwerp

Brussels

RHINE

EMPIRE OF THE

25 July

Brest

Le Havre

Paris

BRITTANY

FRANCE

GERMAN NATION

45⁰

19 September

La Rochelle

Vienna

19 June–22 July

Geneva

SWISS

CAPE
FINISTERRE

12 June

ASTURIAS

21 Sep.

Santander

Bilbao

S. Sebastián

Pasajes

Bayonne

Bordeaux

SAVOY

Turin

Saluzzo

MILAN

VENICE

PARMA

Venice

OTTOMAN

EMPIRE

RAGUSA

10 June

40⁰

GALICIA

La Coruña

Vigo

Porto

PORTUGAL

Burgos

Valladolid

CASTILE

El Escorial

Pastrana

ARAGON

Zaragoza

Marseille

Genoa

Florence

TUSCANY

Rome

PAPAL
STATES

CORSICA

9 June

Lisbon

Madrid

Aranjuez

Barcelona

NAPLES

Naples

Eboli

28 May

Setúbal

TAGUS

Toledo

LA MANCHA

VALENCIA

Valencia

Beja

Elvas

Badajoz

Serpa

SARDINIA

CAPE
ST. VINCENT

Sagres

ALGARVE

Faro

ANDALUSIA

GRANADA

Granada

Sanlúcar

Cádiz

Seville

Málaga

Herradura

Almería

Cartagena

BALEARIC IS.

MEDITERRANEAN

SEA

Palermo

SICILY

Tangier

Gibraltar

Arcila

Larache

Alcazarquivir

Tetuán

Melilla

Oran

Algiers

CUCO

Tunis

MALTA

35⁰

La Mamora

FEZ
AND MOROCCO

Tlemcen

BARBARY STATES

NORTH   AFRICA

5⁰W

0⁰

5⁰E

10⁰E

15⁰E

proceed with the armada to Ireland, if Parma concurred.

The King concluded his instructions by complimenting the Duke on the care he had always shown for costs and expressing his confidence that the Duke would carefully husband the money and stores aboard the armada and look after the health and welfare of the men.

In a separate "secret" instruction, he discussed the eventuality that Parma might have made a successful crossing before the armada arrived, in which case Leyva would land with the six thousand reinforcements carried in the armada and lead them to Parma. In the event that Parma could not cross the Narrows, Medina Sidonia was to attempt if possible to seize the Isle of Wight, which would give him a safe anchorage whence he could operate. In that event, Medina Sidonia and Parma would have to determine what to do next. If, the King added, all were successful, Parma should try to capture Dom António and turn him over to Medina Sidonia, who was to ensure that the restless Portuguese Pretender did not escape.

With these two instructions came a third under seal, which Medina Sidonia either had to hand to Parma when he landed in England or return to the King unopened.[6] In the sealed instructions, the King dealt with the eventuality that Parma had successfully landed his army in England, but matters did not allow an easy solution by force of arms. In this instance, Parma might negotiate peace, using the presence of his army and the armada to intimidate the Queen. The King made clear his terms: first, the free practice of the Catholic faith must be permitted in England; second, the places in the Low Countries the English had occupied had to be restored to him; and third, compensation should be paid for the damages done to his estates and subjects by the English. The last demand Parma could modify as he saw fit to gain the first two. Of the contents of this dispatch Parma never knew, nor, likely, did Medina Sidonia.[7]

For the armada Medina Sidonia issued his own instructions by virtue of his authority as Captain General of the Ocean-Sea.[8] They covered every possible concern: the holy nature of the cause and avoiding blasphemy; discipline and morale; allowing no women aboard; wake-up calls and morning prayers; signals and station-keeping by day and night; passwords; clearing decks for combat, general readiness,

---

Map 3. Western Europe and the armada campaign of 1588. Shaded areas indicate the territories ruled by Philip II. Broken line indicates the route of the armada.

and keeping powder dry once the armada had cleared Cape Finisterre; daily rations; the quartering on board of sailors and soldiers; maintaining lookout for sails and land; and coping with fire at sea. For each ship in the armada, he ordered his secretary to provide a copy, which was to be read aloud to all on board. For *San Martín*, his flagship, the Duke issued specific orders that assigned captains, gunners, soldiers, and crewmen to their battle stations.

About the distribution of rations, a detailed instruction had been prepared by the Factor Francisco Duarte, with the assistance of *contadores* (pursers) Alonso de Alameda and Pedro Coco Calderón and issued to the master of each ship.[9] The basic daily ration was a pound and a half of biscuit or two pounds of fresh bread and a bit over a pint of wine. The wines were to be drunk in order of durability, with the light wines of Medina Sidonia's Condado [de Niebla] and the neighborhood of Lisbon first, the wines of Lamego on the Douro[10] and Monzón[11] next, and the stronger wines of Jerez and Candia, Crete, last. Described as *recio*, which implies strong, the Cretan wine was probably a malmsey; in any case, a ration of it was a half-pint, with a double ration of water. Added to the bread or biscuit everyday were olive oil and vinegar, and on specified days, garbanzos and soup-bones, salt pork and rice, preserved tunny or codfish, octopus or sardines. Water was to be carefully guarded. In issuing food and drink, the oldest or that closest to spoiling was to be used first. No one, regardless of rank or station, was to receive more than an ordinary ration without the explicit permission of the Duke or of the armada's chief *Proveedor* (provisioner), Don Bernabé de Pedroso.

The route the armada would take on its voyage had been carefully determined by the Duke's pilots, and for the captain of each ship he had a copy of a detailed rutter printed.[12] A fascinating example of its kind, it provided for the waters of the English Channel, the Bristol Channel, and southeastern Ireland rich detail about soundings and the seabottom, distances between landfalls, and descriptions of shorelines, landmarks and harbors, tides, and currents. The planned course took the armada to Lizard Point, then in sight of the English shore to the Strait of Dover and the meeting with Parma. The King's instructions make clear why the armada sailed closer to England than to France: the French coast was considered more difficult and dangerous, and it would enjoy more sea room with winds prevailing from the west. The armada's commanders had no illusion about slipping up-Channel undetected, though when the rutter was drawn up they believed the main

English fleet would await them off Dover or perhaps combine with Drake's between Wight and the Channel Islands, but not near Plymouth. Had they thought it would be at Plymouth, they may have kept more to mid-Channel.

Medina Sidonia had some hope on 11 May that the armada would soon be on its carefully planned route, were Oquendo correct about the weather. As night fell, a Flemish flyboat stood into the darkening Tagus and pulled alongside *San Martín*. Aboard the Duke's capitana clambered Captain Francisco Moresin, sent by the Duke of Parma with several pilots who knew the waters of the Channel and Flemish coast. Moresin met with Medina Sidonia and enlightened him about Parma's preparations.

Parma had ready and available for the Enterprise, Moresin stated, 17,000 men and 1,000 cavalry. The shipping collected for their transport amounted to 300 small vessels without oars or topsails.

Medina Sidonia could only have been stunned. Parma was reported to have between 30,000 and 40,000 men for the Enterprise, and as of late December 1587, 74 seagoing ships, 150 playtes, and 70 river-hoys.[13] Idiáquez, when Medina Sidonia in March 1588 requested another eight galleys for landing operations, replied that Parma had for the purpose a "great number" of vessels, "including hoys, playtes and others appropriate to the effect."[14] Parma's seagoing ships were probably for the most part *filibotes*, or flyboats (vlieboots, *not* fluits), two-masted vessels normally ranging from 80 tons to as much as 150.[15] Playtes were flat-bottomed vessels, little better than barges, that had one gaff-sail. Hoys were shallow-draft vessels for river and coastal navigation that ranged in size from 20 to well over 100 tons and could be armed.[16] Medina Sidonia persisted in believing that Parma had enough armed vessels to spearhead the sortie of the invasion flotilla from its ports.

If Medina Sidonia was dismayed by the news Moresin brought from the Duke of Parma, Moresin seemed surprised by the size and strength of the armada assembled at Lisbon, which was more potent than he had expected. What seemed clear was that neither Medina Sidonia nor Parma knew much about the strength the other had mustered. The King and Idiáquez bore the responsibility of keeping the Captain General of the Ocean-Sea and the Governor General of the Low Countries informed of each other's progress, though the two commanders were urged to establish close correspondence when the campaign began.

None of the participants was ignorant of the problem of communications that dogged the whole campaign from its planning stages to its conclusion. The overland journey for a messenger from Madrid to Brussels under the best of circumstances took twelve days, thus nearly a month for return mail, while routine dispatches reached Lisbon in four days and a reply could be received in eight. The volume of correspondence concerning the Enterprise that reached Madrid from Lisbon was therefore greater and more regular, though no more information about the armada seems to have been forwarded to Brussels than intelligence of Parma's doings to Lisbon, and that was little. A dispatch by sea from Lisbon to the Flanders or vice versa could reach its addressee in a fortnight, but given the vagaries of wind and weather, it might take much longer.

For all concerned, keeping up with changing circumstances was difficult, and important information was sometimes seriously out-of-date. Parma had written Philip on 20 March that he had only 17,000 men, so by early April the King certainly knew what Medina Sidonia apparently only found out when Moresin arrived in Lisbon on 11 May. However, the King said nothing new about the shipping available to Parma and what could be expected of it until late June, when it may have been too late, so it remained a particular matter about which there was significant misunderstanding.[17] When Philip did write Medina Sidonia about it, he expressed hope that Moresin had cleared the matter up.

Medina Sidonia might have better understood what Moresin told him about Parma's problems had he been party to the early planning for the Enterprise, about which he protested he knew nothing when he tried to refuse command of the armada. He may have known the plans in crude outline, but it was unlikely that he knew much about the vicissitudes through which they had gone during the three years they had been taking shape.

When Philip II finally decided in the summer of 1587, in response to Parma's concerns and urgings, to send the armada to support Parma's cross-channel invasion rather than against Ireland, Parma had assembled a flotilla to transport his invasion force and spread word that he meant to launch a seaborne offensive against Zeeland. His English and Dutch opponents were in disarray and at odds with each other after he had taken Sluys in mid-August. He expected to regroup his forces by early autumn and cross the Narrows rapidly, in eight to twelve hours, given the right conditions, protected by Santa Cruz's armada against weak and hastily assembled opposition. The armada never came, despite frenzied activity through the autumn and into the winter at Lisbon.

The English and Dutch, attentive to the activities in Lisbon and Flanders, harbored few further doubts that the aim of Philip II's grand design was not Zeeland but rather England, and the Dutch, with English urging, established a close blockade of Parma's shipping to prevent its sortie either for England or Zeeland. Parma's best vessels were bottled up in Antwerp, the rest in Sluys, Nieuwpoort, and Dunkirk. In response Parma enlarged canals and moved vessels from Sluys to Nieuwpoort and Dunkirk, away from the rebel strongholds in Zeeland and as close as possible to England. But neither Dunkirk nor Nieuwpoort was a deepwater port. He could only hope that when the armada arrived off the Flemish coast, the Dutch flyboats that patrolled it might be drawn off. He kept his headquarters at Bruges in an effort to confuse them[18] and planned a sortie by his Antwerp squadron to focus Dutch attention on the Scheldt, away from Nieuwpoort and Dunkirk.

For whatever reason or oversight, no mention seems to have been made to Medina Sidonia about what the Dutch were doing in Flemish waters, though Parma knew and Madrid had been kept informed by him and by Don Bernardino de Mendoza, Philip's ambassador to France and his principal source of news from England. Yet Madrid seemed to discount reports of the Dutch blockade. Why? For one thing, Madrid believed that the English and Dutch were each suspicious of the other and not cooperating. The Dutch were known to fear that Elizabeth in her negotiations with Spain might abandon them. Moreover, given the amount of trade Holland and Zeeland ships did in Spain, in Madrid it was widely held that Dutch shippers preferred to pursue profit rather than involve their ships in risky combat. "The rebels of Holland and Zeeland work only to look after themselves," a court memorandum told Medina Sidonia.[19]

What more Moresin told Medina Sidonia than what the Duke reported to Madrid is not certain. He was with him nearly a month and may have tried to reassure him that Parma would increase the number of available men and have his shipping ready for the crossing. Whatever Moresin told Medina Sidonia about Parma's shipping and its capabilities, Medina Sidonia believed that Parma's flotilla would be able to reach the open sea, where his armada's deep-draft vessels could escort it if necessary to England. He seemed more concerned with tides and shoals than with the Dutch blockade.

The depressing intelligence Medina Sidonia received from Moresin on the evening of 11 May was followed in the morning of the twelfth by a deflating wind from the west that kept the armada penned in the Tagus. It was almost the end of the month when the winds became favorable again. Beginning 28 May, the armada's ships began warping over the bar at the Tagus's mouth, assisted by the galleys. By 30 May its ships were all at sea.

The winds proved erratic and the armada soon fell well south of the Rock of Lisbon. "We had to work to keep from rounding Cape St. Vincent," Medina Sidonia complained.[20] Slowly the armada beat its way northward, taking nearly a fortnight to cover fifty leagues.

Watching the armada's slow progress, the Duke began to receive disturbing reports: much food was bad, more was spoiling, and worse, the water was fast becoming undrinkable. It was not entirely un-anticipated. He had long experience with the problems of the Indies flotas, and during the six weeks the armada's ships remained anchored in the Tagus after the troops had been embarked, he had learned some-thing of the conditions of the ships' stores, much of which had been on board since the previous autumn. Thus he had written to the Marquis of Cerralbo, Captain General of Galicia, to prepare victualers at La Coruña to meet the armada off Cape Prior for the transfer of food and water to its ships. He instructed the four galleys to prepare to assist them. He also requested that Madrid begin to prepare a flotilla to follow the armada with supplies, for which purpose the King ordered Don Sancho Pardo to begin collecting ships at Lisbon.

As the armada passed Cape Finisterre, Medina Sidonia sent Cap-tain Moresin, who carried dispatches for Parma dated 10 June, off to Flanders in a swift, well-armed zabra, accompanied by the flyboat that had brought him to Lisbon. Much information had been committed to his memory, and he had orders to throw the dispatches overboard in weighted bags if overtaken by enemies. "I expect that he will arrive in Flanders fifteen days before the armada," Medina Sidonia informed the King, "which is important so that the Duke [of Parma] can get ready and put all in order for the moment when, God willing, it arrives."[21] He also asked Parma to collect and be ready to send water to the armada. Moresin was with Parma on 22 June.

When the armada arrived at the latitude of La Coruña, Medina Sidonia halted its progress to await the needed supplies. The leading ships stood off Cape Prior, the rearmost off the Isle of Sisargas. On 19 June the victualers had not appeared, and Medina Sidonia, having taken *San Martín* along the line of ships and consulted with his generals, gave signal for the armada to enter La Coruña's extensive system of bays to obtain the needed stores. At nightfall *San Martín* and part of the armada dropped anchor off La Coruña; the remaining ships stood outside the harbor under a waning moon.

During the night a front passed over the darkling ocean; morning came with gales and mountainous waves that forced the vessels that had not entered the harbor to scatter seaward. Some, including most of the urcas, were blown northward to the mouth of the Channel, not far from the Scilly Islands. Other ships ran before the wind to find shelter along Spain's north coast, in ports from Bayona, south of Finisterre, to Laredo, east of Santander.

Bit by bit the Duke received news of his scattered armada. Leyva had arrived safely at Vivero with several other ships; the galleasses *Patrona* and *Zúñiga* had anchored at Gijón; and *Santa Ana de Recalde*, capitana of the Vizcayan squadron with Maestre de Campo Nicolás de Isla aboard, had found haven at Santander. Many ships had suffered damages. At La Coruña Medina Sidonia collected the reports of his captains, arranged for repairs, began to board the needed stores, and maintained order and discipline. The weather only slightly abated and continued contrary.

The Duke appeared indefatigable, but whatever confidence in the Enterprise he may have built since he took command seems to have collapsed. On 24 June he took pen in hand to express his misgivings to the King.[22] The contrary weather he interpreted as a sign from the Lord that obliged him to say what he had previously put off saying, for fear that it would seem only a personal opinion. He begged the King to give credit to his proposals, which he offered with the same love and zeal that he had always shown in the royal service.

He reminded the King of his attempt to refuse command of the armada and admitted that his reason was not so much that he was unsuited for the task, but rather because he believed that the armada assembled in Lisbon was inadequate for the conquest of England, "so large a Kingdom aided by its neighbors," and that the course of negotiation was more suitable to the King's service.

Nonetheless he had accepted the command, made sail, and brought the armada to La Coruña, where it now lay storm-battered and divided. It was, according to all who knew, much inferior to the enemy fleet, lacking many of its best ships and two of the galleasses. The crews were sick and appeared to be dying from rotten victuals, which were not only bad, but barely enough for two months. "And thus Your

Majesty can judge how things will go in this condition, and what depends on the success or failure of this campaign, for which Your Majesty has collected all his forces, in ships, guns and munitions. I see no other way to repair the damage but time, and much of it."

Immediately the King might press more Italian ships for the armada, but Medina Sidonia believed them unsuitable for northern waters. There were no ships left in the Basque provinces, Portugal, and Andalusia, nor artillery. Danger loomed for Portugal and the Indies, and he feared that the States of Flanders would take heart from the failure of the armada to return to rebellion.

> To undertake such great things with equal forces is not right, much less with inferior forces, such as they are now. The men are not as experienced as is necessary, nor are the officials,[23] few or almost none of whom, I say in conscience to Your Majesty, understand or know how to fulfill the obligations of their offices. I have experienced this, and warn Your Majesty in full awareness.
>
> Believe me, Your Majesty, what is here is very weak, and let no one deceive Your Majesty that it is otherwise. Moreover, the few men the Duke of Parma has only supports what I am saying: even if what is here and what is there were joined in a single force, it would be weak. How much worse will it be if we cannot assist each other as planned, I ask Your Majesty, given the circumstances of today?

Medina Sidonia reminded the King of the forces he had raised for the conquest of Portugal, a kingdom that bordered on Castile and in which he had widespread support. "Now, against so large a Kingdom which so many must aid, how can success be expected of this enterprise with what has been assembled?"

Having stated his opinion in what he admitted was a long-winded discourse and commended himself to the Lord, Medina Sidonia urged the King to decide what most suited his royal service under the circumstances: either, he wrote, "take some honorable means with the Queen," then crossed out "Queen" and wrote "enemies," before he continued, "or do what is necessary to assure the outcome of the campaign. The interests of Your Majesty," he added, "also demand looking far ahead in any undertaking, since there are so many who envy your grandeur and states."

Whatever Medina Sidonia might have hoped in response to his letter, he continued in his duties. On 27 June he summoned the available squadron generals, senior infantry officers, and commissary officials to a council of war aboard *San Martín* to decide how best to reassemble the armada.[24] In attendance were the naval generals Recalde, Diego Flores de Valdés, Pedro de Valdés, Oquendo, Moncada, and Bertendona, the Maestre de Campo General Bobadilla, *San Martín's* two principal infantry captains, Juan de Velasco and Gaspar de Hermosilla, and the Veedor General, Don Jorge Manrique. Medina Sidonia told them that he had sent Alférez Esquivel in a pinnace toward the Scillies to search for missing ships and reconnoiter the activities of the English, Alférez Corral in a fast vessel to search the north coast as far as Pasajes, and a galley to Vivero to determine which vessels had made port there. Would it be best, he asked them, to wait in port until the missing ships were found and rejoined or to put to sea in hope of rounding up the stragglers as the armada proceeded?

Don Jorge Manrique, who as Veedor General was inspector and chief administrative officer of the armada, a veteran of the Azores campaigns, provided the others with facts and figures: after counting the ships at La Coruña and close by in Vivero and Ribadeo, some twenty-eight ships were missing and with them 6,000 men. The armada's rolls, he admitted, were inflated with noncombatants, boys and rowers, and aboard the fleet were no more than 22,500 effectives. Thus the loss of 6,000 men from this figure was crippling. He believed that the armada should keep to port.

All agreed except for Pedro de Valdés, who argued that every day lost in port weakened the armada. The English fleet was, he believed, divided into three squadrons, which could be defeated in detail by the armada's ships from La Coruña, Vivero, and Ribadeo which would combine at sea. The missing ships, he was certain, would rejoin the armada under way. Maestre de Campo Bobadilla rebutted that the armada should sail only when reunited, for the sake both of morale and of victory. When the vote was taken, all but Valdés agreed they should remain in port. After the council adjourned, Valdés wrote to the King that he feared the Duke would think badly of him and not give him his due nor take his advice.[25]

Philip II received the first news from La Coruña on the morning of 26 June. Believing that the Duke had entered port only to take on the needed water and stores, he responded, "I am confident that you will without fail depart, as you state, in two days' time." Late the same day the news of the storm and the dispersal of the armada arrived.

Idiáquez in response expressed the court's reaction: "You have given us a terrible shock."[26] He clearly worried about the Duke's morale: "I hope . . . that in this storm all hazards and impediments have been spent and that what follows will be what we wish, through the mercy of God. May Your Lordship, who first discharged your conscience and then accepted this enterprise for the public weal and service of the King, I hope emerge with much honor [*reputación*] and that past travails will lead to the desired day."

In the days that followed came further shocks in reports of damages and missing ships, and finally the plea in Medina Sidonia's own hand that the King consider calling off the Enterprise.

On 1 July the King responded to it from the Escorial.[27] Of the Duke's zeal he was certain, and therefore he would be more open with him than with another. The Duke's arguments had not been based on facts, he wrote, and in order that the Duke might better understand matters, he had ordered a detailed memorandum prepared that he would enclose with his reply. He was confident that Medina Sidonia would persevere in repairing the armada and resuming the voyage as soon as possible. "I have offered God this service, and to assist me in it I have taken you as my instrument. There can be no greater confidence than I have in you; for all you did in Lisbon to weigh anchor you merit the thanks I gave you. What happened in the storm is not at all your fault. For having made repair as quickly as I believe you have, I thank you; from the result of what is to come, may it please God that it bring you much honor."

The accompanying memorandum refuted point by point Medina Sidonia's objections.[28] Who drafted it is not certain, but it seems to have been Moura, rather than Idiáquez, who usually handled such matters. Each wrote separately a note to Medina Sidonia in response to his plea. In his, Moura remarked that he had answered it elsewhere at some length and admonished Medina Sidonia to "eat, sleep and stop believing that you are obliged to give account for what heaven ordains, because it knows better what suits us." In his note, Idiáquez attributed Medina Sidonia's misgivings to his zeal to serve and advised him to comply with the King's orders. He referred simply to the King's letter.[29]

Some of the points of the memorandum, especially those regarding the quality of English ships and the suggestion that the Dutch rebels were not cooperating with the English, reflect surprising ignorance or wishful thinking that is not easy to associate with Idiáquez. Did Idiáquez also waver, so that Philip gave the task to the steadfast and moral Moura? If the expressed opinions were Philip's and widely held at court, the prevalent confidence in the Enterprise makes more sense. There seems little doubt that Philip had become obsessed with the

Enterprise, and as Cabrera de Córdoba remarked, it was Moura who best knew the humor of his master.[30]

The memorandum began with the assertion that His Majesty had gathered his forces in Spain and Flanders primarily in the service of God. The storm that hit the armada might be regarded as punishment for our sins, but it could not be seen as a sign from God to desist in the Enterprise, because the war was just. No great enterprise succeeded without difficulties, which only added to its esteem when they were overcome. Even if the armada lacked some of its ships, it was superior to the fleet that awaited it: "Many of the enemy's ships are old or small, not as good as ours, while our armada enjoys every advantage in its manpower, veterans mixed with recruits, whereas the enemy's forces are untrained, levied from the ordinary population, disorderly and without discipline."

Second, the memorandum dismissed the likelihood that England would be aided by its neighbors: France was rent by dissension, and the few Huguenot corsairs who might sail from La Rochelle were no worry; the rebels of Holland and Zeeland looked only to themselves; the Protestants of Germany were scarcely able to plan a diversion, which would have no effect on the armada; the King of Denmark, the enemy's chief supporter, who might have reinforced the enemy fleet, was dead, and England had no hope for help from there; and from the King of Scotland they who shed the blood of his mother could neither expect assistance.

Third, it was the best month of the year for sailing, and the Duke of Parma was satisfied with his army, which was ready to cross the Narrows when the armada arrived.

Last, the armada at La Coruña was too far away to influence any negotiations, and the enemy would take its absence as a sign of weakness. It would also encourage corsairs to sail for the Indies, with the armada shamefully in port, and threaten the treasure that Alvaro Flores [de Quiñones] had to fetch so that His Majesty could wage war. These were, the memorandum concluded, but some of the many reasons for not desisting in the Enterprise, which had to go ahead with the aid of God.

On 5 July, the King returned to the matter of Medina Sidonia's misgivings. "You have seen clearly my intentions, which are not to desist in this Enterprise," he wrote, and challenged the Duke's disparaging remarks about Levanters and urcas.[31] He ordered him to be ready to sail by the tenth or twelfth, and no later than the twentieth.

On the same day Idiáquez, back in the fold if he had indeed wavered, offered gratuitous advice to stiffen the Duke's sense of authority and self-confidence: "Anticipate what might happen and consider the responses, for it is something that later in action makes for a sure and ready spirit, and permits giving resolute orders with a display of confidence, without having to collect the council [of war] when the time comes to carry out what was decided."[32]

Idiáquez suggested to Medina Sidonia that he form an inner council to assist him aboard *San Martín* but warned him that "of the thousands of men assembled, only Your Lordship is in charge of everything." In a final remark, he added, "The day that Your Lordship received me as your servant, you took me with this fault, of being rather bothersome—perhaps too much so—in the true interests of the persons to whom I have obligations."

However much Idiáquez took the Duke's true interests to heart, what was written to Medina Sidonia soon leaked to the corridors of the court, and courtiers openly criticized the Duke's irresolution and poor seamanship. In his report the Venetian Ambassador stated that the King was unhappy with the Duke, who needed to show more courage, and ordered him to keep a council of war aboard his ship.[33]

Medina Sidonia took the advice given, if he had not considered it already, and established aboard the capitana real a small council of war to give him the advice he often claimed he would need. For nautical matters he appointed Diego Flores de Valdés, General of the Castilian squadron, while for matters involving the embarked infantry and combat, he selected Maestre de Campo General Don Francisco de Bobadilla, whom he brought to the capitana from *San Marcos*. The capitana's sailing master, Captain Marolín de Juan, also provided the Duke with nautical advice, and Don Jorge Manrique, Veedor General, advised him on logistics.

Bobadilla, Marolín, and Manrique had all served with Santa Cruz in the Azores. Diego Flores had never served with him. Why Medina Sidonia turned to him rather than another, perhaps Oquendo or Bertendona, to advise him remains a puzzling question. Medina Sidonia had nothing kind to say about Diego Flores in 1581, when he assisted him in the outfitting of the armada to the Strait of Magellan.

The King and Idiáquez approved Medina Sidonia's choice of Diego Flores and the King perhaps recommended it.[34] He would not have forgotten that Flores served in the armada of 1554 that took him to his marriage to Mary Tudor and thus had some experience of English waters. Bobadilla the King explicitly recommended.[35] But the wording, "it will be well that you order," rather than the direct "I command," would allow for discretion on the Duke's part. In royal orders to those who exercised authority under demanding and changing circumstances, a discretionary clause, "or whatever occurs to you most convenient," was customarily included.

Recalde later claimed that he recommended Oquendo to serve the Duke as nautical adviser, and that he was not pleased with the Duke's choice, whom he did not name.[36] He must not have believed that the King directly ordered Medina Sidonia to choose Diego Flores.

In choosing Diego Flores over Oquendo, Medina Sidonia probably decided to stick with seniority and perhaps also preferred to deal with someone with whom he had already worked rather than one he scarcely knew. Both men were equally difficult, although Oquendo was better regarded by his peers. So maybe the Duke decided that it would be better for all concerned if he personally dealt with the cantankerous Diego Flores, took advantage of his long experience with ships and fleets, and kept him apart from the other generals and even his own squadron.[37]

From court the Secretary to the Council of War for the Sea, Andrés de Alva, hurried to La Coruña, where he arrived on 17 July.[38] He brought verbal orders from the King to Medina Sidonia about selecting advisers. Alva found that the Duke had accounted for almost all his ships, that the necessary repairs had been made, ships careened, and fresh water and stores loaded, and the armada stood ready "for the reduction of [England] to the Holy See."[39] The men of the armada had regained their faith in God's design, since the armada was resuming its voyage stronger than before.

Though bombarded with admonishment, reproof, and fresh orders from court, Medina Sidonia had never ceased working to make the armada ready again for sea. He obtained fresh food for his crews and watched them quickly recover; for those most ill a hospital was established ashore. He supervised in person the replacement of broken masts and caulking of leaky hulls. He embarked several hundred men recruited in Galicia, then let four hundred go as too old or too young, or married men with children whose wives had raised a clamor at dockside. To ensure the spiritual well-being of his men, he landed the armada's clergy on an island in the harbor and had tents erected to serve as chapels, where by 15 July over eight thousand men had confessed and received the Holy Sacrament.

The two principal naval generals who had served under Santa Cruz, Recalde and Oquendo, both wrote to the King praising the Duke. "The Duke makes the greatest haste," the armada's Admiral General stated, "working as he should, to get [the armada] to sea."[40] Oquendo seconded the Admiral, writing that "the Duke attends to everything with much care and great prudence, in such fashion that this armada, by putting into port, has been strengthened in many things, without which it would not have sailed in the best order."[41]

Only weather, blowing from the north, prevented the armada from making sail. Then on 19 July, accompanied by squalls, the winds shifted and began to blow from the southwest.

On the afternoon of the next day Medina Sidonia summoned his generals, maestres de campo, and senior captains to a council of war in the presence of Andrés de Alva.[42] The meeting seems to have been held aboard Medrano's galera real. Medrano, not at the 27 June meeting, was there, and the San Martín's officers at that meeting were not. The clerk taking the minutes, perhaps Alva himself or one of his people, listed the participants in rough order of rank and station after the Duke: Don Alonso de Leyva, Don Francisco de Bobadilla, Secretary Andrés de Alva, Don Jorge Manrique, Admiral-General Juan Martínez de Recalde, Diego Flores de Valdés, Pedro de Valdés, Miguel de Oquendo, Captain Martín de Bertendona, Captain Diego de Medrano, Don Diego Enríquez, and Gregorio de las Alas, Admiral of Diego Flores's squadron. Not present were the general of the galleasses, Don Hugo de Moncada, of the urcas, Juan Gómez de Medina, and of the zabras and pataches, Agustín de Ojeda, who had replaced Don Antonio Hurtado de Mendoza.[43] Ojeda had been serving aboard the capitana and shared with Captain Marolín de Juan responsibility for the ship and its crew.

Don Alonso de Leyva, mentioned for the first time since he rejoined the armada as participating in the council, opened the discussion with questions about the weather. Listed in the 9 May roster as an adventurer, he was about to take command of one of the armada's combat divisions. Had his designation as Medina Sidonia's successor become public? if so, what accommodation was expected of Recalde, the Admiral General and formerly second-in-command? No mention appears.

Leyva soon yielded to Diego Flores de Valdés, who expounded his meteorological lore in a description of the relationship between prevailing winds and phases of the moon. The new moon would be on the twenty-third. According to the signs, the weather would worsen, but after the new moon it could be predicted with more confidence. He admitted that if on the morrow it cleared in the north, the winds would hold from the southwest and the armada might sail, but he feared they might revert to the north. Don Pedro de Valdés in the main agreed with his Asturian kinsman.

The Vizcayan Martín de Bertendona, chief of the Levanters, sharply dissented: the weather already permitted the armada to sail. The pilots concurred with him. The armada might have made sail at midday.

Don Diego Enríquez, son of the former Viceroy of Peru, spoke next. He commanded the embarked infantry of the Castilian squadron. Enríquez related, as had Diego Flores, the likely wind direction to phases of the moon. He believed that the winds were likely to blow from the west or southwest with the new moon as they had with the last, which meant that the armada could sail.

Miguel de Oquendo in his turn stood with the two Asturians. La Coruña, he reminded everybody, was nine or ten leagues from the open sea.

Bobadilla, seeing the naval generals in disagreement, demurred as a landsman. Recalde joined his compatriot Bertendona and argued that the armada might have doubled Cape Prior that night. He quoted an old saw, "There is no bad sign in summer nor good sign in winter," and urged that the armada make sail on the morrow, if the winds held true, without waiting on the moon.

When the meeting adjourned, those present affixed their signatures to the King's copy of the minutes and to the Duke's.

Medina Sidonia had Recalde, Diego Flores, and las Alas assemble the armada's chief pilots to ascertain their views, which they did at seven the next morning. As Bertendona claimed, the pilots believed that the armada could have sailed the day before and swore to it.[44] But that morning, the weather had changed, and the day had broken with squalls and erratic winds. The armada shivered and tossed in port. Later the sky cleared, the sea calmed, and a steady breeze rose from the southwest. At dawn Friday, 22 July, the Duke ordered a piece fired to signal weighing anchors, and a second for the unfurling of sails.

Initially the winds merely tantalized: at two that afternoon, the armada stood becalmed in sight of La Coruña, half surrounded by the green hills of Galicia. With nightfall the winds stirred again. An hour past daybreak Saturday the armada was moving before fair southerly winds. By sunset it was fifty miles at sea.

The last roster taken by name showed 138 ships, galleasses, galleys, and caravels sailing from La Coruña, including 7 feluccas carrying water.[45] Six more ships sailed from nearby ports and were to rejoin at sea. The *Contador* Pedro Coco Calderon, both thorough and reliable, lists a total of 151 by ship type: 23 *galeones*, 43 *naves*, 26 *urcas*, 4 *galeazas*, 4 *galeras*, 20 pataches, 10 zabras, 11 *carabelas*, and 10 *falúas*.[46] In Lisbon six storeships outfitted under Sancho Pardo to follow.

Saturday, Sunday, and Monday brought the armada clear skies and fair winds, the sort of weather Spaniards call *bonanza*. Medina Sidonia was satisfied, though he fussed about the lubberliness of some of his ships: without them his best squadrons would have been in the Channel rather than off the tip of Brittany. On Monday, 25 July, he sent Captain Rodrigo Tello de Guzmán off in a fast patache to inform Parma that the armada was under way for their rendezvous and had reached the 48th parallel.

On Tuesday morning a dead calm descended on the armada and dark clouds gathered in the sky. Then at noon north winds struck, followed by squalls and heavy seas. The armada tacked first east, then west, struggling to maintain its progress. The winds shifted to west-northwest and the seas mounted. The galley *Diana*, shipping water over its low freeboard, made for shore. Don Diego de Medrano, the galleys' chief, warned Medina Sidonia that the seas were a bit "much" and that his remaining three galleys might also have to seek haven. Medina Sidonia sent two pataches to assist Medrano and urged him to persevere. The Duke could see the galleys during the remaining daylight hours but lost sight of them during the night. Medrano had decided to head for the coast, and though Medina Sidonia did not learn it until after his return, he brought his battered galleys back to Spain, save for one which was beached and wrecked at Bayonne.

The rain squalls gradually subsided, but the heavy seas persisted. Hardened mariners protested that they had never seen such high seas in July. In a passage that suggests his familiarity with Virgil's *Aeneid* Medina Sidonia described mountainous waves that seemed to touch the sky, on which ships rose and fell, sometimes passing from sight. Waves came crashing down on decks, and one tore off the stern gallery of *San Cristóbal*, the seven-hundred-tonelada capitana of the Castilian squadron. During "the cruelest night I have ever seen,"[47] he feared yet more damage to the armada, which struggled under sail against the seas.

Thursday dawned clear and sunny, the winds became more favorable, but the seas continued heavy. The Duke counted the ships in sight and found he was missing forty, including the galleys. Worried, he sent off three pataches to locate them. The one he sent ahead in the direction of Lizard Point took soundings and reported back to him a depth of sixty-eight fathoms, which let him know he was not far from landfall.

During the night the seas calmed, while the wind continued light and from the west. At eight in the morning of a bright day the pataches returned with the news that the missing greatships and urcas had been found and were under way to rejoin the rest. Some, including Pedro de Valdés's *Rosario*, had reached the Scilly Islands.

At four that afternoon Medina Sidonia spied Lizard Point. He ordered raised to the masthead a banner bearing a crucifix flanked by Our Lady and the Magdalene, and had three pieces fired. All bowed their heads in a prayer of thanksgiving.

✳ CHAPTER EIGHT ✳

The Armada Campaign: Lizard Point to the Isle of Wight

ON Friday, 29 July (19 July by the Old Style Julian calendar then used in England), shortly before seven in the evening, Medina Sidonia began to write the King a report of the armada's progress.[1] He stated that all the vessels of the armada had reassembled except for the galleys, the greatship *Santa Ana*, capitana of Vizcaya, which had sailed from Santander and never rejoined,[2] and the patache that took Rodrigo Tello to Parma. The Duke could probably count around 140 ships, including caravels and feluccas that accompanied him from Spain, now drawn up for the night.

The next day Medina Sidonia added a few lines to his letter to inform the King that he would resume sailing as soon as the capitana of the galleasses had repaired its rudder, damaged by the heavy seas.[3] About the galleasses he remarked that they were weak vessels for seas as rough as what they had experienced.[4] He admitted that he was very worried about the galleys, of which he had no news, but for the rest, the armada had suffered little harm and morale seemed high.

With his report he enclosed a dispatch in cipher, in which he stated that he intended to shelter off the Isle of Wight until he received definite news from Parma. He wrote nothing about conquering the island. The King had repeatedly instructed him not to attempt to capture a port until after Parma's army had successfully landed in England or it had become clear that Parma could not make the crossing. In such case the King had suggested the Isle of Wight and recommended the eastern approach.

Throughout the planning of the campaign, the armada's chief officers constantly complained that the armada lacked an adequate port for its operations. It might find temporary anchorage off what the King's instructions called the Cape of Margate, between the Kentish coast and Goodwin Sands,[5] or in the lower estuary of the Thames, after the troop landings took place. But eventually a proper port would be necessary. According to Recalde, the closest were Southampton and the Isle of Wight, though he preferred a port further west: Dartmouth, Torbay, Plymouth, or Falmouth, any of which afforded easier communication with Spain.[6] What Medina Sidonia intended, other than to take advantage of the lee of Wight or the vast anchorage of Spithead, is not clear. He must have felt confident that the armada could hold the anchorage and defend itself against the constant English attacks that would have been likely. Reaching shelter in the lee of Wight was now his first objective. After that he would determine when to "join hands" with Parma.

Taking a port or sheltering off Wight was probably a topic of discussion at the council of war held aboard *San Martín* Friday evening or sometime Saturday. No detailed account like that of the last council at La Coruña has been found for the meeting. The record that does exist is of mixed value.[7] Don Alonso de Leyva probably spoke first and seems to have urged an attack on Plymouth. While this appears foolhardy, it fits his experience in the Sicilian galleys. Assaulting ports was a significant dimension of Mediterranean warfare. Medrano's galleys, which unfortunately would not rejoin the armada, could land troops to storm the forts covering Plymouth Harbor, while the powerfully gunned galleasses, under power of oar, would lead a strong squadron of the armada's fighting ships through the harbor's narrow entrance to find, corner, and seize or destroy the English ships there. How many English ships Leyva believed they would find at Plymouth is unknown. He argued that in the confines of the harbor, grappling and boarding them would certainly prove easier than on the open sea. The guns of the harbor forts, were they not taken, would be limited in their effect by the fear the gunners would have of hitting their own ships.

Medina Sidonia referred to his instructions to proceed directly to the rendezvous with Parma and fight only if opposed. To enter Plymouth, he argued, the armada would have to proceed by twos and threes against enemy fire. Inside Plymouth harbor, if the report received at La Coruña were to be believed, were both Drake and the Lord Admiral with perhaps twenty to thirty powerful galleons, each armed with forty bronze cannon, plus a swarm of other vessels.[8] He did not have the galleys; he did not wish to land troops to seize the forts, and thus any effort to force Plymouth's narrow and tricky entrance channel would risk heavy damages and casualties. Most of the other commanders assembled seem to have agreed with him.

The council of war may also have discussed where they would "join hands" with Parma. From what Medina Sidonia wrote the King on 30 July it appears that he planned for the armada to meet Parma's invasion force off the coast of Flanders rather than await it off Margate, as the King's instructions had originally stated. The King had written Medina Sidonia in late June to make sure that he understood from Captain Moresin that the armada would have to clear the passage of the Narrows for Parma's invasion flotilla.[9]

When their business was done, the armada's generals returned to their own ships. Sometime Saturday the galleass capitana completed repair of its rudder and the armada began its march up-Channel.

All day Medina Sidonia could see warning fires and smoke signals ashore. Ahead lay Plymouth. To garner more timely intelligence of English strength, he dispatched Saturday evening Alférez Juan Gil, who spoke English, in a zabra reinforced with twenty sharpshooters. While awaiting Gil's return, he detected through wisps of fog in the growing dusk sails toward land, how many he could not tell. Then an English vessel approached the armada; he ordered Agustín Ojeda to give it chase. Ojeda pursued it to its port, where shore batteries gave him hot welcome.[10]

At midnight Gil returned with a fishing boat in tow. Its crew of four, from Falmouth, reported that they had seen the Lord Admiral Charles Howard and Drake sail from Plymouth that afternoon. The fishermen believed they had ready 120 ships, and that another forty patrolled off Dover. That meant that the bulk of the English fleet was indeed at Plymouth.

Medina Sidonia turned to his inner council for advice. Diego Flores wanted the armada to shorten sail, to maintain the weather gauge and enjoy the advantage of remaining upwind of the English. When the Duke suggested the armada might best come round and work toward the open sea to ensure keeping the weather gauge, Diego Flores and the others on the quarterdeck advised against it, for fear that the armada might become divided in the dark. Medina Sidonia accepted their advice. All agreed that the armada should assume battle formation at daybreak, and the Duke sent a captain round in a patache to relay his order to the armada's squadron generals and ship captains.

For battle, the armada's administrative organization by squadron, which seems to have sufficed during its voyage from La Coruña, gave way to its tactical organization. Aboard each ship in the armada, the senior officer, whether landsman or seaman, or in some cases a prominent noble adventurer, commanded in battle and took responsibility for his ship's conduct. Letting landsmen command has since seemed questionable, but because most of the armada's seamen, save for the naval chiefs and the crewmen of the King's ships, came from the merchant tradition, their willingness to risk offensive combat was suspect. The handling of rudder and sail did remain the business of the ship's master, who relayed orders to helmsman and sailors.

At the call to quarters sailors stood by the rigging while ship's boys made ready water buckets for fighting fire and stood by to assist the sailors. Under some circumstances a ship would lower its longboat to the water with a coxswain, oarsmen, and a couple of musketeers aboard to assist the ship in its maneuvers.

When the ship's crew took battle stations, "pages," or cabin attendants, and the servants of officers and adventurers prepared for a host of small tasks. Some were assigned to assist the ship's surgeon and a few bore arms. The musketeers and arquebusiers of the embarked infantry lined the ship's rails and galleries while pikemen stood by to repel boarders or board the enemy. Incendiary clay pots were made ready to hurl onto enemy decks.

Gunners, assisted by soldiers, ran out their guns and made sure they were securely lashed to the ship's side. Falcons, sakers, and demisakers would open fire first, aiming at the masts and rigging of the enemy ships with shot of ten pounds or less; the big guns, weighing from 2,500 to 6,000 pounds and positioned on the lower decks, would hold fire until the enemy had come within point-blank range, preferably almost hull to hull, before firing their shot, which ranged in size from fifteen to fifty pounds. Gunnery handbooks recommended finding the range by first firing point-blank, and if the shot fell short, then raising the gun, putting the second shot slightly higher and further. For a shot that fell short there always remained the chance that it might skip into its target; an overshot was a lost shot.

The reloading of the gun took time. After each shot, the gun had to be hauled inboard and its bore had to be sponged and wormed to remove all residue from the previous shot. Contador Coco Calderón reported that two gunners aboard his ship were killed by a flash explosion because they failed to sponge their gun well. After thoroughly cleaning the gun bore, the gun crew then either ladled fresh powder into the barrel and tightly but gently packed it with a rammer that pressed a wad against it, or introduced a prepared cloth cartridge filled with powder and carefully rammed it home. For some small guns the cartridge was made of paper. The gunners next sponged the gun barrel again to clean any loose powder grains from the bore. Then the ball, dusted and cleaned, would be rammed home, followed by a second wad. The gun would be run out and lashed in place, then the gun captain would aim the piece at its target; when satisfied, he had an assistant prime the piece and put match to the vent, while he stood apart to gauge where the shot hit.

Well-trained Venetian gunners, the best in Europe, reportedly could reload, sight, and fire a big gun in about two minutes under ideal conditions.[11] For sustained fire, the rate for a big gun in the nineteenth century reached twelve shots per hour, but beyond that, with even the best gun crew, there was the risk of the gun overheating.[12] If the English gunners of 1588 sustained fire at anything like twelve rounds an hour—and during the armada battles they fired their guns at least three times faster than the Spaniards did—the armada's best gunners needed at least fifteen minutes to reload and fire their big guns. Often they took an hour. Because they hesitated to use their heaviest guns outside point-blank range, the Spaniards in action mainly fired pieces that shot balls of ten, six, and four pounds.

Small bronze antipersonnel pieces fired at faster rates than the big guns because they cooled faster, as did the small iron breechloaders. Muskets and arquebuses fired at best a round a minute but had to be allowed to cool after some minutes of sustained firing. Battle conditions aboard the decks of ships under way in varying seas were extremely taxing and demanded tight discipline and steady nerves.

The failure of the armada to do any serious hull damage to the English suggests that under battle conditions the gunners aboard the armada proved wanting. Though Medina Sidonia and his chief officers complained they were short of powder and shot, recently found records show that many of the armada ships returned with substantial quantities of both on board; archaeological excavation of sunken ships too has yielded evidence of sizable amounts of each.[13]

A serious shortage of competent naval gunners seems the best explanation. The Spaniards often had to rely on foreign gunners.[14] Of the fifteen ships pressed in Seville in 1587, listed aboard *Santa Ana*, which belonged to Oquendo and served as his capitana, were twenty-six gunners for its forty-seven rated guns, and aboard *Nuestra Señora del*

Rosario, which became Pedro de Valdés's *capitana*, sixteen for forty-six rated guns.[15] English galleons of similar tonnage had forty gunners. Continuing down the list, one ship has twelve, two have ten, one nine, one eight, two six, two four, two three, and two have two. Because these were ships originally bound for the Indies, their gunners were probably experienced aboard ship. The chief gunner of Seville's Casa de Contratación stated that "handling artillery at sea requires that the gunner also be a seaman, for otherwise, not understanding the pitch and roll of the ship, he cannot achieve the accuracy and effect desired."[16] Medina Sidonia in his later years returned to the same theme: "In my experience, gunners from land are not much good at sea."[17]

Many gunners aboard the armada were probably landsmen, and on too many ships depended on help from musketeers. In action it seems they either did not or could not reload. The gun crews aboard *San Martín* and other principal ships, whose commanders claimed they were running out of ammunition, probably could reload under fire. These were the ships, especially those commanded by the armada's generals, admirals, and maestres de campo, that bore the brunt of the fighting and, for the most part, suffered the worst of the damage. Later Bobadilla would complain to Idiáquez that some twenty ships had done almost all the fighting.

For combat each ship had its assigned place in the order of battle. Medina Sidonia and his senior people intended to deploy the armada *en lúnula*, a vast crescent moon with its tips projected toward the enemy. It was the formation preferred by Spanish and Italian theorists, and the Roman military writer Filippo Pigafetta had it more or less right in a pamphlet published in Rome in August, though some adjustments had clearly been made at La Coruña.[18] All but the smallest ships had places in the battle formation. Don Pedro de Valdés was quoted by Petruccio Ubaldino as stating that the armada had 110 fighting ships, not the 65 or so found in most modern histories, although Valdés had recommended that only the best ships, divided between a vanguard and rearguard, do the fighting and that what he called the useless ships form a third division and keep clear.[19] What he recommended approximates the way the armada in fact often fought after the first day's encounter.

The planned formation en lúnula consisted of the central main battle, or *batalla*, a right wing, fittingly called by Spaniards the *cuerno derecho*, or right horn, and a left wing, the *cuerno izquierdo*, or left horn; behind each was a *socorro*, a smaller second line to serve as relief (fig. 2;

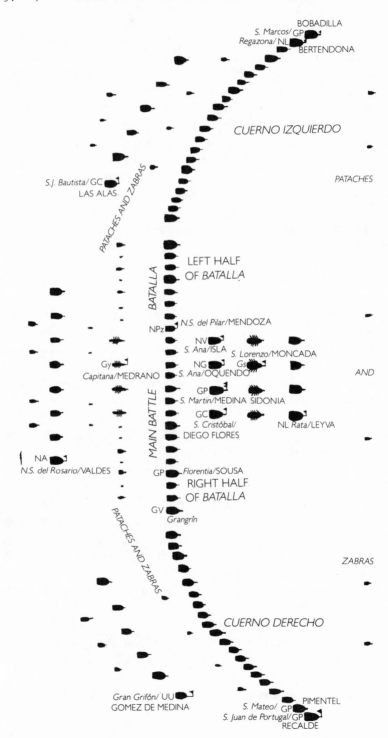

BOBADILLA

S. Marcos/ GP

Regazona/ NL

BERTENDONA

CUERNO IZQUIERDO

PATACHES

S.J. Bautista/ GC
LAS ALAS.

PATACHES AND ZABRAS

LEFT HALF
OF *BATALLA*

BATALLA

N.S. del Pilar/MENDOZA

NPz

NV
S. Ana/ISLA

S. Lorenzo/MONCADA

Gy

NG   Gs
S. Ana/OQUENDO

AND

Capitana/MEDRANO

GP
S. Martin/MEDINA SIDONIA

MAIN BATTLE

GC
S. Cristóbal/
DIEGO FLORES

NL Rata/LEYVA

NA
N.S. del Rosario/VALDES

GP   Florentia/SOUSA

RIGHT HALF
OF *BATALLA*

GV
Grangrín

PATACHES AND ZABRAS

ZABRAS

CUERNO DERECHO

Gran Grifón/ UU
GOMEZ DE MEDINA

PIMENTEL

S. Mateo/ GP

S. Juan de Portugal/GP

RECALDE

see Battle Order of the Armada, pp. 235–243). The capitana real, supported by the galleasses and a small but powerful vanguard, would mass ahead of center of the crescent, while the four galleys were to have sailed directly behind the batalla. This seeming head and tail on the crescent caused Pigafetta to refer to the formation as an *águila* (eagle). The most powerful fighting ships were carefully allocated among the batalla, the cuernos, and the three socorros. Well ahead some pataches and zabras sailed to scout; the remainder of these small fry sheltered behind the batalla, cuernos, and socorros.

The Spaniards intended to bear down on the English, to close and board, not fight a gunnery duel in which they believed they would be at serious disadvantage. With a huge array of ships, large and small, perhaps three dozen of them well gunned or especially handy, the rest not, but all carrying troops, Medina Sidonia and his captains hoped that at least one would be able to grapple with a foe and precipitate the desired mêlée.

Most modern naval historians deride the armada's preferred tactics and contrast them unfavorably to the English decision to rely on gunnery and avoid boarding. The English had more and better guns than the Spaniards did, but even they were not certain in 1588 how effective gunnery alone would prove. Big, wooden sailing ships were not easily sunk. For their purpose, however, they did not have to destroy the armada, only keep it at a distance from England and prevent Parma's crossing; and they hoped their guns would suffice. Their ships could afford to be gun platforms: they were not, like the Spanish, carrying an invasion force and months' worth of supplies for a voyage far from home.

Many historians have gone beyond any clear evidence to infer that the English, in contrast to the massed frontal assault the Spaniards planned, were prepared to give battle by broadsides fired by ships sailing in line ahead, which they insist was the only sensible tactic for sailing vessels after the advent of shipboard gunnery. While glimpses of line ahead sometimes dimly appear in what the English did in 1588,

---

Figure 2. Projected battle formation of the armada, late March 1588. Key to abbreviations: *Squadrons*: A = Andalusia; C = Castile; G = Guipúzcoa; Gs = Galleass; Gy = Galley; L = Levant; Pz = Pataches and zabras; P = Portugal; U = Urcas; V = Vizcaya. *Ship types*: G = Galleon; Gs = Galleass; Gy = Galley; N = Nao/Nave (Greatship); U = Urca (Hulk). (The ships in this and the following figures are not drawn to scale.)

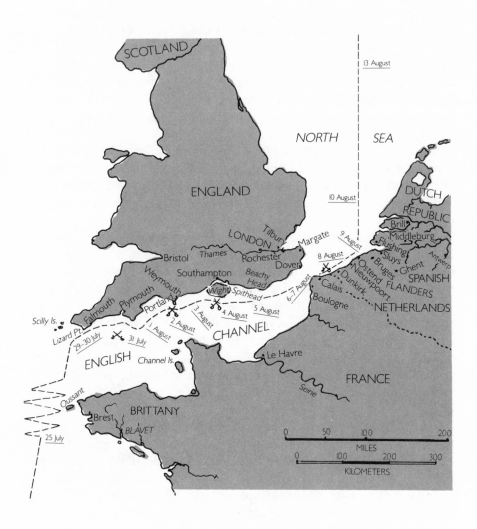

Map 4. The armada in the English Channel, showing sites of the battles.

battle orders that advocate it date from the mid-seventeenth century and later, the period selected by A. T. Mahan for his seminal *Influence of Seapower upon History, 1660–1783* (1890). It seems mistaken to look much earlier for consistent line ahead tactics, and it ought not be forgotten that closing and grappling remained a decisive maneuver through the time of the Battle of Trafalgar, fought in sight of Medina Sidonia's ancestral estates. In that battle, Nelson's *Victory* alone carried more guns firing shot of twenty-four pounds and up than the entire Spanish Armada. The sustained gunnery duel between lines of battle developed when ships came to mount considerably more artillery than the ships on either side did in the armada campaign, and the administration of navies and training of crews had far surpassed the rudimentary state of 1588.

The armada, prepared to fight en lúnula, proceeded along the English coast *en arco*, extended in a similar crescent but with the two cuernos trailing rather than projecting forward. This was not unlike the customary formation of the Indies flotas. The formation en arco was also well regarded by theorists and combat veterans for battle, though lúnula was preferred.[20] The formation en arco in battle was designed to smash first the enemy center, en lúnula to turn first the enemy's flanks. Both were flexible and permitted the necessary communication of commands.

The battle formation the armada prepared to assume in the Channel differed from the original plan only slightly, to reflect shifts in personnel and the absence of some ships. Medina Sidonia in the capitana real still intended to sail ahead of the center of the batalla, flanked to port by Oquendo in his one-thousand-ton capitana *Santa Ana*, but with the Marquis of Peñafiel in *San Marcos* in place of the missing *Santa Ana* of Vizcaya to Oquendo's port; and Gregorio de la Alas, Admiral of the Indies Guard who now commanded Diego Flores's capitana *San Cristóbal*, to his starboard.

Oquendo was responsible for the batalla's left wing. Like the other principal commanders, he enjoyed considerable independence of maneuver when battle was joined and could call on support from the ships under his immediate charge.

Arrayed slightly ahead of the capitana real and her consorts were the four galleasses, and ahead of them four galleons, probably Maestre de Campo Diego de Pimentel in *San Mateo*, Maestre de Campo Agustín Mejía in *San Luis*, and Portuguese captains Gaspar de Sousa in *Florentia* and Antonio de Pereira in *Santiago*. These could combine with Medina

Sidonia in an overwhelming assault on the enemy or, as he explained to the King, be dispatched to reinforce one or the other of the cuernos as needed.[21]

Deployed to port and starboard of this powerful central nucleus was a mixed array of two dozen galleons, greatships, and urcas, with Diego Téllez Enríquez in *San Juan de Sicilia* at one tip and the Levantine almiranta *La Lavia* and the Castilian galleon *Santiago el Mayor* at the other. In command of the main battle's socorro sailed Don Pedro de Valdés in the powerful *Nuestra Señora del Rosario*, with at least seven other stout ships.

The two cuernos indicated in the original battle plan became in the first day's fighting in the Channel the rearguard and vanguard, because of their places running before a northwesterly wind when the armada sighted the English fleet and prepared for action. The right cuerno under Recalde in *San Juan Almiranta de Portugal* was astern of the main battle; the left cuerno, taken by Don Alonso de Leyva in the Genoese carrack *La Rata Santa Maria Encoronada* when Bobadilla went to the capitana real, sailed ahead as vanguard.

In effect Leyva had the place of honor. As Captain General of the Light Cavalry of Milan he was superior in rank to Recalde, Almirante General, as well as to Bobadilla.

But in some compensation to Recalde's pride, command of the rearguard might become command of the vanguard if the armada faced a foe to its stern. His cuerno would again be to the batalla's right, as in fact it was off Plymouth. Whatever his feelings about the matter, Recalde never complained.

The socorro to Recalde's cuerno was commanded by Juan Gómez de Medina in *Gran Grifón*, probably seconded by Francisco de Toledo in *San Felipe*; Marcos Aramburu in the Castilian almiranta *San Juan Bautista* headed the socorro for Leyva's cuerno.

Medina Sidonia's allocation of warships reflects the experience of the Battle of Lepanto (1571) and the Battle of San Miguel (1582). Veterans of both were aboard the armada. Each of the Duke's cuernos had at its extreme tip a powerful ship, Recalde's *San Juan de Portugal* and Leyva's *Rata*, and each would have also had strong ships at its inward tip. Between the tips the remaining ships of each cuerno sailed in echelon, with about fifty yards between each. In the main battle Medina Sidonia concentrated a great deal of power at the center, with the capitana real, the galleasses, and a cluster of battle-worthy galleons, not unlike the concentration of big galleys at the center of Don Juan of Austria's batalla at Lepanto.

As the armada swarmed forward in a broad frontal attack, its ships would fire their bow pieces and some might fire pieces from each broadside in turn if winds and seas permitted, but their chief aim would be to get among the English ships as quickly as possible. Their topside guns would do most of the shooting, aimed to disable enemy masts and riggings. The Spaniards preferred to save their big guns to batter hulls when the ships closed. The chief purpose of gunnery was to cripple the foe and do all damage possible, including killing and wounding crewmen, prior to boarding.

While this tactic was used both at Lepanto and San Miguel, the Battle of San Miguel, fought in 1582 between sailing ships in deep water off the Island of San Miguel in the Azores, provided the model of how sailing vessels might come to close quarters. Because some of Santa Cruz's armada had returned to Cádiz, Medina Sidonia would have learned firsthand about the encounter fought between Santa Cruz's armada of twenty-five sail, twenty in line and five in socorro, and an enemy fleet the Spaniards reckoned at some sixty French, Portuguese, and other hired vessels commanded by Philippe Strozzi and the counts of Brissac and Vimioso, supporters of the Pretender Dom António. It had been a running, desultory affair lasting several days until one of Santa Cruz's galleons, the armada's *San Mateo*, then commanded by Maestre de Campo Lope de Figueroa, which had become separated from the rest, was assaulted by Strozzi's flagship and several other enemy ships. Grappling irons soon bound *San Mateo* to the enemy flagship and two others, and her disciplined soldiery quickly dominated the combat. Meanwhile Santa Cruz closed in with his other ships, pounding the crowded enemy and raking their decks with murderous gunfire until they were forced to surrender. By the end of the battle, ten enemy ships had been captured, sunk, or abandoned and wrecked, and the rest put to flight. Though the Spaniards knew that English ships carried more, bigger, and better guns and were swifter and more maneuverable than any they had faced at San Miguel, most believed they would somehow bring them to close quarters, even though a few skeptics felt that it might require a miracle.[22]

With its fighting order formed soon after daybreak Sunday, 31 July, the armada spread canvas and began to move. The winds blew from the northwest, the tide was running west. The entrance to Plymouth Sound lay ahead to port. Medina Sidonia did not know whether the English would come out to try to block his passage up-Channel or emerge only after the armada had past and seek battle with the weather gauge in hand. The only English ships seen ahead numbered eleven, all beating their way westward close to shore. When the Duke looked astern he saw the main English fleet, which during the night had cleared Plymouth and gained the weather gauge, the advantage of having the westerly winds at their back and the choice of engaging or not engaging at will. It was exactly what he had hoped to avoid.

From the English fleet a pinnace sent by the Lord Admiral danced toward the armada to challenge the Spaniards to battle.

The Duke of Medina Sidonia, Captain General of the Ocean-Sea, ordered the royal standard, Philip II's arms emblazoned on the Cross of Burgundy, raised to the capitana real's foretop. Around him on the quarterdeck gathered his chief advisers plus the Prince of Ascoli, the Count of Gelves, and other noble adventurers, including several of the Duke's kinsmen. Captain Alonso Vanegas, who served aboard *San Martín*, reckoned she carried some nine hundred men.[23]

Medina Sidonia first seems to have turned the batalla in the direction of Plymouth in hope of drawing the English back to defend their harbor, which would allow him to recover the weather gauge. The vanguard and rearguard trailed in the direction of the English fleet, which would have appeared divided into two squadrons that with rare accuracy the Spaniards identified as commanded by the Lord Admiral and Drake.

English sources suggest that the wind was from the southwest rather than the northwest, as Medina Sidonia's account claims. It may have veered: a southwest wind makes more sense of accounts of the fighting. The English squadrons continued to close the armada's vanguard and rearguard. The Duke ordered the batalla about; it majestically formed front in the deep center of the lúnula, with *San Martín* and its nucleus of powerful galleons pushing ahead. The galleasses must have been left astern of them in the direction of Plymouth or sent in pursuit of the eleven English ships inshore because they do not appear in the accounts of the fight that followed. The inshore socorro under Gómez de Medina may have joined them.

The English squadrons approached the projecting tips of the armada's crescent *en ala*, according to Vanegas, who probably perceived them to be echeloned in oblique lines, not, as so often claimed, in line ahead. The Lord Admiral followed by his squadron fell first on the carrack of Don Alonso de Leyva, which was leading his cuerno and had likely taken station inboard to be first in closing the English. The

English mistook *La Rata* for Medina Sidonia's capitana real.

At the same time Drake and his squadron closed Recalde and the armada's rearguard. Closest to shore, it might yet threaten Plymouth. Howard and the ships that followed him did not stop to fight Leyva but rather headed toward Drake, firing at long range at Spanish ships as they passed.

Recalde aboard his flagship shortened sail and turned to bring his guns to bear on the ships attacking him. The remainder of his rearguard continued under sail in the direction of the batalla. Alone and soon surrounded by foes, Recalde may have hoped to precipitate a general mêlée, as had happened at San Miguel. The English did not take the bait. They kept their distance from the 1,100-tonelada Portuguese galleon and pounded it with gunfire. He could see that they behaved as the Spaniards expected they would.

Medina Sidonia saw Recalde's plight as the ships of the rearguard that might have stood beside the almirante general closed with the rest of the armada. While he did not use the word *flight* in his account, other observers did and remarked that the Duke was angered. He headed *San Martín* toward the fight, and the principal ships of the batalla followed (fig. 3).

Recalde's rearguard at last hauled up and came round. First to reach Recalde was *Grangrín* from his own cuerno and *San Mateo*, the closest galleon of the batalla. Don Pedro de Valdés's socorro also headed toward the action. As *San Martín* neared Recalde, Medina Sidonia for a moment thought that the English might yet grapple him, but when he finally fought his way alongside his Admiral the English disengaged. The shooting had lasted some two hours, though it involved few armada ships. Disappointed at not coming to grips with his enemies, Medina Sidonia at least thought he had put fear into them.

Captain Vanegas calculated that the capitana real had fired 120 rounds from her forty-eight guns, or 2.5 rounds per gun in perhaps an hour under fire. Altogether he believed that in the morning's combat the Spaniards had fired 750 rounds and the English over 2,000.[24] Except for damage to the foremast and rigging of Recalde's almiranta real, the armada suffered little.

Medina Sidonia maneuvered the armada in a vain effort to recover the weather gauge, but finding it impossible he ordered his ships to resume course up-Channel. The tide was now running east. As the vessels came about and the vast lúnula became an arco, two calamities struck.

An explosion rent the almiranta of Guipúzcoa, *San Salvador*, send-

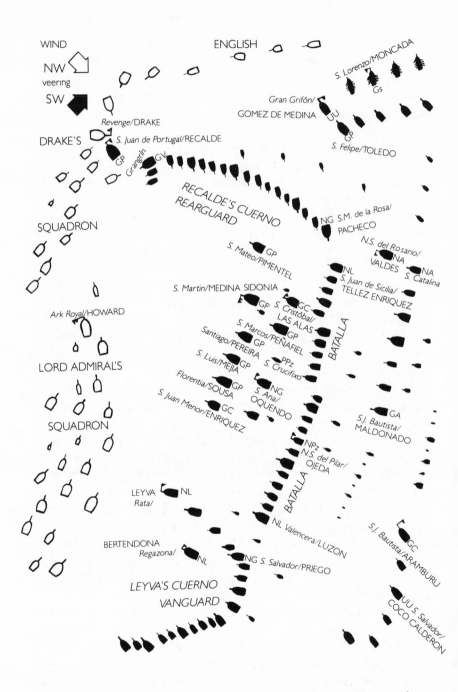

Figure 3. Battle off Plymouth, 31 July. Medina Sidonia and the Batalla go to the aid of Recalde.

ing bodies and fragments into the air, killing more than one hundred men and horribly burning many others. The greatship was taken into tow, though many abandoned her.

The smoldering *San Salvador* wallowed astern off Medina Sidonia's starboard quarter; looking off his port quarter, he could see the other calamity take shape as Don Pedro de Valdés in his capitana *Rosario* became entangled with *Santa Catalina* of his squadron as the two ships returned to station.[25] *Rosario*'s bowsprit broke, and as the vessel lurched about, her unstayed foremast came tumbling down, damaging the main-mast and spilling sail. Medina Sidonia dropped aft in the capitana real to assess the situation. Westerly winds kept the armada moving ahead, soon leaving Medina Sidonia and Valdés behind. The Duke ordered several ships, including a galleass, to assist the damaged *Rosario*, but rising seas made passing cable and keeping the towering vessel under tow almost impossible. The following English fleet approached relentlessly. In the growing dusk the distance between the capitana real, *Rosario*, and her attendant ships and the rest of the armada steadily opened.

Medina Sidonia turned to Diego Flores de Valdés for his opinion. "Though Don Pedro de Valdés is of my blood and a friend," Flores responded, "what matters most is the service of His Majesty." If they became encumbered with the task of rescuing Valdés's ship, the Duke would be lost and the armada endangered.[26]

Don Jorge Manrique disagreed. Not to assist Don Pedro would cost them both honor and the armada. Others on the quarterdeck felt the same way.

The Duke stood with Diego Flores, though he must have remem-bered the controversy that hounded Flores's decision in 1582 to abandon at Rio de Janeiro Sarmiento and his vessels bound for the Strait of Magellan.[27] The old mariner did have long experience with fleets and understood the difficulty of keeping formation, and he had been rec-ommended to the Duke by the King. But Flores's judgment apparently had no room for human considerations and the subtle element of morale. In this he was much like the King. For the sake of many the few might be sacrificed. Reluctantly Medina Sidonia ordered the helm of *San Martín* over to rejoin the armada. He left Agustín Ojeda in his 300-tonelada capitana, four pataches of Ojeda's squadron, *San Francisco* almiranta of the Andalusian squadron, Las Alas in *San Cristóbal*, and a galleass to assist *Rosario*. But his chivalric instincts had yielded to Diego Flores's cold calculation.

Yet it was chivalry, not calculation, that remained the ideal of the sixteenth century, if not always the practice. Throughout the armada men were stunned that a capitana had been left behind and that evening abandoned when Ojeda and the vessels with him retreated before the oncoming English fleet. The distant sound of gunfire echoed briefly in the night, then all fell still. Morale wavered. Contemporaries thought it the Duke's greatest blunder; all that Medina Sidonia attempted and all Valdés's shortcomings in handling his ship were ignored. Lepanto veteran and War Councilor Don Juan de Cardona wrote later that for explaining the defeat of the armada "the principal reason was the loss of the ship of Don Pedro de Valdés, which fell behind . . . while the Duke and the armada continued on its way."[28] In retrospect it must have seemed that had *Rosario* been fought for, the boarding action the armada sought would have occurred and victory been won.

Through the night the armada continued on its way. According to Fray Bernardo de Góngora, who had been sent from *Rosario* by Valdés to seek help, the Duke took little sleep and ate nothing but bread and cheese.[29] The wind and sea ran strong. At daybreak Monday *Rosario* had disappeared from sight, and in midmorning Medina Sidonia decided to scuttle *San Salvador*, whose captain claimed it was sinking. Those still aboard who were able transferred to other ships. An armada paymaster boarded the almiranta of the urcas, also named *San Salvador*, along with his papers and as much cash as he could salvage.[30] Because the English were trailing the armada closely, the stricken ship could not be scuttled. It fell adrift with a few badly wounded people on board. A year later its owner, claiming his ship could have been saved, was suing the Crown for 18,000 ducats.[31]

Though Medina Sidonia did not mention it in his account—nor did anyone else aboard the armada—the English Lord Admiral claimed that he and two of his ships had been close in the armada's wake when day broke, with the remainder of the English fleet hull-down on the horizon. With his vessels he quickly came about to rejoin the rest of his fleet. According to the contemporary Dutch historian Emanuel van Meteren, Don Hugo de Moncada requested permission of Medina Sidonia to attack the isolated Lord Admiral with his galleasses, but was denied. Although some modern historians feel Medina Sidonia regarded it his own prerogative to attack the English Lord Admiral, Meteren simply states that the Duke "was loath to exceed the limits of his commission and charge."[32] If the incident really happened, what makes most sense is that Medina Sidonia was determined to get to the Isle of Wight as soon as possible, and the further behind the armada the English were, the better.

To deal with English attacks on his rear, Medina Sidonia ordered Leyva to join his vanguard to Recalde's rearguard, forming one body or task group to serve as a rearguard for the whole armada. Because Recalde was still repairing damages done to his ship the day before, Leyva for the time held sole command of the newly formed group, which the Duke reinforced with the Portuguese galleons *San Mateo*, *San Luis*, and *Santiago* and the Tuscan *Florentia*, and three of the galleasses. He had written the King that he was prepared to send four galleons and two galleasses to reinforce either cuerno threatened by the English were he caught between their fleets. Now with the greater part of their fleet behind him, he combined the cuernos into a single reinforced rearguard, while his main battle in effect became the armada's vanguard. Because Leyva's force probably sailed en lúnula and Medina Sidonia's proceeded en arco, with the ships of the socorros and the small craft between them, the armada as a whole seemed to form the "roundel" mentioned in contemporary Dutch and English accounts.

That afternoon Medina Sidonia sent off Alférez Juan Gil in a patache to Dunkirk with dispatches for Parma. He urgently wanted news of Parma's preparations, and the armada's big ships needed pilots who knew the coast of Flanders. He described the fight off Plymouth with the English fleet, which continued to dog the armada and harass its rear. He reckoned the English fleet had been reinforced to more than one hundred sail.[33]

Night came and a calm settled over the sea. The moon, three days past the first quarter, would set around two. Shortly after midnight Recalde, Leyva, and Oquendo hurried to the capitana real and urged Medina Sidonia to order Moncada's four galleasses to attack several English ships that sailed apart from the rest. Medina Sidonia concurred and sent Oquendo to Moncada with the promise of a rich commandery at home if Moncada succeeded in closing with them under the cover of darkness to provoke the kind of fight the Spaniards wanted. Moncada seemed agreeable but did nothing.[34]

Why? Perhaps he felt it was too dark, or perhaps it was something more. If indeed the Duke had denied his request of the morning before to attack the English flagship, he may have been smarting; or he may have resented being put under the orders of Leyva and Recalde in the force that protected the armada's rear. Though one of the accounts from the capitana real states simply that the wind came up and the sea turned rough, preventing Moncada from attacking, Medina Sidonia in

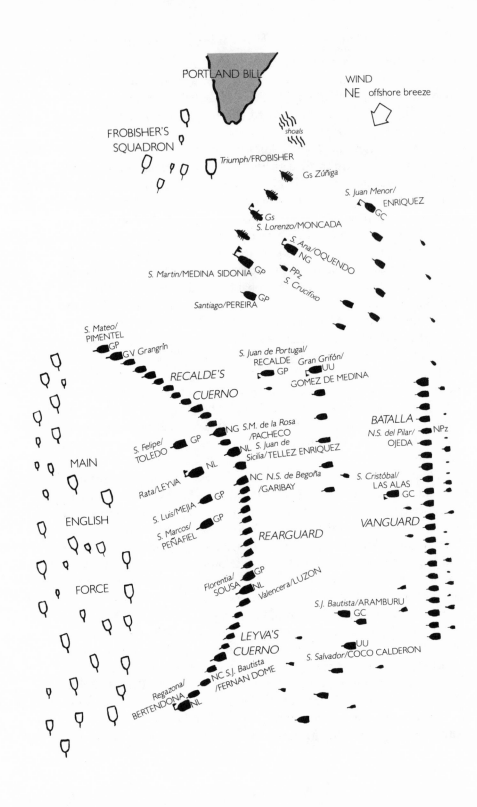

PORTLAND BILL

WIND
NE offshore breeze

FROBISHER'S
SQUADRON

shoals

Triumph/FROBISHER

Gs Zúñiga

S. Juan Menor/
ENRIQUEZ
GC

Gs
S. Lorenzo/MONCADA

S. Ana/OQUENDO
NG

S. Martin/MEDINA SIDONIA GP   PPz
S. Crucifixo

Santiago/PEREIRA GP

S. Mateo/
PIMENTEL
GP
GV Grangrin

RECALDE'S

S. Juan de Portugal/
RECALDE Gran Grifón/
GP   UU
GOMEZ DE MEDINA

CUERNO

NG S.M. de la Rosa
/PACHECO
S. Felipe/ GP
TOLEDO   NL S. Juan de
Sicilia/TELLEZ ENRIQUEZ

BATALLA
N.S. del Pilar/   NPz
OJEDA

Rata/LEYVA NL

NC N.S. de Begoña
/GARIBAY

S. Cristóbal/
LAS ALAS
GC

MAIN

S. Luis/MEJIA GP

S. Marcos/
PEÑAFIEL GP

VANGUARD

ENGLISH

REARGUARD

Florentia/ GP
SOUSA
Valencera/LUZON
NL

FORCE

S.J. Bautista/ARAMBURU
GC

LEYVA'S
CUERNO

UU
S. Salvador/COCO CALDERON

NC S.J. Bautista
/FERNAN DOME

Regazona/
BERTENDONA NL

a note to him later the same day expressed his disappointment that he had not done as expected; he then elaborated the need for a strong rearguard that included Moncada with three of his galleasses, which the Duke had assigned to it when he formed it the previous day.[35]

Waiting vainly on the galleasses, the Duke noticed with daybreak Tuesday that light breezes began to blow offshore to the armada's advantage. In the growing light he could see toward Portland Bill English ships working close inshore to regain the wind, though most of the English fleet remained well out to sea. San Martín was apart from the bulk of the armada and close to the four galleasses. Medina Sidonia decided to join the galleasses to deal with the English inshore and ordered the rest of the armada against the main part of the English fleet with the advantage of the offshore breeze. Pereira in Santiago accompanied Medina Sidonia; Peñafiel in San Marcos joined the rest (fig. 4).

Leyva's cuerno of the rearguard, closest to the English fleet, came about and bore down on them. Leyva in Rata and Bertendona in Regazona were quickly engaged, followed soon by the rest of the principal ships of the enlarged rearguard, including Recalde's almiranta, which had been repaired and had resumed its place at the tip of the inshore cuerno he commanded. The capitana and almiranta of the urcas from the socorros also joined the fighting. The ships of the batalla, which served as the armada's vanguard, were farther from the action and went in piecemeal as ordered by Medina Sidonia.

Medina Sidonia in San Martín, Pereira in Santiago, and the galleasses worked to close the English inshore group, which included their biggest galleon, Frobisher's Triumph. Unable to get past the Spaniards, they hung off Portland Bill. The Duke dispatched Gómez Pérez das Mariñas, Knight of Malta and soon to be Governor of the Philippines, to his fellow Knight Moncada to order the galleasses ahead to cut them off. Soon the galleasses' great sweeps flashed in the morning sunlight as they propelled the elegant warships toward the English vessels inshore. From the great galleon came a murderous barrage of fire. The galleasses checked and wheeled, the steady cadence of their oars broken by the splash and strike of roundshot. Moncada soon found he faced not only shot, but also shoals and treacherous tidal races.

As the morning drew on, the offshore northeast breeze faded, and a wind came up from the southeast, then veered to southwest, giving

Figure 4. Battle off Portland Bill, 2 August, early morning.

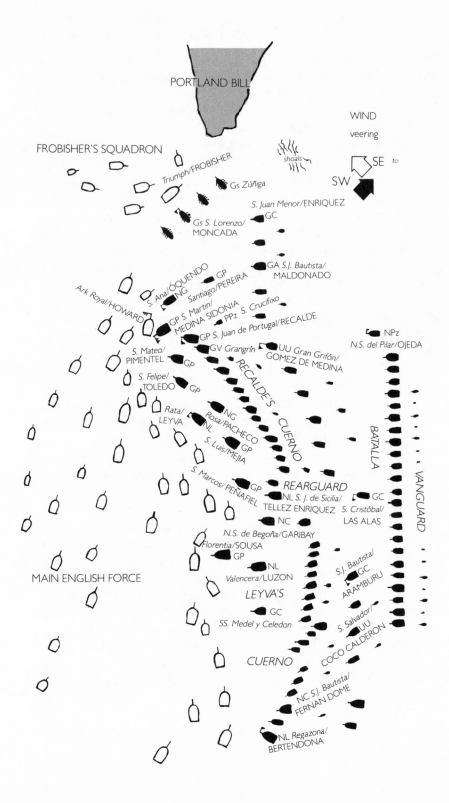

PORTLAND BILL

WIND
veering
SW SE to

shoals

FROBISHER'S SQUADRON

Triumph/FROBISHER

Gs Zúñiga

S. Juan Menor/ENRIQUEZ
GC

Gs S. Lorenzo/
MONCADA

GA S.J. Bautista/
MALDONADO

S. Ana/OQUENDO GP
NG
Santiago/PEREIRA

Ark Royal/HOWARD

GP S. Martin/
MEDINA SIDONIA
PPz S. Crucifixo
GP S. Juan de Portugal/RECALDE

NPz
N.S. del Pilar/OJEDA

S. Mateo/
PIMENTEL
GP

GV Grangrín
UU Gran Grifón/
GOMEZ DE MEDINA

S. Felipe/
TOLEDO
GP

Rata/
LEYVA
Rosa/PACHECO
NL
NG
GP

BATALLA

RECALDE'S CUERNO

S. Luis/MEJIA

S. Marcos/PEÑAFIEL
GP

REARGUARD
NL S. J. de Sicilia/
TELLEZ ENRIQUEZ
GC
S. Cristóbal/
LAS ALAS

NC

VANGUARD

N.S. de Begoña/GARIBAY
Florentia/SOUSA
GP
NL
Valencera/LUZON

S.J. Bautista/
GC
ARAMBURU

MAIN ENGLISH FORCE

LEYVA'S

GC
SS. Medel y Celedon

S. Salvador/
UU
COCO CALDERON

CUERNO

NC S.J. Bautista/
FERNAN DOME

NL Regazona/
BERTENDONA

again the weather gauge to the English. The Lord Admiral moved to assist Frobisher against the galleasses that dogged him but came against Recalde's *San Juan* almiranta at the inshore tip of the armada's rearguard. A furious fight erupted.

Medina Sidonia, hovering between the galleasses and the battle at the armada's rear, turned to the relief of Recalde and dispatched *San Martín*'s sea-captain Marolín in a felucca to order other ships of the batalla to follow him. Shortening sail as he drew near what he believed to be Howard's flagship, the Captain General of the Ocean-Sea invited the Lord Admiral of England to come to grips (fig. 5). The English stood off, their ships exchanging fire with *San Martín* in turn. The Duke claimed his guns had good effect, as the last English ships kept greater distance than the first. He took the battle from Recalde and for a moment stood alone. Warships from both the rearguard and batalla beat to his aid, headed by *San Marcos*, commanded by his cousin Peñafiel. Oquendo too barged into the fight.

It was late afternoon when the English Lord Admiral signaled his fleet to disengage. Medina Sidonia did not know the English were low on powder and shot, but rather felt sure they were receiving steady supplies from shore, even as his own dwindled. What he had still failed to do was provoke a fight at quarters close enough for boarding.

He ordered his ships to resume formation and continue their up-Channel voyage. The day's battle had begun at dawn and raged till nearly sundown. Roundshot had crashed against hulls, ripped through rigging, raked decks, and raised great geysers from the sea. Balls and bullets from swivel guns and muskets had peppered sails and railings and struck down men. Yet for all the roaring and blazing, for all the expenditure of powder and shot that astounded veterans of Lepanto and the Azores, casualties were few and damages hardly crippling. The English had not been able to sink armada vessels from afar with gunfire, as the Spaniards had feared. Gaining an anchorage at Spithead sheltered from foul weather by the Isle of Wight seemed more than ever possible.

When morning came, Medina Sidonia saw that the English trailed at a good distance, though from time to time they closed range to harass the armada with exchanges of fire. One exchange became furious as Juan Gómez de Medina's hulk *Gran Grifón*, flagship of Recalde's socorro, was cut off and pummeled by English gunfire. Medina may

Figure 5. Battle off Portland Bill, 2 August, midmorning.

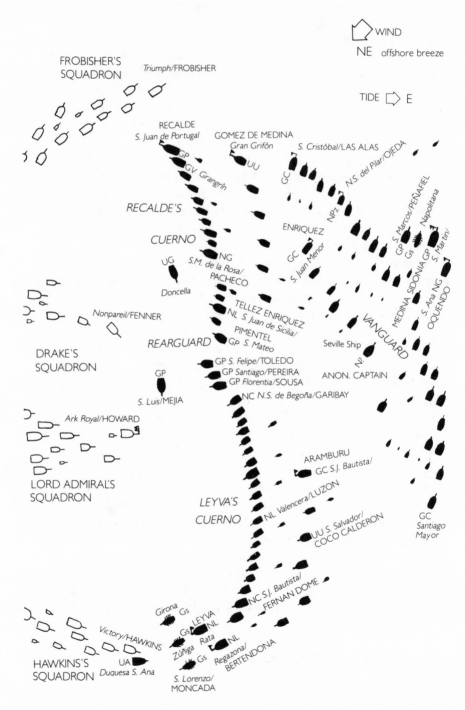

ISLE OF WIGHT

WIND
NE offshore breeze

TIDE E

FROBISHER'S
SQUADRON   Triumph/FROBISHER

RECALDE
S. Juan de Portugal   GOMEZ DE MEDINA   S. Cristóbal/LAS ALAS
Gran Grifón

GP   UU   GC   N.S. del Pilar/OJEDA   S. Marcos/PEÑAFIEL
GV Grangrin   NP²   Napolitana

RECALDE'S   ENRIQUEZ   GP Gs GP   S. Martin/

CUERNO   GC   S. Ana NG
UG   NG   S. Juan Menor   MEDINA SIDONIA   OQUENDO
S.M. de la Rosa/
PACHECO
Doncella
TELLEZ ENRIQUEZ   VANGUARD
NL S. Juan de Sicilia/   Seville Ship
Nonpareil/FENNER   PIMENTEL   Nº
GP S. Mateo
REARGUARD   ANON. CAPTAIN
DRAKE'S   GP S. Felipe/TOLEDO
SQUADRON   GP   GP Santiago/PEREIRA
GP Florentia/SOUSA
S. Luis/MEJIA   NC N.S. de Begoña/GARIBAY

Ark Royal/HOWARD

ARAMBURU
GC S.J. Bautista/
LORD ADMIRAL'S
SQUADRON
LEYVA'S   NL Valencera/LUZON
CUERNO   UU S. Salvador/   GC
COCO CALDERON   Santiago
Mayor

NC S.J. Bautista/
FERNAN DOME
Girona Gs   LEYVA
Victory/HAWKINS   Gs   NL
Zúñiga Rata   NL
HAWKINS'S   UA   Gs   Regazona/
SQUADRON   Duquesa S. Ana   BERTENDONA
S. Lorenzo/
MONCADA

have made a deliberate effort to tempt the English to grapple. Spanish ships, including Medina Sidonia's capitana real, swarmed to his relief, and the galleasses shot the *entena del arbol mayor*, either the main yard or top-mainmast, off what they thought was the English flagship but probably was Drake's *Revenge*.[36] The English withdrew. When the day of desultory fighting ended, Vanegas calculated that both fleets had expended some five thousand rounds of shot.

Medina Sidonia returned in the capitana real to his station at the head of the armada. He appointed Don Diego Enríquez, son of the former Viceroy of Peru, as chief of the Andalusian squadron and the batalla's socorro that Don Pedro de Valdés had commanded. Sailing in *San Juan el Menor* of the Castilian squadron, Enríquez, who seems to have been a fine seaman, had so far been in the thick of the combat.

The next day, 4 August, was the feast of St. Dominic de Guzmán, Medina Sidonia's family's saint. He was nearing the Isle of Wight and needed at least to keep the English at bay till he gained the anchorage at Spithead. He might even inflict a defeat on them, which would prove even more useful. He summoned his council of war to make plans and sent a sergeant major in a pinnace round the armada to advise all captains to keep station and do their duty under pain of death.[37] He had not forgot the confusion of part of Recalde's cuerno in the first day's battle.

Having seen that day an opportunity to close and grapple elude him, and another the day before when Gómez de Medina was surrounded and an English galleon's maintop felled, Medina Sidonia decided to bait a trap.

When morning came on Thursday, 4 August, the armada held its course toward the Isle of Wight, while two or three vessels were left to drift behind. Named were the urca *Duquesa Santa Ana*, which bore the name of Medina Sidonia's revered grandmother,[38] and had been sailing with Recalde's rearguard; the Portuguese galleon *San Luis*, Maestre de Campo Agustín Mejía aboard, and the urca *Doncella* of Oquendo's squadron. However many and whichever they were, they were meant to serve as bait.[39] The principal straggler all agree was *Duquesa*. From the battle that followed, it would seem that Medina Sidonia's intention was for the English to grapple with *Duquesa*, then for Leyva and the galleasses to go to her rescue. Leyva, a former galley general, would

Figure 6. Battle off the Isle of Wight, 4 August, early morning.

know how to use the oared warships. If the desired mêlée ensued, the entire armada would enter the fight; if it did not, he could spearhead entry to Spithead with the fighting ships under his command while Recalde and Leyva held the English fleet at bay.

In preparing for battle, he may have modified the armada's fighting order in line with the recommendation of Pedro de Valdés to concentrate only the better-gunned and more maneuverable ships in the rearguard and vanguard and keep what Valdés called the useless ships apart.

The morning was still, the sea flat. During the night the English had formed their fleet into four squadrons and continued to dog the armada's wake.[40] The ships of the closest squadron—it was John Hawkins's—spotted the straggling *Duquesa Santa Ana*, lowered boats into the water, and under tow began to edge toward her. Aboard the straggler 280 soldiers and a knot of gentlemen adventurers waited. The English appeared to be taking the bait. As they neared her, they opened fire.

Leyva lost no time in responding. He signaled the three galleasses that sailed with the rearguard to head for the beleaguered urca; one took his *Rata* in tow. The galleasses' forecastle guns roared. The remainder of his cuerno followed him, joined by *San Juan de Sicilia*, while more English ships moved to Hawkins's aid (fig. 6). *San Luis*, like *Duquesa Santa Ana* sailing alone, was soon engaged as the English began to put pressure also on Recalde's cuerno, which became the hinge of the day's fighting.

As the battle engulfed Leyva's cuerno and spread to Recalde's, Medina Sidonia saw that another English squadron—it was Martin Frobisher's—had used inshore currents to work past the armada's landward flank and had turned toward him, guns ablaze. The tall galleon from the day before was in the lead. Mistakenly he thought it the Lord Admiral's flagship. When they reached point-blank range, the English opened fire with the big guns of their lowest decks: a shot nicked *San Martín*'s mainmast and killed several soldiers aboard.

With ships from the batalla's socorro Don Diego Enríquez moved against the trailing ships of the upwind English squadron, while Gregorio de las Alas in *San Cristóbal* of Castile and Oquendo in *Santa Ana*, both close astern of Medina Sidonia, closed the towering English galleon. Medina Sidonia believed he might overwhelm Frobisher's squadron and push into Spithead.

San Martín pressed ahead and for a moment stood alone among the enemy. Oquendo soon reached her and drew fire away from his commander-in-chief. As more Spanish ships swarmed into action, the tall English galleon became separated from its squadron and appeared disabled by the furious cannonade. Eleven skiffs worked frantically to tow her clear. The shooting reached musket range and the chance to board seemed near. Medina Sidonia watched the distance to his prey narrow.

Recalde, who believed he had repulsed the English attacking him, headed toward Enríquez to help overwhelm the isolated English squadron. Other ships of his cuerno followed. Medina Sidonia thought the big English galleon had been abandoned by her squadron, which appeared to turn tail. To the captain of a Seville ship, embargoed by the Duke in 1587, it looked like the English fleet had become divided in two and victory lay in the Spaniards' grasp.[41]

As the sun rose higher the winds stiffened and veered in favor of the English. According to the Seville captain, what appeared to him the English flagship (which he thought had withdrawn from the fray) came about and furiously attacked the galleon *San Mateo* where Recalde's cuerno met Leyva's. Sir Julian Corbett in *Drake and the Tudor Navy* decided it had to have been Drake, who is given no mention in the English accounts of the day's fighting. Most historians since have accepted his theory. But Drake was probably out of action, making temporary repairs to his damaged mainmast and rigging.[42]

Hit hard, *San Mateo* gave way and fell back among her crowded fellows. More English ships returned to the fight, guns reloaded. Along the whole of the armada's front action intensified. An observer aboard the galleass *Zúñiga* described the English formation as a half-moon, in other words, a lúnula.[43] The armada ships facing them had come to form an extended arc, from the capitanas of Medina Sidonia and Oquendo south of Wight to Leyva's seaward cuerno. As *San Mateo* reeled, the armada's front began to buckle: the Seville captain feared they would be cornered and destroyed (fig. 7).

The rising wind permitted the English flagship Medina Sidonia had hounded to put on canvas and rapidly pull away. As it sailed clean round the armada, two ships regarded as the armada's fastest, the Levantine greatship *San Juan Bautista*, of Fernán Dome, and another took off in pursuit. Watching them, Contador Coco Calderón thought they seemed at anchor by comparison to the English galleon.

Medina Sidonia had no time to worry about his escaped prey: he had to bring *San Martín* round to keep his buckling front from break-

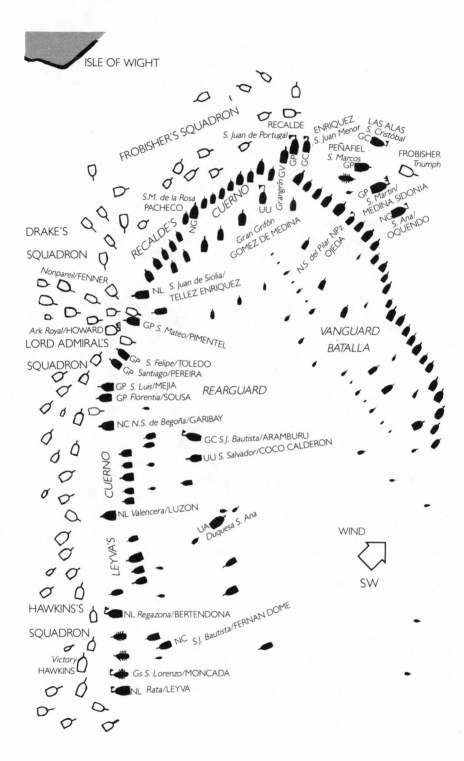

ISLE OF WIGHT

FROBISHER'S SQUADRON

RECALDE
S. Juan de Portugal
ENRIQUEZ
S. Juan Menor
LAS ALAS
S. Cristóbal
GC
PEÑAFIEL
S. Marcos
GP
FROBISHER
Triumph

S.M. de la Rosa
PACHECO
CUERNO
UU
Grangrín GV
GP
GC

GP
S. Martin/
MEDINA SIDONIA
NG
S. Ana/
OQUENDO

DRAKE'S

SQUADRON

RECALDE'S
NG
Gran Grifón
GOMEZ DE MEDINA

N.S. del Pilar NPz
OJEDA

Nonpareil/FENNER

NL S. Juan de Sicilia/
TELLEZ ENRIQUEZ

VANGUARD
BATALLA

Ark Royal/HOWARD

GP S. Mateo/PIMENTEL

LORD ADMIRAL'S

SQUADRON

GP S. Felipe/TOLEDO
Gp Santiago/PEREIRA

REARGUARD

GP S. Luis/MEJIA
GP Florentia/SOUSA

NC N.S. de Begoña/GARIBAY

GC S.J. Bautista/ARAMBURU
UU S. Salvador/COCO CALDERON

CUERNO

NL Valencera/LUZON

UA
Duquesa S. Ana

WIND

SW

LEYVA'S

HAWKINS'S

NL Regazona/BERTENDONA

SQUADRON

NC S.J. Bautista/FERNAN DOME

Victory
HAWKINS

Gs S. Lorenzo/MONCADA

NL Rata/LEYVA

ing. Fighting hard, he and the ships that followed him prevented a collapse—but in doing so he had to abandon his effort to enter Spithead.

In late morning the English, with the advantage of the wind, chose to break off the main action. From their point of view they had done what they had to do, prevent Medina Sidonia from gaining the shelter of Spithead. Even though the armada remained close, the flow of tide made entry out of the question until late in the day. Medina Sidonia knew it and ordered the armada to resume formation. The English fleet stood some distance off, between the armada and the Isle of Wight.

Figure 7. Battle off the Isle of Wight, 4 August, late morning.

✳ CHAPTER NINE ✳

The Armada Campaign: Calais to Santander

O N the afternoon of 4 August, Medina Sidonia was still in view of the Isle of Wight and perhaps retained some hope of yet gaining the anchorage he sought. He drafted a dispatch for the Duke of Parma and sent it off with Captain Pedro de León. He had as yet received no news from Parma and could not know that Parma had dispatched ships to find him, one of which carried Captain Moresin; or that Captain Rodrigo Tello had reached Parma's headquarters at Bruges two days before.

To Parma Medina Sidonia expressed his frustration: "The enemy has resolutely avoided coming to close quarters with our ships, although I have tried my hardest to make him do so. I have given him so many opportunities that sometimes some of our vessels have been in the very midst of the enemy's fleet, to induce one of his ships to grapple and begin the fight; but all to no purpose, as his ships are very agile and mine very ponderous, and he has plenty of men and stores."[1] Medina Sidonia found his own stores dwindling, especially powder and roundshot of ten, six, and four pounds. He begged Parma to find all he could and send it to the armada.

The wind at some time fell off. The night was still. Slowly the armada drifted on the tides and currents. When morning came, the Isle of Wight had disappeared from view, and the armada and the English fleet lay becalmed in sight of one another. When the winds came up, Medina Sidonia set course for Calais Roads, an unsatisfactory anchorage open to wind and tide, where he would have to anchor while he determined what Parma was doing at Dunkirk and Nieuwpoort.

From the letter Medina Sidonia sent Parma with Captain León, he appears to have decided to seek battle whenever he could rather than avoid it as the King had preferred. That seems his practice from the day off Plymouth onward, however much his official log gives the impression that the armada proceeded inexorably toward its rendezvous, fighting only as forced to by the English until he reached the point of "joining hands" with Parma. But Parma's passage across the Narrows would have proved so much more simple had the armada inflicted a serious defeat on the English fleet, which would have required that they come to close quarters. He admitted to Parma that he had deliberately baited the English, though in vain; yet in his official account he only mentioned stragglers and, in the case of the opening battle, hinted that Recalde had been abandoned by his cuerno.

Neither in the official account did he mention his effort to gain shelter in the lee of the Isle of Wight. There, even had he not yet defeated the English, he at least would have had some advance knowledge of Parma's state of readiness and control over the timing of the rendezvous. But the King's instructions had not provided for any delay at Wight and had clearly forbidden trying to seize it until Medina Sidonia had met Parma.

When was the official account compiled? It was dispatched to Spain on 21 August and was for the King's eyes. There were no sacrosanct logbooks then,[2] and while there would have been a daily journal, the account Medina Sidonia sent the King may well have been wholly drafted after the armada had been herded across the North Sea and turned for home. It made the armada's defeat appear to result from dutiful compliance with the King's orders, despite the heroic fight put up by the Duke and his principal officers. The armada had proceeded unswervingly as ordered to its intended rendezvous.

As the armada neared the rendezvous, a climactic battle had become inevitable. The King had never denied that battle might finally be necessary. Medina Sidonia decided to ask Parma, surely after consulting with his principal officers, to send him forty nimble, well-armed, and well-manned flyboats to assist the armada's ungainly ships to come to grips with the English. He sent the request off Friday in the hands of the pilot Domingo Ochoa, who was well suited to explain the problems.

When the armada reached Calais Saturday afternoon at four (fig. 8), Medina Sidonia landed his secretary Gerónimo de Arceo with the same request couched in more urgent language. He could hold the armada at Calais only for a short time and at great risk. "The enemy's fleet [is] on my flank and able to bombard me, whilst I am not in a

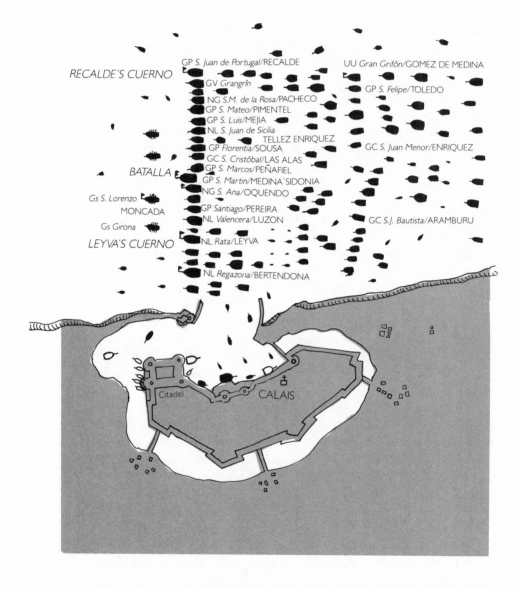

Figure 8. Projected order of the armada at Calais, 7 August.

position to do him much harm."[3] For the Enterprise to succeed, Parma had to send him the flyboats, and his people at Dunkirk and Nieuwpoort had to be embarked and ready to make sail.

Some armada officers did not want even to anchor at Calais. The fighting in the Channel and the failure to find a port convinced them the campaign was already lost, and they urged Medina Sidonia to continue into the North Sea and return to Spain. The course had been plotted already. Medina Sidonia flatly rejected their suggestion and ordered the armada to anchor.[4]

Sunday morning after daybreak a pinnace running before gunfire— it was not certain whether the shooting came from the English or the armada—brought Captain Rodrigo Tello from Dunkirk with the first news of Parma Medina Sidonia had received since leaving La Coruña. Tello had reached Dunkirk and visited Parma at Bruges on 2 August. He stated that his report of the armada's approach had pleased Parma. Tello returned to Dunkirk, but when he boarded ship to depart for Calais Saturday night, Parma had not yet arrived at Dunkirk nor had the assembled troops or requested munitions been embarked.

Medina Sidonia in the meantime sent supply officers ashore to obtain what supplies and munitions he might from the French. The French Governor of Calais proved civil and sent his nephew to visit the Duke aboard the capitana real with a basket of fruit. The French agreed to provide the armada with food and water but proved reluctant regarding munitions.

After conferring with his generals about Tello's report, Medina Sidonia drafted another dispatch for Parma and sent it with his Veedor General Don Jorge Manrique in person to impress upon Parma the danger of the armada's situation and the need for swift action. The English fleet that the Spaniards reckoned to number between 100 and 120 sail had been joined by the Dover Squadron of 38 (which they mistakenly believed Hawkins commanded), giving the enemy a total of 140 to 160 vessels great and small. How many Medina Sidonia had at this point is not clear, but probably close to 130. The armada's 15 to 20 caravels and falúas, save for the falúa that Marolín de Juan used to relay orders off Plymouth and another that carried Domingo de Ochoa to Parma, received no mention apart from the Lisbon and La Coruña rosters.

The armada commanders agreed to hold their ships at Calais as long as they could, which would not be for long. If Parma was not ready, they either had to find an adequate port or return to Spain.

Finding a port had become the chief priority of the campaign no matter what the King's original orders were. What they wanted was Parma's assistance in seizing the Isle of Wight.[5] They needed his flyboats and they needed men. In effect they wanted to change the whole plan for the invasion of England, from a landing on the coast south of Margate to a landing on Wight.

Parma was still at Bruges, trying to cope with Medina Sidonia's ever more urgent requests for pilots, powder, and shot and the prompt embarkation of the invasion force for their rendezvous with the armada. He drafted a letter to the King to give his side of the story.[6] He had received between 2 and 7 August the messages carried by Tello, Alférez Juan Gil, León, and the pilot Ochoa, copies of which he enclosed. He insisted that when Gil arrived he had sent his transport craft to where the troops would embark, but that there was no use embarking them in such cramped and open craft until they were on the verge of sailing. But Medina Sidonia, Parma continued, was mistaken to believe that the shipping he had collected could sail against opposition or in rough seas. While he planned a feint by the ships he had in Antwerp to draw at least some Dutch vessels back to cover Flushing, the waters off Dunkirk and Nieuwpoort were too closely guarded by their enemies for his barges to put to sea.

What Medina Sidonia had long feared was now reality. The armada had arrived off the Flemish coast without defeating the English or finding secure haven, and until the seas had been cleared of the English and Dutch, Parma's army could not cross the Narrows. Most of Parma's flyboats, the vessels Medina Sidonia wanted, were apparently with the flotilla bottled up at Antwerp, although reports claimed that at least twenty-eight more lay at Dunkirk; for whatever reason they were not ready for sea, or, as later claimed, their masters were unwilling to leave port.[7] Thus, even had the armada inflicted a defeat on the English and gained temporary control of the Narrows, its principal fighting ships drew too much water to escort what shipping Parma had assembled for his invasion army through the Dutch blockade. It was for this reason above all that the armada commanders had wanted at least a dozen shallow draft galleys, to escort the invasion flotilla and support its landing with close gunfire.[8] Though repeatedly told by Madrid that Parma's shallow draft flyboats could perform that task, they remained unconvinced, and they could only have found it a dreadful misfortune that unusually heavy seas had forced the four galleys the armada did get to return to Spain; galleys had on other occasions made the same voyage and had also crossed the Atlantic. The Spaniards did not mention using the galleasses as escort. Galleasses were also relatively shallow draft vessels and had supported landings in the Azores. But galleasses were neither as fast nor as maneuverable under oar as galleys, and in the armada campaign were probably regarded as too important in the battle line. The only other suitable vessels with the armada were the pataches and zabras, but they had not been adequately armed to deal with well-gunned Dutch flyboats of 80 to 160 tons.[9]

While the tone of his letters to Parma remained polite, Medina Sidonia could only fret and feel frustrated as he waited aboard *San Martín* off Calais for further reports. That evening around ten he received another, from his secretary Arceo, that stated Parma was still at Bruges and matters at Dunkirk appeared even worse than Tello had suggested. Arceo did not believe Parma would have his people embarked and ready to sail in fewer than fifteen days, though with the help of Pedro López de Soto, who had acted as Medina Sidonia's secretary during the Larache episode, he did obtain Parma's agreement to expedite the powder and shot Medina Sidonia had requested.

Soto had already heard that both sides had fired more than thirty thousand cannonballs and noted that Parma had collected fifteen hundred quintals of powder and five thousand balls for the armada. He looked forward to the meeting of Parma and Medina Sidonia, which he believed would prove cordial, aided by the good offices of the Duke of Pastrana.[10] "God give us fifteen days of calm weather to do what we must, for without it things will be most difficult." Had Soto perhaps said this aloud to Arceo, who misunderstood fifteen days of calm—which Soto seemed to imply was necessary for the Channel crossing and landings—for fifteen days for Parma's troops to embark? Most in fact were embarked by 9 August.

Medina Sidonia, in sending Manrique to Parma, had sent a nobleman of distinguished lineage and the senior administrative officer of the armada. He had to know exactly where Parma stood and make sure Parma embarked his people in all possible haste. Manrique if anyone could get the intelligence Medina Sidonia needed.

However much disturbed about the progress of Parma's preparations, Medina Sidonia immediately had to prepare the armada to fend off a likely attack by fireships. All day the English had seemed up to something. He ordered stout picket boats to take up station to seaward of the armada's vessels anchored in the open roads.

Around midnight, carried by flowing tides and favorable winds, eight incoming fireships appeared from the direction of the English fleet, larger ships than had apparently been expected. The boats posted to fend them off had little luck, and when loaded guns and fireworks aboard the blazing vessels began exploding, they abandoned the effort. Watching the floating infernos bear down on the anchored armada and fearing they might be infernal machines, set to explode like the terrible "Hellburner of Antwerp" that three years earlier blew up a bridge crowded with Parma's soldiers and guns, Medina Sidonia ordered all ships to weigh anchor and get clear. When it was safe to do so, the ships were to return to the anchorage.

With the fireships approaching, the armada's ships got under way in confusion and disorder approaching panic. Rather than weigh anchors, most cut or slipped cables, leaving their anchors behind. The capitana real had some difficulty because other ships were to her windward, while the capitana of the galleasses ran afoul of *San Juan de Sicilia*, and her luckless rudder became entangled with a cable.[11] Yet all ships got clear and the fireships drifted ashore without exploding or doing any direct damage to the armada. Medina Sidonia fired a signal gun to order his ships to return to port, and the capitana real and several ships nearby came round to reenter the anchorage. The other ships continued to drift in the direction of Dunkirk. Medina Sidonia decided to go after them. In the confusion the Prince of Ascoli, who had gone ashore, was left behind, while five pataches remained at Calais and later headed back to Spain.[12]

At dawn Monday the Duke, aboard *San Martín*, stood two leagues off Calais on a northerly course. The armada had cleared the roadstead save for the crippled galleass capitana, which ran for the protection of the French forts.[13] The rest of its ships lay strung out on a northeasterly course offshore from Gravelines. Close by the Duke were Recalde in *San Juan* and two galleasses.

The English fleet had followed the armada closely: Medina Sidonia estimated their number at 136 sail. At eight in the morning they opened fire. *San Martín* was soon surrounded, exchanging shot with what seemed the whole English fleet. Captain Vanegas at one time counted 17 English ships to port and 7 to starboard. The Duke later charged that most of his captains except for the squadron generals and maestres de campo had virtually abandoned him.[14]

The first to succor him was his cousin the Marquis of Peñafiel, who brought *San Marcos* to his aid. A dozen other armada warships soon came about and were hotly engaged, including Recalde's, Leyva's, and

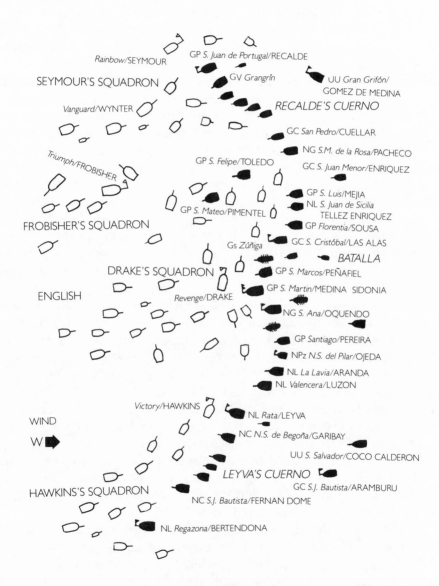

Figure 9. Battle off Gravelines, 8 August. Armada reforms its battle formation.

Oquendo's. Slowly round the capitana real the armada's fighting ships recovered a semblance of their battle formation (fig. 9), though Medina Sidonia claimed that the smoke was so thick he could not see more than two of his own ships at a time. One English officer reckoned they faced some 32 armada ships, 16 to a wing.[15] The range between them shrunk to within arquebus range, some claimed within reach of pike. Men could challenge, shout, and curse between ships through the thick, all-enveloping gunsmoke, but no armada ship succeeded in grappling an enemy.

In previous engagements those aboard the armada believed that they had done the English serious damage; off Gravelines Medina Sidonia complained that the English "had the advantage of artillery, we only in the fire of muskets and arquebuses." For the first time the range was so close that each side could see the damage done the other. *San Martín*, according to Captain Vanegas, fired 300 rounds from her forty-eight guns in the course of the long day, but he says nothing about their effect. If the action can be reckoned at six hours, *San Martín* fired barely a round per gun per hour. She suffered, Vanegas stated, 107 hits from cannot shot in her hull, masts, and sails, and that shot aimed at her waterline penetrated her thick timbers, causing serious leaks that strained her pumps. A padre aboard claimed a fifty-pound ball passed clean through her hull despite her sides being seven planks thick.[16]

The galleon *San Felipe*, Maestre de Campo Toledo in command, worked past Recalde's hard-pressed cuerno and drove into a swarm of English ships. Maestre de Campo Pimentel soon had beside her his *San Mateo*, the galleon that had precipitated the action at close quarters at San Miguel. Toledo and Pimentel wanted to provoke such an action again, and Toledo, according to Coco Calderón, ordered out the grappling irons and taunted the English to board him. The Seville captain who wrote that *San Mateo* had given way off Wight and cost the battle noted that she tried now to make amends for her previous shortcoming.

The English stood clear and blasted the two galleons with gunfire. No ships took a more terrible beating. Recalde in *San Juan de Portugal* and Mejía in *San Luis*, which usually worked closely with *San Felipe*, had to extricate Toledo and Pimentel.

Late in the afternoon a sudden squall interrupted the fighting, and afterward the battle subsided as the English disengaged. According to Vanegas, the armada lost six hundred men killed and eight hundred wounded. Medina Sidonia wanted to pursue the English, but his pilots warned him he could not succeed against the strong currents and stiff winds, now blowing from the northwest. It would be best, they claimed, to gain the more open waters of the North Sea.

In assessing the day's combat, the Duke soon learned that his chief fighting ships ran low on powder and shot, and that *San Mateo* and *San Felipe* seemed close to sinking. Medina Sidonia sent to their relief pataches and an urca, which removed most of the survivors, but the two maestres de campo, infantry colonels true to the custom of the sea, stayed with their galleons and steered them toward the Flemish shore.[17]

During the night the wind stiffened, impeding the armada's progress north. When the winds lessened at dawn, they left the armada dangerously close to the Zeeland Banks. The Duke, with Recalde, Levya, and others of the rearguard, and the three galleasses, sailed a half league from the trailing English fleet. He reckoned them at 109 sail. He sent the three galleasses at them, guns ablaze, and noticed that the English fell off. He could not have known they were running short of ammunition.

He signaled the rest of the armada sailing ahead to keep formation and sent a pinnace to warn them of the Zeeland Banks and the need to luff close-hauled to the wind in order to clear them. But wind and current combined to edge the armada ever closer to the shoals. *San Martín*'s leadsman called seven fathoms, and the pilots warned that only a miracle could save the armada. Some on the quarterdeck talked surrender or abandoning ship, but the Duke and Bobadilla remained confident that "Our Lord and His most glorious Mother" would see them through. The leadsman called six and a half fathoms; *San Martín* likely drew close to five.

According to Coco Calderón, Oquendo's capitana drew alongside the capitana real, and Medina Sidonia shouted, "Señor Oquendo, what shall we do! We are lost!" "Ask Diego Flores," Oquendo retorted. "I shall fight and die like a good man. Send me more roundshot." Medina Sidonia must have taken Oquendo's remark with some humor, because he sent him eighty rounds. Harsher exchanges between the two and between the Duke and Leyva appear in Padre Victoria's less-than-reliable account.[18]

By midmorning, according to Vanegas, the lead marked six fathoms and disaster appeared unavoidable. Then the miracle they prayed for occurred. The wind veered west-southwest, and the armada was able to pull clear of danger.

That afternoon Medina Sidonia called his generals to a council of war to decide what to do next. The English fleet still dogged them. The

Duke's account suggests that he presented the state of the armada, remarked that all the ships that had borne the brunt of the fighting lacked shot, and asked them whether they ought to return to the English Channel or return by way of the North Sea to Spain. Vanegas added that Parma's unpreparedness was also mentioned. Medina Sidonia did not describe the discussion, but other fairly reliable witnesses did. Leyva apparently expressed his frustration at not being able to bring the English to close quarters and stated that his ship was thoroughly battered and had only thirty rounds of shot left, but despite all, he would not fail to do his duty. Recalde suggested holding the armada where it was until the weather permitted their return to Calais.

"There was not lacking," Vanegas continued, "someone who said that it was no time to talk of derring-do [*bizarrías*], but rather of His Majesty's service. How did they think they could cope with the enemy's attacks for three days without enough ammunition?" That someone was probably Diego Flores, about whom the official account remarked laconically after reporting the meeting, "In matters pertaining to the armada and the sea the Duke followed the opinion of the General Diego Flores." Yet according to the Contador Coco Calderón, Diego Flores thought the armada should return to Calais if it could.

Some suggested wintering in Norway, but the Duke objected. Norway he regarded as enemy territory. It was ruled by the King of Denmark, a Protestant ally of England. What seemed to him much more important was not to leave Spain undefended by sea with the English fleet at large. Medina Sidonia could hardly have forgotten Drake's raids in 1585–86 and 1587. Other ports the council may have considered, such as Emden, Enkhuizen, Hamburg, or even Antwerp, would have been ruled out for like reasons.

The participants in the council agreed finally to obey the dictates of wind and weather. If the armada could return to the Channel and Calais, it would; if not, it would sail round Scotland and Ireland and head for Spain. Neither choice was appealing on serious reflection. Even with ammunition redistributed so that the principal fighting ships had some powder and shot, they knew they did not have enough for another all-day fight. At the same time they had discovered that even at close quarters they had been unable to grapple English ships, while they had suffered serious damage and heavy casualties from English gunfire at that range and seen one ship sink and two powerful galleons forced to run for shore. Yet the expressed willingness of the Duke and most of the armada's generals to continue the fight, however suicidal, was more than a statement for the record: it was a willingness rooted in their chivalric values.

With chivalric impulsiveness Medina Sidonia was willing the next day, Wednesday, to risk battle once more. It was the feast of St. Lawrence, the occasion in 1557 of a great victory over the French by Philip II's armies, which included six thousand English. The morning winds blew strong and the sea was choppy, but in the afternoon the wind subsided and the trailing English fleet appeared to close Recalde's rear guard. The Duke brought the capitana real round to join Recalde and ordered the armada to shorten sail and stand by to support them. He arrayed his galleasses and another dozen good ships in line to fight. The English appeared to haul up; no shots were exchanged.

In what must have been a mix of frustration and disappointment, Medina Sidonia then convened a court martial with Bobadilla. All the armada's ships had not responded to his order to shorten sail, and he decided to punish those who failed. He was still smarting from what he perceived to be the failure of many captains to support him and engage the enemy off Gravelines. They did not seem to share the chivalric impulses of the Duke and their generals and had seemed more eager to return to Spain.[19] The differences between what were called valor and prudence created bitterness and led to recriminations among the armada's officers.

When one captain tried to explain why he had not obeyed the order, Medina Sidonia retorted, "Hang the traitor!"[20] Twenty arrests were made of derelict commanding officers, several were condemned to the galleys and two to death. One was Captain Cuellar, who won a reprieve;[21] the other was an urca captain from Puerto Santa Maria, who was executed. Hanging from the yardarm of a patache, the corpse was paraded through the armada as a warning.

When the business of the court martial was done, Medina Sidonia withdrew to his cabin, still upset, according to Cuellar, over the armada's failures at Gravelines and since and the loss of the galleons of Pimentel and Toledo.

The route the armada would follow for a return to Spain round Scotland and Ireland was settled by Medina Sidonia and his pilots: they would proceed to 61°30' north, round the Shetlands, take a southwest course to well west of Ireland, then come to a southeast course to La Coruña. With that long voyage increasingly likely, Medina Sidonia ordered rations shortened for all hands and had some forty horses and forty mules thrown overboard to save water. The English continued trailing the armada to the middle of the North Sea, about 55° north latitude; the Spaniards' sounding of nine fathoms put them over the Dogger Bank. There on 12 August the English fleet disappeared. The armada was far at sea and had made no move toward Edinburgh.[22]

The account of the voyage Medina Sidonia sent to the King on 21 August tells little of what happened after the English were lost from sight. Others offer more detail and sometimes vivid description of the storms that plagued the armada as it struggled toward Spain.

The Contador Coco Calderón aboard the urca almiranta stated that the armada broke into smaller divisions because of foul weather and heavy seas that persisted from 13 till 18 August. At 58° north the weather improved and the winds shifted to northeasterly. Medina Sidonia consulted his pilots and decided to take the armada between the Orkneys and Shetlands. By 21 August he had cleared Fair Island passage and still at 58° prepared to take the southwesterly course. He sent ahead in a patache Don Baltasar de Zúñiga, brother-in-law of his cousin the Count of Olivares, to carry dispatches and an account of the campaign to the King in Spain.[23]

Medina Sidonia informed the King of the sorry state of the armada and asserted that "the best service I can do Your Majesty is to save it." Its defeat he attributed to the better-gunned and swifter ships of the Queen. Aboard were three thousand sick in addition to many wounded. He urged the King to have Andrés de Alva collect the necessary stores and victuals at La Coruña and request the bishops of Galicia to prepare to assist with the infirm. He related what he had heard at Calais of the four galleys and Recalde's *Santa Ana*, that they were in French ports, and asked the King to inform Parma of what had happened, since he had not been able to contact him.

On 24 August Coco Calderón boarded the capitana real to confer with Medina Sidonia and Diego Flores. His urca had sailed for a while with Recalde's group, lost them in squalls and fog, then rejoined the real on the twenty-second. A French pilot the Contador had recommended spread out a chart and indicated that they had the Faroes to the north at 62°30′ and Ireland to the south at 55°. All agreed that they had to give wide berth to the rugged Irish west coast. Medina Sidonia promised the pilot a 2,000 ducat reward if they safely reached Spain.

They discussed the number of wounded and sick aboard *San Martín*, and what do with them. The Contador offered Medina Sidonia victuals and rice from his own stores. Medina Sidonia ordered him to issue them to all ships that carried sick and wounded. At some point

Medina Sidonia brought his cousin Peñafiel and Peñafiel's uncle, Don Alonso Téllez Girón, aboard the real, and they survived the voyage, though *San Marcos*, which Peñafiel had commanded through all the fights, was wrecked in Ireland.[24]

The same day the weather worsened again, with strong winds rising from the southeast. Under darkening skies the armada could make no progress. Storms raged for days on end, and in the heavy seas some ships were scattered as far as 62° north. Padre Góngora, who had come from the *Rosario* with no more than the clothes on his back, suffered in the cold. Medina Sidonia gave him one of his own cloaks. When the storms abated the ships regrouped.

On 3 September, two days after this thirty-ninth birthday, Medina Sidonia counted ninety-five sail, with seventeen missing, including the ships of Recalde and Leyva and others of the armada's best. The armada still stood at 58° north, but the winds had turned favorable, and the Duke hoped for a prosperous southerly voyage. He was concerned for the sick and wounded. Men died daily, including relatives and friends of the Duke. In his cabin both Don Pedro de Zúñiga, the young heir of the Marquis of Aguilafuente, and Don Lorenzo de Mendoza, son of the Count of Orgaz, died within four days of each other.[25] Blacks and mulattos suffered particularly in the harsh northern cold, Captain Vanegas noted. In a report to the King Medina Sidonia concluded, "May Our Lord in His mercy give us fair weather so that we soon make port. This armada goes so short of food that if it be delayed because of our sins, all shall be lost without hope of remedy."[26]

The fair weather did not last in that extraordinary late summer.[27] On 6 September the weather turned foul again. Padre de la Torre's pen described

> great storms on that restless and ever-agitated sea which the human body could scarce survive. Constant tempests and wild waves made a restful night impossible because of the uncontrolled pitching of the ship, and so much worse did they become that I was not alone in losing hope of seeing land again. We expected the mainmast to tumble down or the ship to roll over. Once the lateen yard was half underwater. Blessed be God that He saved us from such dangers, for the ship was coming apart in so many places that it was necessary to bind the hull with three large hemp lines.

After two tempestuous days the weather began to improve. Medina Sidonia counted sixty ships with him on 10 September. Two days later another storm hit and raged through the thirteenth. When it passed, the armada resumed course and reached 45° north, perhaps one hundred miles from La Coruña. Then on the nineteenth a fresh storm broke. The Duke feared all was lost, but it subsided on 21 September. Eleven ships were still in company with *San Martín*. The pilots reckoned they stood at 43°30' north, the latitude of Cape Finisterre, and with westerly winds sailed east till later that morning they sighted what they thought was the Isle of Sisarga in the Gulf of La Coruña. But one of the accompanying caravels had run closer to shore and came out to inform them they stood off Santander. Because of contrary winds and currents, Medina Sidonia decided not to turn for La Coruña. He summoned boats from Santander to assist his ships to haven and late that afternoon went ashore in a pinnace. He left Diego Flores in charge of the capitana real, which anchored according to Captain Vanegas in the Bay of Laredo the next morning, after a rough night at sea. Aided by a galley she entered the narrow harbor of Santander late in the month.

To the eleven ships Medina Sidonia counted when he arrived off Santander, he could soon add over thirty more that entered port over the next few days. The vessels he had counted on 10 September had not separated as completely as he had feared. By the end of the month, forty-six galleons, greatships, pataches, and zabras had anchored at Santander, Laredo, and Castro Urdiales. Most of the ships as they arrived dropped anchor off Laredo because the entrance to Santander was difficult. Only a few ships at a time warped on the tides into its more secure anchorage.

Never comfortable at sea, Medina Sidonia had been sick and feverish during most of the return voyage, but ashore he persisted in his work in spite of his wretched health. He received the close cooperation of the Corregidor of Santander (the *Cuatro Villas*) in organizing the relief of his men and wrote other officials and the bishops of northern Spain to beg their assistance.

On 23 September, two days after he landed, he announced his arrival in a letter to the King and informed him of the grim state of the armada and of his own poor health. Don Baltasar de Zúñiga had reached court the same day to confirm what was beginning to be suspected: that the armada was not only returning to Spain, but had been defeated in battle and battered by storm. Though already gloomy about its fate, the King was plunged into despair; Medina Sidonia's report of the armada's losses and of the condition of the survivors could only have intensified his dejection.

Two days later Medina Sidonia requested license of the King to return to his home. "I am in bed and at the point of dying. I neither understand anything, nor want to. . . ."[28] With his request he dispatched Don Francisco de Bobadilla to court to relate all that had happened to the King.

To Idiáquez he wrote more pointedly, echoing the sentiments he had expressed when he attempted to turn down command of the armada:[29]

My lack of health persists and I am useless for doing anything, and in no way when I am whole and sound again shall I embark. His Majesty has no need to be served as I have done, with no kind of advantage whatsoever to his cause because I know nothing of the sea nor of war. Thus Your Lordship[30] must forget me for any of this business. I pray you, since Our Lord has not been served to summon me to this vocation, not to employ me in it, because neither in conscience nor in obligation can I fulfill it, as I have so often pointed out to Your Lordship, whom I beg, in all truth as your servant, to support me with His Majesty in my fair request. For in his spirit of clemency I hope that he will want only to be done with me, who has in all honesty wished to serve him, and it will be done. Insofar as naval matters go, for no reason and in no manner will I ever take them up, though it cost me my head. That way would be simpler, and save me from dying in some office I can neither fulfill nor understand, having to believe those who advise me, I know not with what aim. I am so weak that I can neither write with my own hand, nor go anywhere.

A series of reports from physicians followed, warning that his life was in danger if he were not treated and allowed to return home to recuperate.[31]

The business of dealing with the shattered ships of the armada and bringing ashore the tattered, sick, and dying survivors was handled by local authorities and such surviving officers as were able. Don Agustín Mejía, assigned custody of the soldiers, was bedridden and explained it would be some days before he could do much. The Contador Coco Calderón arrived in suspiciously good health on 28 September and at once pitched in to assist the others.

Miguel de Oquendo sailed the bulk of his squadron and several other ships, numbering ten plus three pataches, home to San Sebastián and Pasajes. His capitana caught fire in port and burned, and a damaged urca settled at her moorings. He must have sailed close by

Santander since Medina Sidonia knew he was safe. The Duke granted him command of all armada ships in Guipúzcoan ports, but the Duke's request for the 50,000 ducats he believed Oquendo carried brought Oquendo's quick rejoinder that he needed the money for the ships and people he had in Guipúzcoa. Ill and exhausted, Oquendo died on 2 October.

Juan Martínez Recalde arrived on 7 October at La Coruña, where a half dozen other ships had already anchored. Bertendona arrived a few days later. Recalde asked about Medina Sidonia and admitted that he feared for Leyva. Not well when the armada sailed in July, he was close to dying. He told Secretary Andrés de Alva that the armada was defeated because Medina Sidonia had chosen not Oquendo, but rather Diego Flores de Valdés, to advise him. On 23 October Recalde died.

Everywhere it was the same. The survivors, except for Medina Sidonia, blamed Diego Flores for all the armada's failures, though Medina Sidonia did claim, according to the Venetian Ambassador, that he acted only on the advice of his council.[32] The official account says as much: "In handling the capitana in combat the Duke turned to Don Francisco de Bobadilla . . . and in the government of the armada and matters of the sea, the Duke followed the opinion of the General Diego Flores." In August 1589 the King wrote Medina Sidonia to ask "about certain charges they say you made against Diego Flores de Valdés about various things" and requested him to forward them to court. Medina Sidonia responded that he had made none and had nothing more to say about the matter.[33]

Maestre de Campo Mejía also expressed doubt about the steadfastness of Maestre de Campo General Bobadilla. When some had suggested surrender to Medina Sidonia as the armada drifted toward the Zeeland Banks, Bobadilla, so Mejía claimed, did not say no, but only "not now."[34]

When War Councillor Don Juan de Cardona, who had commanded the Sicilian galleys at Lepanto and was badly wounded, conducted his inquiry at Santander, he agreed that Diego Flores was to blame for much, above all for the loss of Pedro de Valdés's capitana, which weakened the morale of the armada and boosted that of the English. But after reviewing the whole campaign, he stated that it seemed pointless to go on seeking who performed well and who did not, though he felt very strongly about the whole thing. "I have found nothing sufficiently certain to be able to accuse anyone, except about the loss of Don Pedro de Valdés." The armada had suffered so much and so many losses, he admonished the King, that it seemed best not to search among the survivors for more to punish. "Praise God and hope that He give Your Majesty victories, as He has on other occasions."[35]

Diego Flores was eventually imprisoned for several years.[36] Of those who had not returned the news trickled in. Don Pedro de Valdés was held captive in England and well treated. He returned to Spain in 1589 in an exchange of prisoners. Others taken by the English included Maestre de Campo Don Alonso Luzón, shipwrecked in Ireland, where most of the common soldiers and sailors and some of the gentlemen who survived the wrecks were killed, either by the English or by Irish chiefs trying to prove their loyalty to Elizabeth. Don Alonso de Leyva died with what a handful of survivors claimed were thirteen hundred people in the wreck of the galleass *Girona* on a rock in Giant's Causeway off the northern Irish coast.[37] He had survived the wreck of *Rata*, and early reports reaching Spain suggested that he was holding out in Ireland with a small army of survivors. Of the two maestres de campo forced to beach their galleons, Toledo escaped and Pimentel was captured by the Dutch and later ransomed. Juan Gómez de Medina, general of the urcas, reached Scotland and returned to Spain in the spring of 1589.

For the failure of the Enterprise, apart from the defeat of the armada, many blamed the Duke of Parma for neither being ready nor having available the flyboats that might have spearheaded his sortie or assisted the armada. According to Padre Victoria, Don Jorge Manrique and Parma almost came to blows. Pimentel, in the hands of the Dutch, also put much blame on Parma.[38] The official account stressed the lack of news from Parma and carried Arceo's statement that Parma could not be ready for fifteen days. While Philip II never directly blamed his nephew, many around him believed that Parma had not carried out his part of the Enterprise well, for whatever reason, and it is likely the King had his own doubts which figured in his decision in 1592 to remove Parma from the government of the Low Countries.[39] Parma died before the order was effected.

In relieving the armada and its wretched survivors at Santander, the town and surrounding country were hard pressed, although survivors with money could buy chicken and meat from villagers nearby. Andrés de Alva and the Marquis of Cerralbo, who had been collecting supplies for the armada's expected return to La Coruña, shipped what they could to Santander. At Santander the officials in charge complained of a shortage of cash, and one stated that of the 50,000 ducats Medina

Sidonia wanted from Oquendo, the Duke intended to keep 34,000 for himself.[40]

Medina Sidonia received the King's license to return to Sanlúcar at the beginning of October. On the fourth, he set out, riding in a litter, with a small caravan. His cousin the Constable of Castile met him on the outskirts of Santander and rode with him to Burgos. There he wrote Idiáquez on 8 October that he had left Santander against the advice of the physicians, and though he suffered from fatigue when he left, he felt better on reaching more "suitable air" and could eat and began to sleep well.[41] He prayed that God would give him help and was glad to hear the news that Recalde had reached port safely.

After this letter, Medina Sidonia's correspondence with Idiáquez seems to have virtually ceased. Did Medina Sidonia come to hold Idiáquez responsible for recommending him to the unwanted command, or did Idiáquez feel that Medina Sidonia had failed his trust? Idiáquez's influence with Philip II diminished following the defeat of the Enterprise, and he seems to have been relegated to the field of diplomacy. The Council of War asserted its independence of him, although he remained a member: Don Hernando de Toledo became its chief spokesman.[42]

After a brief siege of fevers at Burgos Medina Sidonia continued his southward journey, through Valladolid and Medina del Campo and over the Sierra de Gredos. The Count of Oropesa, whose cousin sailed aboard Oquendo's flagship, welcomed Medina Sidonia at his castle on the Tagus, whence the Duke proceeded to the Monastery of Guadalupe, built to celebrate the 1340 victory over the Moors at the Rio Salado. On 21 October the caravan reached the Guadalquivir at Cantillana, and on the twenty-fourth the Duke arrived in Sanlúcar.

Recovering in his palace, Medina Sidonia could hear, so the stories go, the cruel jests of boys in the streets. Padre Victoria said he had gone to sea without gray hairs and came back gray.[43] Whatever he thought about the campaign, he seems to have added nothing more, at least in writing, to what he expressed during his eight months as commander-in-chief of the armada. He believed his survival something of a miracle.

At the age of thirty-nine, Medina Sidonia faced the prospect of living the rest of his life carrying the taint of defeat, his *reputación* impaired, in an age when Spain had lost few battles. Sixteenth-century literature, of which Medina Sidonia was an avid student, conveys well the horror of the loss of honor. "The purest treasure mortal times afford is spotless reputation," exclaims Mowbray in Shakespeare's *Rich-*

ard II: "Mine honour is my life; both grow in one. Take honour from me and my life is done." In Spanish, "point of honor" becomes one word, the oft-used *pundonor*.

According to the rules, Medina Sidonia could defend his honor only when it was directly attacked, and it was not. The attacks and slurs appeared in pamphlets or were spread through gossip and correspondence. It was up to his partisans to serve as his champions, especially in the exchange of broadsheets and booklets such as the "History" of Padre Victoria, who gleefully stated that the Duke's partisans defended the Duke in public while privately agreeing with his critics. But the Duke's friends and associates in Andalusia and at court remained loyal to him. In Madrid Don Pedro de Guzmán upheld Medina Sidonia's good name, while in Rome the Count of Olivares championed his kinsman's honor and conduct against supporters of the Duke of Parma, whose conduct in the Enterprise was also hotly criticized.

What was certainly most important to Medina Sidonia, apart from his own conviction that he had done his duty and the continued loyalty of kin and friends, was the response of the King, who did nothing to dishonor him, continued to treat his opinions with respect, and let him retain the office of Captain General of the Ocean-Sea. Philip II had done all he could to mount the Enterprise, which he knew was a risky affair, however confident he had to appear. He had sincerely believed that God would assure victory and now had to admit that the defeat of the Enterprise reflected the will of God, as punishment for sin. Medina Sidonia, who thought on occasion in the Channel that he might yet bring the English to close quarters, grapple, board, and win, certainly believed the same. By bringing the armada back to Spain, he did all a man could. The storms that wreaked most of the havoc with it were to him and his King unquestionably the work of God, whose purposes are hidden from mortal men.

CHAPTER TEN

Recovery from Defeat

WHEN Medina Sidonia left the capitana real *San Martín* and Santander in October 1588, he did not return to the peaceful life of an Andalusian gentleman "among his orange trees," as Sir Francis Drake had claimed he might wish to do.[1] He returned to all the business that had occupied him in the years before he sailed, under more trying circumstances. He remained Captain General of the Ocean-Sea in more than title, and the title Captain General of the Coast of Andalusia only gave him explicit recognition for many of the myriad tasks he had performed for a dozen years without it and would continue to perform almost to the end of his life.

As Captain General of the Coast he was above all responsible for regional defense. In the King's name he dunned local authorities to muster and drill the local militias and Crown and city officials to maintain coastal fortifications and lookouts. On paper he had the authority to levy fines and penalties as appropriate.

He supervised the levy of soldiers and collection of munitions for the King's armies and, with the authority of both offices, the recruitment of seamen and collecting of ships and stores for the King's armadas and the annual sailings of Indies flotas. In the exercise of both offices he received countless orders but neither salary nor paid staff. He paid many bills from his own revenues.

Medina Sidonia did much more than serve as the King's chief agent for Andalusian military and maritime matters. He also continued to act as an adviser to the Crown for a wide range of concerns. No one not at court wielded more influence than Medina Sidonia in matters of gen-

eral policy regarding the commerce and defense of the Indies or relations with Barbary, and only his successors in the command of the
Ocean Armada enjoyed as much influence in Atlantic naval affairs. The
King and his ministers kept Medina Sidonia well informed and constantly solicited his views; and when they did not, he often volunteered
them.

Medina Sidonia's recovery from the ailments that plagued him during the armada campaign was swift. By the end of the year he was
discharging the responsibilities of his offices and received the compliments of the King for dispositions he had made for the defense of
Sanlúcar and Cadiz.[2] But Medina Sidonia strongly opposed a plan
decided in Madrid in 1584 for the defense of the region, the establishment of a chain of towers along the coast from Gibraltar to the Portuguese frontier to complete the chain that already extended from the
Pyrenees to Gibraltar.[3] Protection against corsair raids was the aim of
the plan, which called for two types of towers: tall *atalayas*, or watchtowers, and massive *torres* that could mount artillery and provide rally-
ing points for local defense. The costs were assigned to the señores and
town corporations along the coast, of which Medina Sidonia lorded
over half. In 1585 he was required to deposit with a royal judge in Seville
8,673 ducats, one quarter of the cost of a tower to be constructed on the
Rio de Loro in his Arenas Gordas. He registered a protest with the
King, claiming that "the salaries being consumed by the judge and his
commissaries are so much that all that was allocated does not supply
them."[4]

When he returned to Sanlúcar from the armada campaign, he found
a royal engineer vested with sweeping authority to continue the building program and hard at work.[5] In January 1591 a new judge-executor
announced what each responsible party had to contribute.[6] Medina
Sidonia owed 29,020 ducats toward the costs of three towers in the
Arenas Gordas and his half of the cost of a tower to be built at Palos,
which he split with the Count of Miranda. Medina Sidonia protested
once more and argued that mounted patrols were sufficient, cheaper,
and more effective against swift corsair raids. His cousin Don Pedro de
Guzmán would take the matter up at court in person.[7] Don Pedro had
become in December 1589 governor to Prince Philip, heir to the throne,
and all save the Prince were pleased "that he was removed from the
power of women."[8]

In May 1591 the Council of War granted Medina Sidonia a delay in
payment for the projected towers and approval to use mounted patrols

of *ginetes*, which they reluctantly renewed in 1593, after he had met with them in person.[9] The Duke did not win further delays, though he continued to object and procrastinate, arguing that the costs should be borne by all who benefited, including Vizcayan shippers.[10]

But in 1589 the first and most urgent problem Medina Sidonia faced had nothing to do with towers, but rather how to meet the expected English counterattack on Spain. The Crown dunned the nobility for donations and the Cortes for increased taxes and ordered Don Juan de Cardona to launch a major new shipbuilding program in the Basque yards. Much needed were masts, both for the new ships and for the repair of such survivors of the 1588 campaign as were deemed seaworthy. Medina Sidonia received orders to embargo several shiploads of masts in Cadiz Bay and persuade their masters to haul them to Cardona and the newly appointed Captain General of the Ocean-Armada, Don Alonso de Bazán, the late Marquis of Santa Cruz's brother.[11] The business of the masts proved tedious and occupied the Duke through the summer and into the next year. He also rounded up and sent off to Cardona and Bazán guns and victuals.

In the same weeks he first embargoed the masts, he supervised the outfitting of the Sanlúcar section of the first flota since 1586 to sail for Tierra Firme and saw to the dispatch of two pataches bound to fetch the 1589 treasure. Two galizabras sailed from the north coast for the same purpose.

A particularly frightening prospect to Medina Sidonia and Madrid was the threat to the treasure route posed by the possible cooperation of the English and the Sharif of Morocco. In Fez the English and Dutch had boisterously celebrated the defeat of the armada and were assaulted by the Spanish Resident Diego Marín and his people. A riot ensued in which three persons were killed. The Sharif arrested Marín, and the conduct of Spain's business at Fez was taken over by a resident merchant, Baltasar Polo. The Sharif, however, continued to be wary of any alliance with Queen Elizabeth against his powerful neighbor.[12] When Dom António's son, Dom Cristovão, came to Fez in 1589 as his father's agent and with Queen Elizabeth's blessing, the Sharif kept him a virtual hostage for three years. As a conciliatory gesture toward the Sharif, Philip II abandoned the puny fortress of Arzila, a step long urged by the Council of War.

At the same time, to keep the Sharif honest, Philip II moved two exiled Moroccan princes with their retinues from Lisbon to Andalusia, whence they might quickly be sent to Morocco to stir up trouble if needed. Philip also had other motives for moving them: he wanted them out of Lisbon, where they had been held since Dom Sebastian's time, in case Dom António and the English were successful in taking the city.[13]

The King lodged one, Mulai ech Sheik, son of the deposed Sharif Muhammad el-Motawakkil, at Carmona; and his uncle, Mulai en Nasir, at Utrera. He put Medina Sidonia in charge of their maintenance. Medina Sidonia had soon spent 800 ducats out of pocket for the *Infantes Moros* and suffered headaches from their "thousand impertinences and wild outbursts."[14]

Concern for the threat posed by Dom António and the English also caused Philip to order Medina Sidonia to be ready to respond to the defense of the thinly populated Portuguese Algarve. In accord with the order, the Duke detailed the Marquis of Gibraleón, his brother-in-law, if summoned by the Viceroy of Portugal, to be prepared to lead over the frontier the militia of his estates plus those of the Marquis of Alcalá de la Alameda, the Marquis of Villamanrique, the Marquis of Villanueva del Fresno, and the lands pertaining to Seville between the Guadalquivir and the Guadiana.[15] Medina Sidonia had a stack of orders at hand bearing the King's signature to use with recalcitrant señores if necessary.

A delicate matter in the arrangements concerned the cooperation of the Marquis of Ayamonte, whose town was the usual place for crossing the frontier. The King was anxious that he show Medina Sidonia and Gibraleón proper respect, which suggests some sort of resentment on Ayamonte's part. All were kinsmen, and Ayamonte's brother Don Luis de Córdoba had served beside Medina Sidonia aboard *San Martín*.[16]

The anticipated English counterattack on the Iberian Peninsula hit La Coruña at the beginning of May.[17] In command was Sir Francis Drake, who had assembled a powerful fleet and sizeable invasion force and brought Dom António with him. On receipt of the news, Medina Sidonia alerted his militia and put several companies of militiamen into Cádiz, where in January he had refereed a jurisdictional dispute between the bishop and the corregidor over responsibilities in the construction of new fortifications. When the English sailed from La Coruña, where they failed to take the fort, War Secretary Andrés de Prada wrote Medina Sidonia, "If the Englishman comes to your region, I hope to God he is as badly treated as he was at La Coruña."[18] Drake had, according to Prada, 120 ships and 20,000 men and had suffered more than 1,000 casualties. He suspected Drake would get fresh supplies from Barbary.

In Cadiz Bay the Adelantado stood ready with his galleys, which Medina Sidonia had reinforced with local recruits. A convoy of pataches and frigates Medina Sidonia had assembled for the voyage to New Spain kept to the safety of the Guadalquivir, and ships bringing veteran troops from Italy were ordered to seek the security of Cartagena and Gibraltar.

Drake landed troops near Lisbon and tried to force the entrance to the Tagus, but the defenses organized by the Viceroy and the Count of Fuentes held, and the feared revolt in favor of Dom António did not materialize. Medina Sidonia's one-time hostage Braganza rallied the Portuguese nobility to Philip of Castile.

Medina Sidonia, on learning that Drake had departed Lisbon, braced for him to attack Cádiz one more time. Madrid feared Drake meant to seize the town, lodge Dom António in it, and get help from Morocco. From Lisbon Drake hit Vigo, then returned to England. In mid-July Medina Sidonia began to discharge the militia companies and send them home. Shipping began to move, and the last two of the six galleasses of Naples[19] arrived in Cadiz Bay en route to join Bazán's armada. To Spain's governors overseas Medina Sidonia sent news and warning of Drake by swift ships whose masters had orders to drop their dispatches overboard in weighted bags if threatened with capture.[20]

On 18 September Medina Sidonia saw the convoy of pataches weigh anchor from the Guadalquivir for Vera Cruz. They carried the new Viceroy of Mexico, Don Luis de Velasco, and the new Governor of the Philippines, Don Gómez Pérez das Mariñas, who had served in the armada aboard *San Martín*.[21] Among the passengers were poor people, given special permission by the Viceroy to sail to Mexico with him.[22]

Expected to arrive at Sanlúcar and Cadiz was a flota that consisted of the New Spain flota of 1588 and a few ships of the Tierra Firme flota that had left in March. Drake had returned to England, but the Earl of Cumberland and a squadron infested the Azores, and the assassination of Henri III of France, about which Indies Secretary Juan de Ibarra informed Medina Sidonia, boded yet new difficulties.[23] In mid-October a dispatch ship arrived with report that the flota had left Havana the second week of September. The Casa de Contratación in Seville complained about the favor Medina Sidonia showed returning passengers by allowing them to disembark in Sanlúcar prior to the Casa's official inspection and wanted to know if the Duke's commission of Captain General of the Ocean-Sea permitted him to do this.[24]

Storms more than enemies imperiled the flota's return; between late October and late November its ships straggled home, including two patches sent for the treasure, which, Secretary Ibarra told the Duke, "alleviated some of the worry with which we live, but the delay of the others is worry enough."[25] The other pair of treasure vessels Medina Sidonia correctly guessed had reached the Azores.

While some ships of the 1589 flota to Tierra Firme had returned with the 1588 New Spain flota, most remained in Cartagena de Indias with their General Diego de la Ribera, in no condition to sail after a hard crossing. The Casa de Contratación started to load two greatships with craftsmen and materials needed for the repair of the flota when Medina Sidonia objected. He persuaded Ibarra that a small, tough armada of patches ought to go to the flota's relief.

As often happened, the plans were combined. Medina Sidonia received orders to outfit a fleet that consisted of the two greatships, the galleon *Santa Maria del Barrio*, a survivor of 1588, the almiranta, and two other greatships of the flota assembling for New Spain, and several patches and zabras. Medina Sidonia placed General Juan de Uribe in command. Needed guns were found for the ships from what was taken from Arzila, and more were loaned them by Medina Sidonia from his own forts. The Duke took the occasion to list the guns he had loaned the Crown over the years, which totaled 65,644 pounds in weight. The guns installed on the ships bound for Cartagena included a cannon of 4,200 pounds, two demicannon of 3,600 pounds each, four demiculverins between 3,200 and 3,300 pounds each, and a saker that weighed 2,000 pounds.[26]

Delays in preparing the ships bound for Tierra Firme prompted the King to order a pair of sturdy *galizabras* under Pedro Menéndez Márquez prepared to fetch the Peruvian treasure. Medina Sidonia saw the convoy for Cartagena and the two galizabras off in mid-May. The court then decided that the galizabras dared not risk returning alone, because of English ships lurking in the Azores, and ordered them to join the great convoy that would form in Havana in June and July. It was hoped that the convoy would sail before 25 July, the last date regarded as safe before the onset of the hurricane season. However, because the King was desperate for the Indies treasure, the royal orders allowed the flotas' commanders to take a vote on whether or not to sail anytime before 10 August. After that date, they were to wait till the next spring. Medina Sidonia sent the orders off in swift vessels on 7 June, but they did not reach the galizabras, which returned to Spain with the Peruvian treasure in August.

In response to the news sent him from court of fresh English squadrons collecting in the Azores, Medina Sidonia urged the King to send Bazán's armada into English and Irish waters to make demonstration and draw the English home.[27] The Ocean Armada had established its principal base at El Ferrol, which made strategic sense but proved a constant logistical problem. Medina Sidonia and Captain Alonso de Vanegas spent weeks early in the year rounding up gunners in Seville for Bazán, and by the beginning of April had nearly ninety, half of them foreigners from Italy, Germany, and even Norway.[28]

The King had other plans for Bazán: he ordered him first to land a tercio in Brittany, then head for the Azores with the full armada to protect the flotas of Uribe and Ribera expected from Havana. Secretary of War Andrés de Prada expressed anxiety for the flotas' safety to the Duke: "They run great risk and it will be a particular miracle if they arrive without serious mishap."[29]

Uribe and Ribera chose not to risk either hurricanes or English squadrons. They remained through the winter in Havana, where more materials had to be sent them from Spain. They did, however, dispatch in February the Mexican treasure in light, swift frigates that reached Lisbon in March. "The frigates are safe and the English are frustrated," exulted Juan de Ibarra in a note to Medina Sidonia, who was busy with the latest relief force, a flotilla of embargoed flyboats.[30]

Coping with the English threats to the Indies route was not Medina Sidonia's entire occupation during these months. In the late summer of 1590 the corsair chief Murad Reis and his galliots terrorized the Andalusian coast and in August conducted a *razzia* (raid) on Terrón, a fishing hamlet near Lepe in the Marquis of Ayamonte's estates. To Medina Sidonia Ayamonte recounted what happened.[31]

The corsairs landed in the wee hours of 17 August and sneaked toward the settlement. They surprised a horse patrolman who approached to investigate, but his companion, a sentry on foot, fled to shout the alarm. When word reached Ayamonte, he, his brother Don Luis de Córdoba, and a few horsemen, each with an arquebusier mounted on his horse's haunches, rode hard for Terrón. More militiamen on foot followed. When Ayamonte reached the hamlet, he "commended himself to God," then led a charge down one street while

Don Luis charged down another. The corsairs massed between two strong houses and put up a hard fight. More militiamen arrived, and the corsairs retreated to their galliots. All the people they had seized were freed but ten, plus the unfortunate patrolman. Seven militiamen and others had been killed, and the bodies of four corsairs were left behind.

In response to the raid Medina Sidonia rounded up people to serve in the Adelantado's galleys, which sailed vainly in hot pursuit of the corsairs. He also provided men and guns to equip a new galleon the Adelantado had built and a pair of greatships he pressed into service to deal with the high-boarded greatships of the English and Dutch that threatened the coast round Gibraltar as they entered and departed the Mediterranean.[32] In 1591, however, because of terrible famine in Italy, Medina Sidonia was sent varying orders to allow Dutch ships carrying grain to pass, although he was to search them for arms and detain them if arms were found.[33]

At the beginning of 1591, Medina Sidonia, who before had seen many English merchants pass through Sanlúcar, welcomed a new sort of Englishman, priests from the English College at Valladolid, returning to England "to preach the gospel." The King ordered him to book passage for them in merchant ships with "much dissimulation."[34]

That year the King intended to send the two regular flotas to the Indies, but the urgent need of vessels to run supplies and men to the flotas waiting at Havana to make the return voyage and the provision of men and materials for the armada and the Adelantado's galleys had stretched the resources of Andalusia thin and made their outfitting difficult. Once more Medina Sidonia dispatched Pedro Menéndez Márquez with swift pataches and galizabras to fetch the treasure, while he complained to Ibarra about the recurring annual problems of dispatching two flotas. He wondered whether or not the two ought to be combined into one, since each one cost so much to prepare: they had become too large and unwieldy and always sailed too late. The armed capitanas and almirantas proved expensive and too loaded with merchandise to be effective. A single combined flota, he argued, should sail early each year, because from May through the summer the ocean was infested by pirates and in the autumn hurricanes threatened.[35]

A month after the Duke had posted his recommendation to Ibarra he learned that the Earl of Cumberland would again be headed with a squadron for the Azores.[36] He urged the King in response to send Bazán with the armada—which he understood numbered twenty-four galleons and greatships, two galleasses, and eight pataches—to intercept the Earl, who, according to the Duke's sources, had only seven large ships.[37] To warn Menéndez, Medina Sidonia sent Captain Juan Gil, promoted from the rank of alférez he held during the 1588 armada campaign, in a fast frigate.[38] A few days later a flotilla of pataches and Flemish flyboats embargoed to take supplies and people to the flotas in Havana weighed anchor.

Medina Sidonia's recommendation that the two flotas be combined made no headway. In 1591 each was ordered to sail as planned. Almost at once Medina Sidonia was forced to advise the King that no matter what else he heard, the New Spain flota would be fortunate to sail by late June. "The lack of sailors is notable: it would be most suitable not to permit small ships to go with the flota and to use their people for the larger ones."[39] In this instance Medina Sidonia's advice was taken, and the flota finally sailed on the first spring tides of July.

At the end of October the flotas that at last had sailed from Havana reached Sanlúcar, badly mauled by a series of storms. Though racked with fevers, Medina Sidonia oversaw the return of fifty-one of seventy-one ships that had left the Caribbean.[40] Bazán's armada, which met them in the Azores, had likewise been storm-battered, but it had driven the English away and in a hard-fought but frustrating victory captured the Queen's galleon *Revenge*, subsequently wrecked by storm.

The Tierra Firme flota was still not ready to sail. About getting two flotas under way in 1591, Medina Sidonia had been right. It did not depart until St Joseph's Day, 1592. A fortnight later, on 2 April, a flotilla of fast frigates went for the treasure. In the meantime rumor reached Sanlúcar that Drake himself was bound for the Indies. In a letter to Ibarra full of advice about how best to respond, Medina Sidonia remarked, "This pirate [*corsario*] is without doubt very experienced in matters of the Indies, a great seaman and gifted soldier." The Duke believed Drake was headed straight for Nombre de Dios. About his advice he added in a telling passage, "Although what I say here may not be worth much, nor taken for anything, I will comply with my obligations until my death, giving advice as I have always done, during what little remains of my life."[41]

Life ended that year for his mother-in-law, the Princess of Eboli, on 2 February at Pastrana. During her last two years she was kept closely guarded after the escape of Antonio Pérez from prison and his part in stirring Zaragoza in Aragon to revolt.

Medina Sidonia could not leave Andalusia until the summer's alarms had passed, but in December he journeyed with the Duchess to Madrid and Pastrana to deal with family affairs. Her brother, the Duke of Pastrana, had found outlet for his swashbuckling temperament by serving as cavalry commander for Parma in the Low Countries, but in late 1589 returned to Madrid, where he become embroiled in arrangements for the marriage of his relative Doña Mencia de Mendoza, daughter of the Duke of Infantado, to the fifth Duke of Alba, contrary to the King's wishes. In the summer of 1590 Secretary Prada had advised Medina Sidonia to keep the matter to himself.[42] The King punished Pastrana with confinement to the town of Talavera, but on his mother's death released him. The settlement of his inheritance led to an ugly suit between him and his brother, the Duke of Francavilla. Not until early 1595 did he return to Flanders as Captain General of the Light Cavalry. In poor health, he remained devoted to duty. Following a brilliant campaign season, he died there the next year.[43] Before he left Pastrana, he and Medina Sidonia arranged for the marriage of his nine-year-old heir to Medina Sidonia's daughter Leonor.

At court Medina Sidonia pressed his personal business. He made another attempt to recover control of the Sanlúcar customs when the contract came due for renewal after ten years, but was blocked by Seville interests. He also met with the Council of War to discuss tower construction and his authority as Captain General of Andalusia. About the Duke's efforts the contemporary historian of Jerez, Padre Rallón, remarked, "The Duke went to Madrid to treat with His Majesty the manner of defending these coasts; it was not very easy for the King had spent all the income of the Kingdom, and all that was being raised was needed for the war in Flanders and the pursuit of his design to make his daughter Queen of France. He thought that with his grand talents that he would be able to influence the ministers. There it became clear that there was no armada to defend the coast and it was a matter of what could be done with infantry and the local militia."[44]

In a memorandum to the Council of War, Medina Sidonia made clear what he wanted regarding the militia.[45] It amounted to a radical change in the way things had always been done. He wished to take the appointment of captains from the local authorities and vest their nomination with the Captain General. Their commissions would be issued by the King. He wanted the militia companies to drill on all holidays and whenever ordered by their captains or the Captain General. Further, he wanted municipal councils to provide the militiamen with powder and shot, dispatch them to the coast when ordered, and pay their expenses until they had arrived on station. Expenses then should be assumed by the Crown and paid until the men returned home.

Medina Sidonia wanted all sentinels and guards posted by señores and towns along the coast to serve at his orders; and to ensure the cooperation of the municipalities in this and other militia matters, he wanted as Captain General to be given a vote on all municipal councils within his jurisdiction in matters that pertained to regional defense. Above all, he wanted it reiterated by royal decree that when he called out the militia or ordered the repair of towers and fortifications, the towns of the Coast of Andalusia were to obey.

The Council of War studied Medina Sidonia's proposals and agreed to everything save for the matter of voting on town councils, which lay outside its competence. Two years later, a royal decree which embodied most of the Duke's recommendations was published.[46] In preparing the decree, the Council of War calculated that the municipalities and señores within Medina Sidonia's jurisdiction, which extended twenty leagues from the coast, would provide 8,200 foot and 1,060 horse, exclusive of the forces of towns and señores on the coast itself and mounted gentleman volunteers, who were expected in considerable number. The decree ordered Jerez to raise five companies of foot of 250 men each and a troop of 100 horse. Seville, much larger but also further from the coast, would send 1,500 men on foot and 200 horsemen. Of the señores, the Duke of Osuna, who had still been Marquis of Peñafiel aboard the armada,[47] had to send the largest number, 1,000 infantry and 1,00 horsemen from his estates round Osuna, Morón, El Arahel, and La Puebla de Cazalla. Medina Sidonia's County of Niebla was assigned 400 foot and 50 horse, a small portion of its 4,600 available militiamen. Most of Niebla's militia would probably concentrate at Huelva, while some were detailed to march to the Algarve if necessary. The militia of Sanlúcar, like the militia of every coastal town—Cádiz, Puerto Santa Maria, Chiclana, Vejer, Conil, Tarifa, and Gibraltar —stood to its own defense, while the men marching from the interior were directed either to Cádiz or Gibraltar, the two places that seemed the most likely targets of major enemy attacks.

Medina Sidonia wanted much from the other señores and the municipalities of his province, but he was also aware of their many preoccupations that soon supplanted their fear of English attack after the threats of 1589 had faded. Harvests had been intermittently bad in Andalusia as well as in Italy, and all complained of financial losses and the high price of bread.[48] Everything that might have been done to carry out the royal decree was not, and Medina Sidonia had too much else to occupy him to do much about it.

One recurring occupation was the problem of the *Infantes Moros*. The younger, Mulai ech Sheik, became Christian[49] and was content to remain in Spain, but his uncle, Mulai en Nasir, living in Utrera, begged Philip II to let him return to Morocco, "to die under his own law and take his sons to their homeland."[50] Philip submitted the request to legal counsel, who advised him that the Prince had first come to Portugal by his own will and should be free to leave. Philip, however, feared the reaction of the Sharif and consulted Medina Sidonia.

The Duke suggested that the King send a "person of quality to explain all to the Sharif, since the situation is so delicate, with the interests of the Turk, the French and the English all involved."[51] To Secretary Martín de Idiáquez he astutely stressed the need for Philip to keep the friendship of the Sharif "lest he throw himself into the arms of the Turk or the Queen of England, which he does not want to do, even though his few favors and inadequate promises do not give His Majesty pleasure."[52]

Philip gave the task to his envoy to Marrakech, the Portuguese Dom Francisco de Acosta, but when Acosta died, he returned to negotiating through the Valencian merchant Baltasar Polo, resident in Fez, to whom he issued credentials. He wanted Polo to make clear to the Sharif that Spain would provide Mulai en Nasir with no support for any design he might have.

Early in 1595, Mulai en Nasir received his license to leave Spain and orders to proceed with his household to Málaga for embarkation to Melilla. He suddenly became reluctant to leave, and Medina Sidonia had to force him from Utrera. He announced to the King, "I have just thrown out Mulai Nasir, because his costs are too much and for one hundred thousand other reasons."[53] The Moorish Prince next appeared on Medina Sidonia's doorstep in Sanlúcar, with a half dozen people, in want and hunger, and was again forced onto the road for Málaga. "He has no support and fears he is lost to his uncle," Medina Sidonia explained.[54]

In May Mulai en Nasir was transported to Melilla with 120 retainers and 22 horses, and sent out into Morocco. At first Medina Sidonia lost track of him, though rumors quickly spread that he had raised 20,000 men and Barbary was in a state of uproar. Repeatedly the Duke urged Philip to allay the Sharif's fears in order to counter at the Moroccan court the machinations of the Turk and the English, who talked of building a fort at Agadir. In the meantime, he saw to the provision of aid to the presidios of Melilla, Ceuta, and Tangier.

Medina Sidonia next learned that the Sharif had sent his son Mulai Muhammad ech Sheik north from Marrakech and quickly followed after him. At the end of August Mulai Sheik defeated Nasir's people in the field, but Nasir escaped. The Sharif arrived in Fez, where he clamped down on dissent and imprisoned Baltasar Polo. Medina Sidonia wrote the Sharif's son to urge Polo's release and remarked about his arrest, "The reason given is debts but something else just may be the cause."[55] When Medina Sidonia raised with the Sharif the matter of Diego Marín, detained since 1588, he responded that he had no idea Marín was still in Morocco.

The release of Mulai en Nasir, however rudely he had been dumped outside the gates of Melilla, put a serious strain on the relations of Philip II with the Sharif; they improved but little after Mulai en Nasir was caught and killed in the spring of 1596, and his head put on display in Fez.

Philip II's relations with the rebellious Dutch also took a new turn in 1595, when Philip decided to impose a total embargo on Dutch commerce with Spain. In 1587–88 he had invoked a partial embargo on Dutch trade with Spain, aimed only at known rebels and heretics. His chief motive had been a need for ships. By the early 1590s that embargo had been relaxed, in part because of the need for grain shipments to relieve famine conditions in Mediterranean Europe and in part because there was little enthusiasm in Spain to deny a lucrative commerce. The value of Spanish commerce to the Dutch, Philip II's officials estimated, had doubled between 1593 and 1594 from 1 million to 2 million ducats.[56] The sum of 2 million ducats would have equaled something over 20 percent of Philip's revenues from Spain and the Indies. In 1595 an official in Seville reckoned that 30,000 ducats in hard cash was leaving Spain each month in ships belonging to Dutch rebels,[57] and though he did not say as much, it would have been known in Madrid that the sum was almost three-fourths the monthly cost of Philip's Army of Flanders that was trying to crush the Dutch revolt.

Late in March 1595 Medina Sidonia as Captain General of the Coast of Andalusia received a secret instruction that announced the new embargo. "I have not tried this measure till now," Philip protested, "in hope that that blind nation might return to what is right. But now it is seen that they show more than ever signs of forgetting their obligations, and in addition to their ordinary impertinency, they arm to join with England and other enemies of my kingdoms."[58]

It commanded Medina Sidonia to detain all ships from Holland and Zeeland, remove their sails, and post guard over their crews. The instruction allowed him to free some who were Catholic, so that they might return home to tell the others of the injury done their commerce and encourage them "to leave their false liberty and return to their obligations to God and their natural lord."

For the supervision of the embargo the Licentiate Armenteros, of the Council of the Indies, came from Madrid to assist the Judge in charge of Andalusian port arrivals, Luis Gaytan de Ayala. The two needed the close cooperation of the Royal Assistant of Seville, Don Luis de Carillo, Count of Priego, and Medina Sidonia, Captain General of the Coast. To assist him in Sanlúcar, Medina Sidonia took Martín de Arriaga, Paymaster of the Adelantado's galley squadron based at Puerto Santa Maria.

Medina Sidonia moved swiftly. On 28 March he reported that twenty-eight vessels suspected of belonging to rebels had been arrested at Sanlúcar and Cádiz. By 3 April the number had increased to twenty-four at Sanlúcar, eleven at Cádiz, and one each at Gibraltar and Huelva, amounting to 7,940 toneladas.[59]

In a separate matter Medina Sidonia received an order to watch for and detain if discovered several ships that belonged to Duke Charles of "Sudermania" (Södermanland, Sweden), accurately described as "a person said to have intelligence with the English, of doubtful loyalty to his king, and an enemy of the Catholic Faith."[60]

Arriaga has provided in a report to the King a good picture of Medina Sidonia at work. "The zeal and care of the Duke is so great that he puts the service of Your Majesty ahead of the interests of his house and the inconvenience to his person. He works at any hour of the day or night on everything, and deigns to put hand to things that persons very inferior do only with reluctance, and thus gives in all his actions the finest example."[61]

The zeal of the Adelantado and his galleys, on the other hand, was considered excessive, and he was told to leave alone German, Flemish, and Norwegian ships come to load salt.[62] No one wanted to jeopardize trade with neutrals.

Despite the suddenness of the embargo and the efforts of Medina Sidonia and others, the King was not pleased with the effect: "The fruit up till now is less than expected."[63] After the first weeks the embargo settled into a routine, and its effects seemed to provide more headaches for the Spaniards than they had expected. Northern merchantmen avoided Andalusian ports, and ships were often hard to find for necessary tasks.

Medina Sidonia wished that more attention were paid to the defense of the coast, which, he confessed to Arriaga, "was unprepared for an enemy fleet or even a handful of Moorish galliots." The twelve Spanish galleys from Puerto Santa Maria left for Lisbon and the campaign in Brittany, and the Duke wanted the King to recommission the five laid up at Cartagena, before "it becomes impossible to sail from Sanlúcar to Cádiz, let alone go out to fish."[64]

Medina Sidonia also worried about the returning Indies flotas. From a Scot questioned in Latin at Sanlúcar he learned that two English fleets were at sea, one under Sir Walter Raleigh and another under Sir Robert Dudley, and that they threatened the treasure route. He detained briefly some German hulks, lest they inform the English that the returning New Spain flota had left Havana early in March and was expected soon.

Madrid expected that twelve galleons hired in Ragusa would reach Cádiz in time to provide escort for the flotas, but they did not. Medina Sidonia armed a few flyboats and put to sea what galleys remained to meet some forty ships that arrived on 8 May from Havana.

With the treasure safe and the embargo in competent hands, Medina Sidonia departed for Conil on the coast south of Cádiz to supervise, as he did whenever he could, his almadraba. At the end of June his sojourn was interrupted by an order from the King to oversee the outfitting and manning of the Ragusan galleons that had been contracted through Pedro de Ibella and arrived in Cadiz Bay.[65] In a separate note, the Secretary Juan de Ibarra apologized for disturbing the Duke and expressed his hope that the Duke was repairing his financial position.[66] Medina Sidonia obeyed and could report on 31 July that the twelve Ragusan galleons had made sail that morning for Lisbon, carrying their 1,700 sailors and 1,280 infantry he had recruited.

In Cádiz and Sanlúcar the Duke discovered that local opposition to the embargo of Dutch ships and goods had come into the open. The Royal Assistant of Seville headed the dozens of prominent citizens who affixed their names to a petition to the King which stated that the embargo was not succeeding as anticipated and caused far more injury to Spaniards and loyal Flemings than to the rebels.[67] As weeks passed, the tone of the petitions became strident: "We are surrounded with calamity which menaces this city and your republic" and "Ships go everywhere but here."[68] Medina Sidonia, who watched the New Spain flota sail in July, claimed that the embargo would hinder the sailing of the Tierra Firme flota.[69]

Souls were also menaced, thought the Bishop of Cádiz, who feared that good Catholic Amsterdamers might feel constrained to swear they were not from Holland.[70] "Your Majesty would better discontinue the embargo than occasion the offense," he admonished.

The two officials in charge of enforcing the embargo, Armenteros and Ayala, agreed in a separate petition that the embargo did not have the desired effect; they suggested that the government of the Low Countries undertake the business of licensing Flemish goods before they were shipped because it was impossible in Spain to determine which goods came from loyal provinces and which came from rebel provinces.[71] Medina Sidonia, who signed the petition they drafted, did admit that an embargo had its use but ought to be employed only against the "biggest rebels and heretics."[72] He believed that the Cardinal-Archduke Albert, newly appointed Governor General of the Low Countries, might well use the embargo as a threat and commerce with Spain as a lure in his negotiations with the rebel provinces.

Medina Sidonia also raised more serious arguments against the embargo. "The cutting of their trade and correspondence with Spain will cause them to find other means to live, for those islanders have so many ships and seamen, and perforce they will turn to piracy (*el corso*) or other hostile acts together with the English and French. This will give us much anxiety and make it necessary to send with every flota a strong armada, and the costs will offset the gains."[73]

Pressed by his Spanish subjects, Philip began to ease his demands for enforcement of the embargo, which local authorities were already relaxing. This, however, did not stop officials in Seville, Cádiz, and Sanlúcar from accusing each other of malfeasance or using its enforcement to local advantage. The result was that enforcement became capricious and reflected motives that ranged from simple greed to inquisitorial zeal.[74] Defending the widespread unwillingness to enforce the embargo after it was three years in effect, Medina Sidonia claimed that dissimulation with the Dutch was necessary, and he repeated the argument he had raised before: "If they are denied trade, they will make the Indies route unnavigable. Even now it is sailed at risk because of the English, without having these rebels also turn to piracy."[75]

The Dutch did turn to piracy on an imperial scale not long after Medina Sidonia penned those words, in part because of the capriciously enforced embargo, and they founded their East and West India Companies to assault the Hispano-Portuguese overseas empires. More immediately, within months after the embargo was decreed, they patched up their strained relations with the English and prepared a joint expedition against Spain.

CHAPTER ELEVEN ✳

The Sack of Cádiz

W HILE Medina Sidonia dealt with the Dutch embargo, assisted in the sailings of the Indies flotas, and fussed over developments in Morocco, he did not lose sight of the war with England or ignore the problems of the Ocean Armada. The English, after the failure of their effort in 1589 to destroy the remnants of the 1588 armada or incite rebellion in Portugal, each year threatened the treasure routes from the New World and India where they passed through the Azores. To cope with the menace, Philip II rebuilt his armada, put it on a permanent footing, and made it more formidable than before.[1] Medina Sidonia wholeheartedly approved.

Many of the galleons that survived 1588 were scrapped because of damages and because their design had been proved wanting, and those that did continue in service, including *San Martín*, were retired or put to sailing in the Indies flotas over the next few years. At the same time new galleons and armed greatships, constructed to the latest designs and similar in appearance to race-built English galleons with their low forecastles, came off the ways to serve in the armada or act as capitanas and almirantas of the Indies flotas. The King kept Medina Sidonia informed about the new construction and asked for his opinions.[2] In July and August 1590 alone, 72,000 ducats were spent on it, while for operations for the rest of the year and the year following the Council of War prepared a budget of more than 1,220,000 ducats.[3] Two galleasses and three galleys supported the landing of a tercio at Blavet in Brittany in the summer of 1590, with the objective of supporting the Catholic League and taking the strategic port of Brest; and in September Don

Alonso de Bazán took thirty-seven galleons and greatships of the Armada of the Ocean-Sea to the Azores to meet the flotas and drive out the English.

As more galleons and other vessels came into service, the King decided it best to establish three armadas to cope with the growing demands of the Atlantic war. The principal Ocean Armada at El Ferrol could operate from the English Channel to the Azores and cover activities in Brittany; a smaller Portuguese Armada at Lisbon would support it and look after Portuguese interests; and the Indies Guard Armada would operate from Cádiz to the Caribbean and back.

Medina Sidonia, at the Escorial in June 1593, was invited by the King to offer his opinions about the reconstituted Armada de la Guarda de la Carrera de las Indias, which had sailed that April under the command of General Francisco Coloma. It consisted of two new galleons and eight other ships, including, it would seem, survivors of 1588.[4] The Duke suggested that the Guard Armada be composed of eight royal galleons of 500 toneladas each and six fregatas.[5]

The Guard Armada that weighed anchor from Sanlúcar early the next year did consist of eight royal galleons. Most were of new construction and bigger than what the Duke recommended, all but one over 750 toneladas. But at the same time, a number of smaller galleons in the 350 to 500 tonelada range were also launched.

To the operating costs of the reconstituted Guard Armada the Crown contributed one-third; the remaining two-thirds were met by a tax, or *avería*, levied on the merchantmen they escorted. Medina Sidonia came to call the Armada of the Guard the "Armada de avería." It sailed with the annual Tierra Firme flota, fetched the treasure, served in the Caribbean to deter pirates, and returned to Spain with the combined flotas from Havana. A few galleys still guarded the chief Caribbean ports, but in line with Medina Sidonia's earlier recommendations, fregatas increasingly took on the tasks of patrol and coast guard in New World waters.

In the summer of 1594 Medina Sidonia learned from Secretary Ibarra, at the King's request, about plans to strengthen the Ocean Armada, for which the King was in search of a new commander.[6] Because of his lackluster performance, Don Alonso de Bazán had been retired to Gibraltar, where his nephew, the second Marquis of Santa Cruz, served as governor.[7] About the problem of finding Bazán's successor, Ibarra confessed, "There are few from whom to choose one."

The plans assigned the twelve Ragusan galleons Medina Sidonia worked with in July 1595 to the Armada of the Ocean-Sea, along with nine other galleons, to give it a core of twenty-one big galleons that carried from twenty-five to thirty heavy guns each. Supporting the core were a dozen armed greatships and five zabras. In early 1596 the King appointed the Adelantado as its Captain General.

The Lisbon armada consisted of two big galleons, six small galleons (galeoncetes) of 300 toneladas each, and thirteen other ships. There was talk of yet another armada in the Strait of Gibraltar, which was customarily patrolled by twelve or more Spanish galleys based on Puerto Santa Maria.[8]

In the autumn months of 1595 Spain's rebuilt armadas faced a major challenge. From England in late August an expedition commanded by Sir Francis Drake—the possibility of which had so alarmed Medina Sidonia in 1592—departed for the Caribbean. With him sailed Sir John Hawkins. Madrid sent orders to Don Bernardino de Avellaneda to take the Lisbon squadron in pursuit. He sailed for the Caribbean at the end of the year. Philip II's armadas could at last respond quickly because they were kept ready, as Medina Sidonia had urged in 1586.

In May news arrived in Spain that the English had been routed from the Caribbean and that Drake had died. Word also came that the Cardinal-Archduke and his army in the Low Countries had taken Calais, and that relations between the English and Dutch were at an impasse. There was talk of a new Enterprise of England. When it was learned in mid-June in Madrid that the Earl of Essex and the Lord Admiral had taken another English fleet to sea, none could imagine where they might head. The Venetian ambassador reported on 25 June that "the Spaniards could not think that after the death of Drake and the scattering of his squadron, coupled with the loss of Calais, the English would think of moving to any great distance."[9]

Medina Sidonia was at Conil, where he had gone to supervise his almadraba. On Saturday afternoon, 29 June, the feast of St. Peter, he was recuperating from a long siege of fevers and taking the sea air in his carriage on the beach. At six in the evening a messenger sent by the President of the Casa de Contratación, Rev. Dr. Pedro Gutiérrez Flores, galloped across the sand to inform the Duke that a hostile fleet of eighty sail had rounded Cape St. Vincent and was headed toward the coast of Andalusia. The President begged Medina Sidonia to hasten to Cádiz, take charge of the defenses, and establish order where chaos suddenly reigned.[10]

The Duke hurried to his residence and drafted dispatches to be delivered to the cities, towns, and señores of the region, ordering that all assigned militia companies, horse and foot, march at once for the defense of the coast and Cádiz. When he had finished, shortly after midnight, he set out for Puerto Real, where he had requested the responsible commanders and officials to meet him after eight Sunday morning. He had been admonished by the King not to risk his person in Cádiz after he had rushed to its defense in 1587.

Since 1587 the fortifications of Cádiz had been only slightly improved. A thick, modern wall built to hold artillery which faced the landward approach to the city was but half-finished, though a new wall fronting the docks had been completed. Close by the landward wall was an old-fashioned citadel that dominated the town, and beyond the far end of the new harbor wall stood the weather-beaten bastion of San Felipe, which faced with its guns the entrance to Cadiz Bay. But westward from San Felipe, there were little more than garden walls, and the city's defense was left to the rugged, rocky coast. Where there was a cove at La Caleta that had a sandy beach suitable for a small landing party, a strong earthwork had been erected, and at the nearby monastery of San Sebastián a tower had been started.

On the mainland opposite Fort San Felipe stood the fort of Santa Catalina del Puerto, which was the responsibility of the Duke of Medinaceli, señor of Puerto Santa Maria. Because Cadiz Bay at this point is over three miles wide, the guns of the two forts together could not begin to mask it effectively.

From Cádiz, two miles down the road that led along the sandspit to the mainland, there was an earthwork that held three old cannon at Puntal, a point that protruded like a spur into Cadiz Bay and divided the inner bay from the outer. From Puntal the sandspit widened and became a broad, flat island, the Isla de León, separated from the mainland by a broad, brackish creek crossed only by the new Suazo Bridge. The bridge, an impressive stone structure, was not yet finished, its center arch spanned only by wooden planks. Medina Sidonia and Hernando de Añasco, the soldier-corregidor of Cádiz in 1590, had started a strong earthwork to defend the bridge, but Añasco's successor, the jurist Antonio Girón, had not continued the project. The defense of the bridge remained with the antique and decrepit Suazo Castle, property of the Duke of Arcos.

In Cadiz Bay a large part of the New Spain flota was fitting out, along with four big galleons of the Guard Armada, *San Felipe*, the capitana of 1,259 toneladas, *San Matías*, *San Andrés*, and *Santo Tomás*, which had been designated to escort it. The Guard General Coloma was in Seville and had left his Admiral, Don Diego de Sotomayor, in charge. In addition to the flota and its escort, there rode in the bay three well-armed fregatas of the type used to run treasure, two privately owned galleons bound for Lisbon with a cargo of grain, three big Levanters, and a host of smaller vessels of every description. Altogether the cognizant officials believed that between forty and fifty vessels worthy of note were anchored in the bay.

Eighteen seaworthy galleys were also in Cadiz Bay, moored at their base, Puerto Santa Maria. Their Captain General, the Adelantado, had just been appointed to the command of the Ocean Armada and was hurrying from Madrid to Lisbon, aware that an English fleet was at sea. In charge of the galleys in Cadiz Bay was his lieutenant, Don Juan Portocarrero. Other vessels, including galleons of the Guard Armada and ships of the New Spain flota, anchored off Chipiona, in the Guadalquivir at Sanlúcar, and upriver toward Seville.

In Cádiz when the alarm arrived, there were 80 soldiers of a garrison supposed to number 300, and the corregidor Girón mustered 510 more people of the local militia in the *plaza de armas*. The militia of Cádiz, as in other maritime towns, formed its companies by nation. In Cádiz there were companies of Spaniards, Basques [Vizcayans], Portuguese, Genoese, and Flemings, in varying numbers. The Council of War in 1592 worried that the population estimated at 400 vecinos was inadequate for its defense and wanted it brought up to 800.[11] The total population may have reached 6,000 because of the large number of transients.[12]

President Gutiérrez summoned Girón, Sotomayor, Portocarrero, the flota's General, Luis Alfonso Flores, and Admiral, Sebastián de Arancivia, and the Casa's Treasurer, Francisco Tello de Guzmán, to meet with him and determine what to do. Each had his own thoughts, Sotomayor and Portocarrero producing conflicting instructions, and little was decided. It was at the end of this meeting that Gutiérrez wrote Medina Sidonia, pleading with him to come quickly and take charge.

Medina Sidonia at daybreak on 30 June, after a journey of some twenty miles traveling in a litter, neared Puerto Real. Outside the entrance to the bay the English fleet waited at anchor, beyond the range of the Spanish guns. The young Marquis of Santa Cruz, who had come from Gibraltar to visit and assumed command of four galleys, took his galleys across the bay from Puerto Santa Maria and worked close along-shore to La Caleta to prevent the English from landing troops in the launches that circulated round their fleet. Spaniards and Genoese from Cádiz hurried to reinforce the earthwork at La Caleta, dragging five pieces of artillery with them. Gutiérrez in the meantime tried to remove the incompetent corregidor from command of the militia and called for the infantry captain of the galleon *San Matías* to come ashore and take charge.

The news that an English fleet was standing at the entrance to Cadiz Bay quickly spread through western Andalusia. By eight in the morning the Corregidor of Jerez, Don Leonardo de Cos, had his companies mustered and on the road for the coast. Close to 200 horsemen, following the cock's tail pennon of the city, and the first company of foot to muster headed for the Suazo Bridge; the four remaining companies of foot marched late in the morning for Puerto Santa Maria to board the galleys for the crossing to Cádiz.

Forty horsemen and a company of arquebusiers from Medina Sidonia's town of Chiclana, the town closest to Cádiz, hurried to the beleaguered city, accompanied by horsemen from other nearby towns. The Duke of Arcos, assigned to the relief of Gibraltar, assembled his people at the Charterhouse near Jerez on a road that led to Gibraltar, but much closer to Cádiz. He stood ready to respond as ordered.

When Medina Sidonia arrived in Puerto Real, his people from Chiclana with their companions were already on the road to Cádiz, and the Corregidor of Jerez and his company of horse were just leaving Jerez. They probably passed through Puerto Real late in the morning and reached Cádiz in midafternoon. The Jerez foot company that followed them did not enter Cádiz till after dark, while the four companies that had marched to Puerto Real found the galleys already out and the waters too choppy for their transfer to Cádiz by launch. Medina Sidonia hoped that they might be shipped to Cádiz Monday morning.

The people who continued to arrive at Puerto Real Medina Sidonia decided to post at the Suazo Bridge, rather than send them into Cádiz after dark. Perhaps 350 militia infantry and 300 horsemen had already reached or were still approaching the city to join the 80 soldiers and 510 militiamen resident there.

From Puerto Real Medina Sidonia saw late in the afternoon the enemy fleet weigh anchor and head into the outermost part of Cadiz Bay. He learned later that many of the ships and a fourth of the soldiers aboard were Dutch. He had always feared and warned about the consequences to Spain if the allied English and Dutch truly cooperated.

While during the armada campaign of 1588 one ally had barely known what the other was doing, for the expedition to Cádiz they joined forces. In 1596 the English feared that Philip II was preparing to resume the Enterprise of England and send aid to rebels in Ireland. A tercio at Blavet in conjunction with holdout Leaguers still threatened Brest,[13] and in 1595 four Spanish galleys raided Penzance. The Queen and her chief advisers determined to frustrate Philip's designs by a preemptive naval strike, such as Drake had carried out in 1587, and she commissioned Essex and the Lord Admiral to burn "the King of Spain's ships of war in their havens, before they should come forth to the seas, and therewith also destroying his victuals and his munitions for the arming of his navy."[14] Though Henri IV begged her to assist him to retake Calais, Elizabeth, who had her own claim on it, would not. The English persisted in their original plan, in which the Dutch willingly joined.

According to Medina Sidonia's later reckoning, the Anglo-Dutch fleet numbered 164 ships, including 30 of the Queen's galleons of more than 1,000 toneladas, 50 ships between 200 and 300 toneladas, 53 hulks and flyboats of Holland and Zeeland, and 31 smaller vessels.[15] A contemporary English relation lists 18 ships and pinnaces belonging to the Queen and a grand total of 128, including a "Flemish" squadron of 24.[16]

To meet the Anglo-Dutch attack the Spaniards had arrayed their best fighting ships and galleys in line across the bay's mouth from Fort San Felipe to Fort Santa Catalina del Puerto. As the enemy fleet advanced there was some exchange of cannon fire between them. In Cádiz itself all was confusion. When the guns of fort San Felipe opened fire, the carriages of three cannon collapsed.

At sunset, the English and Dutch halted their advance for the night. In awe of the discipline and power of their opponents, the chiefs of the flota and its escort galleons, with the approval of Gutiérrez, voted to withdraw to the inner bay beyond Puntal. Gutiérrez explained that "ten ships could grapple each of ours, while the rest could burn the flota. . . . In front of the bastion at Puntal, because it is narrow, three galleons scarcely fit, and with two fregatas in front and the galleys divided on the sides, the entrance would be very difficult or impossible to the enemy."[17] Gutiérrez also repeated his plea for Medina Sidonia to come to Cádiz.

At daybreak Monday, 1 July, Medina Sidonia found time to draft his first dispatch for the King, informing him of his dispositions and of his resolution to go to Cádiz in response to Gutiérrez's pleas, despite the expressed wish of the King that he not do so. From his window he could see the flota anchored in the inner bay and galleons of the Guard Armada moving into position in the narrows between Puntal and Mata Gorda. As he finished the letter, he detected movement on the English side. "At this moment, the English fleet is making sail, entering the bay with a fair wind. . . . Of what happens, I shall keep Your Majesty advised."[18]

As the Spanish galleons took station, the 18 galleys sought to hinder the English advance. Failing in their effort, they fell back under the walls of Cádiz, whence 10 withdrew to Puntal and the other 8 circled back toward Puerto Santa Maria. Surging into the bay, the English and Dutch fired at the galleys, Cádiz, and the forts. By midmorning the chief English ships, including those of Essex, the Lord Admiral, Sir Walter Raleigh, and Lord Thomas Howard, had closed with the three Spanish galleons that blocked the narrows and pounded them with gunfire. A Spanish chronicler of the event, Padre Abreu, observed that the fire of the Spanish galleons was too quick, which seems evidence of weak charges, badly loaded and poorly aimed from light-shotted guns. The English fire in contrast he found steady and powerful.[19]

The Duke had mounted a horse to ride to Cádiz, and with his party stopped to watch the fight from the shore of Mata Gorda, which protrudes toward Puntal. English small craft plied the water offshore, preventing Spaniards from setting out in launches from Puerto Santa Maria and firing with muskets at Medina Sidonia and those with him.

After some hours of cannonading, *San Felipe* capitana and *San Andrés* tried with the help of the galleys to warp round to bring their undamaged broadsides against the enemy but struck bottom in the shallow water. Seeing the Spaniards stuck in the mud, the English warships closed in. Flames from *San Felipe* shot into the sky. Though at the time Medina Sidonia thought the English set fire to *San Felipe*, he learned later that Sotomayor had decided to burn his capitana rather than let the English take it. The crew abandoned ship to swim, wade, or drown in the brackish water. The flames rising from their capitana took the fight from the remaining Spaniards. From galleons and merchantmen sailors fled in small craft or swam for shore. The English promptly seized the abandoned galleons *San Andrés* and *San Matías*.

Leaving the scene of the disaster, Medina Sidonia returned to Puerto Real and drafted another report to the King:[20]

This morning I wrote Your Majesty that the English fleet was entering into the bay, since the flota and galleons of Your Majesty had retired inside of El Puntal, with the galleons and galleys standing in the mouth. There then came swarming round them the best ships of the English, and they have cannonaded them for more than four hours with such great weight of guns that *San Felipe* and *San Andrés*, wanting to turn around, went aground. . . . I have wanted to give account to Your Majesty of how great is the power of this fleet. Little confidence can be put in our people, though they are of the vicinity; about this I have spoken many times to Your Majesty. Now to experience it weighs on my soul.

Great crowds had turned out to watch the events in the bay. Seeing their side worsted, they succumbed to panic and began to flee for the interior. The raw militia companies remained but fretted nervously as they watched the men from the flota and galleons flailing ashore. Medina Sidonia rallied them and collected what soldiers he could from the men who had escaped the ships and ordered them to march for the Suazo Bridge and Cádiz.

The English lost no time getting their people ashore. They left the ships of the flota and other vessels to be rounded up later at will. Launches soon put two thousand English and Dutchmen ashore at Puntal, where, under the command of Essex and veteran officers, they quickly overran the earthwork. Of its three cannon, one blew up when fired. Leaving people to cover the road to the mainland, Essex hurried toward Cádiz with the bulk of the English troops.

Riding for the Suazo Bridge with the people he had rallied, Medina Sidonia late in the afternoon encountered a municipal councilor who had fled Cádiz. He told the Duke that all was lost. The English had overrun everything and blocked the road from the mainland. Medina Sidonia positioned his men at the Suazo Bridge, then proceeded to Chiclana to set up a new headquarters and send a dispatch to the King to inform him of how matters stood.

At the Suazo Bridge, the people of the companies that had fled Puntal raced across it with the English close behind. The English halted at the bridge, tore up its center planking, then turned to attack the Suazo Castle that flanked it. The few defenders the Duke of Arcos's warden had in the castle fled, but the English forces, anxious to depart to plunder Cádiz, began to dissolve. Only a few Englishmen remained behind hastily erected barricades to guard the bridge.

Under cover of darkness, Spaniards began to cross the creek. Encountering little resistance, they took prisoners, cut down stragglers, and reoccupied Suazo Castle. They also garnered news of Cádiz. From Cádiz Monday afternoon the Corregidor of Jerez had led his horsemen in a mad charge against the attackers and was driven back. When the English and Dutch reached the unfinished landward wall, they swarmed over it and soon forced the gate. Most of the defenders retreated to the old citadel and the bastion of San Felipe. The Corregidor of Jerez and his people barricaded themselves in a strong house.

Tuesday morning, after a proper amount of talk and bluster, the Spanish holdouts in Cádiz surrendered and agreed to pay 120,000 ducats ransom for their lives. Gutiérrez, Councilman Pedro del Castillo, and other rich men and civic leaders were held for separate ransom or kept hostage to guarantee the payment of the 120,000 ducats. The remaining citizens were permitted to keep the clothing and jewelry they wore as well as an extra suit of clothing and were allowed to leave the city.

Medina Sidonia, when he had no further hope of saving Cádiz, turned to the task of keeping the disaster from assuming larger proportions. The road from Jerez to Seville lay open, and no militia companies from Seville had yet appeared. The news that the English were at the entrance to Cadiz Bay reached Seville only late Sunday night, though the authorities knew for at least twenty-four hours that the English fleet was in Andalusian waters.

According to royal decree, Seville's militia was to provide six infantry companies totaling fifteen hundred men and two companies of horse, of one hundred riders each, for the defense of Cadiz Bay. As the tocsin roused them in the small hours of Monday morning, the Royal Assistant Priego and the city council met in emergency session. The infantry were short of firearms, and the Factor Francisco Duarte, who was spending a weekend in the country, had to be summoned to find weapons, powder, and shot from the stores assembled for the Indies flotas, which proved no easy task.

On Monday afternoon three companies took the road toward Cádiz only half armed, while the weapons, as they were located, were loaded on lighters to be hurried downriver to Sanlúcar, whence they could be distributed to those who needed them. The half-armed infantry were preceded by swarms of gentlemen-volunteers on horseback. The poet Miguel de Cervantes likened the march of the militia to the parade of confraternities during Holy Week.

At daybreak Tuesday, Medina Sidonia could see that the Suazo

Bridge was for the moment in Spanish hands and under repair, and the Duke of Arcos's warden was again in Suazo Castle. Medina Sidonia and the Judge of the Indies, Francisco Tello, who had been aboard the flota, looked over inner Cadiz Bay, where the flota's largely deserted ships lay, and the outer bay beyond, where the English fleet was anchored with the two captured galleons. They had agreed after Monday's battle that Portocarrero's galleys ought to tow two or three big Levanters to the narrows between Puntal and Mata Gorda and scuttle them, so they would serve as a barricade against the English. The galleys should then patrol the waters round the remaining ships to prevent the English from getting at them in launches, of which Medina Sidonia estimated they had eighty.

But Portocarrero had ignored Tello and did little but patrol and, according to his later court martial, permit his men to loot the abandoned merchantmen. Tuesday morning, when he saw that the Suazo Bridge was safe, his people removed the center planks again and towed the galleys down the shallow creek from the inner bay to Sancti Petri on the coast. Young Santa Cruz was there with the rest of the galleys. Reunited, the squadron sailed to Rota, at the northernmost edge of Cadiz Bay.

Seeing the flota abandoned by the galleys and aware that considerable looting had been going on, Francisco Tello consulted with the flota's General Flores, his officers, and the ships' owners about the next step. The King's officers wanted to burn the defenseless ships, the ships' owners wanted to negotiate with the English for their ransom. Unofficial feelers were put out toward the English with an offer of 2 million ducats. The English purportedly wanted 4 million. Tello went to Chiclana to talk over his dilemma with Medina Sidonia.

Before they had reached any decision, they saw from the Duke's windows fires begin to rise from ships trapped in the inner bay. An estimated 4 million ducats' worth of cargoes burned, without counting the value of the ships and guns.[21] Medina Sidonia reckoned that thirty-four ships were lost, including the royal galleon burned and two captured, three fregatas used to fetch treasure, the two Lisbon galleons, three Levanters, and ships of the flota.

With Cádiz fallen and the ships aflame, Medina Sidonia focused his attention on the defense of Jerez, Sanlúcar, and Seville. The enemy forces he faced seemed immensely strong, and Andalusia lay open to them. He guessed correctly that they also hoped to sack "Porta Reall, Porta Sta Maria, St Lucar and Sherez, as also to burne and take suche shipps and gallies as should be found in the places aforesaide,"[22] and he feared for Seville.

The greatest number of his militia was concentrated at Puerto Santa Maria, which seemed to him the likeliest spot for an English attack, since they could cross the bay at will in launches. Going via the Suazo Bridge was the long way round Cadiz Bay, over marshlands and salt flats, and to march on Jerez and Seville they would still have to pass through Puerto Santa Maria. If he concentrated his forces at the bridge and tried to recover Cádiz, as critics claimed he should have, the English could easily have cut him off by crossing the bay on ships and launches and placing themselves between him and Jerez, Sanlúcar, and Seville. After some discussion about a counterattack on Cádiz, Medina Sidonia headed for Puerto Santa Maria.

To guard the Suazo Bridge, he left some 800 men, 400 of them soldiers who had abandoned the galleons of the Guard Armada, the rest militiamen from Jerez and his own estates, all under the command of the soldiers' captain Don Pedro de Esquivel, another veteran of 1588. While Suazo Castle also remained in Spanish hands, its warden answered to none but the Duke of Arcos. He did accept a few of Esquivel's soldiers.

The first confused reports Medina Sidonia received from the English side gave credence to his suspicion that they intended to move against Seville, possibly by way of the river Guadalquivir. While there were armed ships and galleons in the Guadalquivir off Sanlúcar, Portocarrero's galleys at Rota seemed the best means of defending the broad, shallow mouth of the river, which was flanked by strong bulwarks. He reminded Portocarrero that his eighteen galleys were the only naval force that remained after the loss of Cádiz and the ships in its bay and entreated him not to sail for Lisbon, where he had been ordered, until the English left.

From Puerto Santa Maria Medina Sidonia left for Jerez to establish a central plaza de armas from which he could cover both Puerto Santa Maria and Sanlúcar. He ordered Esquivel and his marine soldiery to join him, leaving only the growing number of militiamen at the Suazo Bridge. When he reached Jerez, he found Francisco Duarte hard at work distributing the arquebuses and munitions he had brought from Seville. The Duke appointed him Veedor General of the assembling forces.

Of the companies arriving from Seville, Medina Sidonia sent three of infantry and one of horse to Puerto Santa Maria, and a company of foot to Sanlúcar, along with a company from his own town of Medina Sidonia. In Jerez he kept Esquivel's 400 soldiers and 110 horsemen, plus 400 militiamen on foot, who had among them only 15 arquebuses.

At Puerto Santa Maria the Duke counted over 800 men, 650 with firearms. Altogether he had on the morning of 4 July a few more than 2,000 men under arms to defend the road to Seville. In Sanlúcar there were perhaps 1,500 more, who likely served under the orders of Don Luis de Fajardo, an officer of the Guard Armada. The Royal Assistant of Seville had come down the Guadalquivir to the anchorage of Las Horcadas, where barricades were erected and equipped with artillery. The ships anchored off Sanlúcar he ordered upriver and their cargoes brought ashore.

Francisco Duarte broadcasted for the sake of the English rumors that Medina Sidonia had mustered 10,000 men; unfortunately for Medina Sidonia's reputation, the rumor traveling the greater distance to Madrid caused many to believe that Medina Sidonia was idling in Andalusia at the head of an army of 25,000.[23]

In Cádiz the English and Dutch seemed well ensconced. The reports that reached the Spanish side described them as plundering the city, mistreating its inhabitants, feasting and drinking, and hearing Protestant services in the cathedral they had desecrated. The hundreds of wretches who fled the city, the rich in boats, the poor on foot, claimed that the English had been decent enough but accused the Dutch of wanton cruelty, conduct hardly surprising given the endless tales, true and otherwise, of Spanish atrocities in the Low Countries.

Medina Sidonia sent emissaries to Essex to discover his intentions and arrange for exchanges of captives. The Spaniards had taken a few Englishmen, usually described as drunk, who had been looting houses near the Suazo Bridge. From the Lord Admiral Medina Sidonia received a polished Latin letter that requested the release of Englishmen pulling oars in Spanish galleys in any exchange of prisoners.[24]

Addressed to "Illustrissimo Principi Duci Medinae de Sidonia," it began, "From some Spaniards I have learned that Your Excellency was in Puerto Santa Maria. Since in anno Domini 1588, in my duties, I was ordered against you and your forces and was at the time appointed sole general, I do not believe that I am unknown to you." Now, he continued, war has come here and your people and places have been taken. He appealed to human decency and referred to the laws of war (*jure belli*), and his desire to free his captives. "You have in your galleys," he then stated, "fifty-one of the Queen's subjects captive, and I have no doubt that you will release them to me, as I shall release yours." He dated it "aboard the royal English fleet at Cádiz, the last of June, *stylo antiquo*," and signed it "Howard."

Medina Sidonia had eight English captives to exchange, and though, as he advised Howard, the galleys came under a different jurisdiction, he requested Portocarrero to release his English rowers. Portocarrero found, freed, and delivered thirty-nine of them.[25]

A matter of more serious concern to Medina Sidonia was the appearance of three Moroccan galliots in Cadiz Bay which, he correctly suspected, brought envoys from the Sharif to talk with Essex. With them, he later learned, came Dom António's son Dom Cristovão. But the feared delivery of Cádiz to the Sharif did not take place: only a few Moorish slaves were freed and returned to Morocco.

After 4 July, Medina Sidonia watched daily streams of men arriving at Jerez, armed and unarmed, mounted and on foot, following their señores, corregidores, and captains from Córdoba, Ecija, Carmona, and far off Jaen, and from the estates of the dukes of Arcos, Osuna, Cardona, and Alcalá de los Gazules.

With growing numbers of men, the counsel given Medina Sidonia became bolder. The city council of Seville suggested that he have the galleys land his men at La Caleta, at the seaward tip of Cádiz, and retake the city; they sent a copy of their suggestion to the King and decently included Medina Sidonia's reply: "What you propose might be carried out with veteran soldiers, but not with the people here, who are all raw. Though they are many, they are not for such things."[26] When the veteran naval commander Don Luis Fajardo came to Jerez on the King's order to advise Medina Sidonia, he proposed that the Duke mass his people at the Suazo Bridge, cross it, and attack the English in Cádiz. Medina Sidonia responded that he could not carry out the proposal because he lacked the people and munitions. Looking for himself, Fajardo saw that the Duke was right.

In addition to suggestions about how to throw the English out of Cádiz, Medina Sidonia received from Seville a request for help in finding the 120,000 ducats ransom asked for the people of Cádiz. Don Antonio Zapata, Bishop of Cádiz, had been in Seville when the city fell, and he begged Seville's city council to find the money for his flock. The council responded that they had neither royal authority to release such a sum, nor were they sure they had it at all, given the expenses of arming and dispatching their militia.[27] Medina Sidonia claimed that he neither could offer Zapata anything. According to Cabrera de Córdoba, he had sent his own treasury from Sanlúcar to Trebujena for safekeeping.

As the English in Cádiz made no new moves, Medina Sidonia began to hope they had no further designs against Andalusia. The men arriving in Jerez, Puerto Santa Maria, and Sanlúcar steadily swelled the number under his orders. A muster of 9 July counted 2,995 infantry, including 744 regular soldiers in Esquivel's companies.[28] Altogether there were 164 officers, 503 musketeers, 1,815 arquebusiers, 213 pikemen, and 280 without arms. The figures for individual militia companies suggested that barely half the men required by the 1595 decree had in fact turned out. The four companies of Jerez that should have numbered 1,000 mustered only 512. Not in this muster are the horsemen or the companies from Medina Sidonia's own estates. His own people were not counted either in his final tally, when Medina Sidonia stated that only 3,600 foot, 430 horsemen, and 300 gentlemen had answered his summons. Padre Abreu gave similar numbers, though he mentioned that "there had gathered much of the nobility of Spain, gentlemen, captains and men of means, all of whom made such a show that no one reckoned there were fewer than 10,000 or 12,000 fighting men, but as it was the beginning of harvest time for cereals, many of those men returned to their lands without being able to stay. . . . Others left because of the terrible heat and little comfort . . . and moreover licenses and passes were given to many, and thus the army diminished notably."

Medina Sidonia's figures seem to reflect only those companies concentrated in Jerez and Puerto Santa Maria. Because the English enjoyed the mobility given them by command of the sea, they could choose to strike anywhere along the coast they wished. Therefore Medina Sidonia had to keep people in Sanlúcar, and he probably alerted his companies from the County of Niebla to respond either to an attack on Huelva or in the Algarve. The Marquis of Ayamonte and the Duke of Béjar, for his Marquisate of Gibraleón, apologized that they needed their people to defend their own shores, which Béjar noted were threatened by corsairs while the English were in Cádiz.[29] Also missing from the musters are the companies of Chiclana, Vejer, and the Duke of Arcos's estates posted at the Suazo Bridge and Castle.

Another place that required defenders was Gibraltar, where Medina Sidonia assigned his militia from Jimena. Command responsibility for Gibraltar he delegated to the Duke of Arcos, to whom he sent seven veteran officers as advisers. It would be safe to estimate that by 9 July some 6,000 militiamen, of the 8,200 foot and 1,060 horse stipulated in the 1595 decree, had turned out in response to Medina Sidonia's orders for the defense of the coast from Ayamonte to Gibraltar. In addition Medina Sidonia had Esquivel's regulars, while Portocarrero had another 500 soldiers aboard his galleys and Don Luis Fajardo had men from the Guard Armada on the Guadalquivir. Regardless of their number, they were no match for the more than 6,000 well-equipped and well-drilled troops carried in the Anglo-Dutch fleet, of whom over 2,000 were veterans of the Low Countries Wars.

Money and munitions Medina Sidonia found more scarce than men. Powder and shot were taken from a Dutch ship embargoed at Sanlúcar, and munitions were sent from Granada and Málaga. Seville claimed it had only 30,000 ducats cash on hand, and Francisco Duarte bought supplies on credit. "All that has been done," Medina Sidonia told the King afterwards, "I do not know how it was even started, since Your Majesty has not seen fit to provide any money, without which things cannot go on."[30]

From the day the English were reported at sea news of them had been trickling to Madrid and to the King, who was at Toledo seriously ill. When the first news arrived that the English had arrived off Cádiz, all in Madrid believed that the land and naval forces available there were sufficient to meet the threat and that the city was in no great danger. Word that the English had taken Cádiz probably reached the King on 5 July, for the next day the Venetian Ambassador in Madrid reported it in his dispatch, adding that Medina Sidonia and his brother-in-law Béjar were feared taken with the city.[31]

At court on 6 July Idiáquez and Moura summoned a *junta de Mar-Oceano* that included themselves, War Councilors Don Juan de Acuña Vela and Don Pedro de Velasco, Secretary Prada, Secretary Ibarra, and one or two others. They could not understand, they informed the King, how "such small forces overcame so many, and so quickly," unless it were punishment from heaven.[32] "This disaster has increased the strength and morale of the enemy and weakened that of Your Majesty, and has put affairs in such great flux that all else must be put aside and not another hour lost in seeking a remedy."

The junta recommended that Velasco raise an Army of Andalusia at Córdoba, for which 200,000 ducats had to be found, plus another 30,000 ducats for the account of the artillery. They designated Hernando de Añasco, former corregidor of Cádiz, Veedor General and dispatched in the meantime several veteran officers, including Don

Sancho de Leyva, the late Don Alonso de Leyva's youngest brother, to the scene of the action.

The junta did not limit its deliberations to Cádiz but also took cognizance of the great sweep of the Atlantic across which the Indies flotas were inching toward the Andalusian ports. The junta shot orders to the Adelantado and his Almirante General Diego Brochero in Lisbon to make ready the Ocean Armada, and to the North Coast ports to outfit more ships for the royal service. And they were ready to withdraw most of the tercio fighting in Brittany and would withdraw all if the Catholic League did not prove more cooperative.

The junta also laid down guidelines for the reform of the militia, which would occupy the Council of War for years to come and affect all the lay and ecclesiastical señores, civic and religious corporations, and *encomiendas* (commanderies) of the Military Orders in the kingdom.[33] It seemed urgent not only to expel the English from Cádiz, but also to prevent such a loss from occurring again.

From Cádiz the English launched on the morning of 10 July what seemed a major attack under Essex with 2,000 foot and 400 horse against the Suazo Castle and Bridge. Arcos's warden was again ready to abandon the castle, but the men provided by Medina Sidonia stood firm, and the English withdrew. The defenders of Suazo Castle and Bridge announced a major victory. They had no way of knowing at the time that the English had already decided to abandon Cádiz, and the attack was a reconnaissance in force to probe the strength of the forces at the bridge and determine if they could threaten the reembarkation.

By 13 July Medina Sidonia, who had received no direct answer about the intentions of the English concerning Cádiz, suspected they would soon sail. That evening he sent a delegation by launch to deal with the Lord Admiral and Essex. The delegates pleaded with the English not to destroy the city and promised to pay its 120,000 ducat ransom in notes to be redeemed by Flemish and German bankers in France or Flanders. Medina Sidonia stated that he would personally guarantee the notes.

The English wanted cash, and Essex announced that regardless of the ransom, he would destroy Cádiz for "reasons of state," the expression, Abreu noted, "of the infamous Machiavelli." After futile argument, Medina Sidonia's delegates won no more than Essex's promise to spare Cádiz's churches, and agreement to release the hostages for half the ransom in cash, a sum they still could not meet.

The delegates returned virtually empty-handed. The next day Medina Sidonia watched the English and Dutch begin to board their ships. By Monday, 15 July, most were aboard, and Cádiz was in flames. All day Tuesday the Anglo-Dutch fleet stood in the bay, awaiting favorable winds. On Wednesday a levanter filled their sails and they headed to sea, in the direction of Cape St. Vincent.

Medina Sidonia sent Don Sancho de Leyva, whom he had made his chief assistant, into Cádiz with 200 sappers to put out the fires. Another 100 soon followed to bury the animals the English had slaughtered. A few days later, after visiting Cádiz, Medina Sidonia estimated that 290 houses had burned, 328 had people living in them, and another 685 were habitable.[34] The cathedral, hospital, and several other religious establishments had been destroyed.

Medina Sidonia's entry into Cádiz was treated by Cervantes in a satirical sonnet about the episode, in which he likened the Duke to a blustering calf.[35] It may have cost him the patronage of the Duke of Béjar, Medina Sidonia's brother-in-law, to whom later Cervantes hopefully dedicated the first part of *Don Quixote*.

Soon after the English sailed, Medina Sidonia discharged most of the militia, though he kept 500 men of the best companies to garrison Cádiz. Of more than 1,000 regular soldiers who had been assembled, he sent 800 aboard Portocarrero's galleys, which sailed on 18 July to trail the English. To the Indies he dispatched swift vessels to warn the returning flotas and the armada of Don Bernardino de Avellaneda. Don Luis de Fajardo took charge of arming several hulks pressed for the Adelantado's armada at Lisbon and plumbed the shallows of Cadiz Bay to recover the guns of the galleon *San Felipe*, the three treasure fregatas, and other sunken vessels.

Assessing the debacle, Medina Sidonia sent a bitter letter to the King: "Your Majesty has ordered neither artillery nor powder nor money. This has endured longer than can be believed. I have on my own account done as much as I can."[36] He begged the King to give Don Pedro de Velasco the necessary authority for his command: "I shall serve only as a soldier in the ranks." He forwarded to court the musters taken of the militia companies, apart from his own, that had responded to the emergency, to be compared with the claims of their señores and municipalities. "These troops were useless," he added.[37] To the King's personal secretary, Don Martín de Idiáquez, Medina Sidonia laid bare his feelings: "I have given His Majesty the best years of my life, endangered and spent along with my fortune in his service."[38] The King responded with a brief letter thanking Medina Sidonia for his zeal.[39]

But King and court remained shocked by the events at Cádiz and were determined to fix blame. Fajardo and the Licentiate Diego Armenteros received a commission to discover the degrees of "culpability on the part of those governing."

Many of those in positions of command when Cádiz fell were now being held hostage in England. Medina Sidonia insisted that he sent them "not orders, but good advice," which they did not follow. Gutiérrez, who was ransomed separately, seems to have been exonerated as a cleric, but he was soon removed as President of the Casa de Contratación, and his post given to Avellaneda, a naval general. On the handling of the galleons and galleys, only Portocarrero and several of his officers were court-martialed for failing to protect the flota and letting their men loot it. The investigators never could fix blame for the burning of the flota, and a consensus developed that its crews had burned it to cover their tracks after they had plundered it. Both its General, Luis Flores, and the Casa's Treasurer, Francisco Tello de Guzmán, denied having given orders to burn it, though they admitted considering doing so in the extremity neither thought had been reached. Tello admitted that he shared in the "general culpability, though I did nothing particularly wrong."[40] He expressed his anger about the investigation and charges to Medina Sidonia: "They know so little of what is prudence that they make accusations because rash deeds were not done or attacks that could have ruined kingdoms were not made. If a thousand men of those we had were lost, there would have been no defense left in the whole land. There were neither arms nor men, only prudence and cunning, about which they who are talking so much know so little."

The investigation launched in August continued through the winter, always skirting round Medina Sidonia, though sometimes coming close. In early January the Duke's case was stated in a letter presented to the King and perhaps drafted by Don Pedro de Guzmán:[41] "Licentiate Armenteros and Don Luis de Fajardo are walking round Cádiz, trying to determine guilt in the loss of the city, and posing questions against the person and deeds of the Duke of Medina Sidonia, something neither he nor his relatives believe is being done at the order of Your Majesty." The letter stated that they were asking witnesses if the city would have been lost if Medina Sidonia had entered it, and ignored the incompetence of the local militia. The author reminded the King that in 1587 he had reprimanded the Duke for entering Cádiz. "In the suddenness of this occasion he could not have entered if he had wanted to."

But Armenteros and Fajardo, the author continued, did not wish to hear the Duke's side of the case and took only unfavorable testimony, not hard to find "with the many enemies the Duke has made in this region, by serving Your Majesty and not looking after private interests, and from his control of the customs of Sanlúcar." And it was not true that the Duke had ignored Cádiz's fortifications: "He had begged Your Majesty for the authority to supervise them, but the Council of War corresponded only with the Bishop, Antonio de Zapata, in this matter, and gave the Duke little support in other pressing matters concerning his authority over the coast."

What the author suggested was that decrees may have been issued, but the means necessary to carry out the decreed authority were lacking. The power over militia appointments and the vote on municipal councils Medina Sidonia wanted were not granted to him. When Medina Sidonia issued orders he depended on officers beholden to others for their positions to carry them out. The corregidores, the naval commanders, and the chiefs of the flota proved uncooperative, and "Don Juan Portocarrero was so jealous of this authority over the galleys that he refused to recognize a superior: I saw him be openly rude." What was worse, in the flota Medina Sidonia had discovered express authority to ignore orders he gave as Captain General of the Ocean-Sea, unless such orders were explicitly approved by the King or his ministers.

The author then defended the Duke's conduct of operations in response to the English attack and stated that "he merits thanks, not an investigation." About Medina Sidonia he concluded, "He has served Your Majesty for many years, and much to his cost; and those occasions that have met with misfortune have been the heavier burden for him, because of the care he has always put into your royal service."

The month after this letter was drafted, Don Cristóbal de Moura assured Medina Sidonia that his case was being well handled by Don Pedro, surely Don Pedro de Guzmán.[42] A month later the Count of Chinchón, who ranked close to Moura and Idiáquez in influence, advised Medina Sidonia not to worry about Armenteros's investigation.[43] He finished with a wish of good health for the Duchess. A few days later the King had a letter drafted for the Duke, in which he admitted that the matter was so serious that neither anyone or anything connected with it could be ignored. But, the draft concluded, "I have always been satisfied with your merits and I still am. I am sure that at all times you will show the zeal which you have hithertofore shown in my service, as is expected of you."[44]

The King seems only fair. The archival record that contains what he and his chief ministers knew supports Medina Sidonia's contentions. The problems were those of an early modern state that had outstripped its limited resources and depended for home defense on an organization of lanzas and militias inherited from centuries earlier that had become moribund during years of domestic peace. The organization had been sorely strained by the rising in 1568 of the Moriscos of Granada and proved unable to mount an adequate response when hit suddenly and hard by the Anglo-Dutch attack of 1596 on Cádiz.

✳ CHAPTER TWELVE ✳

From Philip II to Philip III

T HE ease with which the English and Dutch surprised and
captured Cádiz generated in the councils of the aging Philip
II strident calls for the reform of home defense and the militia. But Medina Sidonia, who had repeatedly urged reform,
found his authority as Captain General of the Coast of Andalusia
restricted rather than enhanced. Men with long military experience
assumed the most important royal offices in Andalusia and had no
desire to be circumscribed in their exercise by the local Captain General. Medina Sidonia had long advocated that a military man rather
than a jurist be given the Presidency of the Casa de Contratación, and
it was, to the naval general Don Bernardino de Avellaneda. Medina
Sidonia had urged repeatedly that a soldier serve as corregidor of Cadiz:
Hernando de Añasco was returned to that office with increased military powers. And as Royal Assistant of Seville, the King provided the
veteran soldier Don Francisco de Bobadilla, now Count of Puñonrostro, who had been in 1588 Medina Sidonia's Maestre de Campo
General.[1]

Military engineers swarmed round Cadiz Bay and the mouth of the
Guadalquivir to design and erect proper fortifications, for which the
estimated bill of 147,000 ducats was to be met one-third by the Crown
and two-thirds by the local powers. The cost of a new fort on the
Guadalquivir Medina Sidonia was to share with Seville.[2]

The señores of the coast, Ayamonte, Béjar for Gibraleón, Medina
Sidonia, Medinaceli, Arcos, and Alcalá were each entrusted with the
defense of his segment of coastline, and Arcos, who had become in 1591
Captain General of Granada, received explicit responsibility for the

defense of Gibraltar. Medina Sidonia had in effect been limited to the defense of Sanlúcar, the Arenas Gordas, and the shores of Conil, Trafalgar, and Zahara.

While Medina Sidonia brought what influence he could to bear at court for the recovery of his authority, he obeyed the new orders for the reform of his militia. He was to muster on his estates all Old Christian males aged eighteen through forty-five and forward the rosters and his nominations for officers to the Council of War, along with suggested ways of paying for the militia in a manner not too burdensome to the householders.[3] The militiamen were to be reassured that they were not required to serve outside the Kingdom of Castile.

To arm his men properly Medina Sidonia requested from the Council of War one hundred muskets and two thousand arquebuses and received the reply "there is not at present [such a quantity] in all the arsenals of Vizcaya."[4] Medina Sidonia turned to the arsenals of Milan and obtained through the Governor General, his cousin the Constable of Castile, a shipment of three hundred muskets and three thousand arquebuses, for which he had to pay 11,765 ducats.[5]

As Philip II and his Council of War undertook to reform the militia, they also prepared a counterattack on England. The armada was ordered to land troops in Ireland to aid a planned rebellion by the Earl of Tyrone. Medina Sidonia assisted in getting nineteen ships and hulks under way from Sanlúcar to Lisbon, to join an armada of eighty-one galleons and transports collected by the Adelantado of Castile, Captain General of the Ocean Armada. In late October 1596 the Adelantado took his armada to sea, under protest, only to have storms that struck it off the coast smash his effort. To Medina Sidonia Andrés de Prada expressed his disappointment: "It has pleased God to send a storm against the armada off Cape Finisterre; Pedro de Ibella and his flagship are lost, along with thirteen others, the best built for Don Juan de Cardona."[6] The losses proved less than at first feared and included only one of Cardona's galleons.[7]

To repair the armada's strength, Medina Sidonia suggested that Don Bernardino de Avellaneda's armada, which had arrived in Lisbon from the Indies, be outfitted at the expense of the avería and then join the Adelantado at El Ferrol rather than return to the Indies.[8]

For fetching the treasure in 1597 he urged the employment of Captain Hierónimo de Ojeda's six new galleons just launched in Vizcaya. When the King responded that Avellaneda's galleons could go for the treasure and the six new galeoncetes from Vizcaya should join the armada, Medina Sidonia answered that Avellaneda's galeoncetes had just returned from two hard crossings and needed overhaul; he emphasized that they too were small galleons and repeated his argument that Ojeda's galeoncetes should fetch the treasure.[9]

In the end Avellaneda brought six royal galleons, only one of them small, to the Guadalquivir for outfitting, and in March 1597, Juan de Garibay, who replaced him as General of the Armada de la Guarda, sailed with the six galleons, two others, and two pataches for the treasure. Medina Sidonia had suggested that they sail by way of the Cape Verde Islands to attack and destroy or chase away some one hundred Dutch hulks he had heard went there for salt, which they could no longer get in Spain.[10] But Garibay sailed too late. It was urgent that the treasure be brought that year to Spain, and Garibay received orders to fetch it and return home as soon as possible. In late 1596 Philip II had declared the third major bankruptcy of his reign.

But to Medina Sidonia the risk of hurricanes seemed a greater danger than the short-term consequences of bankruptcy. He believed it would be September before Garibay could collect all the treasure and be ready to sail from Havana. He urged the King not to permit the galleons to sail till after the hurricane season had ended in November. Garibay should sail in December, after the change of season, which would bring him to Spain at the beginning of February.

Medina Sidonia's urgings were not acted on. Both Garibay's galleons and the New Spain flota sailed from Havana in September and with good fortune reached the Azores safely, where they had to seek shelter under the guns of the great fort of Angra to escape waiting English squadrons commanded by Essex and Sir Walter Raleigh ("ser Gaute Rauli" in Medina Sidonia's correspondence). Medina Sidonia had already learned from Pedro del Castillo, just ransomed from England, that Essex was at sea, and he had warned Madrid accordingly.[11] Castillo claimed that the "headstrong" Essex and the English court learned quickly of developments in Spain through agents of the exiled Antonio Pérez.[12]

With Essex and Raleigh absent from English waters, the Adelantado sailed from El Ferrol-La Coruña in late October with a bigger armada than he had led the year before and headed into the Channel. His object was to land a small army at Falmouth or, if checked in that, at Brest. Once again storms struck and forced him to return to port, but without serious losses. "All possible was done," Philip responded to the news. "God punishes us for our sins."[13]

Essex arrived in England from the Azores, ignorant that the armada was at sea, and was penned in port by the same storm that forced the Adelantado home.

Medina Sidonia saw Garibay's galleons and the flota cross the bar at Sanlúcar on 21 February 1598, after a safe voyage from the Azores under the protection of thirty ships of the Ocean Armada. Soon afterward he left for Madrid on public and personal business.

In Madrid in April he was telling the Venetian Ambassador that an English fleet of 150 sail, of which 40 were Dutch, had sailed to the Caribbean.[14] Owing to persistent and determined efforts that followed the defeat of 1588, the Spanish response was prompt. The Armada of the Guard, with Don Luis Fajardo now in command, sailed for the Caribbean in June, and other powerful forces outfitted in El Ferrol and Lisbon were to follow. In the same months the war with France ended with the Peace of Vervins (2 May 1598), and the Spaniards withdrew from Calais and Brittany.

In the fall the armada saw the treasure safely home and the English departed the Caribbean. The Spaniards relaxed their efforts. Medina Sidonia protested to the King that he ought not relax, but rather should send the powerful forces already collected to the Caribbean to bolster morale and proclaim his resolve to defend his overseas possessions. The King to whom he addressed his letter was Philip III, who succeeded Philip II on Sunday, 13 September 1598.

In his last service to Philip II, Medina Sidonia acted as one of his pallbearers. For the new King Medina Sidonia prepared a gloomy prognosis:[15]

The kingdoms of Spain, supporting others with their money and men, find themselves in the greatest misery I have ever seen. From Your Majesty, *señor* and master, to the lowliest field hand, all suffer. The people are poor, idle and vicious, no longer good at arms. . . .

Navarre, Aragon and Catalonia are open to French invasion. Vendôme [Henry IV] is a gallant King and the best soldier in the world. . . .

Portugal, though inherited legitimately, was in effect conquered by force of arms. The spirit of the Portuguese has always been so hostile and opposed to the Castilians that they cannot bear subjection to this crown. Thus they lean toward Dom Emanuel, son of Dom António. . . . The Azores are similarly inclined.

The coasts of Andalusia, and likewise those of Portugal, Galicia, Asturias, Vizcaya and the Province [Guipúzcoa] are so without defense that, though the inhabitants do their duty, they cannot resist the many enemies Your Majesty has at sea, such as the English, French, Hollanders, Zeelanders, Scots and Danes, without mentioning the Moors and Turks. Moreover, on the coast of Valencia there are many Moriscos.

Regarding the provinces of Flanders, where Your Majesty has consumed most of your treasury, they are far from submitting to Your Majesty's rule notwithstanding a war of long duration. Holland and Zeeland have become so powerful that at sea they are inferior to none in the quantity of ships, seamen and guns they possess, which today is so great they are coming to surpass the English.

The State of Milan is open to the French, because Savoy is weak. . . .

The West Indies are rich but defenseless. Enemies can dominate them whenever and however they wish, and Your Majesty can neither resist nor counterattack by sea. . . . The flotas are in such danger that it is a miracle of Our Lord that they have thus far escaped. . . .

The Philippines are threatened from China and Japan. . . .

To the East Indies the Dutch are going, no longer to Lisbon but to the source of the spices. . . .

Barbary is so close to the undefended coast of Spain, where so many Moriscos live, that it would prove a misfortune if ever the Turks and Moroccans ally. . . .

Having offered his opinion, Medina Sidonia stood ready to serve Philip III as he had Philip II.

The government of Philip III was from the start dominated by the grandee Don Francisco Gómez de Sandoval y Rojas, Marquis of Denia, the royal favorite who became Duke of Lerma in 1599. He and Medina Sidonia would most certainly have known one another for many years. Lerma was four years younger than Medina Sidonia and had been raised in Seville by his uncle, Archbishop Cristóbal de Sandoval y Rojas. His grandfather was Francis Borja, General of the Jesuits,[16] who visited Sanlúcar in 1560, and he married a daughter of the Duke of Medinaceli. At court in 1589 he joined the household of Prince Philip, then newly constituted under Medina Sidonia's cousin Don Pedro de Guzmán.

The regime of Philip III and his *valido* Lerma deserves serious new attention by historians. To disgruntled contemporaries Lerma seemed corrupt, and with some reason. He appears to have been unduly trusting and generous with friends and relations, and munificent with himself. Moreover, the subsequent regime of Philip IV and Olivares had further reasons of its own to denigrate him.

Lerma favored aristocratic government and sought the service of leading noblemen in high office. While his heavy-handed replacement of the aged and austere letrado Rodrigo Vázquez de Arce by a grandee, the Count of Miranda, as President of the Council of Castile is often cited to indicate a wholesale replacement of government personnel, he continued to use many of Philip II's chief ministers, though not always at court. Don Juan de Idiáquez remained to advise him on foreign policy, but Don Cristóbal de Moura was created Marquis of Castel Rodrigo and appointed Viceroy of Portugal and the Count of Chinchón became Ambassador to Rome. A grandee, the Count of Lemos, did at last obtain the office Medina Sidonia once sought, President of the Council of the Indies.

Medina Sidonia received appointments to the prestigious Councils of State and War, though he continued to serve as before, chiefly in Andalusia. He seldom sat with the councils at court. In official correspondence he became again "Your Excellency," the form suppressed under Philip II in favor of "Your Lordship."

Most of his correspondents in the secretarial ranks who had served Philip II continued in office. Juan de Ibarra's brother, Esteban de Ibarra, dealt with Medina Sidonia about naval affairs until 1606, when Antonio de Aróztegui replaced him. Andrés de Prada also remained an important figure with the Council of War, which added several titled nobles to its active membership. But scandal did result from the interference of Lerma's close associate, Don Pedro de Franqueza, in a revived policy of building and hiring armada ships by asiento, which Medina Sidonia had approved. Charges of poor quality erupted, and Franqueza was disgraced in January 1607 and subsequently imprisoned.[17]

Medina Sidonia shared Lerma's view that great nobles should fill the highest offices of state and promoted his heir Don Manuel, Count of Niebla, who married Lerma's daughter in Madrid in November 1598, after the valido had wielded power for a bare two months. Because few at court had any illusions about Lerma's influence with Philip II's heir, the matrimonial alliance had likely been planned before Philip II's death. It stood in the tradition of Medina Sidonia's own marriage to the daughter of an influential minister, though Eboli was a parvenu in comparison to Lerma. At Niebla's wedding, King Philip III and his half-sister, Infanta Isabel Clara Eugenia, acted as sponsors.

Lerma arranged for Philip III to cancel many of the debts Medina Sidonia purportedly owed the Crown, reassert his authority as Captain General of the Coast of Andalusia, and confirm him in the rich encomienda of Habanilla in the Order of Calatrava.[18] Medina Sidonia also regained considerable influence in the collection of customs at Sanlúcar, when he purchased through Lerma the office of chief clerk.[19]

The Count of Niebla obtained in 1603 the office his father had once sought, Captain General of the Galleys of Spain. And increasingly the Count came to share with his father the functions of Captain General of the Coast of Andalusia, which he was authorized to exercise in Medina Sidonia's absence.

Medina Sidonia continued to deal with the concerns he had always dealt with, the defense of Andalusia, the Indies flotas, the armada, and Morocco. The war with England ended only in 1604. The Spanish delegation to the court of James I was headed by Medina Sidonia's cousin, the Constable of Castile, while the English delegation to Spain was led by Medina Sidonia's old opponent, Lord Admiral Howard, now Earl of Nottingham.

The struggle with the Dutch rebels intensified and Barbary remained in a state of perpetual unrest. Corsairs continued to threaten coastal shipping and villages.

After the sack of Cádiz, as before, Sharif Ahmed al-Mansour played Spain along, while treating with the English, Dutch, and Turks and pursuing the conquest of the west African Sudan. He continued to detain Baltasar Polo, and Diego Marín remained in prison, though Polo was able to conduct both diplomacy and business. Medina Sidonia claimed late in 1596 that Polo's influence was greater than ever.[20]

But the Sharif chose to use Polo and Marín to bargain, and he agreed to release them only in exchange for a Reis held captive in the Spanish galleys, who he claimed was old and a friend. He pledged that he would not permit the Reis to resume the career of a corsair. When three Portuguese officers from Tangier were taken captive while out hunting late in 1596, they were added to the scale. The Sharif eventually got his man, and Philip II's subjects were set free. Medina Sidonia urged the King to reward Polo with a monopoly over certain imports from Spain to Morocco.[21]

Sharif Ahmed al-Mansour died in 1603, and Morocco soon plunged into civil war as his three sons struggled for power. Rival Moorish war bands repeatedly threatened the Spanish and Portuguese Moroccan presidios, for which Medina Sidonia had often to find men and provisions.

Algeria suffered from similar unrest. The Turkish Bey of Algiers had little control over the dominant corsair chiefs, whose depradations against shipping and razzias against the coasts of Christian Europe bore little relation to official Ottoman policy. Much of the Algerian hinterland was disaffected and local rulers were in frequent rebellion. In the Khabylie Mountains between Algiers and Bougie [Bejaia] the petty state of Cuco, as Medina Sidonia knew it, repeatedly asserted its independence. In 1601 the Kinglet of Cuco Ahmed sent two of his sons to Spain to propose the conquest of Algiers with his help. Philip III ordered Gian Andrea Doria to prepare a vast expedition against Algiers in support of the Kinglet, but it came to nothing. The next year Don Juan de Cardona was brought from retirement to mount a second attack, which did not materialize either. In 1603 Kinglet Ahmed died, and a struggle among his heirs ensued.

The Kinglet's eldest son, Mulai Sheik, sought the assistance of Spain, and Medina Sidonia's son, the Count of Niebla, received orders to sail with his galleys to Barbary in the prince's support. Aided by the Duke, Niebla put out from Cadiz Bay on 3 August for Cartagena. When he reached Majorca in September, he learned that Mulai Sheik had succeeded in his object and driven his brothers' Algerine support- ers from Cuco.

No longer needed, Niebla returned to Cartagena and late that year paraded his galleys in the harbor of Valencia before Philip III and the Duke of Lerma, who had come to meet with the Cortes of that King- dom. Three years later, he resigned his commission to Don Pedro de Toledo, Marquis of Villafranca, in part because the costs of maintain- ing the galleys had become too much of a burden for the encumbered Medina Sidonia estates. He became *Montero Mayor* (Master of the Hunt) to Philip III and eventually secured the succession to his father's titles of office, which he assumed after the seventh Duke died.[22]

In the office of Captain General of the Ocean-Sea, Medina Sidonia found renewed respect for his advice, which was constantly sought in matters of imperial strategy and the movements of armadas and flotas. The Dutch menace against which he had long warned grew steadily. Dutch warships and merchantmen, pirates and smugglers in Spanish eyes, swarmed over the seas in increasing numbers. They sailed through the Strait of Gibraltar to the Levant, rounded the Cape of Good Hope to India and the East Indies, and voyaged westward to infest the Caribbean.

Medina Sidonia despaired of Spain's ability to respond, either militarily or economically. Around him he could see the demographic catastrophe that formed part of the problem. Andalusia suffered from repeated famines, and in 1601 disease decimated the population.[23] Often foreign vessels had to be hired for the import of necessary grain and ships had to built in foreign yards for Spanish use. Spain's yards could not keep up with the demands of war and empire and the loss to attrition of men and vessels through disease, rot, weather, and shipwreck.[24]

Medina Sidonia wrote a long treatise about shipbuilding in Spain, claiming that ships were not as solid as they once were but were built too quickly and without sufficient care. Shipowners, he stated, were afraid that if their ships were too well built, they would be pressed as capitanas and almirantas of the flotas. That meant a loss of at least 6,000 ducats in cargo to the owner, because gun ports had to be cut, big guns placed aboard, and soldiers carried, who were careless and "not clean."[25] "When big ships arrive from Vizcaya, all wait to see if they are taken as capitana or almiranta, to the harm of the owner, who will not build such good ships in the future." Medina Sidonia believed that the Crown should provide four stout ships for that purpose, two of six hundred toneladas and two of five hundred, and that the remainder of a flota's ships ought to be in the two hundred to five hundred tonelada range for keeping good order in convoy. And in his long observation of ships, he became increasingly impressed by the woods used for shipbuilding in the yards of Havana and Goa.[26]

The shortage of seamen appeared to Medina Sidonia as big a problem as the lack of adequate ships, and the shortage of gunners seemed worse. Having to depend on Flemish, German, and Italian gunners he likened to holding a bomb in one's hands.[27] He proposed an apprenticeship program for poor or vagabond boys of twelve to fifteen years old in the flotas; a letter from the King of 28 February 1607 complimented him on finding ninety-three idle boys (*muchachos baldíos*) to serve as pages, cabin attendants, aboard the New Spain flota.[28] For boys who served as pages Medina Sidonia proposed a school in Seville to train them in the arts of seamanship and gunnery.[29] Gunners who were not experienced seamen, he stated, recalling his own experience of 1588, were not much good at sea.

When Medina Sidonia received for his comments in early 1602 a revived plan for the establishment of an Armada de Barlovento to cover the Windward Islands and patrol the Caribbean, he objected to it, whereas in 1581 he had favored such an armada.[30] In support of his objections he referred to the strategic concepts of Pedro Menéndez de Avilés and argued in favor of a strengthened Armada of the Guard to consist of ten medium-sized galleons and six pataches, carrying eighteen hundred soldiers and thirteen hundred seamen and gunners, that operated from Spain. He wanted the galleons to sail each year in December and leave Havana in July. "No fleet able to match them can be assembled in England or Holland without it being known in time."

While objecting to the Barlovento Armada, Medina Sidonia had long favored an armada of sailing ships in the Strait of Gibraltar. The galleys that were needed to protect the coast from corsair raids in summer were of little use in the rough seas of late autumn, winter, and early spring and were routinely laid up between November and May. The big northern merchantmen had learned to enter the Mediterranean in March and April and leave in November to avoid them. Low in the water and fragile, galleys had, moreover, mixed luck with well-armed, high-boarded merchantmen. When the Adelantado took six galleys to sea from the Anchorage of Herradura at Christmastide, 1601, and sank two and captured six northern merchant ships off Almería, the Council of War proudly proclaimed to Philip III that the galleys had "restored their reputation."[31]

In 1605 Philip III appointed the thoughtful Admiral General of the Ocean Armada, Don Diego Brochero, to the councils of State and War to advise him on naval policy. Like Medina Sidonia, Brochero considered matters of grand strategy as well as the necessary detail of naval administration, but Brochero's war record was more fortunate than the Duke's. A Knight of Malta, Brochero had begun his career in the Mediterranean galleys and came to the Atlantic in 1590 with the last two galleasses to support operations in Brittany. He became Admiral General of the Ocean Armada in 1595. Medina Sidonia had great regard for him and compared him to the late Marquis of Santa Cruz.[32] Brochero respected Medina Sidonia's opinions and routinely sought them in naval affairs. Their correspondence treated the deployment of armadas, the sailings of flotas, the size of ships, and their arming and manning. Both agreed that soldiers aboard ship too often abused the seamen and that the captain of a ship rather than the captain of the embarked infantry ought to enforce military justice over those aboard.[33] Medina Sidonia offered as examples of men competent at sea and war the "intelligent nobles" of the north coast who had been galleon captains and risen to high office in the royal service, such as "Don Pedro de

Valdés, now Governor of Havana, Sancho Pardo Osorio, Diego Flores de Valdés, Diego de la Rivera, Antonio Navarro, Juan Gutiérrez de Garibay, and Juan Gómez de Medina."[34]

A series of significant royal decrees about armadas, the Indies flotas, and shipbuilding followed Brochero's appointment. The status and privileges of those who served at sea, both noble and common, were affirmed in a royal decree of 22 January 1607.[35]

The year before it was definitely decided to establish an Armada del Estrecho to patrol the Strait of Gibraltar. Truce talks had opened in Flanders between the Dutch and the quasi-independent government of Archduke Albert and the Infanta Isabel Clara Eugenia, whom Albert married in 1599 after doffing his cardinal's hat. Madrid wanted to improve the Archduke's bargaining position by cutting Dutch commerce to the Mediterranean, as it had already been denied to Spain and its possessions overseas.

With the Armada del Estrecho the Atlantic armadas or squadrons would number five. The others included what came to be called the Armada de Cantabria, based on Santander and the Basque ports; the Armada del Mar Oceano, since 1604 under Don Luis Fajardo and based on El Ferrol-La Coruña; the smaller Armada de Portugal, based on Lisbon, and the Armada de la Guarda de la Carrera de las Indias.

In the Mediterranean the galley squadrons of Spain, Naples, and Sicily were strengthened at the same time, and under the second Marquis of Santa Cruz, the Marquis of Villafranca Don Pedro de Toledo, and Don Pedro de Leyva conducted aggressive operations against the Ottoman Empire and Barbary States. Four more galleys were based in Portugal, and galleys occasionally served in northern waters.

For his part, Medina Sidonia received orders to supervise the preparation of the new Armada del Estrecho. In addition to cutting Dutch commerce, the new armada would also cover the sailings of the Indies fleets, guard the Andalusian coast, and operate against Morocco, where civil war reopened the matter of Larache.

Medina Sidonia, who was as customary overseeing the preparation of the annual New Spain flota, assembled by the end of 1606 a squadron of twelve small galleons and embargoed ships, several of them foreign. The Crown sent him 70,000 ducats and noted that 60,000 had already been spent.[36] With the arrest of Pedro de Franqueza there followed some confusion, as responsibility for funding the Strait Armada was returned to the Council of War.[37] The Duke found additional guns for vessels that needed them but admitted that many guns were of reinforced iron. To man the new armada he rounded up with the usual difficulty eight hundred sailors of mixed quality and one thousand soldiers and recommended Fajardo's former almirante of the Guard Armada, Juan Alvarez de Avilés, as commanding general. His recommendation was accepted.[38]

Within a few weeks of sailing in March 1607 the Strait Armada had sunk or taken fourteen Dutch merchantmen. Alvarez de Avilés had orders to hang the captains of ships that resisted and send their crews to the galleys. The men of peaceful merchantmen that belonged to rebels were to be detained. Excepted were those ships and men licensed to carry needed grain to Italy, so long as they carried no contraband.

The Dutch, who knew of the Strait Armada's establishment, had already prepared their response. In early January Medina Sidonia wrote the King that he had heard that eighty Dutch ships were outfitting but he understood they would traffic in the Indies. Then on 24 April he learned that a Dutch squadron of thirty-one warships and four provisioners had passed Lisbon and was off Cape St. Vincent. Fajardo had not yet assembled the Ocean Armada for the year and could do nothing. To join Fajardo in Lisbon Medina Sidonia had orders to prepare in Cádiz two Guard galleons returned from the Indies, and soon received further orders to take two galleons from the Strait Armada and send them also to Lisbon.

Because the Dutch brought ships carrying provisions with them, Medina Sidonia assumed they planned a long voyage. He sent some caravels to trail them and others to carry warnings to Spain's overseas governors. At the same time he suggested to the court that Fajardo's armada should be reinforced with the Armada of the Strait, a third surviving Guard galleon, and the two big galleons intended as capitana and almiranta of the New Spain flota, as well as the four galleons already intended for it. With these seventeen vessels, the four galleons and the urca Fajardo had ready to sail in Lisbon, and Don Antonio Oquendo's Cantabrian squadron of ten ships, Medina Sidonia believed that Fajardo would muster sufficient strength to pursue the Dutch. He had heard that the Dutch fleet had few big ships and did not carry many soldiers or guns.

To Alvarez, who had entered Algeciras Bay with his prizes, Medina Sidonia sent warning that the Dutch were off Cape St. Vincent. Two days later, he learned that the Dutch had entered the Strait, attacked the Strait Armada before Gibraltar, and destroyed five of the ten armada ships that were there, including the capitana and almiranta. Alvarez, who had learned about the Dutch fleet only at eight o'clock on the morning of battle, 25 April, was killed, and his son, for whom he had obtained the post of *capitán de guerra* (captain of infantry) aboard his capitana, was taken captive. The Dutch general, Martin van Heemskerck, had also fallen in action. Medina Sidonia's account of the disaster reached the King just as he signed a letter to the Duke expressing his appreciation for Alvarez's good work.

Medina Sidonia quickly tended to the defense of the coast and the security of its shipping. The five survivors of the battle huddled in the safety of Gibraltar's mole, and soldiers were stationed to protect them, as much from looters as from the Dutch, who cruised offshore between Gibraltar and Cape Spartel. Militia companies from Castellar and Jimena joined the regulars on battlements, and horsemen patrolled the beaches. Salvage operations to recover the guns began almost at once. Eventually over forty-five pieces of bronze were salvaged. Those deformed by the intense heat of the burning ships were sent to the royal gun foundry at Málaga to be refounded, while the others were redistributed to ships that needed them.

Two other ships of Alvarez's armada, from which none had yet been detached to sail for Lisbon, had anchored at Fuengirola with a Dutch prize and missed the battle. Medina Sidonia ordered them to Málaga.

Medina Sidonia established his headquarters at Jerez, as in 1596, and called out the Andalusian militia. Cádiz was reinforced, and the ships in its bay and in the Guadalquivir were brought under the protection of forts that had been strengthened since 1596. The Duke's complaints about the response of señores and towns to his summons echoed those of eleven years earlier.

Because five of the Strait Armada's ships survived the fight and two missed the action, Medina Sidonia received orders from court to conduct a close investigation of what had happened, to ensure that all responsible had done their duty. Medina Sidonia himself was widely blamed for the debacle.[39] He learned that Alvarez had called a council of war with his captains and discussed the order for battle if attacked. They agreed to keep close to the mole, under the shelter of the guns of Gibraltar, though some feared being caught in crossfire between the forts and the Dutch in a close fight. In the late afternoon of 25 April the Dutch warships surged into the bay, riding a west wind and scarcely shortening sail. By nightfall they had overpowered the five Spanish ships of the first line and an Emden vessel that fought with them. The five galleons of the second line beached themselves behind Gibraltar's mole, along with the prizes they had taken earlier. The Dutch hesitated to close further and eventually withdrew. Several hundred captured Spaniards were stripped and cast overboard, their hands bound behind them. All involved, Medina Sidonia concluded, had fought well, and the Germans from Emden deserved gratitude and compensation.

The victorious Dutch fleet spent several days off Gibraltar, then sailed north and cruised off the mouth of the Tagus, to keep Fajardo in port and prevent him from receiving reinforcements. It was 1587 again. Fajardo proposed that the Vizcayan squadron of Antonio Oquendo sail far out to sea to avoid the Dutch and then head back for Cape St. Vincent to meet what armada ships could be assembled in Andalusia. The combined squadrons would then head north and Fajardo would emerge from Lisbon. They would catch the Dutch between them.

When advised of Fajardo's plan, Medina Sidonia disagreed. The ten Vizcayans ran too many risks, and if they did reach Cape St. Vincent, the north winds that prevailed off the Portuguese coast in summer would hinder the Spaniards and permit the Dutch to defeat them in detail. He urged that the Vizcayans stay put and that a bigger armada be assembled in Andalusia. More ships could be pressed into service from the New Spain flota, and its sailing delayed as, he added, had been done in the past in times of emergency. He recommended that the Andalusian armada include the seven survivors of the Strait Armada and four ships newly embargoed for it, three galleons he had been outfitting in Cadiz Bay for Lisbon, and the capitana, almiranta, and another six or eight good ships of the flota. Such a force could combine with the ships in Lisbon to challenge the Dutch. Fajardo himself should come overland from Lisbon to command it, because of the lively rivalry between Juan de Garibay, whom the Duke had made general of the Strait Armada, and Don Sancho Pardo, general of the flota. Fajardo could head for the Tagus and combine with the ships there to overwhelm the Dutch. To get infantry for the planned armada Medina Sidonia proposed that six thousand men be recruited from the señores and towns of Andalusia, as in 1587, "about which the Comendador of León [Don Juan de Idiáquez] could enlighten Your Majesty."[40]

To the Council of War and Fajardo the idea seemed promising. Fajardo left his armada in Lisbon under his son, Don Juan de Fajardo, and hurried by land to Andalusia to take charge of the armada proposed by Medina Sidonia. To assist him and cover the Andalusian coast Don Pedro de Toledo was under way from Cartagena with the Spanish galleys, and not far behind sailed a Genoese squadron commanded by Carlo Doria, Duke of Tursi, Gian Andrea Doria's heir.

By mid-July the Dutch had left the Iberian coast and sailed for the Azores in search of treasure fleets. Fajardo headed after them, treating the Andalusian militiamen embarked to a summer cruise.

Madrid now renewed interest in Larache, whose garrison had marched off to take part in the strife between Mulai Muhammad ech Sheik and his younger brother Mulai Zaidan. As in 1581, Medina Sidonia received orders to take charge of an expedition to occupy it. A long plan drawn up by his comrade of 1588 Bobadilla, Count of Puñonrostro and Councilor of War, was forwarded to him for comment. The galleys of Toledo and Tursi would spearhead the enterprise. Because it did not warrant Medina Sidonia's presence, Toledo would be in tactical command. As before, people were recruited in Granada and Andalusia, and the galleys were maintained in a state of readiness. And as before, the plan came to nothing. Depending on the intrigues of rival Moroccan factions and the fortunes of civil war, it was dropped when word came that Larache's garrison had returned and the season became too late.

In October the Genoese galleys left for Italy, and the Indies fleets and armada galleons of their escort reached Andalusia. Problems arose in paying off the Andalusian militiamen, and an inquiry was launched into why so many had not survived the voyage.[41] But for those who had deserted, punishment was sought.

During 1608 peace talks in Flanders led to the Twelve Years' Truce of 1609 between Spain and the States General of the rebel provinces, which ended for the remainder of Medina Sidonia's lifetime the wars that began in the reign of Philip II. But "beyond the line," as they said then, which in men's imagination bounded Europe and its adjacent waters, there was no peace. Hostilities, privateering, and piracy persisted overseas.

As had Philip II in 1559, with the end of war in the north, Philip III and his government turned its attention to the Mediterranean. In a Draconian response to a perceived security problem and widespread local prejudice, Madrid decided to expel to North Africa in 1609 several hundred thousand "New Christian" Moriscos as suspect in religion, a minority that would not be assimilated, and a potential fifth-column. As a Councilor of State, Medina Sidonia, who in 1570 seemed reluctant to lose his Morisco vassals, was asked for his views. He put in writing what he had told the Council earlier.[42]

He acknowledged that the King had already made up his mind what he would do and agreed that the Moriscos, especially those of Valencia, were growing in number and were a threat to Spain's security. He accepted the decision to expel them. The solution to the problem attempted by "the King who is in heaven," Philip II, the dispersal of the Granadine Moriscos throughout the Castilian hinterland had only created tensions with the Old Christians, while the Valencian problem had not been addressed. But Medina Sidonia expressed fear that during the expulsion the Moriscos would be harshly treated and become implacable foes of Spain in Barbary. He urged that the King forbid their maltreatment and assure them adequate provisions.

Already in Spain, he continued, they had been denied access to the clergy, the army, and maritime careers. Yet they were an industrious people and had made the best of their lot. Rather than have them augment the power of the Turks and Barbary States, why, he asked, might not a good number be sent to Florida, Cuba, Santo Domingo, or other hot lands that had suffered depopulation? Of this interesting and relatively humane proposal nothing came.

Fajardo brought the Atlantic armada into the Mediterranean to cover the expulsion and attack Barbary ports, where sailing ships, some from northern Europe, had joined the flotillas of corsair galliots.

Larache was not forgotten. An attempt to surprise it in 1608 had failed, but in 1610, Mulai Muhammad ech Sheik, beleaguered in the town, offered it to Spain in return for aid. Medina Sidonia received orders to give all necessary support to the Marquis of San Germán, Captain General of the Artillery, who was put in charge of the expedition. In November San Germán's expedition succeeded and Larache was occupied.[43]

The corsairs who operated from Larache shifted their base to La Mámora [Medhyia], further south. Among them now were exiled Andalusian Moriscos, implacable in their hatred of Spain, as Medina Sidonia had feared, and they had the support of Mulai Zaidan, ruler of Marrakech. In 1614 Fajardo took La Mámora, but the corsairs relocated to Salé, which became one of the most notorious of all pirate lairs, home of the "Salee rovers." In the last months before his death, Medina Sidonia spent much time in correspondence about the government, garrisoning, and provisioning of La Mámora.

In early 1610 the Duchess of Medina Sidonia died after an illness of some months. The Count and Countess of Niebla had come to Sanlúcar from court to be with her. The Duke, who had neither been well, began

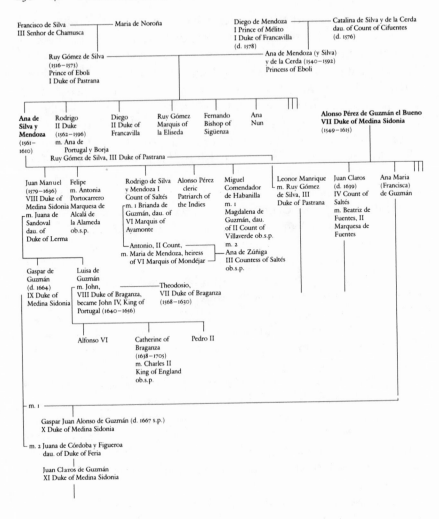

Figure 10. The Descent of the seventh Duke and Duchess of Medina Sidonia and her Ancestry

to withdraw from public life, though he continued to fulfill the routine tasks of his office. In 1611 he begged off accompanying the Infanta Anne of Austria on her planned journey to France to marry Louis XIII, and returning with Louis's sister Elisabeth, who was to marry Prince Philip. "I am old, infirm, and poor," he explained, "and have donned the robe, having placed my children."[44]

Madrid continued to seek his advice. To Don Diego Brochero in December 1610 he apologized for the length of a letter about trade to the Indies and noted that "it has been forty-one years since His Majesty, now in heaven, came down to Seville and ordered me to treat these matters."[45] In Madrid in 1613 he consulted with Brochero about the construction of galleons, their manning and deployment. He once more asked forgiveness for being long-winded, "for I have been interested in this profession so long that I run off at the mouth talking about these matters."[46] In what proved to be the last year of his life, the court still sought his views. On 13 June 1615, the King signed in Valladolid a letter that dealt with arming ships and sweeping the Andalusian coast of corsairs.[47] It was perhaps the last addressed to him, "Duke of Medina Sidonia, cousin, of my councils of State and War, and Captain General of the Ocean-Sea and the Coast of Andalusia."

After 1610 the Count of Niebla gradually assumed most of the burdens of Medina Sidonia's offices and estates. On Pentecost Sunday, 1615, in Sanlúcar, the old Duke placed round his neck the collar of the Golden Fleece, bestowed by Philip III.

Taking up the naval career Niebla left in 1605 was the Duke's third son, Don Rodrigo de Silva y Mendoza.[48] In the fall of 1611 the King wrote Medina Sidonia to congratulate him on Don Rodrigo's success in breaking up a flotilla of Moorish and Dutch pirates. Don Rodrigo received in reward the title Count of Saltés,[49] which eventually passed to his younger brothers in turn, after he became through marriage Marquis of Ayamonte.

The Duke's youngest son, Don Juan Claros de Guzmán, also followed a naval career and in 1624 took a seat on the Council of War. He became by marriage Marquis of Fuentes, and between 1635 and 1639, when he died, was the highly successful Admiral of the Dunkirk squadron.

Medina Sidonia's second son, Don Felipe de Guzmán y Aragón, may have been feebleminded; he married a local heiress, but the marriage was dissolved.[50] Medina Sidonia's fourth son and namesake, Don Alonso Pérez de Guzmán, entered the church and became in time

Patriarch of the Indies. The fifth son, Don Miguel, took the encomienda of Habanilla in the Order of Calatrava, made two good marriages, and left no heir.

Medina Sidonia's eldest surviving daughter, Doña Leonor, married her cousin Ruy Gómez de Silva, third Duke of Pastrana, in 1601 in a ceremony at Sanlúcar, while her younger sister Doña Ana María married, in a practice not limited to royalty, her own nephew Don Gaspar, who became in 1636 ninth Duke of Medina Sidonia. The ninth Duke's sister, Doña Luisa, married Duke João of Braganza, who was proclaimed King of Portugal in 1640, with her connivance. As John IV, he successfully led Portugal to independence from Spain. Their daughter, Catherine of Braganza, great-granddaughter of the armada commander, married King Charles II of England in 1660.

The successful revolt of Portugal engendered in Sanlúcar a family plot to make of Andalusia an independent kingdom with the ninth Duke of Medina Sidonia king. Another descendant of the seventh Duke, Don Francisco de Guzmán, Marquis of Ayamonte, was chief instigator. In 1641 the plot was nipped in bud by yet another Guzmán, Don Gaspar, Count-Duke of Olivares and all-powerful minister of Philip IV. Ayamonte was condemned to death and eventually executed, while his cousin, Medina Sidonia, was humiliated and stripped of his inherited Captain-Generalships and jurisdictions over Sanlúcar.[51]

But in 1610, Don Gaspar de Guzmán was twenty-three years old and had been Count of Olivares for only three years. He was resident in Seville and entertaining poets. His career at court still lay ahead of him. As a cadet of the House of Guzmán, he would certainly have paid visits to the Duke of Medina Sidonia, the head of his family. Both his father Don Enrique and his uncle Don Pedro had proved loyal to Medina Sidonia even in the most difficult of times.

On 26 July 1615 the seventh Duke of Medina Sidonia died in Sanlúcar. Diego Ortiz y Zúñiga, chronicler of Seville, noted simply that he had been "a great promoter of the grandeur and opulence of his House. He lived in peace and took the title of Captain General of the Ocean-Sea and of the Coast of Andalusia."[52]

Medina Sidonia may have lived in peace his last few years, but apart from tending to the "grandeur and opulence of his house," war had been his chief preoccupation. His titles carried heavy responsibilities and in each office he was dogged by defeat, though he had conducted himself well and with honor. But his temper was reflective, not impetuous, and he won his early laurels in the peaceful conquest of the Algarve, which required of him organizational and diplomatic skills.

When it came to battle, he proved prudent and brave, but not daring. Had he been more daring, the two defeats in which he was directly involved would not likely have been victories and might well have proved far more disastrous. Half the 1588 armada might not have been saved (much more would have been were it not for storms and shipwreck), or it might have been penned in some northern port such as Antwerp, leaving the English in far better position to undertake their 1589 campaign against Portugal. Trying to emerge from Antwerp, the armada might have been virtually annihilated, as was the Turkish fleet emerging from Lepanto. Had Medina Sidonia tried to assault Cadiz from the Isla de León in 1596, his militia would probably have been routed, and the English and Dutch would not only have gained more loot in Cadiz Bay, but also been free to attack the shipping in the Guadalquivir and even strike at Seville itself. Yet fortune, as was often said then, favors those who court her, and Medina Sidonia did not. A reasonable man, he did not try his luck even when luck might have been his only chance.

But his reasonableness, if not marked by luck at moments that demanded tactical decisiveness, suited the conduct of grand strategy. Coupled with his experience, it made him a wise counselor. When the campaign of 1588 ended in defeat, those who promoted it knew that the Duke's forebodings and reservations ought to have been heeded. When Cádiz was taken in 1596, Medina Sidonia's warnings about the time-worn and ramshackle arrangements on which home defense depended were confirmed. That the reforms in the armada and home defense he urged were seldom carried out in full remained the fault of the distracted and financially strapped royal government in Madrid, not his.

In his last years he became a senior statesman, appreciated by those closest to the Crown if not by the general public. His memorials to the Crown after 1596, especially his exchanges with Brochero, testify to his having found the role that most suited him in serving the Crown, adviser on naval administration and grand strategy.[53]

Yet in history, the denigration of Medina Sidonia by gossip chroniclers like Padre Victoria prevailed. The prolific Italian writer of histories, Faminius Strada, in *De Bello Belgico decades duae*, claimed that in Medina Sidonia the armada received "a general of gold in place of a general of iron." Cesáreo Fernández Duro, who quoted this description in his *La Armada invencible*,[54] spends pages disparaging Medina Sidonia. He suspected that the Duke's appointment was due to the

King's relations with the Duke's mother-in-law, the Princess of Eboli, and if not that, could be explained only by some other "inexplicable, mysterious and powerful cause."[55] The chronicler of the Escorial, Fray Gerónimo de Sepúlveda, claimed, "I know not what devils counselled the King."[56] The English hispanicist and historian Martin A. S. Hume called Medina Sidonia "a fool and a craven,"[57] and J. K. Laughton, editor of the English armada papers, stated that the King's choice of him to command the armada was made "with a light heart."[58]

Perhaps the first modern historian to assess Medina Sidonia fairly was J. A. Williamson in *The Age of Drake* (1938). The Duke of Maura's *El Designio de Felipe II* (1957) then brought to light Medina Sidonia's career prior to his taking command of the armada and was published in time to be used by Garrett Mattingly in his Pulitzer Prize–winning *Armada* (1959). Mattingly wrote about the restoration of Medina Sidonia's reputation that "it [does not] matter at all to the dead whether they receive justice at the hands of succeeding generations. But to the living, to do justice, however belatedly, should matter."[59]

Ambassador Lippomano's assessment of Medina Sidonia in 1588 seems to hold, though what "only one might desire" must be extended to include more than Medina Sidonia's lack of experience at sea. It must also include the general shortcomings of any early modern state, especially in finance and military organization, and additionally, in the case of the overextended Spain of Philip II and Philip III, shortcomings in ship construction, the manning of ships, and in guns and gunnery. About all these shortcomings the Duke of Medina Sidonia warned, and throughout his life he did what he could to alleviate them. Though at times overcome, they persisted, and the Duke experienced the consequences on several momentous occasions, above all in 1588 in the failed Enterprise of England, with which his name has been forever linked.

Appendix
Battle Order of the Armada

On most Armada lists the ships appear by squadron. Here they are listed in fighting order, based on the *orden de pelear* found in KML *Cartas* 5, doc. 66, which lists thirty ships for the Main Battle (*batalla*) and twenty each for the two wings or horns (*cuernos*); and on the Tuscan ambassador's report, Archivio di Stato, Florence, *Mediceo* 4919/340, which indicates the posts of the chief officers, including the heads of the three relief (*socorro*) squadrons, a four ship-vanguard, and the places of the galleasses and galleys; and accounts of the battles.

Listed here are vessels of more than one hundred toneladas burden. Each appears with that part of the battle formation to which she was assigned, or with which she can be reasonably associated. Ships for which there is insufficient evidence to place them are listed at the end. Pataches, zabras, and pinnaces of less than one hundred *toneladas* are not named below: these vessels were intended to play supporting roles.

Given for ships listed are rated tonnage, the number of soldiers, sailors, listed guns, and the amount of powder aboard by hundredweight. The ratio of guns to the amount of powder provides some indication of the size of guns carried. In some cases, the principal person aboard is indicated. Many ships carried considerable numbers of noble adventurers and their retainers, who augmented the soldiery aboard.

Abbreviations for ship type: G = galleon; Gs = galleass; Gy = galley; N = *nao* or *nave* (greatship); P = Patache; U = *urca* (hulk); Z = *zabra*
Abbreviations for squadron: A = Andalusia; C = Castile; G = Guipúzcoa; L = Levant; P = Portugal; Pz = Pataches and Zabras; U = Urcas (hulks); V = Vizcaya

An asterisk denotes those ships expected to lead in the fighting. These were the best-gunned ships, with principal officers in charge; or in the case of medium-sized Castilian galleons, well-manned and maneuverable, if not very well gunned.

An "S" ending the line with the ship's name indicates the ship survived the campaign; "L" indicates lost; "U," fate unknown.

Ship	Rated tonnage	Soldiers	Sailors	Guns	Powder
BATALLA (MAIN BATTLE)					
RIGHT HALF (The numbers appear in KML *Cartas* 5, doc. 66)					
10. *PG *S. Martín Capitana Real*	1000	300	177	48	140 S
The Duke of Medina Sidonia, Captain General of the Ocean-Sea					
2. *CG *S. Cristóbal Capitana*	700	205	120	36	88 S
Diego Flores de Valdés, General of Castilian Squadron, transferred at La Coruña to *Capitana Real*; his Almirante took charge of *S. Cristóbal*					
3. *GP *S. Luis*	830	376	116	38	69 S
Agustín Mejía, Maestre de Campo, Tercio of Andalusia and Lisbon					
4. *GC *S. Juan Menor*	530	163	113	24	49 S
Diego Enríquez, Captain in Tercio of Indies Armada and son of former Viceroy of Peru					
5. *GP *Florentia (S. Francesco)*	961	400	86	52	75 S
Gaspar de Sousa, Senior Portuguese Captain *Note. Florentia* was some-times listed with the Levantine Squadron.					
6. PPz *Santo Crucifijo*	150	40	29	8	5 S
7. *NL *La Juliana*	860	325	70	32	67 L
8. UU *Castillo Negro*	750	239	34	27	23 U
9. *LN *S.M.de Gracia/ S. J.de Sicilia*	800	279	63	26	69 L
Diego Téllez de Enríquez, son of Comendador Mayor de Alcántara, seems to have been promoted to					

Ship	Rated tonnage	Soldiers	Sailors	Guns	Powder
Maestre de Campo during campaign					
10. UU *Barca de Amburg* (*Hamburg*)	600	239	25	23	31 L
11. UU *Barca de Ancique* (*Gdansk*)	450	200	25	26	29 U
12. GP *S. Cristóbal*	352	300	78	20	22 S
13. UU *Casa de Paz Chica*	350	162	24	15	12 S
14. UU *Santiago*	600	56	30	19	24 L
15. *GV *Grangrín Almiranta*	1160	256	73	28	72 L

LEFT HALF

Ship	Rated tonnage	Soldiers	Sailors	Guns	Powder
1. *NG *Santa Ana Capitana* Miguel de Oquendo, General of Guipúzcoan Squadron; died on return	1200	303	82	47	106 S
2. *NV *Santa Ana Capitana* Nicolás de Isla, Maestre de Campo, Tercio of Extremadura; died of wounds *Note.* Separated from the rest of the armada, lost at Le Havre.	768	323	114	30	71 L
3. *NL *Trinidad Valencera Veneziana* Alonso de Luzón, Maestre de Campo, Tercio of Naples; captured in Ireland and ransomed *Note.* From the list what can be made out is "*qi bel / It^a*", so this listing is not certain. Only she and *Trinidad de Escala* of the Levanters cannot be clearly situated in the formation.	900	307	79	22	41 L
4. UU *Ciervo Volante*	400	200	22	18	19 U
5. *GP *Santiago* Antonio Pereira,	520	300	93	24	46 S

Ship	Rated tonnage	Soldiers	Sailors	Guns	Powder
Portuguese Captain					
6. UU *Falcón Blanco Mayor*	500	161	36	16	24 U
7. NPz *N. S. del Pilar Capitana*	300	109	51	11	18 S
Antonio Hurtado de Mendoza, Chief of Squadron of Pataches and Zabras; died at La Coruña and was replaced by Captain Agustín Ojeda					
8. NG *Santa Cruz*	680	138	36	18	30 S
9. GP *San Bernardo*	352	250	81	21	30 S
10. UU *Paloma Blanca*	250	56	20	12	11 S
11. NA *S. Juan de Gargoriu*	569	165	56	16	21 S
12. UU *S. Pedro Menor*	500	157	23	18	34 L
13. UU *David*	450	50	24	7	8 U
Note. She seems not to have continued from La Coruña.					
14. *NL *La Lavia Almiranta*	728	203	80	30	35 L
Martín de Aranda, Judge Advocate General					
15. *GC *Santiago el Mayor*	530	210	132	24	47 S

THE FOUR GALLEASSES

(posted ahead of Medina Sidonia's *Capitana Real* at the center of the *batalla*)

Ship	Rated tonnage	Soldiers	Sailors	Guns	Powder
*Gs *San Lorenzo Capitana*	500?	262	124	50	132 L
Hugo de Moncada, General of the Galleasses					
*Gs *Zúñiga Patrona*	500?	178	112	50	118 S
*Gs *Girona*	500?	169	120	50	130 L
*Gs *Napolitana*	500?	264	112	50	118 S
Note. Each galleass also had a complement of three hundred rowers.					

VANGUARD OF FOUR SHIPS POSTED AHEAD OF GALLEASSES

Ship	Rated tonnage	Soldiers	Sailors	Guns	Powder
*LN *Rata S.M. Encoronada*	820	335	84	35	80 L
Alonso de Leyva, Captain					

Ship	Rated tonnage	Soldiers	Sailors	Guns	Powder
General of the Light Cavalry of Milan, commander of the landing force and secretly designated as Medina Sidonia's successor. He eventually died in wreck of galleass *Girona*. *Note*. Before the armada entered the Channel, Leyva took command of the *Cuerno Izquierdo*, which was called the Vanguard when sailing in battle order. Another, likely Sousa in *Florentia*, took his position, but this four-ship vanguard of the Main Battle formed only for the battle off Plymouth, if then. The other three ships were likely already listed in the Main Battle.					

THE FOUR GALLEYS (assigned posts astern of the main battle's center. All were forced by weather to turn back before reaching the Channel.)

Ship	Rated tonnage	Soldiers	Sailors	Guns	Powder
Gy *Capitana (Galera Real)*	250?		106 300 rowers	5	15 S
Diego de Medrano, General of the Galleys					
Gy *Princesa*	200?		90 200 rowers	5	15 S
Gy *Diana*	200?	94	5 192 rowers	15	S
Gy *Bazana*	200?	72	5 193 rowers	15	L

CUERNO DERECHO (RIGHT "HORN")

Ship	Rated tonnage	Soldiers	Sailors	Guns	Powder
*GP *San Juan Almiranta General* Juan Martínez de Recalde, Admiral General; died after return	1050	300	177	48	140 S
*GP *San Mateo*	750	277	120	34	82 L

Ship	Rated tonnage	Soldiers	Sailors	Guns	Powder
Diego de Pimentel, Maestre de Campo, Tercio of Sicily; captured by the Dutch and ransomed.					
Note. Before entering the Channel *San Mateo* seems to have exchanged places with the Vizcayan galleon *Grangrín.*					
NV *Santiago*	666	214	102	25	47 S
NV *Concepción de Zubelzu*	468	90	70	16	45 S
NPz *Caridad Inglesa*	180	70	36	12	20 S
NV *Magdalena*	530	193	67	18	38 S
NV *S. Juan*	350	114	80	21	36 S
NV *Maria Juan*	665	172	100	24	61 L
NV *Manuela*	520	125	54	12	30 S
NV *S. Maria de Montemayor*	707	206	45	18	38 S
UU *El Gato*	400	40	22	9	8 S
UU *S. Gabriel*	280	35	20	4	5 S
UU *Falcon Blanco Mediano*	300	76	27	16	19 L
UU *S. Andrés*	400	150	28	14	20 S
UU *Sanson*	500	200	31	18	24 S
NC *Trinidad*	872	180	122	24	48 S
*GC *S. Pedro*	530	141	131	24	48 S
*NG *S. M. de la Rosa* ex-Almiranta	945	225	64	26	80 L
Note. She is also described as the "former *Capitana* of Oquendo." Diego Pacheco, brother of Marquis of Villena					
ZP *Augusta*	166	55	57	13	9 S
UA *Duquesa Santa Ana* Pedro Amaras, Master	900	280	77	23	30 L

CUERNO IZQUIERDO (LEFT "HORN")

*GP *San Marcos*	790	292	117	33	85 L
Francisco de Bobadilla, Maestre de Campo General; transferred at La Coruña to *Capitana Real*					
Note. When Bobadilla left *San*					

Ship	Rated tonnage	Soldiers	Sailors	Guns	Powder
Marcos, she joined the Main Battle under the Marquis of Peñafiel, who also transferred later and was not lost with her. Alonso de Leyva in *La Rata* replaced Bobadilla in charge of the Left *Cuerno*, called the Vanguard in the Channel.					
*NL *Regazona Capitana* Martín de Bertendona, General of Levantine Squadron	1294	244	80	30	35 S
NL *Anunciada*	703	196	79	24	46 L
NL *S. Nicolas Prodaneli* Marino Prodaneli, Master; survived wreck	834	274	81	26	40 L
NL *S. Maria de Visón*	666	236	71	18	67 L
NG *S. Esteban*	936	196	68	26	43 L
*NG *S. Salvador Almiranta* Pedro de Priego, Captain, Tercio of Sicily; abandoned ship	958	321	75	25	130 L
NPz *S. Andrés escocés*	150	40	29	12	14 S
ZP *Julia*	166	44	72	14	10 S
UU *Casa de Paz grande*	600	198	27	26	26 U
UU *S. Pedro Mayor*	581	213	28	29	21 L
UU *Perro Marino*	200	70	24	7	7 S
UU *Ventura*	160	58	14	4	8 S
UU *S. Bárbara*	370	70	22	10	12 U
NG *S. Bárbara*	525	154	43	12	22 S
NG *S. Buenaventura*	379	168	53	21	20 S
*NC *N. S. de Begoña*	750	174	123	24	52 S
*GC *SS. Medel y Celedon*	530	160	101	24	48 S
*NC *S. Juan de Fernán Dome* Fernán Dome or Fernando Mero, Master	652	192	93	24	47 L
*GC *N. S. del Barrio* Juan de Garibay, Captain in Tercio of Indies Armada	530	155	108	24	49 S

Ship	Rated tonnage	Soldiers	Sailors	Guns	Powder

SOCORRO (RELIEF) FOR MAIN BATTLE (eight or more ships)

Ship	Rated tonnage	Soldiers	Sailors	Guns	Powder
*NA *N. S. del Rosario Capitana* Pedro de Valdés, General of Andalusian Squadron; captured and ransomed. His post was given to Diego Enríquez aboard *CG *S. Juan Menor.*	1150	304	118	46	114 L
*NA *San Francisco Almiranta* *Note.* Valdés complained that he was not allowed to appoint an Admiral for his squadron.	915	222	56	21	43 S
NA *Santa Catalina*	730	231	77	23	41 S
*GA *S. J. Bautista* Captain Juan de Maldonado	810	218	89	31	50 S

SOCORRO (RELIEF) FOR RIGHT (six or more ships)

Ship	Rated tonnage	Soldiers	Sailors	Guns	Powder
*UU *Gran Grifon* Juan Gómez de Medina, General of Squadron of Urcas; survived shipwreck in Scotland	650	243	43	38	48 L
*GP *San Felipe* Francisco de Toledo, Maestre de Campo, Tercio *de Entre Miño y* *Duero*; escaped from wrecked ship	800	415	117	40	85 L

SOCORRO (RELIEF) FOR LEFT (six or more ships)

Ship	Rated tonnage	Soldiers	Sailors	Guns	Powder
*GC *S. J. Bautista Almiranta* Gregorio de las Alas, Admiral of Castilian Squadron; died on return *Note.* When Diego Flores trans- ferred to the *Capitana Real*, las Alas transferred to the Castilian *capitana San Cristóbal* and left Marcos de Aramburu, *Proveedor* of the Squadron, in command.	750	207	136	24	53 S
UU *S. Salvador Almiranta* Pedro Coco Calderón, *Contador*	650	218	43	24	40 S

Ship	Rated tonnage	Soldiers	Sailors	Guns	Powder

Each of the following ships most certainly served in one of the three relief squadrons indicated in the Tuscan Ambassador's report, but in which each served does not become apparent from any accounts of the fighting.

Ship	Rated tonnage	Soldiers	Sailors	Guns	Powder
NV *Concepción Menor del Cano*	418	164	61	18	30 S
*GC *S. Felipe y Santiago Menor*	530	151	116	24	47 S
*GC *Ascención*	530	199	114	24	49 S
GC *Santa Ana*	250	91	80	24	29 S
NC *S. Catalina*	882	190	159	24	49 S
NA *Concepción*	862	185	71	20	83 S
NA *La Trinidad*	650	192	74	13	20 S
NA *S. Maria de Juncal*	730	228	80	20	31 S
NA *S. Bartolomé*	976	240	72	27	32 S
NG *Santa Marta*	548	173	63	20	43 S
NG *Maria San Juan*	291	110	30	12	14 S
UG *Doncella*	500	156	32	16	28 S
LN *Trinidad de Escala*	900	307	79	22	41 S
UU *Essayas*	280	30	16	4	5 S

In addition to the 101 ships named here there were 21 pataches, 7 zabras, and 2 pinnaces named, for a total of 131 vessels. In addition, some 20 caravels and feluccas are mentioned, with crews of seven to ten men.

Abbreviations

AGS	Archivo General de Simancas
AGS *Est.*	Estado, plus number of *legajo* (bundle)
AGS *GA*	Guerra Antigua, plus number of *legajo*
AM	*Archivo Municipal*
BL	British Library, London
BL *Add.Mss.*	British Library, Additional Manuscripts, plus volume and folio number
BN Madrid	Biblioteca Nacional, Madrid
BN Paris	Bibliothèque Nationale, Paris
Cabrera	Luis Cabrera de Córdoba, *Felipe II, Rey de España* (1619), 4 vols. (Madrid, 1876–78)
CODOIN	*Colección de documentos inéditos para la historia de España*, 112 vols. (Madrid, 1842ff.)
CSPSp	Volume 4 of *Calendar of Letters and State Papers Relating to English Affairs Preserved in, or Originally Belonging to the Archives of Simancas*, edited by Martin A. S. Hume (London: HM Stationery Office, 1899)
CSPV	*Calendar of State Papers and Manuscripts relating to English Affairs, existing in the Archives and Collections of Venice and other Libraries in Northern Italy*, 39 vols., edited by Horatio Brown and others (London: HM Stationery Office, 1864–1940)
FD	Cesáreo Fernández Duro, *La Armada invencible*, 2 vols. (Madrid, 1884–85), with document number
FD *AE*	Cesáreo Fernández Duro, *Armada Española*, 9 vols. (Madrid, 1895–1903)
HO	Enrique Herrera Oria, S.J., ed., *La Armada invencible*, vol. 2 of Archivo Histórico Español, *Colección de documentos inéditos para la historia de España y sus Indias* (Valladolid, 1929)

IVDJ   Instituto de Valencia de Don Juan, Madrid, with *envío* (packet) number

KML   Karpeles Manuscript Library, Santa Barbara California

KML *Cartas* *Cartas de los Reyes y sus secretarios a los duques de Medina Sidonia y copias de unas respuestas*, vols. 4, 1587; 5, 1588–89; 6, 1590–93; 9, 1604–06; 11, 1608–09

KML *CGA* *Capitanía General de Andalucía, Cartas, Memoriales . . .*

KML *Cuentas* *Capitanía General de Andalucía, Cuentas*

Laughton J. K. Laughton, ed., *State Papers Relating to the Defeat of the Spanish Armada, anno 1588*, 2 vols. (London: Navy Records Society, 1894)

leg.   *legajo* (bundle: documents at AGS are stored by *sección* in numbered *legajos*)

MN   Museo Naval, Madrid

MN *FN*   *Colección de Fernández de Navarrete*

MN *FNG* *Colección de documentos y manuscritos compilados por Martín Fernández de Navarrete*, edited by Julio Guillén Tato, 32 vols. (Nendeln, Liechtenstein: Kraus-Thompson, 1971). Facsimiles of the previous collection.

MN *SB*   *Colección de Sans de Barutell*

MSA   Medina Sidonia Archive, Sanlúcar de Barrameda. The additional letters and numbers used relate to the archive's cataloguing system.

MSA *Cartas* *Cartas de los Reyes y sus secretarios a los duques de Medina Sidonia y copías de unas respuestas*. MSA has only copies for the years held by KML above.

RAH   Real Academia de la Historia, Madrid

RAH *Jes.* Real Academia de la Historia, *Colección Jesuitas*, plus volume number

Notes

Preface

1. Gabriel Maura y Gamazo, *El Designio de Felipe II* (Madrid, 1957).
2. Garrett Mattingly, *The Armada* (Boston: Houghton Mifflin, 1959) [in the United Kingdom titled *The Defeat of the Spanish Armada*].
3. Peter Pierson, "A Commander for the Armada," *MM* 55, no. 4 (1969): 383–400; I. A. A. Thompson, "The Appointment of the Duke of Medina Sidonia to the Command of the Spanish Armada," *Historical Journal* 12, no. 2 (1969): 197–216. Also, Geoffrey Parker, "If the Armada Had Landed," *History* 60 (1976): 358–68; and Colin Martin and Geoffrey Parker, *The Spanish Armada* (London: Hamish Hamilton, 1988).

Chapter One. An Andalusian Grandee

1. *CSPV*, 8:340, 19 February 1588.
2. Ferdinand and Isabella's daughter Juana was mother to Charles V, Philip II's father. Ferdinand's bastard Don Alonso de Aragón, Archbishop of Zaragoza, fathered Doña Ana. See fig. 1.
3. MSA, *Posesiones del Estado y Mayorazgo de Medina Sidonia y Niebla, tomadas en nombre del Señor Duque Don Alonso por muerte del Señor Duque Don Juan Alonso, su abuelo que falleció en Sanlúcar a 26 de Noviembre 1558*.
4. For seigneurial jurisdiction in Castile, see Alfonso María Guilarte, *El régimen señorial en el siglo XVI* (Madrid, 1962).
5. The *Condado* included the *términos* of Almonte, Alonso, Beas, Bollullos, Bonares, Cabezas Rubias, Calañas, Huelva, Las Cruces, Lucena, Niebla, Palos (part), Paymogo, Puebla de Guzmán, Rociana, San Juan del Puerto, Santa Barbara, Trigueros, Valverde del Camino, and Villarasa.
6. The término of Vejer included Zahara de los Atunes; Jimena was lumped together with the término of Gaucín; and close by were the términos of Algotocín and Benarraba, which in 1587 listed sixteen and thirty *vecinos* (heads of households),

respectively; they had been Morisco villages and probably lost much of their previous populations.

7. In the ducal archives I have not encountered a census that gives the population of the ducal estates, but Tomás González, *Censo de la población de las provincias y partidos de la corona de Castilla en el siglo XVI* (Madrid, 1829), provides useful figures from a census taken between 1587 and 1589 by the bishops of Castile, and a census of 1591–94 taken for tax purposes. For the earlier census, the census-takers for the Archbishop of Seville seem far more thorough than those who served the Bishop of Cadiz. A discussion of these and much more appears in Annie Molinié-Bertrand, *Au siècle d'or, l'Espagne et ses hommes* (Paris: Economica, 1985), 11–21, 283–93.

The 1587–89 list of vecinos gives a figure of 11,612; the 1591 census gives figures only for the Kingdom of Seville: González totals 11,746; Molinié-Bertrand, *Au siècle d'or*, p. 285, quotes Jean Sentaurens, with 12,103 vecinos.

Different scholars have used differing coefficients, ranging from 3.5 to as high as 6.0 to determine the number of persons per household from the number of vecinos. Where we do have figures—as in the census for the archdiocese of Seville—that show both vecinos and persons, the ratios vary from about 3.5:1 to 6:1. If we opt for 4.5, we get 52, 254 persons; 4.0 would yield 46,448. A militia muster of about 1590 (AGS, *GA*, 302, *Relación de la última muestra de la gente de cavallo y de a pie que se halla en el estado del duque de Medina Sidonia, toda armada.*) gives a figure of 10,492 men in the eighteen through forty-five age group. In 1590, the population of Medina Sidonia's estates was almost entirely Old Christian, and only the clergy or cripples would be exempt from serving in the militia. If the number of militiamen were roughly 40 percent of the male population, we would have about 26,250 males; and doubling that for females, we have some 52,500 persons.

8. RAH *Jes.*, 109–39, *Relación de la artillería del duque de Medina Sidonia*, lists some forty guns provided to royal ships and expeditions between 1581 and 1590 that ranged in size from 70-lb. falcons to a 4,200-lb. cannon. All together the weight of the guns totaled over 65,000 lbs.

9. Fernand Braudel, *The Mediterranean and the Mediterranean World in the Age of Philip II*, 2 vols. (New York: Harper & Row, 1972), 2: 710.

10. AGS *GA*, 302, *Relación de la última muestra de la gente*. The Condado provided 335 horsemen, 2,306 men with firearms, and 3,017 armed with pikes. In most of the Duke's towns, those with firearms heavily outnumbered those with pikes, giving for the estates as a whole 5,367 men with firearms and 4,376 with pikes, in addition to 749 horsemen.

11. I. A. A. Thompson, "Appointment of the Duke of Medina Sidonia to the Command of the Spanish Armada," *Historical Journal* 12, no. 2 (1969): 213*n*121.

12. Luis Cabrera de Córdoba, *Felipe II, Rey de España* (1619), 4 vols. (Madrid, 1876–78), 3: 269.

13. Modesto Ulloa, *La Hacienda Real de Castilla en el reinado de Felipe II* (Rome, 1963), 162–163.

14. IVDJ, *Envío* 21, n.d., 1583.

15. Gordon Connell Smith, *Forerunners of Drake* (London, 1954), 8, 81–82, 90, 213. For the 1578 figure, (AGS *Est.*, 160, *relación*). The same year thirty-three Breton ships from St. Malo and St. Pol de Leon called, along with fifty-seven other French

ships, from Rouen, Havre de Grace, Dieppe, Normandy, Bayonne (*Bayona de Francia*), and Pasajes [*sic*, probably St. Jean de Luz], fifty-nine Easterlings, from Danzig, Norway, Denmark, and Poland, and four Flemish. English ships may well have continued coming there under false nationality, a not uncommon practice in response to Philip II's several embargoes against English and Dutch shipping.

16. AGS *GA*, 365, a list of English merchants in Spain, "católicos, sospechos o herejes." Those in Sanlúcar regarded as Catholic were Thomas Jaymes and William Davis; as suspect, William Golden and Henry Harkes. For the rest of Andalusia, there were five in Seville, four in Cadiz, one in Puerto Santa Maria, two in Jerez, two in Ayamonte. Compare with eighteen in Lisbon.

17. Cabrera, 3: 269. Ulloa, *La Haciénda Real*, 551, reads the passage to mean that the Duke was robbing Spain, but it seems to me, in spite of Cabrera's usual convoluted prose, that Medina Sidonia, who had come to court, was complaining about another: "haberle puesto otro el rey, sobre que se agraviaba, y el fiscal de que por su barra [the bar at Sanlúcar] entraba la plata y por su ladronia salia y se robaba a España y pedió remedio y castigo."

18. *CSPV*, 9, 23 April 1593, Ambassador Vendramin remarked that Medina Sidonia refused to depart from court, as urged, to organize the defense of the coast until he had been satisfied in his lawsuit over the Sanlúcar customs. MSA L-67 C-21, 29 May 1600, deals with the sale by Lerma of the office of Escribano Mayor de Aduanas.

19. Diego Ortiz y Zúñiga, *Anales eclesiásticos y seglares de Sevilla* (Madrid, 1677), 528.

20. Braudel, *The Mediterranean*, 2, 713.

21. Pedro de Medina, *Crónica de los duques de Medina Sidonia*, published in *CODOIN*, 39: 173. Discussing the original grant in 1356, he claims that in some years one hundred thousand tunny were caught and that the value was more than 40,000 ducats a year. For a description of the fishery, see 277–81.

22. Ulloa, *La Hacienda Real*, 164.

23. Eugenio Alberi, ed., *Relazione degli ambasciatori veneti al Senato* (Florence, 1839–63), series I, vol. 3, 263, gives 80,000 escudos, which equal 74,667 ducats. The problems in determining noble incomes are discussed in Modesto Ulloa, *Las rentas de algunos señores y señoríos castellanos bajo los primeros Austria* (Montevideo, 1971). Medina Sidonia is not among those discussed.

24. Alberi, *Relazione degli ambasciatori*, series I, vol. 5, 228. BL *Harleian Mss.* 588, fol. 94, has 100,000 ducats for 1575, which seems too low.

25. Núñez de Salcedo, *relación* published in *Boletín de la Real Academia de Historia* 73 (1918): 470–91.

26. Maura, *El Designio de Felipe II*, 241–44, 16 February 1588, for this oft-cited figure.

27. *Ibid.*, 113. For the suspension, BM *Add.Mss.* 28,343, fol. 398, s.d., 1582.

28. See Charles Jago, "The Influence of Debt on the Relations between Crown and Aristocracy in Seventeenth Century Castile," *Economic History Review* 26 (1973): 218–36. Helen Nader, another student of the Spanish aristocracy (*The Mendoza Family in the Spanish Renaissance* [New Brunswick: Rutgers, 1979], in papers and conversation has suggested that some aristocrats borrowed at low rates of interest and invested the money in hope of greater gain.

29. See Pedro de Medina, *A Navigator's Universe: The Libro de Cosmografía of 1538*, trans. Ursula Lamb (Chicago and London: University of Chicago, 1972), 9–18. David Goodman, *Power and Penury: Government, Technology and Science in Philip II's Spain* (Cambridge, 1988), 60, carries a portrait of Medina.

30. MN *Mss.* 496–253, memorial of early 1581.

31. See Claude Chauchadis, *Honneur, Morale et Société dans l'Espagne de Philippe II* (Paris: CNRS, 1984).

32. Ibid., 197, 211*n*31.

33. In *CODOIN*, 39, *Crónica de los duques de Medina Sidonia*. A similar chronicle, "Ilustraciones de la casa de Niebla," was written about the same time by Pedro Barrantes Maldonado and is published in *Memorial de la Real Academia de la Historia*, vols. 9–10.

34. MSA, L-41–C-4, 15 June 1572.

35. These and many other population figures come from González, *Censo*. In 1587 the Archbishop of Seville reckoned his diocese to have 123,014 vecinos and 466,929 persons; the Bishop of Cádiz counted 11,800 vecinos in a less detailed census. The region also had a notoriously large population of vagabonds and others who escaped census-takers. Regarding population, see n. 7 above.

36. AGS *Est.* 177, 26 May 1597, Medina Sidonia to King.

37. Carlos Riba García, ed., *Correspondencia privada de Felipe II con su secretario Mateo Vázquez* (Madrid: C.S.I.C., 1959), 253. Memorandum of Vázquez to the King. The purchaser was Bernardino de Salinas.

38. MSA, L-42; for quote, a memorandum to the King by Secretary Mateo Vázquez, BL *Add.Mss.* 28,370, fol. 88; see also 28,355, fol. 338, for the matter in the royal council.

39. Adolfo de Castro, *Historia de Cádiz y su provincia* (Cádiz, 1858), is filled with this sort of antiquarian detail. The dukes of Arcos headed the Ponce de León family and had held previously the title of Marquis of Cádiz.

40. AGS *GA*, 365, report of 23 September 1592. The War Councilors favored eight hundred *vecinos*. Cádiz had been attacked in 1587 by the English and feared another attack in 1589; and the years of 1587–93 were poor for the Indies trade. Molinié-Bertrand, *Au siècle d'or*, 291–93, discusses the population of Cádiz.

41. For instance, MN *Mss.*, 497–253, 19 December 1610, to Don Diego Brochero, a War Councilor.

42. BL *Add.Mss.* 28,370, fols. 85–86, Medina Sidonia to Secretary Mateo Vázquez, 20 March 1583.

43. MSA, L-39, contains the contract of 19 December 1565, which includes the customary 100,000-ducat dowry. Her name is given elsewhere as María Andrea; she seems to have died in late 1589.

44. This Girón was grandnephew of the Pedro Girón who tried to seize the Medina Sidonia estates and who died without descent.

45. *Dépêches de M. de Fourquevaux*, ed. l'Abbé Douais, 3 vols. (Paris, 1896–1904), vol. 1, pt. 1, p. 92.

46. MSA, L-39 C-18, 19, 20. Most documents are 1566, but the continuation of the annuity, given at 937,000 *maravedís*, is 11 October 1574, after Eboli's death.

47. BL *Add.Mss.* 28,335, fols. 27, 28, of 10 and 11 August 1566 for this matter.

48. See Andrew C. Hess, "The Moriscos: An Ottoman Fifth Column in Six-

teenth Century Spain?" *American Historical Review* 74 (1968): 1–25.

49. This and most of what follows regarding Medina Sidonia and the Morisco rebellion can be found in Maura, *El Designio de Felipe II*, 15–26.

50. Chauchadis, *Honneur, Morale*, 139, 159n144.

51. BL *Add.Mss.* 28,343, fol. 398, n.d., 1582, mentions a suit between the Duke and vecinos of the city of Medina Sidonia in the Chancellery of Granada, which may be related to this case.

52. Braudel, *The Mediterranean*, 1070

53. See fig. 11 for Medina Sidonia's heirs and their careers. Alonso López de Haro, *Nobiliario de los reyes y títulos de España* (Madrid, 1621), Libro 1, chap. 10; and Luis Salazar y Castro, *Historia genealógica de la Casa de Silva* (Madrid, 1685), vol. 2, chap. 18, provide considerable detail about the families.

54. Maura, *El Designio de Felipe II*, 30–31; the original source seems to be Francisco Pérez Ferrer, BN Madrid *Mss.* Ee80.

55. Salazar y Castro, *Historia geneálogica*, 2, 571.

Chapter Two. A Career of Service

1. Fray Juan de Victoria, "Noticias de la invencible," *CODOIN*, 81, is full of such anecdotal information, but his reliability is often questionable.

2. The picture hangs in the ducal palace and has been reproduced in Mattingly, *The Armada*, and in several more recent studies.

3. See William S. Maltby, *Alba* (Berkeley and Los Angeles: California, 1983).

4. See I. A. A. Thompson, *War and Government in Habsburg Spain* (London: Athlone Press, 1976) chap. 10. I thank Thompson for alerting me years ago to Medina Sidonia's interest in the galleys. Medina Sidonia later had mixed feelings about the *asiento* system: they are expressed in a *consulta*, c. 1598, that involved him, the Adelantado of Castile, then commanding the Ocean Armada, the Count of Fuentes, Don Juan de Borja of the War Council, and the Naval Secretary Esteban de Ibarra. MN *FN*, 8, fols. 146–54.

5. AGS *GA*, 78, fol. 97, 15 November 1574.

6. RAH *Jes.*, 109, fols. 463–503, consists largely of Medina Sidonia's correspondence with the court over the asiento and related papers.

7. *Ibid.* fols. 503–04.

8. *Ibid.*, fols. 497–98, to Juan de Ovando, n.d., refers to Ovando's of twenty-first of this month.

9. AGS *Est.* 453, n.d. The other letters and consultas of early 1575 are also in this *legajo*.

10. MN *SB*, 5°-45, 24 July 1575. Don Enrique was second Count; his father, Don Pedro, died in 1569.

11. MN *Mss.* 497-253.

12. RAH *Jes.* 109, fols. 471–74, 6 June 1576.

13. Maura, *El Designio de Felipe II*, 28, King to Medina Sidonia about opinions he had expressed to the Marquis of los Vélez, of the Council of State.

14. BN Madrid, *Mss.* 2062, fols. 56–57, copy of a letter dated 20 February 1580 from Medina Sidonia to the Duke of Braganza.

15. Many refused to believe he had died, and "false Sebastians" appeared into

the beginning of the seventeenth century. See Mary Elizabeth Brooks, *A King for Portugal* (Madison: Wisconsin, 1964).

16. MSA, L-40, letters of 2 and 4 September 1578 and 13 November 1579.

17. Gregorio Marañón, *Antonio Pérez*, 7th ed. (Madrid, 1963), 1, 278, letter of 6 October 1578, Juan de Samaniego to Prince of Parma.

18. More precisely for Dom Manuel's descendants, Philip (1527–98) was the son of his eldest daughter, Isabel (1503–39); Dom António (1531–95) was the bastard son of Dom Luis (1506–55); and Catalina (1540–1614), daughter of Dom Duarte (1515–40). An excellent claim that was not pressed belonged to Ranuccio Farnese (1569–1622), son of Alexander Farnese (1547–92), Prince of Parma, and Dom Duarte's older daughter Maria (1538–77). Alexander Farnese was Philip II's nephew and Governor General of the Low Countries (1578–92), a widower when Dom Sebastian fell, loyal to Philip II, and perhaps hopeful of something else. The Venetian ambassadors and others suspected he entertained some hope of Mary Queen of Scots and England.

19. *CODOIN*, 6:214, 29 October 1578. Much correspondence, including Medina Sidonia's, about the annexation of Portugal is printed in this volume, and in volume 27.

20. MN *SB*, 3°-440, 24 August 1579, Council of War.

21. Medina Sidonia's own estates could provide a considerable number of men. A relation of November 1581 in the ducal archive lists 3,750 infantry equipped with arquebuses. For some ten years later, AGS *GA*, 302, *relación de la ultima muestra*, gives the total militia of Medina Sidonia's estates as 10,519: 776 were mounted, of whom only 27 did not have firearms in addition to lance, 5,367 were arquebusiers, and 4,376 were armed with pikes or spears.

22. *CODOIN*, 6:445, 14 June 1579.

23. BN Paris, *Fonds français, Mss.* 16106, fol. 274, 18 September 1579.

24. For this matter, see Marañón, *Antonio Pérez*, and Gaspar Muro, *Vida de la Princesa de Eboli* (Madrid, 1877).

25. Muro, *Vida de Eboli*, 74, doc. 60.

26. The most plausible treatment of the murder is Geoffrey Parker, *Philip II* (Boston: Little, Brown, 1978), chap. 8.

27. Muro, *Vida de Eboli*, 163, doc. 139.

28. Marañón, *Antonio Pérez*, 1:281, Pedro Núñez de Toledo to Vázquez, 25 August 1579.

29. Ibid. See A. Valente, "Un Dramma Politico alla Corte de Filippo II," *Nuova Rivista Storica* 8 (1924).

30. *CODOIN*, 27:221–23.

31. Ibid., 225–26.

32. Ibid., 228.

33. RAH *Jes.*, 150, fol. 19, to Philip II.

34. *CODOIN*, 27:243–44.

35. Ibid., 249–52, 9 January 1580.

36. BN Madrid, *Mss.* 2062, fols. 57–58, 13 February 1580 (copy).

37. Ibid., fols. 56–57, 20 February 1580 (copy).

38. Cabrera, *Felipe II*, 2:575.

39. MSA, L-42, 26 March 1580.

40. *CODOIN*, 27:282-83, 10 April 1580.

41. RAH *Jes.*, 109, contains much material about the dealings of the Duke and Duchess of Braganza both with Medina Sidonia and the Bishop of Cuenca.

42. Maura, *El Designio de Felipe II*, 73-74, puts the letter, n.d., from the Medina Sidonia archive after one of 11 July 1580. CODOIN, 27:245-49, gives the date as 29 December 1579, which makes no sense unless the late King-Cardinal issued it before his death.

43. *CODOIN*, 27:418, 18 August 1580.

44. Ibid., 24:51, 8 September 1580.

45. *Correspondance de Cardinal Granvelle*, ed. Edmond Poullet and Charles Piot, 12 vols. (Brussels, 1877-96), 12:619, Philip's notation on Granvelle's letter of 13 February 1581.

46. BN Paris, *Fonds français, Mss.* 16108, fol. 91, 23 February 1581.

47. BL *Add.Mss.* 28,370, fol. 2, 31 March 1581.

48. Ibid., fols 8-9, 20 May 1581.

49. Ibid., fols. 34-35, 1 June 1581.

Chapter Three. Captain General without Title

1. MN *Mss.* 496-58*bis*, 8 July 1581. Much of the material for this matter is in this volume of transcripts, or in Maura, *El Designio de Felipe, II*, chap. 5-7. More remains in MSA, Sanlúcar. Henri de Castries et al., *Les Sources inédits de l'histoire du Maroc* (Paris, 1905-), 1st series, France, vol. 2, provides some interesting background on Spanish interest in Larache.

2. MN *Mss.* 496-54, 22 May 1581.

3. MSA *Cartas*, 25 July 1581; the date is incorrectly printed 22 July in Maura, *El Designio de Felipe, II*, 88-89, which contains part of the letter.

4. BL *Add.Mss.* 28,370, fol. 78, n.d., among the papers of Mateo Vázquez that relate to Medina Sidonia. Andalusia, save for the "Kingdom" of Córdoba, was included; Granada was regarded as a separate kingdom.

5. MSA *Cartas*, King to Medina Sidonia, 26 August 1581.

6. Muro, *Vida de Eboli*, doc. 190, report of Fray Pablo de Mendoza, March 1582.

7. Ibid., docs. 131, King to Medina Sidonia, 2 September 1581; also 130, La Favara to King, 23 August 1581.

8. MSA *Cartas*, 10 September 1581.

9. RAH *Jes.*, 117-14; next is item 16.

10. AGS *GA*, 109, fols. 404-08, 435. MN *Mss.* 496-253 covers the same topics in letter form.

11. MN *Mss.* 497-253, 19 December 1610.

12. AGS *GA*, 109, contains much correspondence on this. Also Maura, *El Designio de Felipe, II*, 103-10.

13. AGS *GA*, 109, fol. 505, 14 June 1581.

14. MN *Mss.* 496-76; for details on ships and people, MN *SB*, 4°-572.

15. MN *FN*, 20:471, 49.

16. MSA *Cartas*, 27 October 1581; with it Zayas sent a report of 28 September on events in Algiers.

17. Thompson, "Appointment of the Duke of Medina Sidonia," 198.
18. AGS *GA*, 109, docs. 318, 319, 329, 330, 332, 8–16 November 1581.
19. Maura, *El Designio de Felipe, II*, 118.
20. Poullet and Piot, *Granvelle*, 10:72 18 February 1582.
21. Ibid., 9:29, 20 January 1582.
22. BN Paris, *Fonds français*, 16108, 4 June 1581.
23. Maura, *El Designio de Felipe II*, 117–18, 18 February 1582.
24. BL *Add.Mss.* 28,343, fol. 235, 15 May 1582, Don Juan de Alarcón to King.
25. MN *SB*, 4°-626, Medina Sidonia to King, Conil, 21 June 1582.
26. MSA *Cartas*, 19 August 1582; part of letter appears in Maura, *El Designio de Felipe, II*, 123.
27. Ibid., 20 August 1582.
28. Ibid., 24 August 1582.
29. Ibid.
30. Ibid., 18 September 1582.
31. Ibid., 29 August 1582.
32. Maura, *El Designio de Felipe II*, 125–26, 1 September 1582.
33. MSA *Cartas*, unsigned relation.
34. BL *Add.Mss.* 28,370, fol. 88, 22 March 1583.
35. MSA *Cartas*, 27 August 1582, to Juan Delgado.
36. Ibid., 19 November 1582; Maura prints part, *El Designio de Felipe II*, 125–26.
37. Poullet and Piot, *Granvelle*, 10:178, 6 May 1583.
38. Ibid., 360, 10 September 1583. Santa Cruz, writing from the Azores, believed that his next objective would be Larache (FD, 1, doc. 1, 241–43).
39. BL *Add.Mss.* 28,370, fols. 118–20, 18 October 1583.
40. Ibid., 28,262, f. 320, Mateo Vázquez to King, 13 February 1584.
41. Maura, *El Designio de Felipe II*, 139–40, 5 November 1583.
42. A. W. Lovett has written two interesting studies on Vázquez, "A Cardinal's Papers: The Rise of Mateo Vázquez de Leca," *English Historical Review* 88 (April 1973), and *Philip II and Mateo Vázquez de Leca* (Geneva: Librairie Droz, 1977).
43. BL *Add.Mss.* 28,370, fol. 29.
44. Maura, *El Designio de Felipe, II*, 138.
45. MN *Mss.* 496–195, 21 October 1584.

Chapter Four. War Comes to Andalusia

1. BL *Add.Mss.* 28,370, fol. 145.
2. Don Martín de Padilla y Manrique de Lara was almost always referred to as the Adelantado, though he became in 1586 Count of Santa Gadea and was so addressed in official correspondence. He also acquired the title Count of Buendía on the death of his brother.
3. AGS *Est.*, 160. *Relación*, n.d. For the rest, see chapter 1, n. 15.
4. *Dépêches diplomatiques de M. de Longlée (1582–1590)*, ed. Albert Mousset, (Paris, 1912), 172, n.d., August 1585.
5. I have treated these matters in larger scope in my *Philip II of Spain* (London: Thames & Hudson, 1975), 176–80.
6. Martin and Parker, *Spanish Armada*, 110–11. Philip had wanted an invasion

of England in 1571 to coincide with the Ridolfi Plot, but Alba, then Governor General of the Low Countries, proved reluctant (ibid., 88–89). There was talk of invasion in 1574 by Pedro Menéndez de Avilés's armada, which was assembled at Santander to support operations against Dutch rebels, but no plan to do it. See Magdalena Pi Corrales, *"La otra invencible" 1574* (Madrid: Instituto de Cultura y Historia Naval, 1983).

7. *CSPV*, 8:128–32, 1 January 1586.

8. Ibid., 22 March 1586.

9. Ibid., 1 May 1586.

10. I. A. A. Thompson, "The Armada and Administrative Reform: The Spanish Council of War in the Reign of Philip II," *English Historical Review* 82 (1967): 698–725; and *War and Government*, 39–48 and passim, deal with the council and changes in personnel. He sees the politics as an aristocrat versus military professional conflict; I see it as a mix of personal court rivalries, traditional aristocratic factions, and the ambitions of a sort of military establishment.

11. Maura, *El Designio de Felipe II*, 145–46, 30 March 1586.

12. MN *Mss.* 501–235, 11 May 1586.

13. Maura, *El Designio de Felipe II*, 149–151, 28 April 1586, to Duke of Osuna.

14. MN *Mss.*, 496–208, 29 May 1586.

15. Ibid., 496–206, 5 May 1586; see also Maura, *El Designio de Felipe II*, 151–54.

16. KML *Cuentas*, 5, has much material on this matter. Some general remarks on galleys in the Caribbean appear in the introduction and notes to Richard Boulind, "Shipwreck and Mutiny in Spain's Galleys on the Santo Domingo Station, 1583," *MM* 58, no. 3 (August 1972): 297–330. Medina Sidonia had been the first in Spain to learn of the mutiny and was involved in its investigation.

17. MN *Mss.*, 496–219, 18 June 1586.

18. MN *SB*, 4°-813, letter of 29 July 1586 from Francisco Duarte to the King, to inform him that Medina Sidonia had ordered him to break the rules in this case.

19. MN *Mss.* 496–225, 5 July 1586.

20. Ibid. Medina Sidonia's assessment proved correct: the commander was punished with life imprisonment. H. P. Kraus, *Sir Francis Drake: A Pictorial Biography* (Amsterdam, 1970), 202.

21. MN *Mss.* 496–222, 1 July 1586.

22. Ibid., 496–223, 1 July 1586.

23. He regarded them as acceptable for harbor defense and short operations but not for long-range patrols and the pursuit of pirates, for which he favored small galleons and *fregatas*.

24. Goodman, *Power and Penury*, 139–40.

25. MSA *Cartas*, 15 November 1586, in which Idiáquez also mentioned the Duke's "sleepless night."

26. MN *Mss.* 496–241 and 242, 15 October 1586; and MSA *Cartas*, Idiáquez's request, dated 8 October.

27. There is much correspondence on this in MSA, L-3 (A-36, E-2), *Capitán General de la costa de Andalucía*; in *Cartas* for 1587, and MN *Mss.* 496, copies of correspondence for 1587. The ship lists in L-3 provide an interesting look at the traffic and its ports of origin.

28. MSA *Cartas*, 10 March 1587.

29. FD, 1, doc. 7, pp. 150–319.

30. Léon van der Essen, *Alexandre Farnèse*, 5 vols. (Brussels, 1937), 5:163–70, for Parma's plan.

31. For Idiáquez, MN *Mss.* 496–264, 13 February 1587; Medina Sidonia's response, Maura, *El Designio de Felipe II*, 163–67, 22 February 1587.

32. Maura, *El Designio de Felipe II*, 167–68, 28 February 1587.

33. *Usted* is still often abbreviated *Vd.* In 1586 Philip II had an end put to many of the grandiloquent Burgundian and Italian styles of address that had proliferated at his court and restored to an extent what were regarded as the simpler forms of Castile. Ordinary gentlemen became *Vuestra Merced* rather than *Ilustre* or *Magnifico Señor*, and titled noblemen became *Vuestra Señoría* (Your Lordship) rather than *Vuestra Excelencia*.

34. Maura, *El Designio de Felipe II*, 168–72, 5 March 1587.

35. They were in fact coming from Guipúzcoa, but Medina Sidonia, despite his excellent knowledge of geography, often confused the two provinces.

36. In fact only four of the six came in 1587; the others came in 1589.

37. MN *Mss.*, 496–270, 31 March 1587.

38. MSA *Cartas*, "relación de la orden," 20 March 1587.

39. FD, 1, doc. 14bis, 334–35.

40. *CSPV*, 8, Lippomano, 6 May 1587. Osuna had returned to Spain from his tour as Viceroy of Naples, 1582–86, and was in poor health.

41. MN *Mss.* 496–295, n.d., May 1587; Maura, *El Designio de Felipe II*, 211–12.

42. Cabrera, *Felipe II*, 3:247–48; Idiáquez insisted in a letter to Medina Sidonia that the Council of War claimed that Cádiz was well fortified and close to help. MN *Mss.* 496–297, 9 May 1587.

43. MSA *Cartas*, 4 August 1587 and 25 August 1587.

44. FD, 1, doc. 18, 23 May 1587. Maura, *El Designio de Felipe II*, vol. 11, uses well the correspondence between Medina Sidonia and the King for these weeks to dramatize the rapid buildup of Spanish forces after Drake's raid.

45. FD, 1, docs. 16, 19; MN *Mss.* 496–286, 8 May 1587. A detailed list of the fifteen ships and their crews is given in FD, 1, doc. 40.

46. MSA *Cartas*, 30 May 1587.

47. Ibid.

48. FD, 1, doc. 26, letter of 3 June 1587.

49. MN *Mss.* 496–317, 3 June 1587.

50. MSA *Cartas*, 17 June 1587.

51. FD, 1, doc. 29.

52. Ibid., docs. 32–43; also MN 378, correspondence with Santa Cruz; MSA *Cartas*, for 14, 24, and 30 July 1587; and Cabrera, *Felipe II*, 3:249.

53. MN *Mss.* 496–342, King to Duke, 30 July 1587. The value of the English prize was estimated at 40,000 ducats.

Chapter Five. Command of the Armada

1. MN *Mss.* 496–343.

2. Previously Medina Sidonia had expressed his doubt that there was a pas-

sage south of the Strait of Magellan, MN *Mss.* 496–253, fol. 273.

3. MSA *Cartas*, 2 September 1587.

4. Ibid.

5. See Manuel Fernández Alvarez, *Felipe II, Isabel de Inglaterra y Marruecos* (Madrid: C.S.I.C., 1951).

6. MN *Mss.* 496–345, King to Duke, 2 October 1587; MSA *Cartas*, King to Duke, 3 October 1587.

7. Cabrera, *Felipe II*, 3:267–68.

8. MSA *Cartas*, 20 October 1587.

9. *CSPV*, 8, 27 August 1587.

10. HO, docs. 18 and 19, King to Archduke Albert, 14 September 1587 and s.d.

11. Enrique Herrera Oria, *Felipe II y el Marqués de Santa Cruz en la empresa de Inglaterra* (Madrid, 1946), doc. 22, 15 October 1587; also HO, doc. 24.

12. Cabrera, *Felipe II*, 3:267.

13. Herrera Oria, *Santa Cruz*, docs. 24, 25.

14. Cabrera, *Felipe II*, 3:266–67; *CSPV*, 8, Lippomano, 5 November 1587.

15. *CSPV*, 8, Lippomano, 5 and 29 November 1587.

16. Cabrera, *Felipe II*, 3:269.

17. The text of the commission can be found in *CODOIN*, 28:376ff.

18. For the defense of Spain's Atlantic coast, two other new regional captain-generalships were established, one for Galicia, which was given to the Marquis of Cerralbo, and another for the Cantabrian Coast, given to the Constable of Castile. There had long been a Captain General of the Coast of Granada, and the viceroys of Aragon, Valencia, and Navarre and the governor general of Catalonia each held the office of Captain General of his region.

19. MN *Mss.* 496–398, and MSA *Cartas*, 28 and 31 January, and 4 February; for the galleys of Genoa, MN *SB*, Art. 3° doc. 530, to Idiáquez, 6 February 1588.

20. HO, doc. 83, 11 February 1588. For detailed treatment of Medina Sidonia's appointment, see my "A Commander for the Armada," and Thompson, "Appointment of the Duke of Medina Sidonia."

21. The letter has been printed many times, including by Maura, 241–44, FD, 1, doc. 53, and in the *CSPSp*, 4. It is a rambling letter and extremely difficult to translate while remaining true to the text. The Duke's style in general seems convoluted, as he puts down ideas in the order they occur to him, though this is hardly unusual for the correspondence of the era.

22. HO, doc. 89, King to Duke, 20 February 1588.

23. Ibid., 88, 20 February 1588.

24. KML *Cartas*, doc. 114, 24 June 1588; also Maura, *El Designio de Felipe II*, 258–61, and FD, 2, doc. 129.

25. The passage in the Duke's hand from KML *Cartas*, doc. 114, reads "Y, assí, rehusé este servicio por esta causa, y por entender que se facilitava más a V.M. el negocio de lo que algunos entendían, que sólo miravan a su real servicio sin más fines." In *CSPSp*, 4:318, it is Englished, "This was my reason for at first declining the command, seeing that the Enterprise was being represented to your Majesty as easier than it was known to be by those whose only aim was your Majesty's service." Colloquially *facilitar* can mean to oversimplify, but in this case I doubt it; and to get the above translation, Martin A. S. Hume had to do some twisting,

though it does remain plausible. I believe that Philip was not one for whom matters were easily oversimplified, and Medina Sidonia did know him. The negotiations were not taken seriously by many, including Philip, who admitted to Parma they were to serve as a cover; but they were under way in June 1588, and Medina Sidonia probably knew of them. When he received a reply from court to this letter, he was admonished that the armada in port could do nothing to affect any "trato de concierto," certainly peace negotiations (HO, doc. 115). Thompson, "Appointment of the Duke of Medina Sidonia," 200–01, makes much of the possibility that the armada's chief purpose may have been to force England into serious peace negotiations; and Padre Victoria claimed that many in 1588 suspected as much (*CODOIN*, 81:224).

The negotiations were being conducted by Sir James Croft for Queen Elizabeth with delegates appointed by the Duke of Parma. Conyers Read, *Lord Burghley and Queen Elizabeth* (1970), 334–39 and chap. 20 deals with the negotiations from the English side; and van der Essen, *Alexandre Farnèse*, vol. 5, chap. 5 from Parma's. Whether or not the negotiations were serious, Lord Admiral Howard of Effingham had no doubts of Spain's perfidy and complained to Secretary Francis Walsingham of Croft's treachery: see Laughton, 1:47.

26. FD, 1, doc. 65; and 2, doc. 114.

27. Ibid., 2, doc. 186; also *CODOIN* 81, "Noticias de la Invencible."

28. FD, 2, doc. 108. On 14 May 1588 the Duke wrote the King about Eboli, "I shall go on with grief and concern until I hear of the clemency which Your Majesty in his grandeur will command done for me."

29. HO, doc. 89, King to Duke, 20 February 1588, in response to the Duke's of 16 February.

30. HO, doc. 88, to Medina Sidonia, 20 February 1588.

31. See my *Philip II*, 95–97.

32. Mousset, *Longlée*, 353, 15 March 1588.

33. *CSPV*, 9:346; Soranzo, 27 September 1598.

34. HO, doc. 76, a letter from the Count of Fuentes in Lisbon dated 30 January, states that Santa Cruz had been in bed ill for seven or eight days; doc. 68, from Fuentes on 4 February, states that Santa Cruz remained indisposed; doc. 82, from Fuentes on February 9, states that the Marquis's illness had turned for the worse and that he was about to die. It would have been late on 11 February before urgent dispatches posted in Lisbon on 9 February could have reached Madrid. The Marquis died late on 9 February, and the news of his death was sent to Madrid the next morning. The Venetian Ambassador Lippomano heard it as he was completing his dispatch for 13 February; he reported that Santa Cruz had died of "spotted fever." *CSPV*, 8:337–38.

35. AGS *Est.* 165, fol. 79.

36. Mousset, *Longlée*, 347, 15 February 1588.

37. *CSPV* 8:340, 19 February 1588.

38. BL *Add.Mss.* 28,340, fol. 49, 29 April 1579, and note about him by Mateo Vázquez to Philip, fol. 91.

39. HO, *apéndice*, doc. 2, 9 February 1588.

40. *CSPV*, 8:477, Contarini, 23 December 1589. Similar comments appear in Lippomano's dispatch of 6 September 1588.

41. The anger of the Spaniards at the choice of Gian Andrea Doria over Santa Cruz for the post of Captain General of the [Mediterranean] Sea has been mentioned above. From the Italian side come remarks about the 1588 armada by the Venetian Ambassador Contarini, *CSPV*, 8, 24 May 1589: "The failure of the Armada was due to want of experienced Italian men and officers, of whom there was none on board the fleet." Regarding the search for a new commander in 1589 he added, "The truth is there are very few Spaniards for so responsible a position and an Italian will hardly be admitted."

42. He resumed the command in 1602 but died in 1604.

43. HO, doc. 89, pp. 144–45.

44. Lasso de la Vega, Miguel [marqués del Saltillo], "El duque de Medina Sidonia y la jornada a Inglaterra en 1588," *Boletín de la biblioteca Menéndez y Pelayo*, Año XVI (1934): 166–77; the sum in *maravedís* is on p. 169.

Chapter Six. The Armada at Lisbon

1. Thompson, *War and Government*, chaps. 2 and 7, provide an outstanding introduction to Philip II's naval administration. Also see Francisco-Felipe Olesa Muñido, *La Organización naval de los estados mediterráneos y en especial de España durante los siglos XVI y XVII*, 2 vols. (Madrid, 1968).

For Spanish ships see *El Buque en la Armada Española*, ed. Enrique Manera Regueyra (Madrid: Silex, 1981), chap. 4, "La Marina Remica de los Austrias," by José María Martínez-Hidalgo; chapter 5, "La Marina Oceana de los Austrias," by Francisco-Felipe Olesa Muñido; and chapter 6, "La Arquitectura Naval de los Austrias," by Carlos Moya Blanco. Also, Olesa Muñido, *La Organización naval*, vol. 1, chap. 3, which surveys the pertinent literature and draws heavily on contemporary materials; Carla Rahn Phillips, *Six Galleons for the King of Spain* (Baltimore: Johns Hopkins, 1986), an outstanding work that remains useful for 1588 even though it is about the 1620s and 1630s; her "Spanish Ship Measurements Reconsidered: The *Instrucción Náutica* of Diego García de Palacio (1587)," *MM* 73, no. 3 (1987):293–96; and Michael Barkham, "Sixteenth-Century Spanish Basque Ships and Shipbuilding: The Multipurpose *Nao*," in *Postmedieval Boat and Ship Archaeology*, ed. Carl Olof Cederland (Stockholm: Swedish National Maritime Museum Report #20, BAR International Series 256, 1985). Peter Padfield, *Armada* (London: Gollancz; Annapolis: Naval Institute, 1988), chap. 6, offers a fine general treatment of ships.

Much valuable information about armada ships has been gathered recently by underwater archaeologists. *Trésors de l'Armada* (Brussels: Crédit Communal, 1985) sums up much work in contributions by Colin Martin and Robert Sténuit, the two leaders in the field. Also Colin Martin, *Full Fathom Five* (New York: Viking, 1975).

The pertinent sections in Richard W. Unger, *The Ship in the Medieval Economy* (London: Croom Helm; Montreal: McGill-Queens, 1980), Björn Landström, *The Ship* (Garden City: Doubleday, 1961), and Peter Kemp, *History of Ships* (London: Orbis, 1976), are also useful.

2. Menéndez was among those who perished. See Pi Corrales, *Otra Invencible*, 153–56.

3. FD, 1, doc. 69, 19 March 1588, lists the armada's ships then in Lisbon

harbor and notes their state of readiness and what work they need.

4. Ibid., doc. 48, 7 January 1588, lists the fifteen greatships pressed into service in Andalusia in 1587 as a unit; doc. 69, the inspection of 19 March 1588 shows the fifteen reduced to nine, with three transferred to Recalde's Vizcayan squadron and two to Oquendo's Guipuzcoan squadron. One of the ships was Oquendo's own; for the other four there were probably similar reasons of ownership or association. Absent from the list is the *Duquesa Santa Ana*, which reappears on later lists.

5. Phillips, *Six Galleons*, has tables of ratios according to the rules of 1618 and 1626. There is no reason to believe that the galleons of 1588 had greater ratios. See her discussion of the matter, 40–44. In a relation of 1613, Medina Sidonia favored 2.5:1 for ships of the armada and flotas (MN *Mss.* 497–265). In contrast, Horatio Nelson's flagship *Victory* (built 1759–65) had a keel to beam ratio of 3:1 and overall length to beam ratio of 4.5:1.

6. The murals in the Hall of Battles of the Escorial and at Santa Cruz's palace at Viso del Marqués (reproduced in *El Buque en la armada española*) are probably the best depictions of Spanish and Portuguese galleons and greatships before the new construction of 1589. Some galleons of the Castilian squadron ordered in 1581 from Cristóbal de Barros may have had lower forecastles, similar to race-built English galleons, copied by the Spaniards in their 1589 program and after.

7. In the sixteenth century, a ship's tonnage, *tonelada* in Spanish, was an estimate of its carrying capacity, or "burthen," rather than its deadweight or displacement tonnage. The estimates varied nation to nation, as did standards of weight and measure. When the English captured the Spanish *San Salvador*, listed at 958 toneladas, they calculated her to weigh 600 tons burden (Laughton, 2:155). Colin Martin, treats the topic in *MM* 63 (November 1977):365–67.

Converting these tonnages into modern displacement tonnage requires considerable guesswork because we have no detailed plans of sixteenth-century galleons that provide length, breadth, draft, and the ship's configuration below the waterline. If one estimates Medina Sidonia's 1,000-tonelada *San Martín* to have a keel of some 100 feet and an overall length of 150, a maximum breadth of 40 feet and to draw 25 feet of water, and, guessing that the hull's configuration was fairly stubby, we might estimate its displacement at perhaps 50,000 cubic feet. With 35 cubic feet equal to a ton of seawater, that gives a displacement tonnage of about 1,400 tons. The displacement tonnage of a 1941 U.S. wooden-hulled minesweeper, with an overall length of 136 feet, a breadth of 24½ feet, and a draft of 8 feet was, fully loaded, 350 tons (J. C. Fahey, *Ships and Aircraft of the United States Fleet*, 6th ed. (1950). *San Martín* was wider, drew more water, had more superstructure, and carried masts and the weight of canvas, so 1,400 tons makes some sense.

8. See Marco Morin, "La Battaglia di Lepanto: il determinante apporto dell' Artiglieria Veneziana," *Diana ARMI*, anno IX, no. 1 (January 1975):54–61.

9. Ibid. A probable description of the placement of the big guns carried by the Venetian galleasses that fought at Lepanto exists in the Venetian archives and has been dealt with by Morin. Braudel, *La Méditerranée* (Paris, 1966), 2, pl. 40, carries a sketch and gun plan of a late sixteenth-century Venetian galleass.

10. Santa Cruz left Naples early in 1578. The two galleasses that joined him in 1583 for the conquest of the Azores were not the Neapolitans, but hired from the Grand Duke of Tuscany (MN *SB* 4°-353, printed in Ignacio Bauer Landauer, *La*

Marina Española en el Siglo XVI: Don Francisco de Benavides (Madrid: Jesús López, 1921), 411–14). A depiction of a Tuscan galleass in the Azores appears in the Hall of Battles of the Escorial. Of the 1588 armada's four, one, the *Zúñiga*, took its name from Don Juan de Zúñiga, Viceroy 1579–82, and a second, *Girona*, from Girón, the family name of the Duke of Osuna, Viceroy 1582–85. The depictions of them that appear in paintings of the 1588 battles belonging to the National Maritime Museum, Greenwich, and the Worshipful Society of Apothecaries, London, are of uncertain accuracy and have been frequently reproduced.

11. The figure for the armada's galleasses is derived from the figure of 1,200 for the number of rowers, FD, 2, doc. 109 (p. 65). Sténuit, *Trésors de l'Armada*, thinks there were eighteen oars to a side (p. 48). Olesa Muñido, *Organización naval*, 1:245, refers to an early seventeenth-century source, Joseph Furttembach, who states that six or seven rowers pulled each oar on a galleass.

12. FD, 1, doc. 39, dated 9 July 1587, gives detailed lists of men, guns, munitions, and stores carried aboard the four galleasses and the two greatships that sailed with them.

13. For galleys in general, see J. F. Guilmartin, *Gunpowder and Galleys* (Cambridge, 1973); Olesa Muñido, *Organización naval*, and *La Galera en la navigación y el combate*, 2 vols. (Madrid, 1971).

14. Because tonnage was then a matter of cargo-carrying capacity, tonnages for war galleys were not given. J. E. G. Bennell, "English Oared Vessels of the Sixteenth Century," *MM* 60, no. 1 (1974), mentions 200 tons for the *Galley Subtle* and 100 tons each for four galleys built in 1601–02, figures he does not find reliable. Working from estimated displacement, 200 tons seems quite possible for the sort of reinforced galley the Spaniards used in the Atlantic.

15. The difference between a *nao* and a *nave* is not clear. There must have been some because on lists the terms sometimes change abruptly. Because both have similar displacements, and some of each come from both Atlantic and Mediterranean ports, it was most likely detail in masts or rigging that set them apart. I have never found an adequate explanation. Compare the lists in FD, 1, doc. 69 and 2, doc. 109.

16. Martin, *Full Fathom Five*, discusses these differences in some detail, 127–35.

17. The problems in dealing with sixteenth-century guns are well treated by I. A. A. Thompson, "Spanish Armada Guns," *MM* 61, no. 4 (1975): 355–71; and Guilmartin, *Gunpowder and Galleys*. In the 1988 studies of the armada campaign by Martin and Parker, *Spanish Armada*, and Padfield, *Armada*, guns and gunnery get much attention.

18. The list printed in HO, pp. 384–405, gives the number of shot and the quantity of powder in quintals for each ship in the armada. Martin and Parker, *Spanish Armada*, 287–88, remarks and notes to chap. 11, have found detailed lists for many armada ships in the archives of Simancas and Seville.

19. See *Trésors de l'Armada*, Martin, *Full Fathom Five*, and Robert Sténuit, "Priceless Relics of the Spanish Armada," *National Geographic* 135, no. 6 (June 1969): 745–77.

20. Martin and Parker, *Spanish Armada*, 215–25, treat artillery at length and reproduce a 1594 plan of land, and sea and fortress carriages. KML *CG*, 2 and 3, have much about the guns and carriages of the fifteen ships Medina Sidonia

embargoed in 1587. Two terms are used for carriages: *encabalgamiento* and *cureña*, which are sometimes described as new or used. Wheels are described as spoked, solid wood, and iron-rimmed. The term *encabalgamiento* suggests a horse-drawn field carriage; was the second more specific for shipborne guns? The painting of the Azores campaign in the Escorial's Hall of Battles shows carriages with two wheels aboard the Tuscan galleass and some armed greatships. While the wheels seem fairly large, the trails look short, unlike the long trails of field carriages.

21. Albert Manucy, *Artillery through the Ages* (1949; repr. Washington: U.S. Government Printing Office, 1956), 49.

22. Thompson, "Spanish Armada Guns," 370, "What seems certain is that the Spanish Armada was at such a decisive disadvantage in firepower in both weight of shot and range, that it was probably incapable of winning the sea battle on whatever terms it fought."

23. For the number of guns, see Thompson, "Spanish Armada Guns," 367–68. Also, figures for gun and shot sizes given by Guilmartin, *Gunpowder and Galleys*, 157–75 and appendixes 2 and 3. Guilmartin's focus is on guns founded in the Mediterranean region, where most of Spain's naval artillery came from.

24. For the English, a full culverin fired a fourteen- to seventeen-pound shot, and a demiculverin, a seven- to nine-pound shot. Mediterranean type culverins fired shot up to sixty pounds.

25. Guilmartin, *Gunpowder and Galleys*, 172–73 and appendix 2.

26. Ibid., 173, esp. n. 4. Also see Martin, *Full Fathom Five*, chap. 7, "Master Remigy's Guns," which touches a special case of a fifty-pounder cannon called in English a curtow, which weighed about 5,500 pounds and was just under ten feet long. Guilmartin, *Gunpowder and Galleys*, 168, diagrams a Spanish fifty-pounder cannon about twenty-three feet long and, 171, gives the weight for such a piece as ranging from 5,000 to 8,000 pounds; on 173 he notes that Spanish cannon tended to be heavier for the same sized shot than Venetian.

27. Guilmartin, *Gunpowder and Galleys*, 166–70. The use of stone shot faded from north to south as wages for skilled labor rose. Great quantities of stone shot can still be found in museum-fortresses in the lands of the former Ottoman Empire.

28. Alberto Tenenti, *Cristoforo da Canal: La Marine Vénetienne avant Lépante* (Paris: Ecole Practique de Hautes Etudes, 1962), 36. Also, Morin, "La Battaglia di Lepanto," 54–61.

29. Manucy, *Artillery*, 63, states "4½ feet of 'sound and hard' oak" but gives no specific source or date.

30. FD, 1, doc. 76, 26 March 1588.

31. Ibid., doc. 48.

32. Ibid., doc. 71, 20 March 1588.

33. HO, p. 135, 4 February 1588.

34. FD, 2, doc. 99.

35. Ibid., doc. 194, pp. 473–74.

36. MN *Mss.* 497–116, 26 April 1601: "poca limpia."

37. FD, 1, doc. 83, 4 April 1588.

38. Philip II never acknowledged any bastards, unlike his father the Emperor, who acknowledged two. The current rumor about Ascoli was the improbable story that his mother, Doña Eufrasia de Guzmán, had been made pregnant by the King,

who forced the Prince of Ascoli to marry her as a cover and then had him poisoned.

39. Laughton, 2 21.

40. Martin and Parker, *Spanish Armada*, 40.

41. FD, 1 doc. 66. KML *CGA* 2 and 3 inventories the guns for 1587.

42. KML *Cartas*, n.d, March.

43. Thompson, "Spanish Armada Guns," 358–59.

44. Ibid., 365.

45. Martin and Parker, *Spanish Armada*, 198–200.

46. KML *CGA* 4, doc. 46, 11 April 1588, and 47, 12 April 1588.

47. The best copy of the roster is published in HO, 384–435, from a printed copy in Simancas. Martin and Parker, *Spanish Armada*, 179n10, have found a note of 3 June 1588 by Philip II to Mateo Vázquez, expressing his displeasure. Mattingly, *The Armada*, 248–49, treats the roster's dissemination.

48. FD, doc. 53; Maura, *El Designio de Felipe II*, 243. *Nuestra Señora* or *Santa María de Begoña* takes its name from a renowned church and district of Bilbao, though confusion with the Slavic names of Ragusan ships does occur. See J. de Courcy Ireland, "Ragusa and the Spanish Armada of 1588," *MM* 64, no. 3 (August 1978): 251–62.

49. In MN *FNG*, 22, doc. 78, Juan Martínez de Recalde wrote to the King, 4 July 1584, that the eight new galleons of the Guard were not well armed. Ibid., doc. 42, f. 147, lists guns normally found aboard ships on the Indies route around 1576. They range from *falconetes* firing two-pound balls up to *medias culebrinas* that fired nine-pound balls.

50.. See Martin, *Full Fathom Five*. Martin argues that Mediterranean-built vessels had largely replaced the Atlantic-built vessels of these squadrons. Tracking the armada over the period 1586–87 through the Spanish correspondence, I find this unlikely, although these squadrons, as did most of the others, probably carried some Levanters on their lists. Martin thought that *Santa Maria de la Rosa* of the Guipuzcoan Squadron was of Levantine construction (128–35), but later in *Trésors de l'Armada*, he states she was built in 1586–87 in San Sebastián (18).

51. Martin, *Full Fathom Five*, 133–34, argues convincingly that much of the artillery added to what the armada carried had, in the last weeks before sailing, been mounted aboard the big Levanters.

Chapter Seven. Lisbon to the Channel

1. FD, 2, doc. 108, 14 May 1588.

2. Ibid., doc. 107, 11 May 1588.

3. Ibid., doc. 94. For the 14 September 1587 plan, see HO, docs. 18–24, and also Herrera Oria, *Felipe II y el marqués de Santa Cruz*, docs. 17–21.

4. The many writers who disparage the theological side to Philip's instructions—such as David Howarth, *The Voyage of the Armada* (New York: Viking, 1981), who finds Philip II's instructions "more suited to a Sunday school picnic than a fighting fleet" (49)—would do well to review Sir Walter Raleigh's Instructions of 1617, which begin with enjoinders to praise "Almighty God," sing psalms, and avoid blasphemy, in J. S. Corbett, ed., *Fighting Instructions, 1530–1816* (London: Navy Records Society, 1905).

5. Martin and Parker make a good point of this (*Spanish Armada*, 51).

6. FD, doc. 96; also *CSPSp*, doc. 253.

7. Van der Essen, *Alexandre Farnèse*, 5:217–18. He wonders how the two commanders would have proceeded if they had known these terms.

8. FD, 2, doc. 99.

9. Ibid., doc. 105.

10. This is the area where the grapes for modern Port grow, in the sixteenth century a source of strong reds. The Port known today was developed in the eighteenth century.

11. It is not clear whether this refers to Monzón in Aragon or Monzón del Campo in Old Castile. Neither is known for wine, and in each case it would have to be shipped by river to the sea. A wine of Monzón del Campo seems the best candidate, since it could be shipped by barge down the Duero to the Atlantic.

12. HO, docs. 93, 94, 155–80. Howarth, *Voyage of the Armada*, 105–10, has a nice discussion of the rutter in relation to Wagenhaer's contemporary *Mariner's Mirror*. His claim that Philip II issued these sailing instructions on misinformation (110) seems to me mistaken; the rutter in question here was issued by Medina Sidonia with charts, and copies were sent to the King, who compared them with his own maps. The meticulous attention to detail that appears in so many of Philip's instructions results not from him, but from the experts who drafted them for his signature. What is striking is how much Philip did know about detail in so many departments; in this case his notations on the document are interesting. But he was hardly the sort to draft a rutter rather than have it done by expert navigators; he was aware of his limits.

13. Figures for how many ships Parma had collected, and of what kind they were, vary. These come from FD *AE*, 3:16, taken from AGS *Est.* 592; and match the painstaking researches of J. L. Motley, *History of the United Netherlands* (New York, 1860; ed. of 1888), 2:322, who offers the same figures from Simancas, "seventy-four vessels of various kinds fit for sea-service, one hundred and fifty flat-bottoms (playtas), and seventy river-hoys." Victoria, "Noticias," *CODOIN* 81:183, states 280 sail, with 54 "heavy" ships and 100 flyboats. Lord Henry Seymour estimated on 28 June 1588 that Parma had no more than "40 sails of flyboats and 220 bylanders;" Laughton, 1:231.

14. FD, 1, 80, 28 March 1588.

15. R. W. Unger, *The Ship*, 262, for vlieboots.

16. An English mariner, William Courtney of Dover, recommended that the arming of 15 or 20 hoys of 120 tons burden would provide an adequate defense at less cost and with fewer people than six greatships. Laughton, 1, 127–29.

17. HO, doc. CX. Martin and Parker, *Spanish Armada*, 179–85, deal with this misunderstanding and bring in the Dutch interrogation of Diego Pimentel, a maestre de campo they captured, who, like Medina Sidonia, believed that Parma had armed vessels that could spearhead his sortie into the Channel.

18. Martin and Parker, *Spanish Armada*, 185.

19. Court memorandum of 1 July 1588, HO, doc. 115. Much of the correspondence about the embargoes of Dutch "rebel" shipping in 1585 and 1595 argues that allowing the Dutch to trade in Spain would let them see the advantage of returning to obedience to Philip II. The general attitude of Philip II's court, which can be

traced back to the era of the Burgundian dukes and appears in Granvelle's correspondence, seems to have been that the Dutch lacked nobility and preferred commerce to war and that the revolt was the work of a few heretics and malcontents headed by the House of Orange and supported covertly from the start, and openly from 1585, by Queen Elizabeth and her heretical government.

20. FD, 2, doc. 118, to Parma, 10 June 1588.

21. Ibid., doc. 120, 13 June 1588.

22. The best version in print is Maura, *El Designio de Felipe II*, 259–61; FD, 2, doc. 129, is flawed. The latter, based on an eighteenth-century copy, is at variance with the former in two important respects. Maura's represents his work in the ducal archive with the copy in the Duke's own hand that the Duke kept for himself, which is now in KML *Cartas*, vol. 5. Working from it, Maura, p. 260, has "naves de Italia," which Medina Sidonia abbreviated "It^{as}"; FD, p. 136, has "naves de flota." Philip's discussion in his letter of 5 July (HO, doc. 117, 217) of the Duke's complaints that "naos levantiscas" were unsuited for northern waters makes it clear they were talking of ships from Italy. The second variance is a matter of sense: Maura, p. 261, prints "con tomar algún medio honroso con los enimigos, o asegurando más esta jornada; FD, 2, 136, "con tomar algunos medios honrosos con los enimigos, asegurando más esta jornada," without the "o". Medina Sidonia had originally written "con la Reyna," then crossed it out and wrote in "los enimigos." The "o" appears in the Duke's draft between two slashes. "/o/-Asegurando más . . . ."

23. "Oficiales." The Duke is probably referring to the officials in charge of supply and provisions. If referring to military and naval officers, he would probably have written captains, sergeants, masters, and such. Certainly all the senior military and naval officers were veterans.

24. AGS *Est*. 455, a fair copy; KML *Cartas*, vol. 6, a working copy with much interesting material about the search crossed out; from this came FD, 2, doc. 131, without the material that had been crossed out.

25. *FD*. 2, doc. 133, 5 July 1588. His dissent was appended to the minute of the council. He had also disagreed with the others about the armada's battle formation and on 15 July wrote the King to urge him to command the adoption of what he proposed as well as to lodge further complaints that Medina Sidonia did not give him his due (AGS *GA*, 225/55).

26. KML *Cartas*, vol. 5, doc. 116. "Gran sobresalto nos ha dado el despacho de 21 con la nueva de la tormenta."

27. HO, doc. 116. This and the accompanying memorandum have been Englished from what seem to be the originals sent to Medina Sidonia and are now in the National Maritime Museum, Greenwich, for George P. B. Naish, ed., "Documents Illustrating the History of the Spanish Armada," *Naval Miscellany*, vol. 4 (Navy Records Society, 1952). I thank Geoffrey Parker for this observation.

KML *Cartas*, vol. 5, has notes of the same date from Moura and Idiáquez that parallel the above, which at some time before the middle of the last century were removed from the Medina Sidonia archive.

28. HO, doc. 115 comes from the court's copy, AGS *Est*. 165. For the National Maritime Museum's version, see n. 27 above.

29. KML *Cartas*, vol. 5, docs. 123, 124, both dated 1 July 1588.

30. Cabrera, *Felipe II*, 3:217, 229.

31. HO, doc. 118.

32. HO, doc. 119.

33. *CSPV*, 8, Lippomano, 14 July 1588.

34. Was Medina Sidonia directly ordered to consult Flores de Valdés? In a letter of 12 July, HO, doc. 121, the King wrote Medina Sidonia that he was pleased to learn from Idiáquez that Medina Sidonia had brought Diego Flores to his galleon, while doc. 192, a letter by War Councilor Don Juan de Cardona dated 20 November 1588, quotes Don Jorge Manrique as saying the Duke told him Diego Flores had been sent to him by the King ("quien V.Md. le avia enbiado"). FD, doc. 185, Captain Vanegas's account, states, p. 379, that Diego Flores had been posted to the Duke by the King's order. Victoria in his history, hostile to the Duke, states that the Duke had the express order of the King to consult Flores de Valdés.

The King's instructions to Andrés de Alva read that Medina Sidonia "is to order those whom you, acting on my behalf, will direct, to go over to his galleon, together with those whom he may deem most useful and who may be least missed from the vessels in which they are now serving" (Naish, *Naval Miscellany*, 4:29). But these are dated 9 July, and Alva did not reach La Coruña till 17 July.

In HO doc. 181, Andrés de Alva reports that Juan Martínez de Recalde told him after the defeat that Medina Sidonia should have selected Oquendo and that he was not satisfied with the "person" the Duke chose. Alva makes no comment.

An account from the capitana real, FD, doc. 168, dated 21 August 1588, described the Duke as bringing Flores to the capitana because of his great experience.

35. HO, doc. 121, 12 July 1588, in the same letter in which he approved the Duke's choice of Diego Flores.

36. Ibid., doc. 181.

37. As stated in n. 26 above, Andrés de Alva's instructions concerning the selection of advisers included "those who may be least missed." Diego Flores had been promoted by the King to command the galleons of the Guard over its popular Admiral Gregorio de las Alas when its former General, Alvaro Flores de Quiñones, left it to fetch the 1588 Indies treasure. When Flores went aboard *San Martín*, las Alas took over the Guard capitana, *San Cristóbal*, while Marcos Aramburu took command of the Guard almiranta, *San Juan Bautista*.

38. Naish, *Naval Miscellany*, 4:25–30, prints translations of Alva's instructions, dated 9 July 1588. Alva, who had a long career as a naval administrator, assumed the office of Secretary of War for the Sea in 1586; at the same time the equally experienced Andrés de Prada became Secretary to the Council of War for the Land (*Tierra*). Previously the council had only one secretary. The War Secretary Juan Delgado, with whom Medina Sidonia corresponded about Portugal and Larache, died in 1585. See Thompson, *War and Government*, 39–40.

39. HO, doc. 129.

40. FD, 2, doc. 140.

41. HO, doc. 127.

42. KML *Cartas*, vol. 5, doc. 137, 20 May 1588; FD, 2, doc. 153, based on a transcript, has "galeón real" and misses Pedro de Valdés.

43. Mendoza died at La Coruña.

44. KML *Cartas*, vol. 5, doc. 139. The pilots' signatures and marks are clustered round the word "juramos," "we swear."

45. FD, 2, doc. 150, 13 July 1588.
46. FD *AE*, 3:455; in English, *CSPSp* 4:439.
47. FD, 2, doc. 159, letter to King, 30 July.

Chapter Eight. Lizard Point to the Isle of Wight

1. This part of the campaign, during which three major engagements and considerable random shooting took place, has been much studied. The chief Spanish student of the campaign remains *Capitán de Navío* Don Cesáreo Fernández Duro. The accounts in English are legion. Older authors (see bibliography for titles) include J. L. Motley, who used Dutch materials; Sir Julian S. Corbett, whose study remains a classic account; William Laird Clowes, who juxtaposed the chief English and Spanish relations; and J. K. Laughton, who edited the chief English documents of the campaign. More recent studies include those by Garrett Mattingly, Michael Lewis, David Howarth, Colin Martin and Geoffrey Parker, and Peter Padfield.

To reconstruct the battles with certainty from the surviving accounts is close to impossible. To understand something of the problem, compare any study of the armada campaign with N. J. M. Campbell, *Jutland: An Analysis of the Fighting* (London: Conway, 1986), in which the battle is reconstructed shot by shot from meticulous logbooks from participating ships on both sides and subsequent dockyard surveys, as well as countless histories and memoirs. Yet, given the contemporary accounts and what is known of the ships, weapons, and waters of the armada campaign and of contemporary theory and practice, many have tried and often prove convincing. What I offer has been carefully plotted with markers for each ship; the results appear in my figures.

The Spanish accounts I have preferred include:

From Capitana Real San Martín:

Diario, 22 July–20 August, written at sea, 58°N, and sent ahead to King with Don Baltasar de Zúñiga. HO, doc. 127 from AGS *Est.* 431, ff 46–50.

Diario, 22 July–20 August, written at sea, 58°N. Almost identical to the above. FD, 2, doc. 165, taken from transcript in MN *SB*.

Diario, Englished: Close to the above accounts, taken from AGS *Est.* 455, by Martin A. S. Hume, in *CSPSp* 4, doc. 402.

Diario of 22 July–21 August, written at sea "off coast of Scotland." Published in FD 2, doc. 168, taken from RAH *Jes*.

Vanegas, Alonso, captain (of artillery), 22 July to mid-October, written at Santander. FD, 2, doc. 185, from Bib. de la Marina, col. *Zalvide*, now Museo Naval. Particularly good for gunnery.

Bobadilla, D. Francisco de, Maestre de Campo General, letter to Don Juan de Idiáquez, 20 August 1588, published in F. Belda y Pérez de Nueros, marqués de Cabra, *Felipe II: cuarto centenario de su nacimiento* (Madrid, 1927). Padre Victoria states that the narrative in his *capítulo* 26 (*CODOIN*, 81), comes from the *diario* Bobadilla gave the King.

Manrique, Jorge de, Proveedor General, went ashore at Calais and covers only 30 July–8 August. HO, doc. 130, from AGS *Est.* 594. Englished in *CSPSp*, 4, doc. 383 from the same *legajo*.

Anonymous, *relación*, 30 July–13 August. Reads very much like the preceding by Manrique, in content and emphasis and differs only in a few words or turns of phrase. HO, doc. 138, from AGS *GA*, 222; also FD, 2, doc. 166, from MN *SB*. A very similar document has been Englished in *CSPSp* 4, doc. 391, from AGS *Est*. 839.

Miranda, Luis de, caballero in Medina Sidonia's suite, 29 July–18 August, written at sea, *canal de Escocia, 58°N*, FD, 2, doc. 169, from RAH *Jes*.

Torre, Gerónimo de la, Padre. Chaplain. Letter to Padre Alonso Daza, 22 July–30 September, Santander. FD, 2, doc. 185bis, from BL *Add.Mss*. 20,915, ff 41–48.

Góngora, Bernardo de, Fray. Chaplain aboard *Nuestra Señora del Rosario*, went to *San Martín*. Letter to Fray Martín de los Angeles, covers 22 July–18 August. Harvard University, Houghton *fMs*. Sp. 54.

Accounts from other ships:

Coco Calderón, Pedro, *Contador* aboard urca almiranta *San Salvador*, 22 July–23 September, written in Santander. FD *AE*, 3, Appendix 1, from AGS via J. Paz, *Revista de Archivos, Bibliotecas y Museos* (1897). Englished by Hume, *CSPSp* 4, doc. 439, from AGS *GA*, 221.

Seville Captain (*maestre de una de las naos de Sevilla*), 29 July–24 September, written in Santander, n.d., FD, 2, doc. 170, RAH *Jes*.

Anonymous, aboard an urca, certainly the capitana *Gran Grifón*, perhaps by General Juan Gómez de Medina, though, given the number of references to saints' days and other religious concerns, it seems more likely to have been written by a cleric aboard), 22 July–27 October, written in Scotland after shipwreck. FD, 2, doc. 171, from RAH, *Salazar*.

Zúñiga, galleass, account from, covers 27 July [*sic*]–4 October, written at Havre de Grâce (Le Havre). *CSPSp* 4, doc. 449, from BN Paris, Archives K 1568 (now AGS K 1568).

Cuellar, Francisco de, Captain, first aboard galleon *San Pedro de Castilla*, then transferred after court-martial to Levanter *La Lavia* and shipwrecked. Letter written from Antwerp, 4 October 1589, which commences with the action of 8 August 1588, then relates his shipwreck and his escape from Ireland. FD, 2, doc. 184, from RAH, *Salazar*.

Valdés, Don Pedro de. Examination of, 4 August 1588 (O.S., 13, N.S.), Laughton, 2:27–29; and letter to King, 30 August 1588 (21, O.S.), 133–36. Also, in the second narrative by Petruccio Ubaldino, (published in Naish, *Naval Miscellany*, Valdés is used as an authority for the Spanish side.

Victoria, Padre Juan de, "Noticias de la Invencible," *CODOIN*, 81, seems preferable to the version printed in FD, 2, doc. 186, which leaves out material that he believed duplicated material he had from other sources. But there are some variations that prove interesting. Victoria collected much material that ranged from fact to hearsay, and his account must be used with caution. Both *CODOIN* and FD versions are drawn from Victoria's manuscript history of the kings of Spain in BN Madrid.

2. The *Santa Ana* ended her days in Le Havre, as far as she got in her attempt to rejoin the armada. Maestre de Campo Nicolás de Isla died of massive injuries received when a spar fell on him during a fight with the English.

3. HO, doc. 130, prints a letter dated 29 June 1588, taken from AGS *GA*, 241,

which mentions neither Saturday nor the problem with the galleasses; FD, 2, doc. 159, is dated 30 July 1588 and proceeds from MN *FN*, 30 (now MN *Mss.* 496); *CSPSp* 4, has the same letter, Englished, from AGS *Est.* 455.

4. In 1591 the Council of War decided that the galleasses had not worked out as expected and recommended that those that remained be disarmed, and their guns and crews redistributed (AGS *GA*, 337, 19 January 1591).

5. HO, appendix, doc. 7, prints a discourse on the campaign by the theorist Bernardino de Escalante, dated 3 April 1588, that specifically mentions anchoring in the shelter of the "bancos de Godina," p. 372.

6. FD, 2, doc. 140.

7. Medina Sidonia does not mention it. For what we have see FD, 2, doc. 185, Vanegas's *relación*, pp. 374–75; doc. 186, Victoria's "Noticias," *CODOIN* 81:204–05: he claimed to get it from one Julian de la Piedra, supposedly one of Oquendo's captains, but whose name appears nowhere else; and Laughton, 2:28, examination of Pedro de Valdés.

8. HO, doc. 126, interrogation of Domingo de Lago, a fisherman of La Coruña who had been captured in May and taken by the English to Plymouth; released, he returned via a French ship to Lisbon, then on foot to his home.

9. HO, doc. 110, 21 June 1588. The King sent this letter to Flanders, believing the armada to be on its way, and expressed hope that when Medina Sidonia received it he would have already joined with Parma. When the King learned that Medina Sidonia at anchored at La Coruña to take on supplies, he sent him copies of it (HO, doc. 111, 26 June 1588). Andrés de Alva, when he arrived at La Coruña, could certainly have clarified this and other concerns of the court.

10. FD, 2, doc. 185, Vanegas, who writes "Fairquez" (375), which would probably be Fowey.

11. Guilmartin, *Gunpowder and Galleys*, 211.

12. Manucy, *Artillery*, 82, states that twelve rounds an hour was "good practice" for big guns during the U.S. Civil War, 1861–65, in the last period of muzzle-loaded, black-powder gunnery, when guns used fixed and semifixed ammunition. The rate might be upped to twenty.

13. Martin and Parker, *Spanish Armada*, 198–201.

14. A list of 1590 of gunners hired in Seville shows about half to be foreign: Italians, Germans, and Flemings. KML *CG*, 5, doc. 148.

15. FD, 1, doc. 40.

16. FD *AE*, 3:189–90.

17. MN *Mss.* 497–149, 15 February 1604.

18. Filippo Pigafetta, *Discorso sopra l'Ordinanza dell' Armata Catholica* (Rome, 1588), dealt with in detail by Corbett, *Drake and the Tudor Navy*, 2 vols. (London: Longmans, 1898), 2:197–202. Martin and Parker, *Spanish Armada*, 31, publish a copy of the armada's projected formation sent by the Tuscan ambassador to the Grand Duke that closely matches Pigafetta's description. In KML *Cartas*, vol. 5, doc. 66, on two sheets with deletions and additions, are the names of twenty ships for each *cuerno* and thirty for the *batalla*, fifteen to a side, that seem to have been drawn up by Medina Sidonia and Recalde in late March and approved by a Council of War in Lisbon. These lists coincide in important ways with what the Tuscan ambassador described. FD, 2, doc. 100, has the cuernos, though with some mis-

takes. The mixup of ships from the Vizcayan and Guipuzcoan squadrons is carried over from the original.

19. Ubaldino in Naish, *Naval Miscellany*, 4:59. About the formation agreed to in Lisbon, Don Pedro de Valdés, as in other instances, disagreed with his fellows and complained about it to the King. See AGS *GA*, 225/55, 15 July 1588, for which I thank Professor Parker.

20. Olesa Muñido, *La Galera en la navigación*, 2:130–39, discusses these formations for galleys, but it seems clear to me from all descriptions of the armada actions, that similar formations were used.

21. FD, 2, doc. 113, 28 May 1588.

22. Mattingly, *The Armada*, 217, "We are sailing against England in the confident hope of a miracle." He thinks it Recalde; Martin and Parker, *Spanish Armada*, 285n27, believe it to be Bertendona.

23. FD, 2, doc. 185, p. 373. One man per tonelada was regarded acceptable for a short voyage.

24. Ibid., doc. 185.

25. All accounts but Valdés's own agree on this. Valdés claimed that he fell afoul of a Vizcayan ship while trying to assist Recalde and that Medina Sidonia ignored and abandoned him (Laughton, 2:133–36). His claim that he resisted the English all night until Drake appeared is not borne out by Ubaldino's second narrative, which benefited from conversations with Drake (*Naval Miscellany*, 4:58–59).

26. The quote comes from what Don Jorge Manrique told War Councilor Don Juan de Cardona, HO, doc. 192, 352.

27. See chapter 3 for these events.

28. HO, doc. 192, 20 November 1588.

29. Houghton Library, Harvard, *fMS Span* 54.

30. Most accounts state that only some of the reputed 50,000 crowns aboard were saved. The pursuing English salvaged *San Salvador* and towed it to Weymouth. Its powder, shot, and better guns were dispatched to the English fleet for use in the battle. The English did not find the cash, but there were reports of looting aboard. The explosion was probably caused by a disgruntled German gunner, struck, according to Coco Calderón (FD *AE*, 3:457–58), by the captain. In the narrative by Ubaldino (*Naval Miscellany*, 4:57), it is stated that the gunner was Flemish and that the captain had made advances to his wife. In Laughton, 2:153, a German ("Almain") woman is listed among the survivors.

31. MSA *Cartas*, 17 July 1589.

32. Corbett, *Drake and the Tudor Navy*, 2:220–21; Mattingly, who quotes Meteren up to this line, *The Armada* 292–93; and Howarth, *Voyage of the Armada*, 133. Meteren's account of the armada campaign, translated from Latin, appears in Hakluyt's *Voyages* (1600). Meteren would likely have heard the story from one of the many armada survivors who continued to serve in the Low Countries, perhaps from a survivor of Moncada's galleass, which was beached and wrecked at Calais.

33. *CSPSp*, 4, doc. 360, 361, 31 July and 1 August 1588.

34. Vanegas's account, FD, 2, doc. 185.

35. *CSPSp*, 4, doc. 362; the account that blames the wind is in FD, 2, doc. 168.

36. In the survey of the Queen's ships taken in October 1588, the mainmast of

the *Revenge* had to be replaced because it was "decayed and perished with shot" (Laughton, 2:252). Drake would likely have fixed a jury-mast to remain in the campaign, which probably explains why he was not mentioned in any account for the fighting on August 4; Recalde took over a day to repair similar damage to his mast and rigging: Drake probably took as long and may even have put into port. Corbett, *Drake and the Tudor Navy*, 2:230n1, believes it was the *Revenge* but does not link his conjecture to the survey.

37. Some believed that those ships not commanded by a senior officer or person of quality had shirked their duty, and Bobadilla insisted that the fighting was chiefly done by about twenty ships. But from narratives such as Captain Cuellar's and the Purser Pedro Coco Calderón's it seems that many other ships fought well. Most of the narratives, like medieval chronicles, tended to emphasize only the ships on which distinguished persons sailed.

38. Pierre et Huguette Chaunu, *Seville et l'Atlantique* 8 vols, (Paris: A. Colin, 1955–59), 3:348, quotes a letter from Arias Maldonado to the Casa de Contratación that Medina Sidonia had bought an urca and the galleon *Netuno* or *San Juan* for the Crown. Though I have yet to find clear evidence, I believe the nameless urca became *Duquesa Santa Ana*, named by Medina Sidonia for his pious grandmother, who was Philip II's second cousin.

39. Medina Sidonia in his letter to Parma, 4 August 1588, makes it clear that he was letting ships become surrounded by the English in hope that the English would come to close quarters and could be grappled. *CSPSp*, 4, doc. 364.

40. Historians, conjecturing what Drake did (his activities are not mentioned in any English account), have ordinarily assigned the squadrons in order from landward to seaward, to Frobisher, the Lord Admiral, Hawkins, and Drake. My belief is that the English sailed in an order determined by rank. Howard and Drake would have taken the center squadrons, with Howard on his own right, Hawkins, who ranked third, to Howard's right, and Frobisher on the extreme left. The English "Relation of Proceedings" mentions Hawkins pursuing a Spanish ship that was "southwards," and Frobisher being "northward" (Laughton, 1:13–14).

41. FD, 2, doc. 170.

42. Sir Julian Corbett, *Drake and the Tudor Navy* 2:233–41; also see n. 36, 40 above. Corbett believed the attack fell on the armada's seaward edge, aimed to force it toward the shoals called the Owers. But such a blow might also have pushed the armada into the anchorage Medina Sidonia sought, from which it might not easily have been dislodged without risk of a boarding action. Moreover, I do not think *San Mateo* was on the armada's seaward flank. From the various sources it seems to me the English hit hard at what amounted to the center of the armada line, which was sufficient to bring Medina Sidonia and his batalla to keep it from breaking. The weight of the English assault thus pushed the armada away from Wight and Spithead.

43. *CSPSp*, 4, doc. 449, p. 460.

Chapter Nine. Calais to Santander

1. *CSPSp*, 4, doc. 364. I have changed a couple of words from Hume's Englished text to make what I believe more sense of the statement.

2. A modern ship's logbook, especially a naval logbook, is a legal document

that records to the second a ship's maneuvers, and in its "remarks" occurrences on board; it cannot be changed. The officer of the deck for each watch and the captain must affix their signatures to it. Mistakes can only be lined out, thus remaining legible, and then initialed.

3. *CSPSp*, 4, doc. 368.

4. HO, doc. 192, inquiry of Don Juan de Cardona, 9 November 1588.

5. *CSPSp*, 4, doc. 380, Parma to the King dated 10 August 1588.

6. Ibid.

7. The failure of Dunkirk to assist in 1588 led to bitter complaints. In 1604 an Admiralty of Flanders and a Dunkirk squadron were established, and in Spain trade concessions were given Dunkirk skippers. In 1605 that squadron fought fiercely against the Dutch in the Channel. Medina Sidonia's son Juan Claros de Guzmán, Marquis of Fuentes, conducted effective operations with the squadron in 1635–39 (FD *AE.*, 3:229–30, and 4:407–12).

8. In 1596, after his armada was dispersed by storm, the Adelantado Mayor of Castile wrote the King, "Many bad nights I have passed thinking of how the conquest of England would be achieved most easily, most quickly and at the least cost," and proceeded to recommend the collection of one hundred galleys, eighty caravels, and sixty pinnaces in Flanders, and a sudden strike at London (AGS *Est.* 177, 28 November 1596).

9. Bigger zabras and pataches, such as those that went for the 1588 treasure were sometimes very well armed, but the armada's were not because its commanders had expected Parma to have flyboats available.

10. HO, doc. 133, Soto to Martín de Idiáquez, 7 August 1588, with a postscript of 8 August, before he learned that the armada had abandoned Calais.

11. So state the accounts from *San Martín*. The report from the galleass *Zúñiga* states that the galleass capitana ran afoul of the galleass *Girona* and the Levanter *La Rata*. Both these and *San Juan de Sicilia* were subsequently lost. All were anchored close together.

12. Ascoli's explanation to the King, *CSPSp*, 4, doc. 386, 12 August 1588; for the five pataches which left Calais on 7 September and arrived in Ribadeo on 15, HO, doc. 148, 18 September 1588.

13. The galleass beached and was attacked by the English, who killed Moncada. The Governor of Calais took the wreck into custody, and its guns were eventually given to Parma.

14. Don Juan de Cardona's investigation, HO, doc. 192.

15. William Wynter, cited in Laughton, 2:10.

16. FD, 2, doc. 185bis, Gerónimo de la Torre, 30 September 1588.

17. Both ships were wrecked; the Dutch captured Pimentel, who was later ransomed. Toledo escaped capture in a launch and reached Nieuwpoort. Both continued in the royal service.

18. "Chickens, to the tunny fisheries!" is one of Oquendo's supposed taunts that Victoria offers.

19. HO, doc. 192, 20 November 1588, Don Juan de Cardona in his investigation mentioned the charges the Duke had sent to court.

20. FD, 2, doc. 185[bis].

21. Captain Cuellar later survived shipwreck, probably of the Levanter *La*

Lavia on the Irish coast, and escaped his English captors to return to Antwerp and write a narrative of his adventures. FD, 2, doc. 184, which has been several times Englished; see Niall Fallon, *The Armada in Ireland* (Middletown, Conn.: Wesleyan; London: Stanford Maritime, 1978), 106–26 and bibliography.

22. This seems not even to have been considered by Medina Sidonia or his advisers.

23. FD, 2, docs. 164, 165. Zúñiga later served as ambassador to the Empire, as Councilor of State (1617–22), and briefly became first minister of Philip IV, just before his nephew Don Gaspar de Guzmán, Count and soon to be Count-Duke of Olivares, openly assumed power. He died in 1622.

24. *San Marcos*'s fate remains unknown, but she does not appear to have returned to Spain. She was so badly damaged that cables were used to hold her together. Fallon (*Armada in Ireland*, 143–49), believes that she was wrecked on a reef between Mutton Island and Lurga Point, near Spanish Point, Co. Clare. His case, however, rests on a captured Don Felipe de Córdoba, whom he mistakenly identifies as the son of Philip II's *caballerizo mayor* (grand equerry), who sailed aboard *San Marcos* but who, according to Spanish accounts, had his head shot off by a cannonball in the fight off Gravelines.

25. FD, 2, doc. 167, 3 September 1588. Mendoza had been aboard *San Felipe* with his uncle, Toledo. Victoria blamed Medina Sidonia for causing his death by feeding him fowl and meat cooked in seawater (FD, 2, p. 433).

26. FD, 2, doc. 167; and *CSPSp*, 4, doc. 415. How Medina Sidonia sent this to the King is not known.

27. H. H. Lamb and C. Loader, *A Meteorological Study of July to October 1588: the Spanish Armada Storms* (Norwich, 1978; University of East Anglia Climatic Research Unit Publications, vol. 6), noted in Martin and Parker.

28. HO, doc. 155, 25 September 1588. FD, 2, doc. 173, published his letter of 23 September 1588.

29. FD, 2, doc. 174, 27 September 1588.

30. Idiáquez had become Comendador Mayor of Leon in the Order of Santiago and thus graduated from *Vuestra Merced* (Your Grace) to *Vuestra Señoria* (Your Lordship).

31. AGS *Est.* 455. Dr. García Vergara and Licentiate Francisco Gómez de las Casas, 30 September 1588, and Dr. Juan de Atienza, 3 October 1588.

32. *CSPV*, 8, Lippomano, 24 December 1588.

33. MSA *Cartas*, King to Medina Sidonia, 11 August 1589 and 8 September 1589.

34. HO, doc. 175.

35. Ibid., doc. 192.

36. In 1589 he was asking the Council of War for license to go out to hear Mass (AGS GA, 272, n.d.).

37. See Sténuit, *Trésors de l'Armada*; also "Priceless Relics of the Spanish Armada" and *Trésors de l'Armada* (Brussels, 1985), with articles by Sténuit and Colin Martin about armada wrecks.

38. Martin and Parker, *Spanish Armada*, 182.

39. See my *Philip II of Spain*, 174.

40. *CSPSp*, 4, doc. 436, Garcia de Villejo to Andrés de Prada, 10 October 1588.

Medina Sidonia wanted 20,000 as a gift promised by the King, 7,000 in salary and 6,000 in reimbursement for what he had loaned the hospital at Santander, plus 1,000 for a grant to Bobadilla. In his letter of 23 September to the King, Medina Sidonia remarked that he had no money for the armada because all 50,000 ducats had been with Oquendo.

41. AGS *Est.* 455.

42. See my *Philip II*, 97-99, 184. Toledo died in 1592, after which Don Juan de Cardona, Don Alonso de Vargas, Don Pedro de Velasco, and Don Juan de Acuña Vela seem to have been the council's dominant members.

43. FD, 2, doc. 186, p. 441.

Chapter Ten. Recovery from Defeat

1. Laughton, 1:364, Drake to Sir Francis Walsingham: "He shall wish himself at St. Mary's Port among his orange trees."

2. MSA *Cartas*, 10 January 1589.

3. MSA, leg. 42, contains interesting materials on the program of tower building. For the sort of thing Madrid had in mind, the best example was Granada. See Alfonso Gámir Sandoval, "Organización de la defensa de la costa del Reino de Granada," *Boletín de la universidad de Granada*, (June-October 1943): 259–337, December 1944): 367–401, and February-December 1947): 3–152.

4. MN, *Mss.* 496–219, 5 July 1586.

5. MSA *Cartas*, copy of letter from the King to Juan Pedro Livadore, 9 September 1588.

6. MSA, *leg.* 42, assessment by Don Gabriel de Busto, 27 January 1591, pursuant to royal decree of 24 December 1590.

7. MSA *Cartas*, 27 January 1591.

8. Ibid., Secretary Juan de Ibarra to Duke, 6 December 1589.

9. AGS *GA*, 387, 12 May 1593, and MSA *Cartas*, letter from King, 26 May 1593.

10. MSA, *leg.* 42., passim., 1600–10. A document of 5 November 1600 notes that he spent 13,959 ducats and 342 *maravedís* on towers in the Arenas Gordas and Vejer.

11. MSA *Cartas*, 24 February 1589.

12. See Fernández Alvarez, *Felipe II, Isabel de Inglaterra y Marruecos* for the general problem.

13. Medina Sidonia heard that Dom António's son promised the Sharif to turn the two princes over to him when Dom António recovered Portugal. AGS *Est.*, 166, letter to Don Martín de Idiáquez, 19 November 1589.

14. Ibid., letters of 22 June, 12 September and 6 November 1589.

15. MSA *Cartas*, 4 February 1589.

16. I do not believe that Don Luis is the same person taken prisoner in Ireland following the wreck of *Falcon Blanco Mediano*, as is often claimed. The Don Luis de Córdoba whom Laughton states was Ayamonte's brother (2:299–302) was a company commander, who admitted to having an older brother who was "a gentleman of 1,000 ducats per annum" (*CSP Ireland, Elizabeth*, August 1588–September 1592 (London: PRO, 1885), 50–51). Ayamonte's income was about 30,000, and moreover, lists of prisoners usually identified those related to titled nobles. The name of

the captive Don Luis's nephew, Don Gonzalo Fernández de Córdoba, suggests that they were of the large Fernández de Córdoba clan of the Córdoba region.

Ayamonte's family name was Zúñiga y Guzmán; the name of his brother derives from their mother, Doña Ana de Córdoba, a daughter of the Marquis of Comares.

17. R. B. Wernham, *After the Armada* (Oxford, 1984) is now the standard work for the English perspective of the Spanish War, 1589–95. Corbett, *Drake and the Tudor Navy*, however, remains useful.

18. MSA *Cartas*, 27 May 1589.

19. Of the four galleasses that sailed with the armada, one was lost at Calais, and the *Girona*, with Leyva aboard, was wrecked. *Zúñiga* reached Le Havre and eventually Spain and *Napolitana* returned with Medina Sidonia to Santander, but both seem to have been disarmed and broken up. The two new galleasses were employed in 1590 in Brittany, but in January 1591 the Council of War ordered them disarmed (AGS *GA*, 337, 19 January 1591), and they spent the remainder of their days ferrying supplies.

20. RAH *Jes.* 109, fols. 552, 548, Medina Sidonia to masters Gonzalo Jiménez and Pero Díaz, 8 July 1589; also MSA *Cartas*, 31 July 1589.

21. Each was allowed to hire a thirty-tonelada *fregata* to carry personal effects, because they found the pataches too small. Das Mariñas continued his voyage in the Manila galleon from Acapulco. He later died fighting Chinese pirates.

22. MSA *Cartas*, 1 September 1589.

23. Ibid., 2 September 1589.

24. Ibid., 22 October 1589.

25. Ibid., 6 December 1589.

26. RAH *Jes.*, 109, fol. 639, *relación* of 1590.

27. MN *Mss.* 497–40, 25 June 1590.

28. KML *CGA*, 6, docs. 148, 152, 145, and MSA *Cartas*, King to Medina Sidonia, 31 March 1590.

29. MSA *Cartas*, 12 August 1590.

30. Ibid., 25 March 1591.

31. AGS *GA*, 298, copy of letter of Ayamonte to Medina Sidonia, 18 August 1590. In it, Ayamonte refers simply to "mi hermano," his only brother, whom Medina Sidonia knew well. Don Luis went on to a distinguished naval career, became general of the Guard Armada, and was lost at sea in 1606 when his capitana sank off Cuba.

32. MN *Mss.* 497–34, 23 February 1591.

33. MSA *Cartas*, 14 January, 24 August, October 2, 11 December 1591.

34. Ibid., 2 December 1590.

35. MN 497-31, 19 January 1591.

36. Ibid., 497-33, 23 February 1591, "el conde de Comerlan."

37. Ibid., 497-44, 10 May 1591.

38. RAH *Jes.*, 109, fol. 58, 18 May 1591, to Menéndez, "por Capitán Juan Gil de la Salde."

39. MSA *Cartas*, 22 May 1591.

40. About the Duke's health, MN *Mss.* 497–54, Ibarra to Duke, 6 November 1591. RAH *Jes.*, 106, fols. 22–23, contains a harrowing relation of the voyage from Havana.

41. MN *Mss.* 497–60, 12 March 1592.

42. MSA *Cartas*, 12 August 1590.

43. Pastrana died at Thionville in January 1596, awaiting the arrival of Archduke Albert, the new Governor General. Cabrera de Córdoba described Pastrana as "valiant and swashbuckling" (bizarro).

44. Esteban Rallón, *Historia de Jerez de la frontera* (c. 1600), 5 vols. (Jerez, 1890), 4:719.

45. MSA *Cartas*, 3 February 1593, and AGS GA, *leg.* 437, 9 February 1593.

46. Ibid., decree of 16 April 1595; with details in AGS *GA*, 437, *consulta* of 23 February 1595. The impact of the decree on Jerez can be seen in its Archivio Municipal, *Actas*, April 1595, fols. 499–500, 503.

47. Peñafiel succeeded his father as Duke in 1590.

48. RAH *Jes.*, 109, fol. 602, a letter dated 29 August 1590 from Medina Sidonia to the King describes "a general shortage of bread in Andalusia" and "the land lost and barren." He urged the King to export no grain, but rather order those who receive grain in rent to distribute it as needed.

49. He took the name Felipe de Africa.

50. AGS *Est.* 174, 27 October 1593.

51. MSA *Cartas*, 25 January 1594

52. AGS *Est.* 174, 4 March 1594.

53. Ibid., 28 March 1595.

54. Ibid., 15 April 1595. The rest of this episode can be followed in the same *legajo*.

55. Ibid., 24 October 1595; also letter to King of same date.

56. Ibid., *relación de aduanas*, 28 April 1585. Fernand Braudel, *El Mediterráneo*, Spanish ed. (Mexico: Fundación de Cultura Económica, 1953), 1:535, quotes this figure, but I have not seen it in the second edition. Braudel treats the Mediterranean grain crisis in *Mediterranean* (1972), 1:584–606.

57. AGS *Est.* 174, Licenciado Armenteros to Consejo Real, n.d., 1595.

58. MSA *Cartas*, 18 March 1595.

59. AGS *Est.* 174, 3 April 1595, in a detailed list of ships, masters, crews, and armament.

60. MSA *Cartas*, 20 March 1595. As Regent of Sweden, Duke Charles upheld the Lutheran Church against the efforts of his nephew Sigismund III, who was also King of Poland, to reintroduce Catholicism. In 1599, the Duke deposed his nephew in Sweden, and in 1604 became King of Sweden as Charles IX. AGS *Est.* 174 carries Medina Sidonia's response, 28 March.

61. AGS *Est.* 174, 5 April 1595.

62. Ibid.

63. Ibid., 12 April 1595.

64. Ibid., 16 April 1595.

65. For Ragusan ships in Spanish service, see J. de Courcy Ireland, "Ragusa and the Spanish Armada of 1588," *MM* 64, no. 3 (1978): 251–62, and for these twelve, my note, *MM* 67, no. 1 (1981): 91–92. Also, Thompson, *War and Government*, 193. Pedro de Ibella, as he was called in Spain, was Petar Ivelja (or Iveglia) of Ragusa-Dubrovnik.

66. MN, *Mss.* 497–75, 16 June 1595.

67. AGS *Est.* 174, 28 June 1595.

68. Ibid., 28 July 1595, and n.d. The *legajo* contains many other petitions, complaints, and comments about the embargo for July and August 1595.

69. Ibid., 9 July 1595.

70. Ibid., *Est.* 178, 17 October 1597. The Bishop had learned of the problem from "a Catholic cleric of Amsterdam."

71. Ibid., *Est.* 174, 12 July 1595.

72. Ibid. 8 August 1595, signed with Ayala.

73. Ibid., n.d., July 1595.

74. Ibid., *Est.* 178, 16 January 1597, the Inquisitor General thought that Germans aboard their ships should be asked about their religion.

75. Ibid., to the King, 16 January 1598

Chapter Eleven. The Sack of Cádiz

1. Thompson, *War and Government*, 191–95.

2. KML *CGA*, 4, has a number of detailed relations about ship construction sent to Medina Sidonia for his comment.

3. AGS *GA*, 302; 3 September 1590 and *relaciones* of 16 November 1590 and 1 October 1590.

4. From the closeness of the given tonnages they would be *San Juan Bautista*, the Castilian almiranta (754–750) (*sic*), *Santa Marta*, which had sailed with the Guipuzcoan squadron (540–48), and *San Juan Bautista Menor* of Castile (526–30), which is usually thought to have been wrecked at Streedagh Strand, Ireland, but is listed "safe" on Medina Sidonia's list, KML *Cartas*, vol. 5, doc. 157; see FD, 2, doc. 180, and also 181, which lists it lost. Because it became customary for the Armada of the Guard to sail each year with the Tierra Firme flota, this flota later came to be known as the galeones.

5. AGS *GA*, 387, 16 June 1593.

6. MSA *Cartas*, 13 August 1594; also MN *Mss.* 497–68.

7. Bazán did resume the post after the Adelantado's death in 1602; he died in office in 1604. The second Marquis of Santa Cruz had an illustrious naval career.

8. From retirement Bazán suggested that ten well-armed sailing vessels be pressed into service to guard the Strait in the late spring and early autumn, when the Dutch and English entered and left the Mediterranean. During the rest of the year, he argued, they might engage in fishing to meet their costs. He was willing to take command of them. AGS *GA*, 465, *memorial*, n.d.

9. *CSPV*, 9, Agostino Nani, 25 June 1596.

10. *CODOIN*, vol. 36, contains much on the sack of Cádiz, while Padre Pedro Abreu, *Historia del saqueo de Cádiz por los ingleses en 1596* (c. 1600), ed. Adolfo de Castro (Cádiz, 1866), provides a vivid contemporary account. Much of the following narrative is based on these sources.

11. AGS *GA*, 365, 23 September 1592. In 1588 the Bishop had estimated 900 *vecinos*.

12. A report of destruction in Cádiz dated 26 July 1596 gives a count of 1,303 houses, AGS *Est.* 177. Allowing 4.5 persons to a house gives 5,854; 5 to a house gives 6,515.

13. For this matter from the English perspective, see Wernham, *After the Armada*, chaps. 23, 24.

14. Quoted in Stephen and Elizabeth Usherwood, *The Counter Armada, 1596* (Annapolis: Naval Institute, 1983), 18.

15. *CODOIN*, 36:205.

16. Usherwood, *The Counter Armada*, 42. Other figures for the Anglo-Dutch side give 11 Queen's galleons, 11 London men-of-war, and 18 larger Dutch fighting ships. One "official" list gives 110 ships total, most popular accounts, 150. See Julian S. Corbett, *Successors of Drake* (London, 1900), 56–59 and footnotes.

17. *CODOIN*, 36:214–15, 30 June 1596.

18. Ibid., 222.

19. Abreu, *Saqueo de Cádiz*, 92.

20. *CODOIN*, 36:223, 1 July 1595.

21. Ibid., 419. Abreu gives a similar figure (*Saqueo de Cádiz*, 160). Regarding the 34 ships, the Chaunu, *Seville et l'Atlantique*, 4:12–15 list 19 ships for the New Spain flota, of which they find that only 14 burned. Gutiérrez stated that 5 of the ships were off Chipiona; 1 went aground and the other 4 safely reached Sanlúcar.

22. Usherwood, *The Counter Armada*, 130.

23. MSA *Cartas*, Pedro de Guzmán to the King, 5 January 1597.

24. The text appears in *CODOIN* 36:325–26.

25. MSA *Cartas*, a letter of Philip to Medina Sidonia, 1 May 1596, mentions forty English captives sent to the galleys.

26. AGS *GA*, 457, Seville to King, 12 July 1596, and Medina Sidonia to Seville, 10 July 1596.

27. Ibid., 10 July 1596. Philip II's chief minister, Don Juan de Idiáquez, was surprised by Seville's response and wanted to know why they had not found the money, *Ibid.*, GA 466, minute of 16 July 1596.

28. AGS *GA*, 457.

29. Ibid., Ayamonte to King, 26 July 1596; Béjar, 10 July 1596.

30. *CODOIN*, 36:292–94, 19 July 1596.

31. *CSPV*, 9, dispatches of Agostino Nani, 6 through 23 July 1596.

32. AGS *GA*, 466.

33. Thompson, *War and Government*, pt. 2, deals with the topic at length; for the effect of the loss in 1596 of Cádiz, p. 128.

34. AGS Est. 177, 26 July 1596.

35. The sonnet reads as follows:

> Vimos en Julio otra Semana Santa
> Atestada de ciertas cofradías,
> Que los soldados llaman compañías,
> De quien el vulgo, y no el inglés, se espanta.
>
> Hubo de plumas muchedumbre tanta,
> Que en ménos de catorce ó quince dias
> Volaron sus pigmeos y golías
> Y cayó el edificio por la planta.
>
> Bramó el becerro, y púsolos en sarta;
> Tronó la tierra, oscurecióse el cielo,

Amenazando una total ruina.
   Y al cabo en Cádiz, con muestra harta,
Ido ya el Conde, sin ningun recelo,
Triunfando entró el gran Duque de Medina.

   We saw in July another Holy Week,
As attested by some confraternities,
That soldiers called companies,
Which made the vulgar, but not the English, afraid.
   There was such a vast crowd of plumes,
That for at least fourteen or fifteen days,
Their pygmies and goliards took flight,
And the edifice collapsed to the ground.
   The calf bellowed and they formed ranks;
The earth shook, the sky darkened,
Menacing a total ruin.
   And at last in Cádiz, with a tough display,
The Earl* already gone, with no fear,
Triumphantly entered the great Duke of Medina.

(*The Spaniards referred to English earls as counts, the equivalent Spanish title.)

36. *CODOIN*, 36:388–90, 17 July 1596.

37. AGS *GA*, 457, 26 July 1596.

38. *CODOIN*, 36:395, 19 July 1596.

39. MN *Mss* 497–91, 31 July 1596. Fernández Asís, in his *Epistolario de Felipe II* (Madrid, 1943), item 1383, added to mention of the sack "por Drake," which is not in the cited manuscript, and caused A. L. Rowse, *Expansion of Elizabethan England*, 311, to comment mistakenly that the King somehow believed the pirate he knew was dead had again attacked Cádiz.

40. *CODOIN*, 36:434–35, to Medina Sidonia, 20 August 1596.

41. MSA *Cartas*, 5 January 1597. The author claimed to be a member of the same house or family. Another who might have been author of this letter was Francisco Tello de Guzmán, who was distantly related to Medina Sidonia, but the next reference makes me believe it was Don Pedro. Richard Boulind, who catalogued the Medina Sidonia papers acquired by H. P. Kraus, attributed the defense of Medina Sidonia to one Alonso de Hurrientos.

42. Ibid., 25 February 1597.

43. Ibid., 22 March 1597.

44. AGS *Est.* 178, minute of letter, 24 March 1597.

Chapter Twelve. From Philip II to Philip III

1. The Council of War on 20 April 1598 discussed Puñonrostro's request to be made Captain General of Seville, which they were willing in effect to grant him, along with authority over the Coast of Andalusia in Medina Sidonia's absence. IVDJ, *Envío* 43/264.

2. AGS *GA*, 499, *consultas* of 30 and 13 January, and 7 and 11 February 1597.

3. MSA *Cartas*, 10 September 1596.

4. Ibid., 31 October 1596. Jerez had ordered 4,000 arquebuses, 1,000 muskets, 300 pikes and 300 lances and received 1,000 arquebuses and 1,500 pikes, "but no more, because they are needed elsewhere." AM Jerez, *Actas*, 25 September 1596 and C(*ajón*)-20, 30 December 1596.

5. Ibid., 17 May and 20 June 1597. The sum was given as 11,030 escudos, which for consistency is given here in equivalent ducats.

6. Ibid. Ibella's flagship and three other Ragusan galleons alone of the twelve that came to Spain were deemed fit for Atlantic service and kept by the armada. The other eight were discharged. Thompson, *War and Government*, 193. Ibella perished along with 140 of the people aboard; 384 were saved.

7. Among the ships lost were two royal galleons: *Santiago*, a 900-tonner of Cardona's program, and 1588 survivor *San Felipe y Santiago*. Eighteen of the twenty-five ships reckoned lost were hired hulks, and with them about 1,700 people. See FD *AE*, 3:129–31, for the episode and figures.

8. AGS *Est.* 177, 16 November 1596.

9. MN *Mss.* 497–94, 3 December 1596, and AGS Est. 177, 8 December 1596.

10. AGS *Est.* 177, 30 January 1597.

11. Ibid., 177, 3 September 1597.

12. According to Abreu, *Saqueo de Cádiz*, 146–47, the Spaniards taken at Cadiz had discussed Pérez with their English captors. When the English said he was "admirable," the Spaniards called him a "Judas, who should be burned, not a gentleman, but of low birth, the son of a cleric who was the son of a Jew." The English then admitted that the Queen abhorred him and gave him no credit "because they found him sometimes involved with boys, and he has committed the nefarious sin for which he goes miserably and with disfavor." Marañón, *Antonio Pérez*, treats this latter aspect of Pérez's character in chap. 13.

13. AGS *Est.* 178, to Adelantado [Count of Santa Gadea], 4 November 1597.

14. *CSPV*, 9, Nani, 4 April 1598.

15. MN *Mss.* 497–107, n.d., 1598.

16. As the widowed Duke of Gandia, Borja abdicated his dukedom to his son and became a Jesuit.

17. Thompson, *War and Government*, 195–96, 266–67. Through Lerma Franqueza obtained in 1603 the title Count of Villalonga.

18. MSA A38 E6, n.d., 1598; *Collection Edouard Favre*, Bibliothèque Publique et Universitaire, Geneva, LXVII, 102, s.d., lists the commanders and knights, including Medina Sidonia.

19. MSA, L67 C21, 29 May 1600, *Venta por el duque de Lerma del oficio de Escribano Mayor de Aduanas*.

20. AGS *Est.* 177, 30 October 1596.

21. Ibid., 179, 4 November 1597.

22. MN *FN*, 3, 327/44, n.d., 1602 for Captain General of the Coast of Andalusia, and 434/56, 14 March 1612, for Captain General of the Ocean-Sea.

23. MN *Mss.* 497–115, Medina Sidonia to King, 22 April 1601, "esta tierra esta tan tocada de peste."

24. See the appendices in FD *AE*, vols. 2, 3, for lists of losses to shipwreck and storm during these years. Carla Rahn Phillips, *Six Galleons*, treats the matter superbly throughout her fine work.

25. MN *Mss.* 497–116, 26 April 1601.

26. See *CODOIN*, 81:304–05, letter of 10 February 1605 about a ship built by Don Pedro de Valdés in Havana.

27. Ibid., 497–149, 15 February 1604.

28. *CODOIN*, 81:315.

29. MN *Mss.* 497–147, 186, 190, 193, 196.

30. Ibid. 497–120, 6 June 1602; he returned to the topic in a letter of 22 June 1604, 497–153.

31. FD *AE*, 3:238.

32. MN *Mss.* 497–253, 19 December 1610.

33. Ibid., 497-176, 26 June 1606, Duke to King, and especially 497–253, Duke to Brochero, 19 December 1610.

34. Ibid., 497–176, 26 June 1606.

35. *CODOIN*, 81:277–78.

36. Ibid., p. 261, letter of 2 January 1607. Volume 81 contains Medina Sidonia's correspondence with the Crown for 1607, taken from the library of the Marquis of Fuensanta del Valle.

37. Ibid., 292, Andrés de Prada to Medina Sidonia, 29 January 1607, and 307, Antonio de Aróstegui to same, 12 February 1607.

38. FD, *AE,* 3:232–36 treats what followed and offers a list of sources. Fernández Duro lets his disdain for Medina Sidonia affect his narrative. The printed documents in *CODOIN*, vol. 81 that includes Medina Sidonia's correspondence give a different picture.

39. Royal orders to keep to shelter and avoid battle were dated in Aranjuez, 29 April: the battle took place 25 April.

40. Ibid., 429.

41. Ibid., 531–33, King to Medina Sidonia, 20 November 1607.

42. KML *CGA* 11, doc. 179, draft dated 6 July 1609.

43. Spain abandoned Larache in 1689, after a long siege, six years after England had abandoned Tangier, part of Catherine of Braganza's dowry for her marriage to Charles II.

44. AGS *Est.*, K-1428. The bridal journey in fact did not take place until 1614.

45. MN *Mss.* 497–253, 19 December 1610.

46. Ibid., 497–264, 22 January 1613, "se me calienta la boca en ablando"

47. Ibid., 497–270.

48. Family names had not yet been standardized, and he took the name of his uncle the Duke of Pastrana, who was probably his godfather.

49. The domain is an island downriver from Huelva in the Medina Sidonia patrimony.

50. In a curious letter of 26 October 1597, Moura wrote, "I want the business of Señor Don Felipe finished and Your Lordship free of the worries that these matters bring with them. I shall do what I can." Did it refer to Medina Sidonia's second son, then about eighteen and marriageable?

51. See J. H. Elliott, *The Count-Duke of Olivares* (New Haven: Yale University Press, 1986), 616–20; also Adolfo de Castro, *Historia de Cádiz*, 437–38.

52. *Anales eclesiásticos y seglares de Sevilla* (Madrid, 1677) 618.

53. Fernández Duro persists in this opinion in deriding the Duke's role as an

adviser and suggesting that Diego Brochero consulted him only in order to protect his own influence. FD *AE*, 3:207–08, 227.

54. FD, 1:225.

55. *Ibid.*, 219–31.

56. Quoted by F. Pérez Mínguez, *Don Juan de Idiáquez* (San Sebastian, 1935), 232.

57. A. S. Hume, *The Year after the Armada* (London, 1896), 4.

58. Laughton, 1:xxviii.

59. Mattingly, *The Armada*, 375.

Glossary

ADELANTADO. A noble title, rare; historically the office of a frontier governor.

ADUANAS. Customs duties.

ALCABALA. A tax on sales and other business transactions, in theory 10 percent, but in practice between 3 and 7.

ALCALDE. A mayor or senior magistrate.

ALFÉREZ. A subaltern officer; ensign bearer.

ALMADRABA. Tunny fishery.

ALMIRANTA. Flagship of an admiral, second-in-command of a fleet.

ALMOJARIFAZGO MAYOR. The customs collection agency of Seville.

ASIENTO. Contract.

ATALAYA. Watchtower.

AUDIENCIA. High Court of Appeals.

AUDITOR. Judge Advocate.

AVERÍA. A tax or a fine.

BERGANTINA. A small vessel with sail and up to ten banks of oars.

CABALLERO. Gentleman or knight; horseman.

CAPITANA. Flagship of a General; commanding officer of a fleet.

CARAVEL (Spanish *carabela*). A small sailing vessel of 80–120 tons burden.

CASA DE CONTRATACIÓN. House of Trade, Seville.

CÉDULA. Royal order.

CONSEJO. Council.

CONSULTA. A document containing recommendations and advice.

CONTADOR. Purser.

CONVERSO, CONFESO. A "new" Christian of Jewish ancestry.

CORONELA. Regiment of Italian Infantry.

CORREGIDOR. An official who represented the King in the government of a town under direct royal jurisdiction; the lord in a town under seigneurial jurisdiction.

CORTES. The representative assembly in a Spanish kingdom. By Philip II's time delegates of only eighteen royal towns attended the Cortes of Castile.

CHALUPA. A large fishing boat.

DON (Portuguese *Dom*). Sir; a polite form that precedes a gentleman's Christian name.

DOÑA. The equivalent of *Don* for women.

DUCAT (Spanish *ducado*). A unit of account, worth 375 *maravedís*. Four ducats approximately equaled a contemporary English pound sterling.

ESCUDO. A gold coin worth 400 *maravedís* (1566–1609).

FALUA. A Felucca. A harbor tender of 20–30 tons burden.

FIDALGO. A Portuguese gentleman.

FILIBOTE (Dutch *vlieboot*). Flyboat. A shallow-draft, fairly slender vessel with usually two masts that weighed between 60 and about 160 tons burden.

FLOTA. A merchant fleet, as opposed to an armada, a war fleet.

FREGATA (later *fragata*). Vessel in transition from a small coaster of oar and sail to a sturdy, oceangoing vessel. References make it seem similar to a *galizabra*.

FUSTA. A small, oared vessel with one sail, often used by corsairs.

GALEONCETE. A small galleon, 300 tons burden or less.

GALIZABRA. A vessel that combined the sailing features of Basque zabras but had a slim 4:1 keel to beam ratio, weighed 150–200 tons, and had the potential to be rowed. Used for treasure runs 1589–92.

GALLEASS (Spanish *galeaza*). A large, three-masted warship that carried up to thirty banks of oars. It had some broadsides artillery. See discussion of them in chap. 6.

GALLEON (Spanish *galeón*). A sailing warship of medium to large size. See discussion of them in chap. 6.

GALLEY (Spanish *galera*). A long, slender warship with two masts, lateen rigged, that carried twenty-five to thirty banks of oars. Its chief guns were mounted in the bow.

GALLIOT (Spanish *galeota*). A small galley with fifteen to twenty banks of oars.

GENERAL. Officer in command. When it follows a rank or title, it implies overall responsibility.

GINETE. A light horseman, often mounted on a mule or jennet.

GRANDEE (Spanish *Grande de España*). One of the chief noblemen of Spain. At the death of Philip II there were 32 out of perhaps 150 titled nobles. A grandee was addressed by the King as *primo*, "cousin," and was permitted to wear his hat, after briefly doffing it, in the royal presence. Whether titled Duke, Marquis, or Count, they took precedence over all other noblemen.

HACIENDA. Household; also Treasury.

INFANTA. Spanish or Portuguese royal princess.

INFANTE. Spanish or Portuguese prince, except for the heir to the throne, who was Prince of Asturias in Spain and Prince of Brazil in Portugal.

JURO. Interest-paying bond.

LETRADO. Lettered; lawyers and clerks.

MAESTRE DE CAMPO. Field Master; in Elizabethan English, camp-master. The commanding officer of a *tercio*, up to three thousand infantry. The equivalent of a modern colonel, but unlike colonel, or the ranks of captain or alférez, used only for one in actual command of a tercio.

MAR-OCEANO. The Ocean-Sea, now the Atlantic. In the sixteenth century it was sometimes called the *Mar de Poniente*, or Western Sea.

MARAVEDÍS. The traditional Spanish unit of account that had become so out of date that sums were often reckoned in the millions or billions. A ducat equaled 375 maravedís.

MAYOR. After a title, indicates chief or senior.

MAYORAZGO. Primogeniture and entail.

MORISCO. A "new" Christian Spaniard of Moorish ancestry.

MULAI (Spanish *Muley*, French *Moulay*). A Moroccan or Barbary prince.

PARECER. Opinion.

PATACHE. A small, two-masted sailing vessel of 60–120 tons burden.

PINAZA. Pinnace, a small, slender sailing ship of 40–60 tons burden.

PRESIDIO. Fort or garrison.

PROVEEDOR. Provisioner.

REIS (Spanish *Arraez*). A North African corsair captain.

SALINA. Salt flat.

SEGUNDÓN. Cadet of a titled house.

SEÑOR. Lord. The term was used to address the Lord, the King, as with Sire, a noble or a gentleman.

SEÑORÍO. Domain; territory under the jurisdiction of a *señor*.

TERCIO. An infantry unit of up to three thousand men, the equivalent of a modern regiment.

TÉRMINO. Township.

TIERRA FIRME. The Spanish Main, now Colombia and Panama.

TÍTULO. A titled nobleman who was not a grandee. He was addressed by the King as *pariente*, "kinsman."

TONELADA. Ton of burden; see chap. 6, n. 5.

TORRE. Large defense tower that can hold cannon.

URCA. Hulk, a generic term for North Sea and Baltic merchantmen. I have usually used the Spanish word *urca* to avoid the connotation "hulking" found in English.

VECINO. Neighbor, resident, and for census purposes, head of household.

VEEDOR. Superintendent. In the armada, the *Veedor General* was the chief supply officer.

ZABRA. A small, stout, Basque-built two-masted sailing ship of 80–180 tons burden.

Select Bibliography

A. ARCHIVAL AND MANUSCRIPT SOURCES

Archivo del palacio de los duques de Medina Sidonia, Sanlúcar de Barrameda (abbreviated MSA in notes to the text).

Much correspondence with the Crown is contained in the bound
volumes of *Cartas de los Reyes y sus Secretarios a los duques de Medina
Sidonia y copias de unas repuestas*, arranged by date. For the seventh Duke,
the archive holds both originals and transcripts of correspondence
through 1585; and for subsequent years, some originals and always transcripts. (Most originals for 1587, 1588–89, 1590–93, 1604–06, and
1608–09, along with much other material, have been acquired by the
Karpeles Manuscript Library (see below).

There is a great deal more in separate files, related to family matters,
estate accounts, the office of Captain General of the Coast of Andalusia,
and so forth. Some of these papers have also over the years been acquired
by other collections, but the archive still contains one of the richest
private collections in Spain and holds letters, records and accounts,
catalogued topically, on all aspects of the dukes' activities from the middle ages to modern times.

The ducal archive also holds the papers of the marquises of los Vélez
and Villafranca del Bierzo.

Archivo General de Simancas. Letters from or related to the seventh Duke
of Medina Sidonia appear frequently in the sections *Estado* and *Guerra
Antigua*.
Archivo General de las Indias, Sevilla.
Archivo Municipal, Jerez de la Frontera.
Biblioteca Nacional, Madrid.

Bibliothèque Nationale, Paris.

British Library, London. *Add. Mss.* 28,334–28,503. *Add. Mss.* 28,370 in particular has much correspondence between Medina Sidonia, Mateo Vázquez, and the King. Catalogue by Pascual de Gayangos. This forms part of the Altamira Collection of working papers and memoranda of Philip II and his secretaries, above all Mateo Vázquez. The collection is now largely divided into four parts: the British Library; the Bibliothèque Publique et Universitaire, Geneva, *Collection Edouard Favre*; the Instituto de Valencia de Don Juan, Madrid; and the Archivo de la Casa de Heredía Spinola, Madrid.

Instituto de Valencia de Don Juan, Madrid. Papers from the Altamira Collection, for which see British Library above.

Karpeles Manuscript Library, Santa Barbara, California. Much material acquired by H. P. Kraus, of Kraus-Thompson Organization, Ltd., has been obtained by the private Karpeles Manuscript Library. For the seventh Duke its holdings include volumes 4–6 (1587–93), 9 (1604–06), and 11 (1608–09) of the *Cartas de los Reyes*, four volumes of business with the Casa de Contratación of Seville, and nine volumes of matters related to the Capitanía General de la Costa de Andalucía y Mar Oceano.

Museo Naval, Madrid. The documents used for this study are late eighteenth- and nineteenth-century transcripts made for the Ministerio de la Marina from originals in Simancas, the Real Academia de la Historia, and private archives, including that of the dukes of Medina Sidonia. In the eighteenth century the archives of the houses of Medina Sidonia, Alba de Tormes, los Vélez, and Villafranca del Bierzo came together through marriage and inheritance, and many of the papers were housed in Madrid; subsequently the Medina Sidonia, los Vélez, and Villafranca papers settled in Sanlúcar. A guide to many of the Museo Naval's transcripts for the period of Philip II is V. Fernández Asis, *Epistolario de Felipe II sobre asuntos de Mar.* Madrid, 1943.

Real Academia de la Historia. The *colección Jesuitas*, especially volume 109, has interesting material relating to Medina Sidonia.

B. DOCUMENTS IN PRINT

Calendar of Letters and State Papers Relating to English Affairs Preserved in, or Originally Belonging to the Archives of Simancas. 4 vols. London: H. M. Stationery Office, 1899. Abbreviated *CSPSp.*

Calendar of State Papers and Manuscripts relating to English Affairs, existing in the Archives and Collections of Venice and other Libraries in Northern Italy. 39 vols. London: H. M. Stationery Office, 1864–1940. Abbreviated *CSPV.*

Colección de documentos inéditos para la historia de España. 112 vols. Madrid,

1842ff. Abbreviated *CODOIN*. Index by Julián Paz, 2 vols. Madrid, 1931. Volumes that have material concerning Medina Sidonia include 6, 24, 27, 28, 36, 39, and 81. He also receives mention in volumes 12, 15, 30–35, and 51.

Granvelle, Antoine Perrenot, Cardinal de. *Correspondance du Cardinal Granvelle*. Edited by Edmond Poullet and Charles Piot. 12 vols. Brussels, 1877–96.

Fernández Duro, Cesáreo. *La Armada invencible*. 2 vols. Madrid, 1884–85. While this has a text, three-fourths consists of documents. Abbreviated FD in notes. Fernández Duro worked in the Museo Naval chiefly with the eighteenth- and early nineteenth-century transcripts made for the Ministerio de la Marina from originals in Simancas and in private collections.

———. *Disquisiciones náuticas*. 6 vols. Madrid, 1876–81.

Fourquevaux, Raymond de Rouer, Baron de. *Dépêches de M. de Fourquevaux*. Edited by l'Abbé Douais. 3 vols. Paris, 1896–1904.

Herrera Oria, Enrique, S. J., ed. *La Armada invencible*. Volume 2 of Archivo Histórico Español, *Colección de documentos inéditos para la historia de España y sus Indias*. Valladolid, 1929. Abbreviated HO in notes.

Laughton, J. K., ed. *State Papers Relating to the Defeat of the Spanish Armada*. 2 vols. London: Navy Records Society, 1894.

Longlée, Pierre de Ségusson, Sieur de. *Dépêches diplomatiques de M. de Longlée*. Edited by Albert Mousset. Paris, 1912.

Maura, Gabriel Maura y Gamazo, duque de. *El Designio de Felipe II y el episodio de la Armada invencible*. Madrid, 1957. Maura worked from several sources, including originals from the Medina Sidonia ducal archive. It would seem from comparison with documents printed by Fernández Duro, taken from Museo Naval transcripts, that some of the originals were those now in the Karpeles Manuscript Library. In the section titled "Purpose of the Work" (Razón de la obra), which he wrote in May–July 1957, Maura mentions "circunstancias fortuitas" that allowed him the opportunity to work with the documents that year, in which the twentieth Duke of Medina Sidonia died and the twenty-first Duchess succeeded to the title.

Naish, George P. B., ed. "The Spanish Armada." In Christopher Lloyd, ed., *The Naval Miscellany*, vol. 4:1–84. London: Navy Records Society, 1952. These translations come from both originals and copies in the [Sir Thomas] Phillipps MS 25342, held since 1949 by the National Maritime Museum, Greenwich. In the same volume appears a translation of Petruccio Ubaldino's "second narrative" that presents the campaign from the English perspective.

Relazioni degli ambasciatori veneti al Senato. Edited by Eugenio Alberi, 15 vols. Florence, 1839–63.

Riba García, Carlos, ed. *Correspondencia privada de Felipe II con su secretario Mateo Vázquez, 1567–1591.* Madrid: C.S.I.C., 1959.

Les Sources inédits de l'histoire du Maroc. Edited by Henri de Castries, Robert Ricard, and Chantal de la Veronne. 21 vols. Paris, 1905ff.

C. CONTEMPORARY AND NEAR-CONTEMPORARY NARRATIVES

Abreu, Pedro de. *Historia del saqueo de Cádiz por los ingleses.* c. 1600. Reprint. Edited by Adolfo de Castro. Cádiz, 1866.

Barrantes Maldonado, Pedro. *Ilustraciones de la casa de Niebla.* Vols. 9 and 10 of *Memorial de la Real Academia de la Historia.* Madrid, 1850.

Cabrera de Córdoba, Luis. *Felipe II, Rey de España.* 1619. Reprint. 4 vols. Madrid, 1876–77.

———. *Relaciones de las cosas sucedidas en la corte de España desde 1599 hasta 1614.* Madrid, 1857.

Hakluyt, Richard. *The Principal Navigations, Voyages, Traffics and Discoveries of the English Nation.* 1600.

Herrera y Tordesillas, Antonio. *Historia general del mundo del tiempo del señor Rey don Felipe el Prudente.* Valladolid-Madrid, 1606–12.

———. *Cinco Libros de la Historia de Portugal y la conquista de Islas Azores.* Madrid, 1591.

López de Haro, Alonso. *Nobiliario genealógico de los reyes y títulos de España.* Madrid, 1622. This contains much interesting material about the nobility, their careers, marriages, and interrelationships.

Medina, Pedro de. *A Navigator's Universe: The Libro de Cosmografía of 1538.* Translated with an introduction by Ursula Lamb. Chicago and London: University of Chicago Press, 1972.

Ortiz y Zúñiga, Diego. *Anales eclesiásticos y seglares de Sevilla.* Madrid, 1677.

Porreño, Baltasar. *Dichos y Hechos del Rey D. Felipe II.* 1628. Reprint. Madrid, 1942.

Rallón, Esteban de. *Historia de Jerez de la frontera* c. 1600. Reprint. Edited by Melchor García Ruíz. Jerez, 1890.

Salazar y Castro, Luis de. *Historia genealógica de la casa de Silva.* 2 vols. Madrid, 1685. Medina Sidonia's in-laws.

Usherwood, Stephen, and Elizabeth Usherwood, eds. *The Counter Armada, 1596: The Journall of the "Mary Rose."* Annapolis: Naval Institute, 1983.

D. MODERN BOOKS AND ARTICLES

Abun-Nasr, Jamil M. *A History of the Maghrib.* Cambridge, 1971.

La Andalucía del Renacimiento 1504–1621. Vol. 4 of *Historia de Andalucía.* Madrid, 1980.

Andrews, K. R. *Elizabethan Privateering*. Cambridge, 1964.

Atienza, Julio de. *Nobiliario Español*. Madrid: Aguilar, 1959.

Barbadillo Delgado, P. *Historia de la ciudad de Sanlúcar de Barrameda*. Cádiz, 1942.

Barkham, Michael. "Sixteenth Century Spanish Basque Ships and Ship-building: the Multipurpose *Nao*." In *Postmedieval Boat and Ship Archaeology*, edited by Carol Olof Cederland. Stockholm: Swedish National Maritime Museum Report #20, BAR International Series 256, 1985.

Bauer Landauer, Ignacio. *La Marina española en el siglo XVI: Don Francisco de Benavides*. Madrid, 1921.

Bleiberg, Germán, ed. *Diccionario de la Historia de España*. 2d ed. 3 vols. Madrid: Revista de Occidente, 1968.

Boxer, C. R., *The Portuguese Seaborne Empire*. London: Hutchinson, 1969.

Braudel, Fernand. *The Mediterranean and the Mediterranean World in the Age of Philip II*. 2 vols. London: Collins; New York: Harper and Row, 1973. Translated from the second French edition, *La Méditeranée et le monde méditerranéen à l'époque de Philippe II*. 2 vols. Paris: Armand Colin, 1966.

———. *El Mediterráneo y el mundo mediterráneo en la época de Felipe II*. 2 vols. Mexico: Fondo de Cultura Económica, 1953. Revised and emended from first French edition of 1949.

El Buque en la Armada Española. Edited by Enrique Manera Regueyra, Madrid: Silex, 1981.

Caro Baroja, Julio. *Los Moriscos del Reino de Granada*. Madrid, 1957.

Castro, Adolfo de. *Historia de Cádiz y su provincia*. Cádiz, 1858.

Cerezo Martínez, Ricardo. *Años cruciales en la historia del Mediterráneo (1570–1574)*. Madrid, 1971.

Chauchadis, Claude. *Honneur, Morale et Société dans l'Espagne de Philippe II*. Paris: CNRS, 1984.

Chaunu, Pierre, and Huguette Chaunu. *Seville et l'Atlantique*. 8 vols. Paris, 1955–60.

Clowes, William Laird. *The Royal Navy*. 5 vols. London, 1897–1903. Vol. I.

Corbett, Julian S. *Drake and the Tudor Navy*. 2 vols. London, 1898.

———. *The Successors of Drake*. London, 1900.

Danvila (y Burguero), Alfonso. *Felipe II y el rey Don Sebastián de Portugal*. Madrid: Espasa Calpe, 1954.

———. *Felipe II y la sucesión de Portugal*. Madrid: Espasa Calpe, 1956. This and the above are reprinted from his *Diplomáticos españoles: Don Cristóbal de Moura*. Madrid, 1900.

Domínguez Ortiz, Antonio. *La Sociedad española en el siglo XVII*. Madrid, 1963.

———. *Golden Age of Spain*. London: Weidenfeld and Nicholson, 1971.

———, and Bernard Vincent. *Historia de los Moriscos*. Madrid: Revista de Occidente, 1978.

Durme, Maurice van. *Cardenal Granvela*. Barcelona, 1957.

Elliott, John H. *Imperial Spain*. London: Arnold, 1963.

———. The Count-Duke of *Olivares*. New Haven: Yale University Press, 1986.

Escudero, José Antonio. *Los secretarios de estado y del despacho*. 4 vols. Madrid: Instituto de Estudios Administrativos, 1969.

Fallon, Niall. *The Armada in Ireland*. London: Stanford Maritime; Middletown: Wesleyan University Press, 1978.

Fernández Alvarez, Manuel. *Felipe II, Isabel de Inglaterra y Marruecos*. Madrid: C.S.I.C., 1951.

Fernández Duro, Cesáreo. *La Armada española*. 9 vols. Madrid, 1895–1903.

———. *La Armada invencible*. 2 vols. Madrid, 1884–85.

Graham, Winston. *The Spanish Armadas*. London: George Rainbird, 1972.

Guilarte, Alfonso María. *El Régimen señorial en el siglo XVI*. Madrid, 1962.

Guillamas y Galiano, Fernando. *Historia de Sanlúcar de Barrameda*. Madrid, 1858.

Guilmartin, J. F. *Gunpowder and Galleys*. Cambridge, 1974.

Hardy, Evelyn. *Survivors of the Armada*. London: Constable, 1966.

Herrera Oria, Enrique, S.J. *Felipe II y el Marqués de Santa Cruz en la empresa de Inglaterra*. Madrid, 1946.

Hess, Andrew C. "The Moriscos: An Ottoman Fifth Column." *American Historical Review* 74 (1968): 1–25.

———. "The Battle of Lepanto and its Place in Mediterranean History." *Past and Present*, no. 57 (November 1972): 53–73.

———. *The Forgotten Frontier: A History of the Sixteenth Century Ibero-African Frontier*. Chicago: University of Chicago Press, 1978.

Howarth, David. *The Voyage of the Armada*. New York: Viking, 1981.

Jago, Charles. "The Influence of Debt on the Relations between Crown and Aristocracy in Seventeenth Century Castile." *Economic History Review* 26 (1973): 218–36.

Julien, Charles André. *Histoire de l'Afrique du Nord*. 2d ed. 3 vols. Paris, 1964.

Kamen, Henry. *Spain 1469–1714*. London and New York: Longman, 1983.

Koenigsberger, Helmut. *Practice of Empire*. Ithaca: Cornell, 1971. [Emended ed. of *The Government of Sicily under Philip II*. 1951]

Lasso de la Vega, Miguel [marqués del Saltillo]. "El duque de Medina Sidonia y la jornada a Inglaterra en 1588." *Bolentín de la biblioteca Menéndez y Pelayo*, año 16 (1934): 166–77.

———. *Historia nobiliaria española*. 2 vols. Madrid, 1951.

Lewis, Michael. *The Spanish Armada*. New York: Macmillan, 1960.

Lovett, Albert. "Juan de Ovando and the Council of Finance (1573–1575)." *Historical Journal* 1 (1972).

———. "A Cardinal's Papers: The Rise of Mateo Vázquez de Leca." *English Historical Review* 88 (April 1973).

———. *Philip II and Mateo Vázquez de Leca*. Geneva: Librairie Droz, 1977.

Lynch, John. *Spain under the Habsburgs*. 2 vols. Oxford: Blackwell, 1963–69.

Maltby, William S. *Alba*. Berkeley and Los Angeles: California, 1983.

Manucy, Albert. *Artillery through the Ages*. 1949. Reprint. Washington: U.S. Government Printing Office, 1956.

Marañón, Gregorio. *Antonio Pérez*. 7th ed. 2 vols. Madrid: Espasa-Calpe, 1963 (abridged English translation, 1954).

Martin, Colin. *Full Fathom Five: Wrecks of the Spanish Armada*. New York: Viking, 1975.

———, and Geoffrey Parker. *The Spanish Armada*. London: Hamish Hamilton, 1988.

Mattingly, Garrett. *The Armada*. Boston: Houghton Mifflin, 1959 [published in the U.K. as *The Defeat of the Spanish Armada*].

Maura y Gamazo, Gabriel, duque de Maura. *El Designio de Felipe II*. Madrid, 1957.

Merriman, R. B. *The Rise of the Spanish Empire in the Old World and in the New*. 4 vols. New York, 1918–34.

Molinié-Bertrand, Annie. *Au siècle d'or, l'Espagne et ses Hommes*. Paris: Economica, 1985.

Morin, Marco. "La battaglia di Lepanto: il determinante apporto dell' Artiglieria Veneziana." *Diana ARMI*, anno 9, no. 1 (January 1975): 54–61.

Motley, J. L. *History of the United Netherlands*. 4 vols. New York, 1888.

Muro, Gaspar. *La Princesa de Eboli*. Madrid, 1877.

Olesa Muñido, Francisco-Felipe. *La Galera en la navigación y en el combate*, 2 vols. Madrid, 1971.

———. La *Organización naval de los estados mediterráneos y en especial de España durante de los siglos XVI y XVII*. 2 vols. Madrid, 1968.

Padfield, Peter. *Armada*. London: Gollancz; Annapolis: Naval Institute, 1988.

Parker, Geoffrey. *Army of Flanders and the Spanish Road*. Cambridge, 1972.

———. *Philip II*. Boston: Little Brown, 1978.

———. "If the Armada Had Landed." *History* 60 (1976): 358–68.

———. *The Spanish Armada*. See under Martin, Colin, above.

Parry, J. H. *The Spanish Seaborne Empire*. London: Hutchinson, 1966.

Pérez Mínguez, F. *Don Juan de Idiáquez*. San Sebastian, 1935.

Phillips, Carla Rahn. *Six Galleons for the King of Spain*. Baltimore: Johns Hopkins, 1986.

———. "Spanish Ship Measurements Reconsidered: The *Instrucción*

Náutica of Diego García de Palacio (1587)." *Mariner's Mirror* 73 (August 1987): 293–96.

Pierson, Peter. *Philip II of Spain*. London: Thames & Hudson, 1975.

———. "A Commander for the Armada." *Mariner's Mirror* 55 (November 1969) 383–99.

Pike, Ruth. *Aristocrats and Traders: Sevillian Society in the Sixteenth Century*. Ithaca: Cornell, 1972.

Ranke, Leopold von. *The Ottoman and Spanish Empires in the Sixteenth and Seventeenth Centuries*. London, 1843.

Rebello de Silva, Luis Augusto. *Historia de Portugal nos seclos XVII e XVIII*. 2 vols. Lisbon, 1862.

Rowse, A. L. *The Expansion of Elizabethan England*. London: Macmillan, 1955.

Schäfer, Ernst. *El Consejo Real y Supremo de las Indias*. 2 vols. Seville, 1934–47.

Sténuit, Robert. "Priceless Relics of the Spanish Armada." *National Geographic* 135, no. 6 (June 1969): 745–77.

———. *Treasures of the Armada*. Newton Abbot, 1972.

Stirling Maxwell, William. *Don John of Austria*. 2 vols. London, 1883.

Suárez Fernández, Luis. *Nobleza y Monarquía*. Valladolid, 1959.

Suárez Inclán, Julián. *Guerra de Anexión en Portugal*. 2 vols. Madrid, 1897–98.

Tenenti, Alberto. *Cristoforo da Canal: La Marine Vénetienne avant Lépante*. Paris: Ecole Practique de Hautes Etudes, 1962.

———. *Piracy and the Decline of Venice, 1580–1615*. London, Longmans: 1967. Trans. of *Venezia e i corsari, 1580–1615* by Janet and Brian Pullan. Bari, 1961.

Terasse, Henri de. *Histoire du Maroc*. Casablanca, 1950.

Thompson, I. A. A. *War and Government in Habsburg Spain*. London: Athlone Press, University of London, 1976.

———. "The Armada and Administrative Reform: The Spanish Council of War in the Reign of Philip II." *English Historical Review* 82 (1967): 698–725.

———. "The Appointment of the Duke of Medina Sidonia to the Command of the Spanish Armada." *Historical Journal* 12, no. 2 (1969): 197–216.

———. "Spanish Armada Guns." *Mariner's Mirror* 61 (1975): 355–71.

Trésors de l'Armada. Brussels: Crédit Communal de Belgique, 1985. Contains essays by Colin Martin and Robert Sténuit on armada wrecks.

Ulloa, Modesto. *La Hacienda Real de Castilla en el Reinado de Felipe II*. Rome: Sforzini, 1963.

———. *Las rentas de algunos señores y señoríos castellanos bajo los primeros Austria*. Montevideo, 1971.

Unger, Richard W. *The Ship in the Medieval Economy*. London: Croom
Helm; Montreal: McGill-Queens University, 1980.
van der Essen, Léon. *Alexandre Farnèse, Prince de Parme*. 5 vols. Brussels,
1935.
Williamson, J. A., *The Age of Drake*. 5th ed. London: A. & C. Black,
1965.

Index